This BOOK is from the library of
David G. Kryscynski

EXPLORING POSITIVE
RELATIONSHIPS AT WORK

*Building a Theoretical
and Research Foundation*

LEA'S ORGANIZATION AND MANAGEMENT SERIES

Series Editors

Arthur P. Brief, *University of Utah*
James P. Walsh, *University of Michigan*

Associate Series Editor

Sara L. Rynes, *University of Iowa*

Ashforth (Au.) • *Role Transitions in Organizational Life: An Identity-Based Perspective*

Bartel/Blader/Wrzesniewski (Eds.): *Identity and the Modern Organization*

Bartunek (Au.) • *Organizational and Educational Change: The Life and Role of a Change Agent Group*

Beach (Ed.) • *Image Theory: Theoretical and Empirical Foundations*

Brett/Drasgow (Eds.) • *The Psychology of Work: Theoretically Based Empirical Research*

Chhokar/Brodbeck/House (Eds.) • *Culture and Leadership Across the World: The GLOBE Book of In-Depth Studies of 25 Societies*

Darley/Messick/Tyler (Eds.) • *Social Influences on Ethical Behavior in Organizations*

Denison (Ed.) • *Managing Organizational Change in Transition Economies*

Dutton/Ragins (Eds.) • *Exploring Positive Relationships at Work: Building a Theoretical and Research Foundation*

Elsbach (Au.) • *Organizational Perception Management*

Earley/Gibson (Aus.) • *Multinational Work Teams: A New Perspective*

Garud/Karnoe (Eds.) • *Path Dependence and Creation*

Jacoby (Au.) • *Employing Bureaucracy: Managers, Unions, and the Transformation of Work in the 20th Century, Revised Edition*

Kossek/Lambert (Eds.) • *Work and Life Integration: Organizational, Cultural and Individual Perspectives*

Lampel/Shamsie/Lant (Eds.) • *The Business of Culture: Strategic Perspectives on Entertainment and Media*

Lant/Shapira (Eds.) • *Organizational Cognition: Computation and Interpretation*

Lord/Brown (Aus.) • *Leadership Processes and Follower Self-Identity*

Margolis/Walsh (Aus.) • *People and Profits? The Search Between a Company's Social and Financial Performance*

Messick/Kramer (Eds.) • *The Psychology of Leadership: Some New Approaches*

Pearce (Au.) • *Organization and Management in the Embrace of the Government*

Peterson/Mannix (Eds.) • *Leading and Managing People in the Dynamic Organization*

Rafaeli/Pratt (Eds.) • *Artifacts and Organizations: Beyond Mere Symbolism*

Riggio/Murphy/Pirozzolo (Eds.) • *Multiple Intelligences and Leadership*

Schneider/Smith (Eds.) • *Personality and Organizations*

Thompson/Choi (Eds.) • *Creativity and Innovation in Organizational Teams*

Thompson/Levine/Messick (Eds.) • *Shared Cognition in Organizations: The Management of Knowledge*

For more information about books in this series, please contact LEA at www.erlbaum.com

EXPLORING POSITIVE RELATIONSHIPS AT WORK

*Building a Theoretical
and Research Foundation*

Edited by

Jane E. Dutton

University of Michigan

Belle Rose Ragins

University of Wisconsin-Milwaukee

Psychology Press
Taylor & Francis Group

New York   London

First Published by Lawrence Erlbaum Associates, Inc., Publishers
10 Industrial Avenue
Mahwah, New Jersey 07430

Reprinted 2009 by Psychology Press

Cover design by Tomai Maridou

Library of Congress Cataloging-in-Publication Data

Exploring Positive Relations at Work: Building a Theoretical and Research foundation

   ISBN 978-0-8058-5388-9 — ISBN 0-8058-5388-X (cloth)
   ISBN 978-0-8058-5389-6 — ISBN 0-8058-5389-8 (pbk)
   ISBN 978-1-4106-1539-8 — ISBN 1-4106-1539-1 (e book)

Copyright information for this volume can be obtained by contacting the Library of Congress.

Printed in the United States of America
10 9 8 7 6 5 4 3

To our partners in life—
Lloyd Sandelands and Erik Thelen

Contents

Series Foreword

Dutton and Ragins's book opens with the following words: "What makes life worth living? For most people, the answer is relationships: friends, family, and loved ones. Too often work relationships are not included in this list." The collection of chapters they put together constitute an "invitation" (to use their metaphor) to scholars to better understand why work relationships too often are missing from the list and how this state-of-affairs can be changed. The approaches to positive work relationships offered are broad, innovative, and provocative. How positive work relationships fuel self-discovery and self-actualization, how conflict and learning can drive positive work relationships, and how familial relationships enter into the equation represent a bit of the enticing territory covered. We are confident Jane and Belle's invitation will be accepted by many, hopefully leading to workplaces becoming settings more characterized as protective, comforting, and stimulating. We are so pleased to be involved in delivering their invitation to you.

—Arthur P. Brief
University of Utah

—James P. Walsh
University of Michigan

Acknowledgments

This book represents the hard work of many individuals. First and foremost, we would like to thank Janet Max, the Projects Coordinator at the University of Michigan's Center for Positive Organizational Scholarship. Janet did a spectacular job designing and executing the book-building conference that served as a foundation for this volume. We would have been lost without her help coordinating the myriad of details and deadlines surrounding this book. We would also like to thank doctoral students Brianna Barker Caza, Marlys Christianson, Jacoba Lilius, and Sandy Lim for their meticulous work documenting the ideas and insights that emerged in our book-building conference. We extend deep appreciation to Lawrence Erlbaum Associates, Publishers, ICOS at the University of Michigan, The Institute for Diversity Education and Leadership (IDEAL) at the University of Wisconsin–Milwaukee, and the Stephen M. Ross School of Business at the University of Michigan for their financial support for the book-building conference. Last, but certainly not least, we would like to thank the contributors to this volume for bringing their creativity, energy, and wisdom to this project. This book was a labor of love with many participants, and we are grateful for their efforts.

About the Contributors

Deborah Ancona is the Seley Distinguished Professor of Management at the MIT Sloan School of Management and the faculty director of the MIT Leadership Center. Her research focuses on distributed leadership, teams, and timing. She studies how teams manage both their internal and external dynamics to obtain high performance in a structure called an X-team. She also examines entrainment, showing how teams respond to multiple pacers in the environment. This work has been published in *Administrative Science Quarterly, Academy of Management Journal, Academy of Management Review, Organization Science,* and *Sloan Management Review.* She received her BA and MS in psychology from the University of Pennsylvania and her PhD in management from Columbia University.

Wayne Baker is professor of management and organizations and director of the Center for Positive Organizational Scholarship at the Stephen M. Ross School of Business at the University of Michigan. He is also Professor of Sociology at the University of Michigan. He earned his PhD in sociology from Northwestern University. His research foci include energy networks in organizations; positive social capital and generalized reciprocity; and values, religion, and spirituality. His latest book, *America's Crisis of Values: Reality and Perception,* was published by Princeton University Press in 2005.

Ruth Blatt is a PhD candidate in Management and Organizations at the Ross School of Business at the University of Michigan. She has a BA in psychology from Swarthmore College and an MS in organizational behavior from Tel Aviv University. Her research examines how individuals proactively create conditions for excellence in their work lives through meaning making and positive relationships, particularly when they work in nonstandard employment arrangements or in nascent organizations.

Carl T. Camden is President and Chief Executive Officer of Kelly Services, Inc., a *Fortune* 500 company. He previously worked for KeyCorp as their senior vice president and director of corporate marketing, served as Copresident of Wyse Advertising in Cleveland, and was Cofounder of North Coast Behavioral Research Group. He also served as associate professor at Cleveland State University and received his doctorate in communications from Ohio State University.

Martin N. Davidson is associate professor of leadership and organizational behavior at the Darden Graduate School of Business at the University of Virginia. His research on the impact of culture and ethnicity on conflict management and on career development appears in academic and managerial outlets including *Administrative Science Quarterly, Research on Negotiation in Organizations, Journal of Personality,* and *Review of Educational Research.* His recent research examines critical competencies for managing effectively across national boundaries. He is the Chair of the Academy of Management's Gender and Diversity in Organizations Division. He received his doctorate from Stanford University and his AB from Harvard University.

Kurt T. Dirks received his PhD from the University of Minnesota and is currently an associate professor of organizational behavior at the Olin School of Business at Washington University in St. Louis. His research is focused on trust in the workplace. He also conducts research on feelings of ownership. His research has appeared in the *Journal of Applied Psychology, Academy of Management Review, Organization Science, Organizational Behavior and Human Decision Processes,* and the *Journal of Organizational Behavior.*

Steve Duck is a professor of communication studies and the Daniel and Amy Starch Research Chair at the University of Iowa. He is the founding editor of the *Journal of Social and Personal Relationships* and the editor or author of 45 books on personal relationships. In addition, he founded the International Network on Personal Relationships (now merged into the International Association for Relationship Research) and two series of international conferences on relationships.

Jane E. Dutton is the William Russell Kelly Professor of Business Administration and professor of psychology at the Stephen M. Ross School of Business at the University of Michigan. She received her PhD from Northwestern University. Her research interests include organizational compassion, high-quality connections, resilience and thriving at work, and positive organizational scholarship.

Joyce K. Fletcher is professor of management at the Simmons School of Management in Boston, affiliated faculty at the Simmons Center for Gender in Organizations, and a Senior Research Scholar at the Jean Baker Miller Training Institute at Wellesley College. Author of *Disappearing Acts: Gender, Power and Relational Practice at Work* (MIT Press), Fletcher is a frequent speaker at national and international conferences on the topic of women, power, and leadership.

Kathy GermAnn earned her PhD in organizational analysis from the University of Alberta School of Business. In her research, she seeks to understand the human(e) dimensions of organizing. She is particularly interested in studying dyadic and collective patterns of relating among organizational members and how these shape possibilities for people to experience well-being through working. Prior to her academic career, GermAnn worked extensively in the Canadian health system.

Mary Ann Glynn earned her PhD from Columbia University and is professor of organization studies at Boston College. She studies cognitive and cultural processes of meaning making, identity formation, and symbolic management, as they relate to organizational change and innovation. She has published in leading management, marketing, psychology, and sociology journals and served on several editorial boards. Currently, she is an officer of the Managerial and Organizational Cognition Division of the Academy of Management.

Karen Golden-Biddle is professor of organizational behavior at Boston University. Her research examines the processes and symbolics of organizational change, and the sociology of organizational theorizing. She has published numerous articles and book chapters, and has coauthored the book, *Composing Qualitative Research* (2nd edition, 2006). Golden-Biddle has served on numerous editorial boards, and was recently elected to the Board of Governors of the Academy of Management.

Jerald Greenberg received his PhD in industrial/organizational psychology from Wayne State University in 1975. He currently is Abramowitz Professor of Business Ethics at the Ohio State University's Fisher College of Business. Greenberg has authored more than 20 books and 150 chapters and journal articles, most of which focus on organizational justice. He has received numerous research awards, including the Heneman Award for Career Achievement from the HR Division of the Academy of Management, and the Distinguished Research Award from the Society of Industrial-Organizational Psychology.

Emily Heaphy is a doctoral candidate in management and organizations at the Stephen M. Ross School of Business at the University of Michigan. She earned her BA at Wellesley College. Her research focuses on how people's relationships at work, emotions, and bodies affect how they perform their work roles.

Monica Higgins is an associate professor in Harvard Business School's Organizational Behavior Unit. She earned her PhD in organizational behavior and MA in psychology from Harvard University and her MBA from Tuck Business School at Dartmouth. Her research interests include career and leader development, mentoring, and strategic human resources management. Her book, *Career Imprints: Creating Leaders Across an Industry*, focuses on the leadership development of executives in biotechnology. Her work has also appeared in journals such as *Academy of Management Review*, *Organization Science*, and *Strategic Management Journal*.

William Isaacs is a senior lecturer at Massachusetts Institute of Technology's Sloan School of Management, and founder and president of Dialogos, a consulting and leadership transformation company based in Cambridge, MA. His book *Dialogue and the Art of Thinking Together* (Doubleday) was featured in *Fast Company* as a guide to "the secret of good informal conversation." He lectures and consults around the world. He received an AB from Dartmouth College, an MSc from the London School of Economics, and an MPhil and DPhil from Oxford University.

Erika Hayes James is an associate professor of leadership and organizational behavior at the Darden Graduate School of Business Administration at the University of Virginia. She earned her BA in psychology at Pomona College and her master's and PhD in organizational psychology at the University of Michigan. Her research interests include crisis leadership, change management, and workplace diversity. She has combined these interests into a stream of research examining firms' strategic responses to discrimination lawsuits. In addition, James studies the role of crises in producing organizational change and innovation. She has published in academic journals, including *Strategic Management Journal, Organization Science, Journal of Applied Psychology,* and *Organizational Dynamic,* and her work has been featured in the popular press. She is the editor and a contributing author of the book *An Executive Briefing on Crisis Leadership.*

William A. Kahn is professor of organizational behavior at Boston University's School of Management. He earned his PhD in psychology from Yale University. His work focuses on the dynamics of caregiving organizations, with particular attention to relational dynamics that facilitate or undermine organizational change and development. Kahn has published articles in a wide variety of academic journals and recently published a book entitled *Holding Fast: The Struggle to Create Resilient Caregiving Organizations* (Brunner-Routledge, 2005).

Kimberly Ling is a doctoral student of organizational behavior and theory at the Carnegie Mellon University Tepper School of Business. Her research interests include positive organizational scholarship, the role of emotions in decision making, and the impact of social support on health and well-being. She explores these areas using a neuropsychological and physiological approach in addition to traditional methods.

Kathleen L. McGinn is the Cahners-Rabb Professor of Business Administration at Harvard Business School. She focuses her research on interpersonal relationships and their role in negotiations, conflict, and resource allocation within and between organizations. Before going to Harvard, McGinn taught at Cornell University's Johnson Graduate School of Management and Northwestern University's Kellogg Graduate School of Management.

Michael G. Pratt earned his PhD in organizational psychology from the University of Michigan. He is a James F. Towey Fellow and associate professor at the University of Illinois, Urbana-Champaign. His research centers on issues of identity, meaning, and knowing. He has published in several journals including the *Academy of Management Journal, Academy of Management Review,* and *Administrative Science Quarterly.* He recently coedited a book, *Artifacts in Organizations.* In addition to his service on editorial boards, he is an associate editor at the *Journal of Management Inquiry,* and division chair-elect for the Managerial and Organizational Cognition Division of the Academy of Management.

Gladys Procyshen held senior health system leadership positions for 35 years. Of those, 25 years were dedicated to public health, her area of passion, which notably included 12 years as Chief Executive Officer of the Wetoka Health Unit in central Alberta, Canada. She continues to voluntarily mentor others as an extension of her lifetime commitment to developing and supporting a positive and inclusive corporate culture where respect for all people, continuous learning, quality improvement, and development of leaders at all levels are hallmarks.

Ryan W. Quinn earned his PhD in organizational behavior and human resource management from the University of Michigan Business School in 2003. He served on the faculty at the Olin School of Business at Washington University in St. Louis, and then at the Darden Graduate School of Business at the University of Virginia. He studies high-impact conversations—conversations, for example, that coordinate, that energize, that transform, that create capabilities for courageous action, and conversations that people experience as high-performing.

Belle Rose Ragins is a professor of management at the University of Wisconsin–Milwaukee (UWM) and the Research Director of the UWM Institute for Diversity Education and Leadership (IDEAL). Her research interests focus on mentoring and diversity in organizations. She has received a number of national awards for her research, including the Sage Life-Time Achievement Award for Scholarly Contributions to Management, the Academy of Management Mentoring Legacy Award, the American Society for Training and Development Research Award, and the American Psychological Association Placek Award. She is a Fellow of the Society for Industrial-Organizational Psychology, the American Psychological Society, the Society for the Psychology of Women, and the American Psychological Association.

Trish Reay is an assistant professor at the University of Alberta School of Business in the Department of Strategic Management and Organization. Her research interests include organizational change, organizational learning, and institutionalization of new practices. Currently, she conducts research in the context of health care and family businesses. Her work has appeared in journals such as *Academy of Management Journal, Organization Studies,* and *Human Resource Management.*

Laura Morgan Roberts is an assistant professor of organizational behavior at the Harvard Business School. She received her PhD in organizational psychology from the University of Michigan. Roberts examines the pathways by which individuals become extraordinary within work organizations. Her research identifies systems and practices that build competence, agency, and purposeful connection across dimensions of difference. Her work has been published in the *Academy of Management Review, Harvard Business Review,* and the *Journal of Organizational Behavior.*

Denise M. Rousseau received her PhD in industrial/organizational psychology from the University of California at Berkeley. Her research focuses on ways to create effective change and mutuality in the employment relationship. Her 1995 book, *Psychological Contracts in Organizations,* won the Academy of Management's Terry Award. Her most recent book, *I-Deals: Idiosyncratic Deals Employees Bargain for Themselves,* examines the role employees play in shaping their relations with an employer. She is a fellow in the Society for Industrial/Organizational Psychology, the American Psychological Association, the Academy of Management, and the British Academy of Management. She is a past president of the Academy of Management and Editor-in-Chief of the *Journal of Organizational Behavior*.

Amy Klemm Verbos is a PhD candidate in management at the University of Wisconsin–Milwaukee. She also holds a JD from the University of Wisconsin Law School, and an MPA from the University of Wisconsin–Milwaukee. Her research focuses on the psychological processes in mentoring relationships.

Krysia Wrobel is a doctoral student studying social psychology at Emory University.

PART

I

INTRODUCTION

CHAPTER

1

Positive Relationships at Work: An Introduction and Invitation

Belle Rose Ragins
Jane E. Dutton

What makes life worth living? For most people, the answer is relationships: friends, family, and loved ones. Too often, work relationships are not included in this list. Yet people spend most of their time at work, and work relationships are central not only for how work gets done, but also for the quality of our lives. Like other relationships, work relationships reflect the full spectrum of quality. At their best, they can be a generative source of enrichment, vitality, and learning that helps individuals, groups, and organizations grow, thrive, and flourish. At their worst, they can be a toxic and corrosive source of pain, depletion, and dysfunction. Despite the criticality of work relationships for individuals, groups, and organizations, organizational scholars have yet to understand the dynamics, mechanisms, and processes that generate, nourish, and sustain positive relationships at work.

This book is designed to put the field of positive relationships at work on the research map by crafting a multidisciplinary volume that uncovers the mechanisms and dynamics of positive work relationships. We envision positive relationships at work (PRW) as a rich new interdisciplinary domain of inquiry that focuses on the generative processes, relational mechanisms, and positive outcomes associated with positive relationships between people at work. PRW examines the conditions, processes, and mechanisms in organizational relationships that increase the capacity for growth, learning, generativity, and resilience in individuals, groups, and organizations.

This introductory chapter starts by giving the reader a brief overview of how positive relationships at work relates to the positive scholarship movement. We then examine why this book is needed and provide the reader with the mission, vision, and objectives of the book. Next, we offer a foundation for defining positive relationships at work based on a distillation of the approaches used by the contributors to this volume. From there, we give the reader a practical overview of the roadmap of the book. This is followed by an appreciative summary of the book chapters that invites our readers to explore this rich new research frontier.

POSITIVE RELATIONSHIPS AT WORK
AND THE POSITIVE SCHOLARSHIP MOVEMENT

As a new area of inquiry, the field of positive relationships at work builds on the positive psychology (Seligman & Csikszentmihalyi, 2000; Snyder & Lopez, 2002), positive organizational (Cameron & Caza, 2004; Cameron, Dutton, & Quinn, 2003), and positive organizational behavior (Luthans, 2002; Luthans & Youssef, 2004) scholarship movements by shifting the lens from models that explain deficiencies to models that explain states of abundance. These positive scholarship movements offer the observation that by focusing on the problems, pathologies, and limitations associated with the worst of conditions we fail to capture the processes, states, and outcomes associated with the best of conditions. In a nutshell, we need to shift our perspective from the shadow to the light, from "what is wrong" to "what is right."

The field of positive relationships at work applies this paradigm to work relationships, and builds on the positive psychology view that relationships are a central source of life satisfaction, enrichment, development, and personal growth for individuals (cf. Berscheid, 1999; Reis & Gable, 2003; Snyder & Lopez, 2002). It also builds on a positive sociological lens (e.g., Baker, Cross, & Wooten, 2003) that suggests that certain patterns of relationships are more generative, enriching, and enhancing than others.

However, we envision PRW as offering organizational scholars more than just a positive perspective on relationships in organizations. PRW seeks to explain how relationships affect organizations through multiple levels and mechanisms and therefore deepens our understanding of the *role of relationships in organizational life*. Relationship science scholars observe that human behaviors do not occur in a vacuum, but take place within the context of relationships (cf. Berscheid, 1999). PRW embraces this perspective by viewing relationships as "front and center" in organizational life. Under this view, relationships represent not only the essence of meaning in people's lives, but they also reside deep in the core of organizational life; they are the means by which work is done and meaning is found in organizations.

WHY THE TIME IS RIGHT FOR THIS BOOK

There are three key reasons why the time is right for a book on positive relationships at work.

We Need to Build Bridges Across Silos of Scholarship

To date, our knowledge of positive work relationships has been obtained through isolated pockets of theory and research that are scattered across fields and disciplines. The idea of positive work relationships, for example, is central in theories of social capital (Coleman, 1988), mentoring (Kram, 1985), network theory (Burt, 1992), leader–member exchange (Graen & Scandura, 1987), trust (Kramer & Tyler, 1996), social support (Uchino, Cacioppo, & Kiecolt-Glaser, 1996), learning (Lave & Wenger, 1991), and psychological growth (Miller & Stiver, 1997). Although attention to this topic spans a broad swath of literature, our understanding of positive relationships at work is limited by silos of scholarship that rarely speak across levels, dependent variables, or fields of inquiry. We need a platform that allows us to reflect the richness of positive work relationships by weaving together threads from different disciplines, levels of analysis, and perspectives.

We Need to Put Relationships at the Foreground of Organizational Studies

Relationships are central to the meaning and being of life. As Berscheid (1999) so eloquently observed, "... relationships with other humans are both the foundation and the theme of the human condition: We are born into relationships, we live our lives in relationships with others, and when we die, the effects of our relationships survive in the lives of the living, reverberating throughout the tissue of their relationships" (p. 261).

In spite of the centrality of relationships to our life experience, relationships traditionally are placed in the background of organizational life (cf. Gersick, Bartunek, & Dutton, 2000; Kahn, 1993, 1998, chap. 10, this volume). This perspective not only ignores the significance of workplace relationships but also takes a needlessly segmented view of people in the workplace; that although relationships are central to employees' lives they are somehow able to turn off this need once they enter the workplace. In contrast, a holistic approach understands that relationships are central to life both within and outside the workplace, and that the need for authentic relationships is not left at the workplace door.

We Need to Extend Our Boundaries of Knowledge About Relationships in Organizations

Our knowledge about relationships in organizations is limited in at least three ways. First, the dominant theoretical paradigm that has been applied to the study of relationships, social exchange theory (e.g., Blau, 1964; Homans, 1974), is limited in explaining processes in positive work relationships. Social exchange theory views relationships as a means for exchanging resources for the purpose of achieving utility or power. This perspective uses an economic model of social interactions and fails to address communal norms evident in high-quality relationships (cf. Ragins & Verbos, chap. 5, this volume). In addition, a social exchange perspective assumes fixed resources and fails to acknowledge processes in positive work relationships that generate and create new resources (cf. Baker & Dutton, chap. 18, this volume), thus expanding "the pie" of individual and organizational resources (cf. Rousseau & Ling, chap. 20, this volume).

Second, we have a limited understanding of how positive work relationships interact with other aspects of social life within and outside organizations. Our research is often artificially constrained by organizational boundaries and we have failed to examine the effects of internal and external communities on organizational relationships (cf. discussion by Blatt & Camden, chap. 13, this volume; McGinn, chap. 14, this volume) and behaviors (e.g., Ragins, in press). We have not considered the symbolic meaning of relationships and how work relationships become institutionalized in organizational contexts and cultures (cf. Glynn & Wrobel, chap. 17, this volume; Golden-Biddle, GermAnn, Reay, & Procyshen, chap. 16, this volume). We have a limited understanding of relationship building and repair (cf. Pratt & Dirks, chap. 6, this volume) and the effects of gender, diversity, and identity on relationships in organizations (cf. Davidson & James, chap. 7, this volume; Fletcher, chap. 19, this volume; Roberts, chap. 2, this volume).

Third, our knowledge about relationships in organizations needs to be expanded to take into account the changing landscape of work and careers. Workplaces and work itself are increasingly interdependent, making connection the norm and relationships the means by which work occurs. Sustainable organizational performance and effective individual development are therefore increasingly dependent on the quality of relationships between people at work. In addition, with the rise of the protean career (Arthur & Rousseau, 1996; Hall, 1996), employees are tied less to organizations and more to relationships that are developmental and growth enhancing

(Ragins & Kram, in press). Consequently, loyalty and commitment to organizations are grounded more on social and relational than economic bases. Finally, as relationships take a more primary role in organizational life, we need to be able to transform relationships from states of just "getting by" and surviving to states of thriving (cf. Harvey & Pauwels, 2003; Spreitzer, Sutcliffe, Dutton, Sonenshein, & Grant, 2005).

PURPOSE OF THE BOOK:
OUR MISSION AND VISION

The goal of this book is to put Positive Relationships at Work on the research map. We do this by composing a volume that builds a solid foundation for this promising new area of scholarly inquiry. Our vision is to offer a multidisciplinary exploration of how relationships at work become a source of growth, vitality, learning, and generative states of human and collective flourishing.

To pursue this expansive adventure we knew we had to approach this topic from multiple levels: individual, dyadic, group, organizational, and community. Each level offers critical and useful insights into the dynamic and generative processes underlying positive relationships in organizations.

Although a multilevel perspective is vital for offering a comprehensive view of positive work relationships, we also recognize the need to weave the threads from different levels together so that we can offer readers a theoretical tapestry that reflects the dynamic richness of positive relationships in the workplace. Our goal is to give our readers an invitation to engage in a new multidisciplinary area of research, but also provide a broad perspective that allows us to build insights across levels of analysis.

Last, we want to breathe new life into established areas of scholarship by applying a PRW lens to established areas of organizational research. We want to inspire future scholars by offering a research agenda that links established areas with the promising new field of positive relationships at work.

With these visions in mind, this volume is designed to meet three key objectives:

1. To establish Positive Relationships at Work as a new interdisciplinary, multilevel domain of inquiry.
2. To facilitate the application of a Positive Relationships at Work perspective to new and established areas of organizational behavior, organizational theory, and organizational strategy.

3. To offer an engaging invitation and multilevel map for guiding future research on positive relationships at work.

We selected a stellar group of multidisciplinary scholars and invited
them to apply their knowledge, insight, and expertise toward creating a volume that achieves these ambitious objectives. In the fall of 2004 these scholars, who represent such fields as interpersonal relationships, interpersonal
communication, organizational strategy, organizational theory, organizational behavior, and a variety of psychological disciplines (industrial-
organizational, clinical, community, and social psychology), came to Ann
Arbor, Michigan, to participate in a book-building conference. Our goal was
to generate a new field of research on positive relationships at work by
crafting a foundation-setting book. These vanguard scholars took this task
to heart, and the result is a collection of thought-provoking chapters that
define the emerging research domain of positive relationships at work.

Our first challenge was to define PRW. Let us now turn to an overview of
the key aspects of this construct.

DEFINING POSITIVE RELATIONSHIPS AT WORK

For years, interpersonal relationship scholars have struggled to define
what precisely constitutes a *positive relationship* (cf. Berscheid, 1994, 1999;
Duck, 1994; Reis & Gable, 2003). We soon discovered a similar challenge in
defining positive relationships at work. Like other positive relationships (cf.
Berscheid & Reis, 1998; Miller & Stiver, 1997; Reis & Gable, 2003), positive
work relationships can be defined in terms of the states or processes in the
relationship, the experienced quality of the relationship, or the outcomes of
the relationship. We asked the authors in this volume to try to include their
definition or perspective on positive work relationships in organizations in
their chapters, and we quickly discovered that although there is some common ground, there is also significant diversity in the approach to this construct. Perhaps there is no single "best" definition of PRW that reflects an
absolute consensus across levels and disciplines. Given that the field is in
its research infancy, we believe that an expansive approach that incorporates a full range of perspectives is appropriate and needed; an approach
that opens rather than closes doors to future research.

With these caveats in mind, we would like to offer readers a basic foundation for defining positive relationships at work that reflects the common
ground discovered through building this book. We then offer a brief bird's-
eye overview of how the contributors to this volume defined PRW with an
eye toward articulating some of the complexities in defining this construct.

A Foundation for Defining Positive Relationships at Work

Focus on Relationships. At its most basic level, positive relationships at work are *relationships* between individuals that can occur at the dyadic, group, community, and organizational level. Traditionally, relationships are defined as a sequence of interactions between two people that involves some degree of mutuality, in that the behavior of one member takes some account of the behavior of the other (Hinde, 1979). Relationships are dynamic and fluid; present interactions are affected by past interactions and may influence future interactions. Relationships do not reside in the individual but are reoccurring interconnections that exist within the tissue or oscillating rhythm of interactions between two people (Berscheid, 1999). They are therefore invisible and are often discerned by observing the effects of the relationship.

Focus on the Organizational and Work Context. Positive relationships at work are a type of relationship that exists within the context of organizations, work, and careers. Positive work relationships, which some of our contributors used interchangeably with the term *positive organizational relationships,* are connected to the organization in some way, but may be situated within or outside of organizational boundaries. They may include relationships between individuals who work together in the same organization as well as relationships that are focused on work and careers that extend beyond the organization's boundaries. Positive relationships at work may therefore include developmental networks and mentoring relationships that span organizational boundaries, as well as relationships between individuals sharing a common profession, occupation or work community that is tied to the organization. Finally, positive relationships at work are not restricted to face-to-face interactions; like other work relationships, positive work relationships may be developed or sustained as virtual or electronic relationships.

Focus on Positive. What distinguishes *positive* work relationships from other work relationships is the notion of "positive." Although the definition of positive varies with different disciplines, lenses, and social constructions, we offer the idea of *positive work relationships as a reoccurring connection between two people that takes place within the context of work and careers and is experienced as mutually beneficial, where beneficial is defined broadly to include any kind of positive state, process, or outcome in the relationship.* This definition, however, just brushes the surface of positive relationships at work. The contributors to this volume flesh out this basic definition and deepen our understanding of the nuances and facets of PRW. Let us now examine how our authors defined PRW with an eye toward identifying the common ground and complexities in defining this construct.

Approaches to Defining Positive Relationships at Work

Positive Work Relationships as High-Quality Connections. Many of the contributors to this volume (see Heaphy, chap. 3; Higgins, chap. 11; Quinn, chap. 4; Baker & Dutton, chap. 18) define positive relationships at work as a *high-quality connection.* According to Dutton and Heaphy (2003; see also Dutton, 2003) high-quality connections (HQCs) involve short interactions or long-term relationships that are marked by vitality, mutuality, and positive regard. HQCs have three key features. First, HQCs have higher *emotional carrying capacity* than other relationships and interactions. Emotional carrying capacity reflects the expression of more emotions as well as a greater range of positive and negative emotions in the relationship. Second, HQCs have greater levels of *tensility,* which is the relationship's ability to bend and withstand strain in the face of challenges or setbacks. Finally, HQCs are distinguished from other relationships and interactions by their capacity for *connectivity,* which involves generativity and openness to new ideas and influences, as well as the ability to deflect behaviors that terminate generative processes.

Experiences, Processes, and Outcomes. Other contributors offer complementary perspectives by defining positive work relationships in terms of the experience and processes of the relationship. Kahn (chap. 10, this volume) views positive work relationships as those that *enable* individuals to personally engage in their work. He explains that positive work relationships meet members' *relational needs* and allow them to be authentic, present, and intellectually and emotionally available at work. Roberts (chap. 2, this volume) builds on this idea by defining positive work relationships as involving a sense of *relatedness and mutuality* that creates the possibility for greater self-discovery, heightened sense of self-efficacy, and identity enhancement. Quinn (chap. 4, this volume) points to the importance of *energy* in positive work relationships and observes that although positive relationships are more than energy, without energy there could not be positive relationships. Pratt and Dirks (chap. 6, this volume) remind us that positive work relationships offer support not only when times are good, but also in the face of adversity. They define positive relationships in terms of relationship resiliency and the capacity to *build and repair trust.* Duck (chap. 9, this volume) points out that, like other interpersonal relationships, positive relationships at work are *socially constructed* relationships, and that their dynamic natures make them fluid works in progress rather than static final states. Blatt and Camden (chap. 13, this volume) define positive relationships in terms of positive connections that lead to feelings of *inclusion*, a felt sense of being important to others, experienced mutual benefit, and shared emotions. They contend that positive work relationships can occur in the present and do not require a shared history or a future of interactions, although other contributors disagree and hold that positive work relationships require a history, a present, and an anticipated future (cf. Golden-Biddle et al., chap. 16, this volume).

Some contributors offer guidelines for assessing whether a work relationship is positive. Applying Stone Center Relational Theory (Miller & Stiver, 1997), Fletcher (chap. 19, this volume) defines positive work relationships as ones in which *mutual growth-in-connection* has occurred, and offers specific evaluative criteria for assessing this state. In particular, relationships are positive when both members experience the "five good things" of zest, empowered action, increased sense of worth, new knowledge and the desire for more connection. Grounded more in organizational settings, Greenberg (chap. 8, this volume) defines positive work relationships as both involving and leading to states of *positive organizational justice.*

Teams, Organizations, and Communities. Positive relationships can also be defined from the vantage point of relationships that are nested within teams, organizations, and communities. Ancona and Isaacs (chap. 12, this volume) define positive relationships in teams as a *structured pattern of interrelating* that creates an overall generative pattern of healthy team functioning. Golden-Biddle and her colleagues (chap. 16, this volume) define positive organizational relationships as patterns of interacting that are characterized by a recurring but not necessarily intimate bond in which groups of people develop a sense of mutuality, positive regard, and respect for one another. McGinn (chap. 14, this volume) examines work relationships within positive communities, and explains that positive communities involve *networks of supportive relationships.* According to McGinn, a community is positive when its members recognize and rely on their membership as a valuable resource.

Resource Perspective. Positive organizational relationships can also be defined as a resource for individuals, groups, and organizations. Baker and Dutton (chap. 18, this volume) view positive work relationships as a form of positive social capital that expands the generative capacity of people and groups, thereby helping them achieve their goals in new and better ways. Through HQCs and generalized reciprocity, positive work relationships increase the *resource-producing capabilities* of individuals and groups. Rousseau and Ling (chap. 20, this volume) point out that positive relationships expand the resources organizations exchange with their members; positive work relationships take a generative role in creating, expanding, and sustaining re-source-rich interactions between organizations and their members.

Relationship Type. Finally, some contributors define particular types of positive relationships in organizations, such as diverse work relationships (Davidson & James, chap. 7, this volume), leader–member dyads (Fletcher, chap. 19, this volume) and mentoring relationships (Ragins & Verbos, chap. 5, this volume). These chapters illustrate that although there are common themes that define positive work relationships, the type of relationship plays an important role in how positive work relationships are defined, perceived, and evaluated. For example, Davidson and James (chap. 7) point to the critical role that conflict and learning play in overcoming stereotypes and developing positive relationships across differences. Along similar lines, Fletcher (chap. 19) observes that cultural constructions of gender influence the views, expectations, and evaluations of relationships involving female leaders. Ragins and Verbos (chap. 5) point to the importance of relational schema and cognitive processes in members' perceptions, expectations, and evaluations of the quality of their relationship.

Summary. This preview illustrates the diversity and complexity involved with defining positive relationships at work. Positive relationships at work can be defined in terms of processes, experiences, and outcomes. They can be viewed as embedded relationships that occur in groups, organizations, and communities. They can be defined in terms of meeting people's needs—needs that continually change based on the constellation of other relationships in the organization and community. Positive work relationships are therefore fluid relationships that evolve and change over time, people, context, and culture. Understanding these relationships requires a holistic approach that incorporates multiple levels and relationships that occur outside the organizations' boundaries. Finally, the very concept of positive may be shaped not only by the external social, organizational, and cultural context, but also by the internal, psychological, and cognitive processes that drive members' perceptions, expectations, and evaluations of the relationship.

Now that we have a preliminary definition of positive relationships at work, let us turn to an overview of the structure and contents of the book.

ROADMAP FOR THE BOOK

We know that positive work relationships may both affect and be affected by individual attributes, dyadic properties of the relationship, properties of groups and communities, and the broader organizational context. With this in mind, *Exploring Positive Relationships at Work* is organized into three parts that span the micro-to-macro spectrum: (a) individuals and dyads, (b) groups and communities, and (c) organizations and organizing.

A unique feature of the book is the use of a *connecting commentator chapter* at the end of each of these three parts. The commentator chapters uncover and discuss integrative themes that emerge within the sections. The commentators invited to take the lead writing these chapters (Duck, Kahn, and Rousseau) are preeminent scholars in their respective fields, and their connecting chapters weave together themes, theories, and perspectives within each level of analysis.

The contributors to this volume represent a select group of scholars who have deep expertise in their field or on some aspect of positive relationships at work. To provide coherence and integration across chapters, we asked our authors to write their chapters with two goals in mind. First, they were asked to integrate and build on each others' chapters across and within levels of analysis. Our book-building conference provided a substantive platform for achieving this goal, which was further reinforced by posting chapter drafts on our book Web site. Second, to stress the importance of linking their area of expertise to the new domain of positive relationships at work, we asked contributors to address three questions in their chapters. First, how does their chapter advance the construct of positive relationships at work? Second, what are the processes or mechanisms underlying positive relationships at work? Last, how does their perspective on positive relationships at work invite future research?

The book concludes with our summary chapter, which summarizes the theoretical mechanisms underlying positive relationships at work, articulates the value of a positive relationship at work perspective for organizational scholarship, and sets the course for navigating future research in this exciting new area of inquiry.

We now focus our attention to an overview of the chapters in this book. In particular, we offer our readers an appreciative summary that attempts to capture the core essence and unique contributions of each chapter.

AN APPRECIATIVE SUMMARY OF THE CHAPTERS

Individual and Dyad Section

The book begins with an examination of the individual and dyadic factors that affect and are affected by positive relationships at work. The authors in this part break new ground and offer new perspectives on positive work relationships by uncovering and exploring a rich and diverse range of topics, such as identity, the body, energy, trust, mentoring, diversity, and justice.

We start with Roberts's chapter (chap. 2), which offers critical insights into the *identity processes* underlying PRW. Positive relationships are associated with a range of positive outcomes, and Roberts uncovers the identity mechanisms that may drive this relationship. She observes that by providing psychosocial support, inspiration, and feedback, positive work relationships allow individuals to learn more about the valued and distinctive aspects of their own identities. She suggests that positive relationships create identity enhancement by allowing individuals to discover their sources of strength, competence, and contributions. According to Roberts, this creates a generative process; as individuals become more aware of their strengths, they change their self-views to be aligned with the positive appraisals of others. Even more intriguing is the proposed interplay between identity and positive relationships. Roberts identifies this as a mutually reinforcing cycle: As relational identities are enhanced and enriched, the relationship becomes even more positive. Her account offers a compelling explanation for the mechanisms underlying positive relationships at work and explains, from an individual perspective, how relationships can be transformed from damaging disconnections to growth-enhancing connections.

Heaphy's chapter (chap. 3) breaks important new ground by examining the relationship between PRW and the *human body*. Heaphy draws on a full range of physiological literature, and her chapter opens an exciting portal into a new area of scholarship on physiology and relationships. She presents three ways of conceptualizing the human body that offer insights into the physiology of positive organizational relationships. First, by viewing the body as a physiological system, she examines how organizational relationships affect physical health through the mechanism of relationship quality. Second, she examines the effects of bodily cues as subjective indicators of the quality of the relationship. She observes that bodily cues allow individuals to make sense of their relationship and that the skillful use of bodily cues is a form of interpersonal competence that emerges in positive relationships. Heaphy astutely observes that we underestimate the importance of bodily cues in organizational life, and her analysis allows us to view the body not as a threat to individual's work performance, but as a source of competence. Last, she offers an assessment of how cultural contexts offer interpretative frameworks that help individuals make sense of the role of bodies in relationships at organizational, institutional, and societal levels. The Heaphy chapter offers a provocative analysis of the body and thoughtful directions for future research on the physiological outcomes associated with positive relationships at work.

Quinn's chapter (chap. 4) analyzes the role of *energy* in positive connections and relationships at work. Energy is defined as a positive affective experience involving the feeling of being eager to act and capable of acting. Quinn contends that energy is necessary for the development of high quality connections and offers a dynamic model of the reciprocal relationship between energy and positive connections at work. He explains that the quality of a connection affects the experience of energy, and energy in turn is necessary for the development of high-quality connections. His chapter offers a thorough and perceptive analysis of three primary mechanisms through which energy influences the quality of workplace connections: mutual resource creation, feedback, and attachment. These mechanisms involve three ideas: that employees build new valuable resources when they are energized, that attachment develops when parties experience energy in an interaction, and that members then use this energy as feedback to infer information about the quality of their interaction. A key insight from this chapter is that energy represents a source of transformation and change in relationships, and that employee energy and the quality of work connections engage in a dynamic feedback relationship that evolves over time.

Ragins and Verbos (chap. 5) examine the natural connection between *mentoring* and positive relationships at work. They observe that the field of mentoring can inform, and be informed by, a focus on positive relationships at work. At its best, mentoring personifies positive relationships at work, and their chapter begins with insights from mentoring research that deepen the understanding of positive relationships at work. They observe that positive work relationships are needs-based relationships that are nested within a constellation of other career relationships that may transcend organizational boundaries. They explain that like mentoring relationships, positive relationships at work may evolve through life cycles that transform over time and through states of relational quality. Ragins and Verbos then turn the table and apply a positive lens to the mentoring arena. They critique the mentoring literature and present the construct of relational mentoring as the most positive state in the continuum of mentoring relationships. The second part of their chapter then offers a theoretical model of mentoring schemas that integrates relational cognition theory, relational schema theory, and models of relational self to explicate the processes underlying schema development and expectations in positive relationships. They propose that individuals develop particularlistic and generic relational schema about positive relationships that serve as a mental guide for developing and sustaining relationships. These schemas are formed through sources of relational knowledge and involve feedback loops that perpetuate the creation of positive relationships at work. Their model of mentoring schemas offers a useful bridge between social cognition theory and our understanding of the psychological and cognitive processes underlying positive relationships at work.

Pratt and Dirks (chap. 6) offer a compelling appraisal of the role of *trust* in positive relationships at work. They begin by observing that trust is central to all positive relationships. They go on to observe that positive relationships are more resilient than other relationships in that positive relationships can offer their members support even in the face of adversity. Pratt and Dirks reason that if positive relationships are characterized by resilience, it is important to understand not only the role of trust in positive relationships, but also the processes involved with the breaking and repair of trust. They make the case that traditional social exchange perspectives do not address how trust is repaired and regained in relationships, and thus fall short in capturing processes in positive relationships. As an alternative to social exchange perspectives, Pratt and Dirks use a relationship-based commitment perspective that focuses on members' commitment to the relationship. They explain that whereas social exchange perspectives allow for the positive and negative aspects of a relationship to cancel each other out, a commitment-based perspective allows members to experience both positive and negative elements simultaneously, leading to a state of ambivalence. They contend that the resolution of this ambivalence becomes the fuel for trust, and that the ability to manage positive and negative elements simultaneously gives the relationship energy and resilience. Pratt and Dirks reconceptualize trust as a volitional acceptance of the existence of both the vulnerability and the benefits associated with being in the relationship. By offering a new lens on the building and rebuilding of trust, this thought-provoking chapter offers a powerful explanation for the resiliency underlying positive relationships at work.

Davidson and James (chap. 7) tackle a critical dilemma in the *diversity* arena: How can employees transform diverse relationships steeped in cynicism, mistrust, and enmity into relationships that are productive, nurturing, and energizing? They offer a key insight that this transformation occurs through two primary mechanisms: conflict and learning. They observe that salient differences between members in diverse (cross-difference) relationships trigger schemas, stereotypes, and expectations that set the stage for conflict. They examine the positive nature of conflict in cross-difference relationships, and propose that the opportunity to transform this conflict into learning is the only means by which high-quality relationships across differences emerge. Their chapter offers a penetrating examination of how individuals move beyond stereotypes and conflict to a learning approach. They propose that the path to learning begins with an individual's personal experiences with members of diverse groups, but is also influenced by the members' investment in the relationship and hinges on core skills or relational competencies that allow members to move the relationship from a state of conflict to a state of growth, learning, and engagement. Developing high-quality relationships across differences is often a daunting task, and this chapter gives sharp insights into how conflict generated in diverse relationships can be transformed into a generative source of learning and personal growth.

Greenberg (chap. 8) takes a fresh perspective by applying a positive lens to the domain of *organizational justice*. He observes that the field of organizational justice has focused more on the avoidance of injustice than on the attainment of justice as a positive outcome of organizational relationships. Greenberg identifies the need to bring balance to the study of organizational justice by refocusing attention from the individual's negative reactions of injustice to the positive side of the spectrum. Toward that goal, he offers the idea of positive organizational justice, which he defines as "deliberate efforts to promote, enhance, and sustain perceived fairness in the workplace in a manner that develops the positive capacities of individuals and organizations." He reviews the three established forms of justice (distributive, procedural, and interactional) with a positive organizational justice lens and offers an incisive critique of the strengths and limitations of these perspectives as they relate to positive relationships at work. His chapter identifies the underlying states and conditions that promote positive organizational justice and offers the idea of a self-regenerating cycle of positive organizational justice. This chapter offers breadth and balance to field of organizational justice and will be a catalyst for future research on positive organizational justice.

The part on individual and dyadic elements of positive relationships concludes with an insightful *commentator* chapter by Duck (chap. 9). As a renowned scholar in the field of personal relationships, Duck draws on more than 20 years of scholarship to integrate the chapters in this section and to offer a number of key insights on positive relationships at work. First, he reminds us that relationships exist in a state of interdependence, and although the chapters in this section focus on the individual and dyadic level of analyses, these levels are embedded in other levels involving groups, organizations, and communities. Second, he observes that relationships are social constructions that are not inherently positive or negative. He points out that the construct of positivity is socially grounded and therefore the qualities associated with positive relationships reflect assumptions embedded in the organization and in the broader societal context. Third, he observes that the fluid, continuous, and dynamic nature of relationships makes them "open-ended enterprises" that reflect "unfinished business" rather than final states. He reminds us that positivity is not a perpetual state, but rather a predominant form of the relationship; we cannot expect individuals to view positive relationships as positive all the time. Finally he points out that positive work relationships differ from other types of relationships in terms of intimacy, length, and whether they are voluntarily formed. By drawing on the related field of personal relationships, Duck's chapter deepens and broadens our understanding of positive relationships at work.

Groups and Communities Section

In this part we shift our attention from individual and dyadic aspects of the relationship to aspects of positive relationships that are embedded within the broader context of groups and communities. Although relationships are often viewed from a micro perspective, the contributors to this part push the boundaries and expand our vision by viewing positive relationships as nested within the context of networks, teams, groups, and communities.

We start with Kahn's chapter (chap. 10), which offers a rich analysis of how *constellations of positive relationships* help workers become attached to their organizations. He stresses the fundamental point that relationships are central to organizational life and individual's workplace experiences. He then identifies five dimensions of meaningful connections among people at work (task accomplishment, career development, sense making, provision of meaning, and personal support) and observes that these dimensions enable people to build relationships that meet instrumental, expressive, cognitive, identity, growth, and relatedness needs. Kahn uses this framework to examine the structure of relational constellations, which are defined as sets of relationships that individuals draw on to meet their needs. He explains that relational constellations vary in effectiveness, and identifies four types of constellations that vary by scope and the degree to which they meet members' relational needs. He makes the case that positive relational constellations bring a sense of psychological attachment that generalizes to the workplace. Kahn offers the idea that meaningful connections at work are not only sources of attachment, but also allow workers to bring their true authentic selves to the workplace. This conceptual insight offers exciting new possibilities for future research on relational constellations, organizational attachment and the development of authentic selves in the workplace.

Higgins's chapter (chap. 11) navigates new terrain by presenting a contingency perspective on *developmental networks* and PRW. Working within the mentoring arena, her chapter shifts the level of analysis from dyadic relationships to constellations of relationships within relationship networks. Higgins points out that prevailing perspectives on mentoring fail to examine how constellations of relationships and network structures affect a given mentoring relationship. Whereas traditional perspectives take a "more is better" approach and assume that the more help that is given in a relationship the better, or that larger networks are better than smaller networks, Higgins observes that the helpfulness of a given mentoring relationship depends on the unique needs of the protégé as well as the structure and quality of the other developmental relationships in the protégé's network. She uses specific scenarios to illustrate her contingency framework. Under this framework, developmental relationships are affected not only by the needs of the individual but also by the patterns of other relationships that exist within social arenas involving work, home, community, and professional associations. Her chapter highlights the interdependence of relationships as embedded within social networks and offers a much-needed holistic perspective on the development of positive relationships across work, life and professional arenas.

Ancona and Isaacs (chap. 12) take a bold step across disciplines by using family systems theory as a paradigm for understanding the *positive side of teams*. They start by critiquing traditional models of team functioning. They point out that these models are mechanistic and take a narrow input–process–output perspective in which the whole is viewed as the sum of its parts. Under this view, the key to high-performing teams involves simply moving or changing a given part (i.e., putting the right people on the team, offering the right incentive, or changing a given behavior), thus failing to analyze the underlying structures that create team behavior or explain the generative processes that characterize effective teams. Ancona and Isaacs address these deficits by offering an alternative paradigm: a "living system" perspective on teams. Under this view, teams are seen as living, self-regulating systems that reflect on their own functioning and engage in creative actions that lead to generative processes and structural balance. Ancona and Isaacs explain that a positive or balanced team has a set of structures that continuously monitor, correct, and produce healthy team outcomes. They develop this idea by applying a family systems lens, which views families in terms of self-regulating systems. Using the family systems "four-player model," Ancona and Isaacs examine how four central acts that occur in teams work together to create a system of structural balance and health in teams. They explain that it is not just the existence of all four acts, but the unique sequence and dynamics across acts that determine team effectiveness. By using family systems theory to understand team dynamics, this innovative chapter expands our vision and understanding of positive relationships in teams.

Blatt and Camden (chap. 13) explore the role of positive relationships in cultivating a sense of *community at work*. Their chapter addresses a pressing dilemma in the new economy: Given the increase in temporary workers, how can organizations cultivate a sense of community among workers who have no past, no future, and no membership in the organization? Blatt and Camden explain that a sense of community, which is defined as a subjective state of belonging, meets workers' fundamental needs of belonging and offers a powerful source of attachment and connection to the organization. However, they observe that the methods used to cultivate community with permanent workers (i.e., strengthening markers of identity and culture) exclude rather than include temporary employees. Blatt and Camden used indepth interviews to uncover the experience of community among temporary employees, and found that temporary workers' sense of community is developed through small acts of positive connecting with other coworkers, rather than through the macro-organizational practices that are frequently used with permanent workers. They found that temporary workers reported that their sense of community did not develop over time, nor was it expected to last; it developed swiftly and involved positive in-the-moment connections that offered feelings of inclusion, a felt sense of importance, perceptions of mutual benefits, and the experience of shared emotions. Their study illustrates that positive connections can enable the experience of belonging at work, even in the absence of a shared past or an anticipated future. This chapter offers critical insights for understanding how positive relationships at work influence community in workforces blended with permanent, temporary, part-time, and virtual workers. It also points to the fact that even as work life becomes infused with discontinuity, people's need for positive relationships remains constant.

McGinn (chap. 14) further extends our vision of positive relationships at work by offering an analysis of the role of *positive communities* in workers' lives. She explains that a community is a set of individuals that share or hold something in common, and may therefore be geographical, conceptual, or behavioral. McGinn uses a case study of a community of longshoremen in San Pedro, California, to examine how positive communities help workers deal with external changes that threaten their livelihoods and lifestyles. She observes that positive communities are characterized by mutually supportive relationships that are recognized as a valuable resource by their members. McGinn discovered that through shared history, shared structure, and shared communication practices, positive communities offer workers a source of identity, a base for interpretation of events and a channel of influence. Her rich analysis illustrates that communities can shape the ways members think about themselves and one another, their work, and their workplaces. This chapter offers the valuable insight that the positive relationships developed in communities can be a tangible, vital, and influential force in the workplace, and further dispels the notion of nonpermeable work–community boundaries.

Drawing on the chapters in this section, Kahn's *commentator chapter* (chap. 15) identifies the underlying conditions that create and sustain positive relationships in groups and communities. He observes that positive relationships at work sustain, and are sustained by, work groups and communities. He explains that groups and communities sustain positive relationships by offering their members *good harbors* that offer shelter from the storms of organizational life. Good harbors allow people to work with each other in bounded and safe ways, allow them to be vulnerable and authentic, and offer shape and meaning to their work experiences. Kahn offers the core insight that positive relationships in groups and communities are created through *positive spirals,* endlessly looping positive acts that are ongoing, self-regulating, and self-perpetuating. He explains that positive spirals are marked by "begetting"—a positive movement from one group or community begets another until the acts take on a life of their own and become woven into the life of the group or community. Through positive acts, groups and communities create an abundance of connection with one another, stockpiling goodwill and positive energy that members can draw on in the course of their work. In this thoughtful and perceptive chapter, Kahn reminds us that positive relationships are difficult to create and sustain, and that they are both "a marvelous and a fragile thing."

Organizations and Organizing Section

The final part of the book approaches positive work relationships from an organizational level and tackles the challenge of exploring how organizations affect, and are affected by, positive relationships at work. By viewing positive relationships through a macro lens, this section offers an important bridge between positive relationships and such topics as organizational culture, identity, effectiveness, and change.

Golden-Biddle et al. (chap. 16) leads off this section with a rich examination of the complex dynamics underlying the relationship between *organizational culture* and positive relationships at work. They explain that culture consists of symbolic forms through which individuals experience and express meaning in the workplace. Symbolic forms are representations involving language, goals, beliefs, and mission. Their case analysis of a Canadian health care organization offers keen insights into how cultural symbols shape organizational members' capacity to cultivate and sustain positive organizational relationships. Golden-Biddle and her colleagues discovered that culture not only shapes positive relationships, but that positive relationships shape culture by keeping symbolic forms alive and reinfusing them with meaning and significance. When capitalized on by leaders, this interdependence helped the organization transition through times of turmoil and change. These scholars found that positive relationships became a life-enriching and energy-producing resource that broadened organizational members' repertoires for dealing with change, and helped members reframe experiences from helplessness and lack of control to hope and purposeful action. This chapter offers the critical perspective that positive work relationships affect not only dyads and groups, but are also cultural products with symbolic meaning that can reflect and revitalize organizational culture.

Glynn and Wrobel (chap. 17) break important new ground by applying an institutional perspective to the study of positive family relationships at work. Their chapter examines the identity and institutional mechanisms that make *family relationships an endogenous resource for organizations.* Endogenous resources come from within the organization, usually through its people or cultural values. Glynn and Wrobel propose that family relationships can give an organization an identity when the family of the founder, CEO, or other prominent figure is displayed as part of the identity of the organization (e.g., Levi-Strauss, Harley-Davidson, Hewlett-Packard). According to Glynn and Wrobel, these positive family relationships become a form of social capital for the organization; they signal the firm's expertise, abundance, and trustworthiness. Glynn and Wrobel propose that positive family relationships can characterize, enliven, and legitimate a firm and its offerings to public audiences. The chapter addresses a critical gap in the literature by examining how organizational identities are grounded in personal identities that spring from positive family relationships. Their analysis of how identity mechanisms claim familial relationships as core attributes of the firm offers an innovative appraisal of the intertwining of personal and organizational identities. Another creative aspect of the chapter is their use of institutional theory to understand how institutional mechanisms serve to graft one social institution (family) to another (the firm). This chapter offers a fresh theoretical perspective on the use of positive family relationships as an endogenous resource over the life cycle of the firm and makes an important link between institutional and identity theory and organizational outcomes associated with PRW.

Baker and Dutton (chap. 18) expands our understanding of positive relationships at work by offering a new framework for understanding how *social mechanisms and organizational practices* foster the development of *positive social capital* at work. They start with introducing the concept of positive social capital. They explain that social capital is positive if it expands the generative capacity of individuals and groups and helps them achieve their personal and professional goals in new and better ways. They then explore how two forms of positive social capital (high-quality connections and reciprocity) increase the resource-producing capabilities of individuals and groups. A key insight of this chapter is the connection between positive social capital and organizational practices. Baker and Dutton offer the idea that different organizational practices activate and affirm employees' motivation to participate in generative connections and systems of relationships. They ground this framework by identifying clusters of human resource practices (selection, socialization, evaluation, rewards) as well as other everyday work practices (conduct of meetings, collaborative technologies, practices of interpersonal helping) that, through motivation and opportunity mechanisms, enable the development of positive social capital in organizations. This chapter offers a powerful framework for understanding how organizational systems and patterns of "everyday doing" can create or destroy positive social capital in organizations.

Fletcher (chap. 19) brings a vital new lens to the topic by conceptualizing leadership as a type of positive work relationship that is influenced by *gender, power, and societal dynamics*. The chapter applies a psychological model of human growth and development, the Stone Center relational theory (SRT), to the leadership arena to develop the concept of *relational leadership*. Fletcher explores the components of relational leadership, and proposes that it influences the relational climate of organizations through a spiraling process that leads to relational outcomes at multiple organizational levels. A key contribution of this chapter is its emphasis on societal factors that affect positive relationships at work. SRT offers a feminist orientation that deals directly with the issue of power differences in relational interactions, and Fletcher applies this perspective to leadership relationships. Fletcher explains that relational behaviors may be misinterpreted as displays of powerlessness for women and other groups with a history of less power in society. The experience and consequences of relational leadership may therefore be affected by the power associated with group membership. This chapter offers the necessary insight that systemic societal dynamics associated with power and group membership may influence organizational members' ability to develop, nurture, and sustain PRW.

The last part of this volume concludes with a commentator chapter by Rousseau and Ling (chap. 20) that deepens our understanding of positive relationships at work as a *resource for organizations*. Drawing on the chapters in this part, Rousseau and Ling offer an incisive analysis of the connection between positive organizational relationships and the resources exchanged by organizations and their members. They observe that positive organizational relationships are a critical form of resource exchange that serves as an intervening mechanism between situational and individual features and organizational responses. They capture the idea that positive work relationships make their participants "resource-rich" by creating efficiencies in the use of resources and by generating new resources that are scarce and valued. Rousseau and Ling point to the generative essence of positive organizational relationships, and make the critical point that positive relationships "substantially multiply the potentialities of people and organizations" and are generative in their ability to expand the array of available organizational resources ("the pie"). Their chapter also offers an interesting historical perspective by pointing out that a positive relationship at work perspective reclaims and resurrects themes of human growth and development that were prevalent in organizational research in the 1950s but were downplayed as organizational studies moved from social sciences to business schools. This insightful chapter not only illustrates the mechanisms through which positive work relationships create resources in organizations, but also highlights the importance of reclaiming a humanistic perspective that recognizes the influence of positive relationships in organizational life.

THE INVITATION

As this appreciative overview illustrates, the chapters in this volume offer a rich and multilayered foundation for building and nourishing positive relationships at work as a new field of inquiry. As a multidisciplinary and multilevel area of scholarship, PRW offers an abundant vista of exciting new research possibilities. We invite you to join us in exploring this promising new research frontier.

REFERENCES

Arthur, M. B., & Rousseau, D. M. (Eds.). (1996). *The boundaryless career: A new employment principle for a new organizational era.* New York: Oxford University Press.

Baker, W., Cross, R., & Wooten, M. (2003). Positive organizational network analysis and energizing relationships. In K. S. Cameron, J. E. Dutton, & R. E. Quinn (Eds.), *Positive organizational scholarship: Foundations of a new discipline* (pp. 328–342). San Francisco: Berrett-Koehler.

Berscheid, E. (1994). Interpersonal relationships. *Annual Review of Psychology, 45,* 79–129.

Berscheid, E. (1999). The greening of relationship science. *American Psychologist, 54,* 260–266.

Berscheid, E., & Reis, H. T. (1998). Attraction and close relationships. In D. T. Gilbert, S. T. Fiske, & G. Lindzey (Eds.), *The handbook of social psychology* (Vol. 2, 4th ed., pp. 193–281). New York: McGraw-Hill.

Blau, P. M. (1964). *Exchange and power in social life.* New York: Wiley.

Burt, R. S. (1992). *Structural holes.* Cambridge, MA: Harvard University Press.

Cameron, K. S., & Caza, A. (2004). Introduction: Contributions to the discipline of positive organizational scholarship. *The American Behavioral Scientist, 47,* 731–739.

Cameron, K. S., Dutton, J. E., & Quinn, R. E. (2003). Foundations of positive organizational scholarship. In K. S. Cameron, J. E. Dutton, & R. E. Quinn (Eds.), *Positive organizational scholarship: Foundations of a new discipline* (pp. 3–13). San Francisco: Berrett-Koehler.

Coleman, J. S. (1988). Social capital in the creation of human capital. *American Journal of Sociology, 94*(Suppl.), S95–S120.

Duck, S. (1994). *Meaningful relationships: Talking, sense, and relating.* Thousand Oaks, CA: Sage.

Dutton, J. E. (2003). *Energize your workplace: How to create and sustain high-quality connections at work.* San Francisco: Jossey-Bass.

Dutton, J. E., & Heaphy, E. D. (2003). The power of high-quality connections. In K. S. Cameron, J. E. Dutton, & R. E. Quinn (Eds.), *Positive organizational scholarship: Foundations of a new discipline* (pp. 263–278). San Francisco: Berrett-Koehler.

Gersick, C. J., Bartunek, J. M., & Dutton, J. E. (2000). Learning from academia: The importance of relationships in professional life. *Academy of Management Journal, 43,* 1026–1045.

Graen, G. B., & Scandura, T. A. (1987). Toward a psychology of dyadic organizing. In L. L. Cummings & B. M. Staw (Eds.), *Research in organizational behavior* (Vol. 9, pp. 175–208). Greenwich, CT: JAI.

Hall, D. T. (1996). Protean careers of the 21st century. *Academy of Management Executive, 10*(4), 8–16.

Harvey, J. H., & Pauwels, B. G. (2003). The ironies of positive psychology. *Psychological Inquiry, 14,* 125–128.

Hinde, R. A. (1979). *Towards understanding relationships.* New York: Academic.

Homans, G. (1974). *Social behavior: Its elementary forms.* New York: Harcourt, Brace & Jovanovich.

Kahn, W. A. (1993). Caring for the caregivers: Patterns of organizational caregiving. *Administrative Science Quarterly, 38,* 539–563.

Kahn, W. A. (1998). Relational systems at work. *Research in Organizational Behavior, 20,* 39–76.

Kram, K. (1985). *Mentoring at work: Developmental relationships in organizational life.* Glenview, IL: Scott, Foresman.

Kramer, R. M., & Tyler, T. R. (Eds.). (1996). *Trust in organizations: Frontiers of theory and research.* Thousand Oaks, CA: Sage.

Lave, J., & Wenger, E. (1991). *Situated learning: Legitimate peripheral participation.* New York: Cambridge University Press.

Luthans, F. (2002). The need for and meaning of positive organizational behavior. *Journal of Organizational Behavior, 23,* 695–706.

Luthans, F., & Youssef, C. M. (2004). Human, social, and now positive psychological capital management: Investing in people for competitive advantage. *Organizational Dynamics, 33,* 143–160.

Miller, J. B., & Stiver, I. (1997). *The healing connection.* Boston: Beacon Press.

Ragins, B. R. (in press). Disclosure disconnects: Antecedents and consequences of disclosing invisible stigmas across life domains. *Academy of Management Review.*

Ragins, B. R., & Kram, K. (Eds.). (in press). *The handbook of mentoring at work: Theory, research and practice.* Thousand Oaks, CA: Sage.

Reis, H. T., & Gable, S. L. (2003). Toward a positive psychology of relationships. In C. L. M. Keyes & J. Haidt (Eds.), *Flourishing: Positive psychology and the life well-lived* (pp. 129–159). Washington, DC: American Psychological Association.

Seligman, M. E. P., & Csikszentmihalyi, M. (2000). Positive psychology: An introduction. *American Psychologist, 55,* 5–14.

Snyder, C. R., & Lopez, S. J. (Eds.). (2002). *Handbook of positive psychology.* New York: Oxford University Press.

Spreitzer, G., Sutcliffe, K, Dutton, J., Sonenshein, S., & Grant, A. M. (2005). A socially embedded model of thriving at work. *Organization Science, 16,* 537–553.

Uchino, B., Cacioppo, J. T., & Kiecolt-Glaser, J. K. (1996). The relationship between social support and physiological processes: A review with emphasis on underlying mechanisms and implications for health. *Psychological Bulletin, 119,* 488–531.

POSITIVE RELATIONSHIPS:
INDIVIDUALS AND DYADS

From Proving to Becoming: How Positive Relationships Create a Context for Self-Discovery and Self-Actualization

Laura Morgan Roberts

In a real sense all life is interrelated. All [people] are caught in an inescapable network of mutuality, tied in a single garment of destiny. Whatever affects one directly affects all indirectly. I can never be what I ought to be until you are what you ought to be, and you can never be what you ought to be until I am what I ought to be. This is the interrelated structure of reality.

—Rev. Dr. Martin Luther King, Jr. (Foner, 1972)

Identity is inherently linked to relationships; it is difficult to separate identity, or the self-system that explains ourselves to the world and to ourselves (Gecas, 1982), from the social relationships in which it is embedded. These relationships provide the context for self-definition as well as direct feedback about our strengths, weaknesses, similarities, and differences. Take the scene in the childhood fairy tale *Snow White,* where the Queen must literally consult a mirror every morning to affirm her own greatness, asking "Mirror, Mirror on the wall, who's the fairest of them all?" Such a simple refrain profoundly illustrates the link between reflected appraisals and identity; that is, the importance of using reflections of the self to discover one's relative strengths, weaknesses, commonalities, and distinguishing characteristics.

It is well established that human beings have a pervasive drive to form and maintain lasting, positive, and significant interpersonal relations (Baumeister & Leary, 1995; Lawrence & Nohria, 2002). Rejection, exclusion, or being ignored leads to anxiety, grief, depression, loneliness, and jealousy, whereas acceptance leads to positive emotions of happiness, elation, contentment, calm, and personal growth (Baumeister & Leary, 1995; Fletcher, 1998; Kram, 1996). Therefore, in work organizations, individuals seek to form and maintain mutually beneficial relationships with peers, superiors, and subordinates to gain instrumental assistance and social support (Gersick, Bartunek, & Dutton, 2000; Higgins, 2001; Higgins & Kram, 2001; Kram, 1996; Thomas, 1993).

In charting a new terrain of research on the nature and implications of positive relationships, it is especially important to understand the process by which positive relationships influence individuals' identities. Dutton and Heaphy (2003) argued that "the quality of the connection [between individuals] matters to the content and evaluation of the identity that employees form, claim and express at work" (p. 270). A considerable amount of research on identity–relationship causal links has focused on the properties of dyadic relationships that negatively impact the self-concept. Although we take for granted the notion that identities are inherently social, research has only begun to address the differential impact of positive versus negative relationships on one's sense of self. Further, we have a limited understanding of how one's sense of self can affect the potential for relational growth and development in work organizations.

This chapter highlights the generative, identity-enhancing dynamics that can emerge in the context of positive relationships. I describe the mechanisms by which positive relationships can enhance identities, which in turn, can strengthen the quality of the connection between individuals. Specifically, positive relationships enable people to learn more about themselves (in particular, the valued and distinctive aspects of their identity) and provide the inspiration and social support to achieve fulfilling, identity-congruent outcomes. I then offer that identity enhancement may be a powerful mechanism for transforming relationships from a state of damaging disconnection to one of growth-enhancing connection. These hypotheses regarding the link between positive relationships and positive identity raise a host of questions that may guide future research in this domain. I conclude the chapter with potential avenues for future research on the positive relationship–identity link.

ENABLING CONNECTIONS: HOW POSITIVE RELATIONSHIPS ENHANCE AND ENRICH IDENTITIES

Numerous researchers have validated the claims that identities are socially constructed and that one must wear the eye of the beholder to truly discover one's own identity. For example, Cooley's (1902) construction of the "looking glass self" suggested that others' reactions to our behavior and self-expressions constitute the viewpoint from which we define our own performance and attributes. We answer the question, "Who am I?" based on the imagination of our appearance to the other, the imagination of his or her judgment of our appearance, and the feeling of pride or mortification associated with that external judgment. Research on symbolic interactionism continued in this vein of anchoring the self-concept in interpersonal interactions. Goffman (1959) and Mead (1934) extended the notion of the looking glass self from a present to a future orientation. They did so by suggesting that people define themselves by taking the responses of others into account; specifically, by adopting the perspective of the generalized other, transforming others' reactions into anticipatory capacities for self-regulation, and then performing roles according to normative expectations of who they should be and who they should become.

Based on this research, one might assume that a relationship that enhances and enriches one's identity is positive, whereas an identity-threatening relationship would be negative. To better understand identity-enhancing functions of positive relationships, it is critical that we first provide greater specificity about the characteristics of positive relationships. Further, it is important to identify the mechanisms by which certain relationships can enhance and enrich people's sense of self.

A positive relationship is one in which there is a true sense of relatedness and mutuality. It is not enough to believe that one is cared for or has others on whom he or she can rely—one must also experience giving and receiving, mutual caring, and safety in times of distress (Baumeister & Leary, 1995). In work environments, four dimensions of mutuality are critical in forming positive relationships: mutual benefit, mutual influence, mutual expectations, and mutual understanding (Blau, 1964; Gabarro, 1987; Luft, 1984; Miller & Stiver, 1997). A positive relationship enhances the quality of life for both parties. Both parties in the relationship experience themselves as being "better off" and being better people as a result of the relationship. In a positive relationship, both parties also have mutual influence on one another, so that both people are learning from one another through the connection. Mutuality is also important with respect to expectations; both parties have clarity and agreement on roles and boundaries in the relationship. Fourth, in a positive relationship, both parties understand one another's intentions and are aware of the impact of their behavior on the other party. Mutuality is essential for generating identity-enhancing outcomes. In positive relationships, people are likely to become more self-aware of strengths and limitations, to feel affirmed, and to become more open to continued growth and development.

Mutual understanding, influence, benefit, and expectations create the possibility for greater self-discovery and a heightened sense of self-efficacy.

When both parties feel that they are known and understood, they are more likely to trust, respect, and like one another (Cole & Taboul, 2004; Kahn, 2001; Miller & Stiver, 1997; Polzer, Milton, & Swann, 2002; Swann, Polzer, Selye, & Ko, 2004). Moreover, when people are clear about what is expected of them in a relationship, they are better able to meet those expectations, which can build trust, liking, respect, satisfaction, and commitment (Dabos & Rousseau, 2004; Davidson & James, 2006). As such, positive relationships are often associated with fulfilled relational expectations and genuine appreciation for what each party contributes to the relationship and to the social environment (Young & Perrewe, 2000).

In the context of such positive relationships, people may be more likely to learn about when and why other people experience them positively, and how they can generate such positive reactions in the future. Mutuality may lead to a more frequent and rich exchange of feedback regarding how each party benefits from the others' presence. For example, intimate relationships are characterized by a greater likelihood to give and receive feedback (Lundgren, 2004), which may increase the self-awareness of both parties in a positive relationship. Specifically, positive relationships increase the salience of positive aspects of one's identity (Dutton & Heaphy, 2003) and can help individuals to discover their sources of strength, competence, contribution, and added value at work (Roberts, Dutton, Spreitzer, Heaphy, & Quinn, 2005). Over time, this heightened salience can lead to identity change. As people become more aware of their strengths and contributions, they may begin to see themselves more favorably, internalizing positive feedback and changing self-views to be more consistent with others' positive appraisals (Drigotas, Rusbult, Wieselquist, & Whitton, 1999; Kernis & Johnson, 1990; Malloy, Albright, Kenny, Agatstein, & Winquist, 1997; Tice & Wallace, 2003).

One might imagine a disconcerting scenario in which two parties provide one another with only positive feedback, feeding into one another's delusions of grandeur and fueling destructive behavior. In such a scenario, both parties would be less open to learning about themselves or to using new self-knowledge for growth and development. However, research suggests that the opposite is likely to occur in relationships that are characterized by mutual expectations, influence, benefit, and understanding. Such affirmation can actually provide the psychosocial resources required for personal growth and identity change.

The absence of mutuality leads to a state of disconnection, in which individuals are more likely to perpetrate and to experience a host of identity threats: processes that threaten the perceived adequacy or integrity of the self (Breakwell, 1986; Clair, Beatty, & Maclean, 2005; Roberts, 2005; Steele, 1988, 2004). Identity threat narrows attention and eats away at one's ability to learn, show initiative, and take risks (Crocker & Park, 2004; Dutton, 2003).

On the contrary, positive relationships facilitate the willingness and capacity to learn and experiment (Davidson & James, 2006; Dutton, 2003; Fletcher, 1998). These positive relationships also facilitate the constructive exchange of critical feedback, by buffering feelings of anxiety and defensiveness that normally accompany feedback processes.

Mutual understanding requires that both parties inquire about the impact of one's actions on the other, separate from one's intent, to reveal blind spots (Luft, 1984; Stone, Patton, & Heen, 1999). Even with noble intentions, one may inadvertently cause another person hardship or distress. One must accept personal responsibility for the positive and negative impact of their actions if a relationship is to meet the criteria of mutual understanding. When people feel known, understood, and affirmed, they are more likely to proactively seek performance feedback because they have fewer impression management concerns (Ashford, Blatt, & Van de Walle, 2003). They are also more likely to trust that positive and negative feedback are accurate and well-intended. For example, Cohen, Steele, and Ross (1999) found that people were more likely to accept criticism when they were told that they were being evaluated on high performance standards and that the evaluator believed that they had the capability to reach such standards. Visualizing close, positive relationships makes people more receptive to additional feedback about newly discovered performance and intellectual deficiencies (Kumashiro & Sedikides, 2005).

Positive relationships also provide the psychosocial support and inspiration required for identity change and growth. When one experiences affirmation, relational satisfaction, and positive expectancies, one is also likely to experience positive emotions. Positive emotions facilitate discovery and experimentation by expanding one's thought–action repertoire, leading one to consider a wider range of possibilities for what may occur and whom one can become (Fredrickson, 1998). For example, positive emotions can inspire individuals to enact their reflected best-self, employing their strengths in a way that creates a positive experience for them and a constructive experience for others (Roberts et al., 2005).

Positive relationships may also provide a secure base for learning and becoming, which leads to increased growth and development (Bolwby, 1982; Edmondson, 1999; Kahn, 2001). When mutuality exists, people are less likely to experience identity threats and more likely to experience identity affirmation. Positive relationships may invoke a learning orientation (Grant & Dweck, 2003), such that people can experiment with new skills, tasks, and even identities without the challenge of proving their legitimacy and worth to an audience that holds negative expectations. People may be less likely to engage in withdrawal and ego-preservation tactics that focus on validating self-worth, and more likely to consider failures, criticism, and negative feedback as opportunities to learn and improve (Crocker & Park, 2004).

When individuals experience a sense of being known and understood, they may also be encouraged to experiment with new identities, a critical component of self-discovery and self-actualization (Ibarra, 2003). In sum, positive relationships provide people with the desire, agency, and capacity to fully utilize their strengths, make important contributions, and grow and develop. Mutuality enables people to view themselves as capable of making important contributions in the lives of those around them and to consider how they might grow and develop to make these contributions more often.

The identity-enhancing and enriching functions of positive relationships often create a mutually reinforcing cycle. As people experience themselves as being known, understood, and affirmed, they are more likely to build trust. Across disciplines, the common definition of trust is "a psychological state comprising the intention to accept vulnerability based upon positive expectations of the intentions or behavior of another" (Rousseau, Sitkin, Burt, & Camerer, 1998, p. 395). When trust exists, people are likely to engage in more self-disclosure and reveal their vulnerability (Aron, 2003; Kahn, 1992; Miller & Stiver, 1997; Reis & Patrick, 1996). This self-disclosure, in turn, can strengthen the tie between parties by generating even more mutual understanding and calibrating expectations. In addition, people who have a greater sense of agency may have a greater capacity to make significant contributions to others' lives, which can enhance the sense of mutual benefit. Ultimately, as identities are enhanced and enriched, relationships become even more positive.

REVERSING THE TIDE: IDENTITY ENHANCEMENT AS A MECHANISM FOR RELATIONAL TRANSFORMATION

The previous section focused primarily on the direct relation between positive identities and positive relationships. There is also a less obvious dimension to the identity–relationship link. Not only do positive relationships enhance identities, but identity enhancement may be a vehicle for repairing and restoring negative relationships.

Relationships that are characterized by a considerable degree of psychological or emotional disconnect between individuals can have a profound impact on how both parties think and feel about themselves. In the midst of interactions, people often experience a sense of disconnection from the person with whom they are interacting, which arises from feeling misperceived, misunderstood, or invisible in the other person's eyes (Dutton, 2003; Ellemers, Spears, & Doosje, 2002). In Dutton's (2003) words, even "small acts of exclusion and the simple lack of recognition chip away at a sense of self-worth and competence" (p. 9). A negative relationship with one's boss, colleague, or client, in which one is seen as illegitimate, inadequate, or unworthy, can severely inhibit the quality of one's work and can undermine one's overall experience at work. As long as someone is dependent on another person for his or her livelihood or career advancement, he or she must find ways to establish functional working relationships.

People frequently employ two types of identity-enhancement strategies—self-focused and other-focused—to build and restore working relationships. Self-focused identity-enhancement strategies are often motivated by a desire to prove oneself: proving that one's own identity claims are legitimate and others' perceptions are inaccurate. For example, individuals may seek to repair their damaged identities by engaging in self-presentational behaviors that correct misperceptions and disconfirm negative expectations (Baretto & Ellemers, 2002; Branscombe & Ellemers, 1998; Jones & Pittman, 1982; Roberts, 2005; Shih, 2003; Tedeschi & Melburg, 1984). These self-enhancement strategies generate a number of favorable personal and career outcomes, including self-verification, client satisfaction, and career promotion (Baumeister, 1982; Ibarra, 1999; Leary & Kowalski, 1990; Rosenfeld, Giacalone, & Riordan, 2001; Schlenker, 2003).

Despite these potentially favorable benefits, attempts to defend and prove one's identity can lead to a number of costly outcomes in work organizations. First, proving might lead to an inordinate focus on monitoring and changing others' perceptions of self, which can ultimately interfere with performance goals. A natural consequence of threat is heightened vigilance and narrowed focus (Staw, Sandelands, & Dutton, 1981), and potential targets of identity threat pay more attention to others' perceptions of them than people who are in high-status or favorably regarded positions (Fiske, 1993; Kanter, 1977; Lord & Saenz, 1985). In some cases, such monitoring can enable one to be seen as likable (Miller, Rothblum, Felicio, & Brand, 1995; Miller & Myers, 1998). However, monitoring others' perceptions and focusing on preserving one's own ego can be cognitively distracting, inhibiting one's ability to focus on task performance (Baumeister, Bratslavsky, Muraven, & Tice, 1998; Ely & Meyerson, 2006). Ironically, attempts to prove oneself may actually backfire by confirming negative expectations, as in the case of stereotype threat, where individuals become so concerned with being viewed stereotypically that they are less able to demonstrate their ability (Steele, 2004). People who are deeply invested in proving their own ability and ensuring that negative stereotypes are not applied to them are more likely to underperform on diagnostic tasks (e.g., standardized tests) than those who are less concerned with proving their ability (Steele & Aronson, 1995).

A proving stance not only impairs current task performance, it may also inhibit one's ability to improve performance on future tasks. Individuals who are subject to identity threat are less likely to engage in constructive feedback-seeking behaviors; instead of directly inquiring about their own performance, they rely on monitoring for implicit cues (Ashford et al., 2003; Roberson, Deitch, Brief, & Block, 2003). Such individuals are also more likely to reject feedback about one's identity that may potentially threaten one's identity (Cohen et al., 1999; Crocker & Major, 1989; Crocker, Voelkl, Testa, & Major, 1991). Thus, people in a defensive or proving stance may become less willing or able to learn anything about themselves, remain rigidly fixated on their own self-concepts, and focus even more on validating abilities to feed their own egos (Crocker & Park, 2004).

Third, one who is focused on proving his or her worth and legitimacy may even suppress important information about the self, thereby deceiving others about one's identity. For example, a medical resident may not tell an attending physician that he is unsure about a patient's diagnosis to prevent the likelihood that she will think he is unqualified for his position. People who present themselves in an inauthentic manner experience dissonance between their external behavior and internal values (Baumeister, 1982; Bell, 1990; Ibarra, 1999). They are also less likely to receive self-verifying feedback from others and are more likely to limit others' opportunities to know who they really are (Polzer, Milton, & Swann, 2002; Swann et al., 2004). Moreover, the targets of such impression management behavior may become aware of the inauthenticity and feel manipulated or deceived (Roberts, 2005; Rosenfeld, Giacolone, & Riordan, 1995). Instead of creating a connection based on mutual understanding, this type of inauthentic behavior can actually create a more damaging disconnect, deepening the divide between two people.

In sum, the risk of employing self-focused identity-enhancement strategies is that they often lead to an inordinate focus on proving one's worth at all costs, which creates barriers for personal and relational growth. When one is stuck in a cycle of proving his or her worthiness or legitimacy to others, it becomes difficult to entertain ideas of personal change. Rather than become consumed with receiving validation and affirmation, one must remain open to learning about, learning from, and affirming others to transform relationships from a state of disconnection to true relatedness and mutuality. Thus these self-focused strategies must be balanced with other-focused identity-enhancement strategies.

If other-focused identity enhancement is to successfully transform relationships, it must be motivated by a sincere desire to help another person see himself or herself more favorably. One could easily mistake all acts of ingratiation, flattery, and deference for other-focused identity-enhancement strategies. These behaviors involve helping others to see themselves as accomplished, benevolent, and powerful (Baumeister, 1982; Jones, 1964; Rosenfeld, Giacalone, & Riordan, 1995). Yet, these behaviors are often employed to serve self-enhancing motives; one might compliment her boss so that the boss will think she is a kind person. If the underlying motive is to enhance one's own identity, these behaviors would fall under the former category of self-focused rather than other-focused identity enhancement. Further, if one does not sincerely believe that another person is worthy of admiration or respect, but behaves as if he or she does, this inauthenticity will limit the capacity for other-focused identity enhancement to transform the relationship. At best, only one party will experience the positive emotions that result from affirmation; at worst, both parties will be aware of the deception, and will associate negative affect with the relationship. Most of all, mutuality will not increase unless both parties genuinely understand, appreciate, and benefit one another.

Other-focused identity enhancement is most effective when it is based on a deep understanding and appreciation of another person. Research has consistently demonstrated that perspective-taking is a key mechanism for increasing mutual understanding and enhancing identities. Perspective-taking involves cognitive and emotional processes for imagining another's thoughts and feelings from that person's point of view (Mead, 1934). Engaging in active perspective-taking leads to greater empathy, concern, identification, and pleasure with another's achievements (Parker & Axtell, 2001; Williams, 2001). Perspective-taking generates other-focused identity enhancement through three mechanisms: positive attributions, self-target overlap, and self-verification. Perspective-taking leads people to recognize external circumstances that can lead to failure and to acknowledge the internal characteristics that enable another's success (Galper, 1976; Parker & Axtell, 2001; Regan & Totten, 1975). When people engage in perspective-taking, they are also less likely to stereotype others, because they perceive more commonalities between how they see themselves and how they see others (Davis, Conklin, Smith, & Luce, 1996; Galinsky, Ku, & Wang, 2005; Galinsky & Moskovic, 2000). Positive attributions and self–other overlap enable people to see others more favorably, which may also lead others to see themselves more favorably based on more sincere and frequent affirmation. Adopting another's perspective also enables one to learn which aspects of the other's identity are most valued. This knowledge can increase the likelihood of identity confirmation (Swann et al., 2004), because one can reflect back the personal and social identity characteristics that are most meaningful and verifying to the other.

Taken together, this research suggests that a combination of self-focused and other-focused identity enhancement strategies is required for relational growth. One must communicate and agree on expectations, ensure that both parties are benefiting from the relationship, help others to understand one's own intentions while learning about the impact of one's own actions, and balance power dynamics so that both parties have influence.

The reason proving falls short of generating a positive relationship in these terms is because it focuses largely on advocating for oneself without learning about the other party. Attempts to convince others of the significance of one's own contributions are often thwarted by others' lack of desire or interest in observing or taking seriously those contributions. Before one can prove oneself, one must engage the other party in a way that enhances his or her desire to learn more about you and his or her openness to see you differently. Self-focused identity enhancement is important, but it must often be preceded by other-focused identity enhancement. The catalyst for relational transformation often lies in helping others to see how they add value; sincere appreciation for another's perspectives and contributions can open the door for clarifying expectations, being influenced, deepening understanding, and receiving mutual benefits from engagement.

FUTURE RESEARCH DIRECTIONS FOR POSITIVE RELATIONSHIPS AND IDENTITY

There are a number of personal and organizational benefits of positive relationships, particularly with respect to their positive impact on identity. As described in this chapter, positive relationships not only buffer inhibiting mechanisms such as threat, suppression, and defensiveness, but they also create new opportunities for enhancing one's conception of self and inspiring individuals to live in accordance with their best self.

It is important to note that much of this chapter is based on inferences drawn from extant literature rather than explicit, detailed studies of the positive relationship–identity link. Many more empirical studies have been conducted that directly test the deleterious impact of negative relationships on identity than those that document how relationships can enhance and enrich one's sense of self. As such, the chapter should be read as a series of propositions rather than conclusive findings, intended to spark interest in systematic investigations of the positive relationship–identity link. Several questions remain unanswered; the following list is designed to sketch possible pathways for future research in this domain.

The first pathway for future research in this domain is identifying contingencies of the positive relationship–identity link. More exploration is needed to learn under what conditions positive relationships enhance identities and positive identities strengthen relationships. For example, must all four criteria of mutuality be present for a relationship to positively impact one person's identity? Must all four criteria be present to positively impact the identities of both parties in the relationship? One proposition is that important or significant relationships, such as those with a romantic partner, an important client, a supervisor, or a subordinate, carry greater potential for shaping identity. As Rosenberg (1979) stated, "Not all significant others are equally significant, and those who are more significant have greater influence on our self-concepts" (p. 83).

Competing hypotheses have been offered regarding the impact of relationships on the self-concept. Research on the self-fulfilling prophecy suggests that others' perceptions are correlated with self-perceptions and actions; in keeping with the principle of reflected appraisals, studies find that when individuals are viewed negatively, they will see themselves and behave in accordance with negative expectancies (Darley & Fazio, 1980; Snyder & Stukas, 1999). An equally compelling stream of research supports that others' reflections inform and shape, but do not determine, one's self-concept. When individuals are consciously aware of others' perceptions, they engage in an agentic and deliberate process of cocreating their own identities. By cognitively and behaviorally resisting the internalization of negative perceptions, people are able to maintain psychological ownership of their self-concept (Crocker & Major, 1989; Hilton & Darley, 1985; Leary & Kowalski, 1990; Lundgren, 2004; Miller & Myers, 1998; Steele, 2004; Swann, 1987). The same resistance may prevent some positive relationships from enhancing one's self-concept.

Further, a dichotomous characterization of relationships as being unitarily bad (negative) or good (positive) adds to the complexity of differentiating identity-enhancing from identity-threatening relationships. In reality, most relationships are likely to have positive and negative moments, in which there are states of more or less connection. For example, Ragins and Verbos (chap. 5, this volume) complicate our understanding of mentoring by discussing mentoring states along a relationship continuum.

Most relationships also contain the capacity for both identity-threatening exchanges and identity-enhancing exchanges to occur; for example, bosses usually deliver critical and affirmative feedback to their employees. Ibarra (2003) described how some intimate relationships may actually constrain one's identity, limiting one's ability to consider new possibilities for who one can become. Moreover, the principle of tough love, often utilized by sports coaches, suggests that performance-enhancing benefits result from withholding affirmation. Therefore, more sophisticated criteria are needed for capturing the qualities of relationships that, on balance, contain a greater proportion of identity-enhancing experiences than identity-threatening experiences, and lead to the virtuous cycle of positive identity change and relational growth. Experimental, event-sampling, and longitudinal methodologies would be appropriate to determine if and when positive relationships enhance identities, and when identity enhancement enables relational growth.

The discussion of relationships and identity in this chapter is also limited in its conceptualization of relationships at the dyadic level. Both social network and social support research suggests that the constellation of one's dyadic relationships influences career and well-being outcomes (Higgins, 2001; Higgins & Kram, 2001). In the future, research might explore how social networks influence identity, and whether certain properties of social networks (diversity, range, size) and status (centrality) are more likely to enhance and enrich one's identity (see Higgins, chap. 11, this volume). For example, one might expect that people with more high-quality connections with people at work would also have a strong sense of identification with their work group, organization, and professional identity, as well as a deep awareness of and appreciation for their strengths and limitations. Such a network might also buffer the impact of potentially threatening experiences that could otherwise undermine one's sense of worth and legitimacy at work.

It would be interesting to explore whether the proportion of nonwork to work-related high-quality connections influences the potential for identity change. Can a strong network of relationships outside of the work environment, yet characterized by mutuality, effectively buffer the impact of identity threats that one might experience at work? Can such relationships grant one the courage and confidence required to engage in vulnerable self-disclosure and perspective-taking, such that one would be more open to seeking true relatedness? Would such a strong, outside network sufficiently fulfill one's desire for belongingness, and reduce one's willingness to make oneself vulnerable and open to perspective-taking with work colleagues, clients, superiors, and subordinates? Moreover, the context of one's relationships (work or nonwork) may increase the salience of different aspects of one's identities (Ashforth, 2001). Many outside work relationships may enhance the positive aspects of one's personal but not professional, identity.

In this realm, one might consider whether the quality of relationships among work groups impacts one's sense of self. Research on work teams documents how psychological safety enhances group learning by creating the freedom to make mistakes without being judged or socially ostracized (Edmondson, 1999). It is possible that psychological safety in one's work group may reduce the likelihood of personal identity threats and generate opportunities for mutual identity enhancement to occur among teammates. Milton and Westphal (2005) extended research on identity confirmation to social networks; they found that the pattern of identity confirmation networks among group members affects cooperation and group performance. These studies suggest that it is important to consider how positive relationships among work groups and social networks might enhance identities.

It is also important to extend research on positive relationships and identity beyond personal identity characteristics to social identity characteristics. The significance and meaning that individuals associate with social identity groups may influence their willingness to build positive relationships across dimensions of difference in work organizations. For example, homophily, the desire to affiliate with similar others, often restricts network formation to same-race ties among Whites and ethnic minorities in the workplace (Ibarra, 1995; Mehra, Kilduff, & Brass, 1998). This desire for similarity is compounded by stereotypes that negatively influence people's expectations about members of racial groups other than their own (Devine, 1989). Davidson and James (chap. 7, this volume) suggest that many of the same identity-enhancing dynamics that were offered in this chapter (e.g., learning orientation, appreciating strengths) may be important in establishing and enriching high-quality relationships across difference.

Finally, the research agenda on positive relationships and identity should focus on linking theory to practice by informing organizational design decisions. Ely and Meyerson (2006) characterized organizations as contexts for identity construction and relational development that create the context where positive relationships can flourish. Additional research in this domain might help to shed light on the following questions, each of which is important for individual, group, and organizational functioning. How do organizations create a culture of connection, where it is valid and normative to reveal and reflect positive attributes? How do organizations encourage individuals to reveal positive and authentic aspects of their identities to others and to mirror and reflect others' positive and/or authentic identities to them? It is especially important to consider the implications of this research on identity and positive relationships in increasingly diverse organizations within an increasingly global society. The answers to these questions will provide the pathway toward creating organizations that catalyze, nourish, and sustain both positive relationships and positive identities. Through systematic research using the lens of identity, we might discover how to truly unleash the power and possibility of positive relationships in work organizations.

REFERENCES

Aron, A. (2003). Self and close relationships. In M. R. Leary & J. P. Tangney (Eds.), *Handbook of self and identity* (pp. 442–461). New York: Guilford.

Ashford, S. J., Blatt, R., & Van de Walle, D. (2003). Reflections on the looking glass: A review of research on feedback-seeking behavior in organizations. *Journal of Management, 29,* 773–799.

Ashforth, B. (2001). *Role transitions in organizational life: An identity-based perspective.* Mahwah, NJ: Lawrence Erlbaum Associates.

Baretto, M., & Ellemers, N. (2000). You can't always do what you want: Social identity and self-presentational determinants of the choice to work for a low-status group. *Personality and Social Psychology Bulletin, 26,* 891–906.

Baumeister, R. F. (1982). A self-presentational view of social phenomena. *Psychological Bulletin, 91,* 3–26.

Baumeister, R., Bratslavsky, E., Muraven, M., & Tice, D. (1998). Ego depletion: Is the active self a limited resource? *Journal of Personality and Social Psychology, 74,* 1252–1265.

Baumeister, R. F., & Leary, M. R. (1995). The need to belong: Desire for interpersonal attachments as a fundamental human motivation. *Psychological Bulletin, 117,* 497–529.

Bell, E. L. (1990). The bicultural life experience of career-oriented Black women. *Journal of Organizational Behavior, 11,* 459–477.

Blau, P. M. (1964). *Exchange and power in social life.* New York: Wiley.

Bowlby, J. (1982). *Attachment and loss: Vol. I. Attachment* (2nd ed.). New York: Basic Books.

Branscombe, N. R., & Ellemers, N. (1998). Coping with group-based discrimination: Individualistic versus group-level strategies. In J. Swim & C. Stangor (Eds.), *Prejudice: The target's perspective* (pp. 243–266). San Diego, CA: Academic.

Breakwell, G. M. (1986). *Coping with threatened identities.* New York: Metheum.

Clair, J., Beatty, J., & Maclean, T. (2005). Out of sight but not out of mind: Managing invisible social identities in the workplace. *Academy of Management Review, 30,* 78–95.

Cohen, G., L., Steele, C., & Ross, L. (1999). The mentor's dilemma: Providing critical feedback across the racial divide. *Personality and Social Psychology Bulletin, 25,* 1302–1318.

Cole, T., & Taboul, J. C. (2004). Non-zero-sum collaboration, reciprocity, and the preference for similarity: Developing an adaptive model of close relational functioning. *Personal Relationships, 11,* 135–160.

Cooley, C. H. (1902). *Human nature and the social order.* New York: Scribners.

Crocker, J., & Major, B. (1989). Social stigma and self-esteem: The self-protective properties of stigma. *Psychological Review, 96,* 608–630.

Crocker, J., & Park, L. (2004). The costly pursuit of self-esteem. *Psychological Bulletin, 130,* 392–414.

Crocker, J., Voelkl, K., Testa, M., & Major, B. (1991). Social stigma: Affective consequences of attributional ambiguity. *Journal of Personality and Social Psychology, 60,* 218–228.

Dabos, G., & Rousseau, D. (2004). Mutuality and reciprocity in the psychological contracts of employees and employers. *Journal of Applied Psychology, 89,* 52–72.

Darley, J., & Fazio, R. (1980). Expectancy confirmation processes arising in the social interaction sequence. *American Psychologist, 35*(10), 867–881.

Davis, M., Conklin, L., Smith, A., & Luce, C. (1996). Effect of perspective-taking on the cognitive representation of persons: A merging of self and other. *Journal of Personality and Social Psychology, 70,* 713–726.

Devine, P. (1989). Stereotypes and prejudice: Their automatic and controlled components. *Journal of Personality and Social Psychology, 56,* 5–18.

Drigotas, S., Rusbult, C., Wieselquist, J., & Whitton, S. W. (1999). Close partner as sculptor of the ideal self: Behavioral affirmation and the Michelangelo phenomenon. *Journal of Personality and Social Psychology, 77,* 293–323.

Dutton, J. (2003). *Energize your workplace: How to create and sustain high quality connections at work.* San Francisco: Jossey-Bass.

Dutton, J. E., & Heaphy, E. D. (2003). Coming to life: The power of high quality connections at work. In K. Cameron, J. Dutton, & R. E. Quinn (Eds.), *Positive organizational scholarship* (pp. 263–278). San Francisco: Berrett-Koehler.

Edmondson, A. (1999). Psychological safety and learning behavior in work teams. *Administrative Science Quarterly, 44,* 350–383.

Ellemers, N., Spears, R., & Doosje, B. (2002). Self and social identity. *Annual Review of Psychology, 53,* 161–186.

Ely, R., & Meyerson, D. (2006). *Unmasking manly men: The organizational reconstruction of men's identity.* Best Paper Proceedings of the Academy of Management Meetings.

Fiske, S. T. (1993). Controlling other people: The impact of power on stereotyping. *American Psychologist, 48,* 621–628.

Fletcher, J. (1998). Relational practice: A feminist reconstruction of work. *Journal of Management Inquiry, 7,* 163–186.

Foner, P. S. (Ed.). (1972). Speech by Martin Luther King, Jr. at Indiana University. In P. S. Foner (Ed.), *The voice of Black America*. New York: Simon and Schuster.

Fredrickson, B. L. (1998). What good are positive emotions? *Review of General Psychology, 2,* 300–319.

Gabarro, J. J. (1987). *The dynamics of taking charge*. Boston: Harvard Business School Press.

Galinsky, A., Ku, J., & Wang, C. (2005). Perspective-taking and self–other overlap: Fostering social bonds and facilitating social coordination. *Group Processes and Intergroup Relations, 8,* 109–124.

Galinsky, A., & Moskovic, G. (2000). Perspective-taking: Decreasing stereotype expression, stereotype accessibility, and in-group favoritism. *Journal of Personality and Social Psychology, 78,* 708–724.

Galper, R. E. (1976). Turning observers into actors: Differential causal attributions as a function of "empathy." *Journal of Research in Personality, 10,* 328–335.

Gecas, V. (1982). The self concept. *Annual Review of Sociology, 8,* 1–33.

Gersick, C., Bartunek, J., & Dutton, J. (2000). Learning from academia: The importance of relationships in professional life. *Academy of Management Journal, 43,* 1026–1044.

Goffman, E. (1959). *The presentation of self in everyday life*. New York: Anchor Doubleday.

Grant, H., & Dweck, C. (2003). Clarifying achievement goals and their impact. *Journal of Personality and Social Psychology, 85,* 541–553.

Higgins, M. C. (2001). Changing careers: The effects of social context. *Journal of Organizational Behavior, 22,* 595–618.

Higgins, M. C., & Kram, K. (2001). Reconceptualizing mentoring at work: A developmental network perspective. *Academy of Management Review, 26,* 264–288.

Hilton, J., & Darley, J. (1985). Constructing other persons: A limit on the effect. *Journal of Experimental Social Psychology, 21,* 1–18.

Ibarra, H. (2003). *Working identity: Unconventional strategies for reinventing your career*. Cambridge, MA: Harvard Business School Press.

Ibarra, H. (1995). Race, opportunity and diversity of social circles in management networks. *Academy of Management Journal, 18,* 56–87.

Ibarra, H. (1999). Provisional selves: Experimenting with image and identity in professional adaptation. *Administrative Science Quarterly, 44,* 764–791.

Jones, E. (1964). *Ingratiation: A social psychological analysis*. New York, Appleton-Century-Crofts.

Jones, E., & Pittman, T. (1982). Toward a general theory of strategic self-presentation. In J. Suls (Ed.), *Psychological perspectives on the self* (pp. 231–262). Hillsdale, NJ: Lawrence Erlbaum Associates.

Kahn, W. A. (1992). To be fully there: Psychological presence at work. *Human Relations, 45,* 321–349.

Kahn, W. A. (2001). Holding environments at work. *Journal of Applied Behavioral Science, 37,* 260–279.

Kanter, R. M. (1977). *Men and women of the corporation*. New York: Basic Books.

Kernis, M., & Johnson, E. (1990). Current and typical self-appraisals: Differential responsiveness to evaluative feedback and implications for emotions. *Journal of Research in Personality, 24,* 241–257.

Kram, K. (1996). A relational approach to career development. In D. T. H. A. Associates (Ed.), *The career is dead—Long live the career* (pp. 132–157). San Francisco: Jossey-Bass.

Kumashiro, M., & Sedikides, C. (2005). Taking on board liability-focused information: Close positive relationships as a self-bolstering resource. *Psychological Science, 16,* 732–739.

Lawrence, P. R., & Nohria, N. (2002). *Driven: How human nature shapes our choices*. San Francisco: Jossey-Bass.

Leary, M. R., & Kowalski, R. M. (1990). Impression management: A literature review and two-component model. *Psychological Bulletin, 107,* 34–47.

Lord, C. G., & Saenz, D. S. (1985). Memory deficits and memory surfeits: Differential cognitive consequences of tokenism for tokens and observers. *Journal of Personality and Social Psychology, 49,* 918–926.

Luft, J. (1984). *Group process: An introduction to group dynamics.* Mountain View, CA: Mayfield.

Lundgren, D. C. (2004). Social feedback and self-appraisals: Current status of the Mead–Cooley hypothesis. *Symbolic Interaction, 27,* 267.

Malloy, T., Albright, L., Kenny, D., Agatstein, F., & Winquist, L. (1997). Interpersonal perception and metaperception in nonoverlapping social groups. *Journal of Personality and Social Psychology, 72,* 390–398.

Mead, G. H. (1934). *Mind, self and society: From the standpoint of a social behaviorist* (Ed. with intro by C. W. Morris). Chicago: University of Chicago Press.

Mehra, A., Kilduff, M., & Brass, D. (1998). At the margins: A distinctiveness approach to the social identity and social networks of underrepresented groups. *Academy of Management Journal, 41,* 441–452.

Miller, C. T., & Myers, A. (1998). Compensating for prejudice: How heavyweight people (and others) control outcomes despite prejudice. In C. Stangor & J. Swim (Eds.), *Prejudice: The target's perspective* (pp. 191–218). San Diego, CA: Academic Press.

Miller, C. T., Rothblum, E., Felicio, D., & Brand, P. (1995). Compensating for stigma: Obese and nonobese women's reactions to being visible. *Personality and Social Psychology Bulletin, 21,* 1093–1106.

Miller, J. B., & Stiver, I. P. (1997). *The healing connection: How women form relationships in therapy and life.* Boston: Beacon Press.

Milton, L., & Westphal, J. (2005). Identity confirmation networks and cooperation in work groups. *Academy of Management Journal, 48,* 191–212.

Parker, S., & Axtell, C. (2001). Seeing another viewpoint: Antecedents and outcomes of employee perspective-taking. *Academy of Management Journal, 44,* 1085–1100.

Polzer, J., Milton, L., & Swann, W. (2002). Capitalizing on diversity: Interpersonal congruence in small work groups. *Administrative Science Quarterly, 47,* 296–324.

Regan, D. T., & Totten, J. (1975). Empathy and attributions: Turning actors into observers. *Journal of Personality and Social Psychology, 32,* 850–856.

Reis, H., & Patrick, B. (1996). Attachment and intimacy: Component processes. In E. T. Higgins and A. W. Kruglanski (Eds.), *Social psychology: Handbook of basic principles.* New York: Guilford.

Roberson, L., Deitch, E., Brief, A., & Block, C. (2003). Stereotype threat and feedback seeking in the workplace. *Journal of Vocational Behavior, 62,* 176–188.

Roberts, L. M. (2005). Changing faces: Professional image construction in diverse organizational settings. *Academy of Management Review, 30,* 685–711.

Roberts, L. M., Dutton, J., Spreitzer, G., Heaphy, E., & Quinn, R. (2005). Composing the reflected best-self portrait: Building pathways toward becoming extraordinary in work organizations. *Academy of Management Review, 30,* 712–736.

Rosenberg, M. (1979). *Conceiving the self.* New York: Basic Books.

Rosenfeld, P., Giacalone, R., & Riordan, C. (2001). *Impression management: Building and enhancing reputations at work.* New York: International Thompson Business Press.

Rosenfeld, P., Giacalone, R., & Riordan, C. (1995). *Impression management in organizations: Theory, measurement and practice.* New York: Routledge.

Rousseau, D., Sitkin, S., Burt, R., & Camerer, C. (1998). Not so different after all: A cross-discipline view of trust. *Academy of Management Review, 23,* 393–405.

Schlenker, B. R. (2003). Self-presentation. In M. Leary & J. Tangney (Eds.), *Handbook of self and identity* (pp. 492–518). New York: Guilford.

Shih, M. (2003). Positive stigma: Examining resilience and empowerment in overcoming stigma. *Annals of the American Academy of Political and Social Science, 591,* 175–185.

Snyder, M., & Stukas, A. A. J. (1999). Interpersonal processes: The interplay of cognitive, motivational, and behavioral activities in social interaction. *Annual Review of Psychology, 50,* 273–303.

Staw, B. M., Sandelands, L. E., & Dutton, J. E. (1981). Threat-rigidity effects in organizational behavior: A multilevel analysis. *Administrative Science Quarterly, 26,* 501–524.

Steele, C. M. (1988). The psychology of self-affirmation: Sustaining the integrity of the self. *Advances in Experimental Social Psychology, 21,* 261–302.

Steele, C. (2004). Kenneth B. Clark's context and mine: Toward a context-based theory of social identity threat. In G. Philogene (Ed.), *Racial identity in context: The legacy of Kenneth B. Clark (Decade of Behavior)* (pp. 61–74). Washington, DC: American Psychological Association.

Steele, C. M., & Aronson, J. (1995). Stereotype threat and the intellectual test performance of African Americans. *Journal of Personality and Social Psychology, 69,* 797–811.

Stone, D., Patton, B., & Heen, S. (1999). *Difficult conversations: How to discuss what matters most.* New York: Penguin Putnam.

Swann, W. B. (1987). Identity negotiation: Where two roads meet. *Journal of Personality & Social Psychology, 53,* 1038–1051.

Swann, W. B., Polzer, J., Seyle, D., & Ko, S. (2004) Finding value in diversity: Verification of personal and social self-views in diverse groups. *Academy of Management Review, 29,* 9–27.

Tedeschi, J. T., & Melburg, V. (1984). Impression management and influence in the organization. *Research in the Sociology of Organizations, 3,* 31–58.

Thomas, D. (1993). Racial dynamics in cross-race developmental relationships. *Administrative Science Quarterly, 38,* 169–194.

Tice, D. M., & Wallace, H. (2003). The reflected self: Creating yourself as (you think) others see you. In M. R. Leary & J. P. Tangney (Eds.), *Handbook of self and identity* (pp. 91–105). New York: Guilford.

Williams, M. (2001). *Seeing through the client's eyes: Building interpersonal trust, cooperation, and performance across organizational boundaries.* Unpublished doctoral dissertation, University of Michigan, Ann Arbor.

Young, A., & Perrewe, P. (2000). What did you expect? An examination of career-related support and social support among mentors and protégés. *Journal of Management, 26,* 611–632.

3

Bodily Insights: Three Lenses on Positive Organizational Relationships

Emily D. Heaphy

Human bodies are an integral part of human relationships. Our bodies' physiological systems are highly responsive to social relationships. Bodily gestures constitute a majority of interpersonal communication (Mehrabian, 1972). How we navigate our bodies through physical space guides our bodies toward, or away from, one another and the potential for interactions. Our visceral experience of our bodies provides a constant hum of signals that help us make sense of our surroundings, including our social relationships. Bodies and body-related symbols evoke potent yet varied meanings in every cultural context, affecting who we relate to and how we relate to them. Even our ability to be physically and emotionally present with others requires a human body. Yet, the body is notably absent from most scholarship on organizational relationships.

The body's absence is not surprising. Our social theories are deeply influenced by the Cartesian dualisms that split the mind from the body. Scholars have spent centuries elaborating, debating, and criticizing this premise, but no one doubts that the body has received far less attention than the mind and the cognitive processes associated with it. Organizational theories, too, are based on the hypothesis that bureaucracy would free organizations from all personal, individual influence (Weber, 1948/ 1991). Thus, many of our theories assume that workers are "bodiless" and universal (Acker, 1990), and that any bodily concerns are outside the domain of work. To the extent that the field does theorize about bodies, it is primarily as physical labor (Marx, 1977; Taylor, 1911).

The cultural forces that have kept our attention away from human bodies are waning, however. Feminist scholars began turning the tide by challenging Cartesian dualisms' deleterious effects on women. Since then, scholars across many disciplines have developed alternative ways of conceptualizing the body. For example, the body has been studied as a physiological system (Uchino, Cacioppo, & Kiecolt-Glaser, 1996), as a tool used in the process of managing impressions (Goffman, 1959), and as a potent symbol with cultural meanings that encode social logic (Douglas, 1996). In the meantime, cross-cultural research has shown that cultural assumptions about bodies are far from universal (e.g., Hall, 1966; Kasulis, Ames, & Dissanayake, 1993).

The project of developing the domain of positive organizational relationships[1] provides us with an opportunity to learn from and extend the rich literatures on the body. The purpose of this chapter is to present three different ways of conceptualizing the human body to better understand the antecedents, outcomes, mechanisms, processes, and indicators of positive organizational relationships. I call these three lenses to convey that each brings a particular aspect of the body into focus. Each of the lenses allows us to see the linkages between the human body and positive organizational relationships in a different way. My hope is that this will enable readers to incorporate the body into theory and research on organizational relationships. Considering how much of our work is accomplished by our bodies, it is surprising that it doesn't have a more prominent place at our scholarly table.

The first lens focuses on the physiology of positive organizational relationships, highlighting the powerful physiological responses of the body to social relationships. The physiology lens helps us unpack relationship processes, such as conflict, and outcomes, such as physical health. The second lens draws attention to our own subjective, visceral experiences of our bodies. Subjective experience of one's own body refers to individuals' perceptions, feelings, and beliefs about his or her own body (Pennebaker, 1983). Bodily cues, such as feelings of energy and exhaustion, often remain in the background, while at other times they jump to the foreground as critical signals. This lens helps us see how these visceral experiences affect our sensemaking and meaning making at work. Finally, the third lens turns to-

---

[1]Following Dutton and Heaphy (2003), positive organizational relationships can include enduring relationships as well as momentary interactions between two people, such as connections. Connections can develop into longer term, enduring relationships, but they need not. I assume that the body matters during connections as well as relationships. When connections and relationships are positive, the individuals in them experience a heightened sense of vitality, positive regard, and mutuality. Within the connection or relationship, individuals have the potential to (a) express and experience a wide range and intensity of emotion, (b) stay connected across a number of circumstances, including conflict, and (c) find a high degree of openness and generativity within the connection.

ward the cultural meaning of bodies. Cultures are full of norms and rules about how and when and which bodies should relate. These norms, in turn, affect the patterns of relationships that form. Next, I describe each of these lenses and the research opportunities they provide in detail.

LENS 1: THE BODY AS A PHYSIOLOGICAL SYSTEM

Physiological research focuses on the study of the normal biological functions and activities of living organisms. Physiological measures, such as blood pressure, release of hormones, and strength of immune cell response, are exquisitely responsive to social relationships, including positive organizational relationships (Heaphy & Dutton, 2006; Seeman, 2001). For organizational scholars, conceptualizing people as having physiological systems deeply responsive to social relationships presents some exciting prospects. I focus on three.

First, the physiology lens provides us with important insights into relationship processes, such as trust building, recovery from conflict, and emotional contagion. These processes, in turn, help us understand the dynamics of work relationships, which undergo changes over time. Second, the most detailed studies find that some but not all work relationships have physiological effects. This presents a puzzle not just for organizational theorists, but researchers across many disciplines who grapple with how social context, including organizations, influences the physiological effects of relationships. Thus, this lens presents an opportunity for the study of positive organizational relationships to contribute to interdisciplinary conversations. Finally, the physiology lens uncovers new ways to theorize about physical health, by proposing that organizational structures and practices affect physical health through how they structure relationship quality.

Two robust findings anchor the physiology lens. First, evidence across a number of studies reveals that when individuals interact with people at work who they view positively, key physiological measures respond immediately (for a review, see Heaphy & Dutton, 2006). Cardiovascular measures, such as blood pressure, decrease (e.g., Brondolo et al., 2003). The immune system, as measured by natural killer cell activity, strengthens (e.g., Levy et al., 1990). Anabolic hormones, such as oxytocin, are released into the blood stream (e.g., Zak, Kurzban, & Matzner, 2004), and lower levels of catabolic hormones are released (e.g., Adam, 2005).[2] Second, over time, these mo-

---

[2]Anabolic hormones are a group of growth-promoting and sex hormones, including growth hormone (a specific growth-promoting hormone), insulin-like growth factor (IGF-1), insulin, and estrogen. Catabolic hormones are stress-related hormones, such as cortisol and catecholamines (Epel, McEwen, & Ickovics, 1998).

mentary physiological changes can accumulate into significant effects on physical health. The effect of social relationships on physical health is comparable to standard medical variables such as blood pressure, physical activity, and smoking (House, Landis, & Umberson, 1988). These findings, found across a number of disciplines, form the foundation for this lens.

The most developed positive relationship construct in this research area is social support. Specifically, perceptions of emotional support, such as a sense of comfort, belonging, and acceptance, have the most reliable and substantial effects on health (Uchino, 2004). However, researchers find similar results using a number of different measures. For example, a study of working mothers showed that they had healthier cortisol (a stress-related hormone) patterns throughout the work day when they had more positive relationship functioning, or general attitudes toward social relationships (Adam & Gunnar, 2001). (For a complete review, see Heaphy & Dutton, 2006.) In the following sections, I outline three ways the physiology lens can be used to understand positive organizational relationships.

Physiological Mechanisms of Relationship Dynamics

Positive organizational relationships are not static, but are dynamic and change over time. Thus, the quality of coworkers' relationships may vary substantially over time, punctuated by disagreements and conflicts that provide internal challenges to the relationship, as well as bonding experiences that bring people closer together, like working well together on a successful project. Scholarship on work relationships has only begun to examine these dynamics, such as trust repair (Pratt & Dirks, chap. 6, this volume), disconnection (Kanov, 2005), emotional contagion (Barsade, 2002), and relationship life cycles (Ragins & Verbos, chap. 5, this volume). Some of the most insightful physiological studies of nonwork relationships focus on just such processes (Gottman, 1998; Gottman, Coan, Carrere, & Swanson, 1998; Kiecolt-Glaser, Bane, Glaser, & Malarkey, 2003). Thus, this is a useful area with which to focus the physiology lens and integrate physiological measures into the study of positive organizational relationships. I focus on two such research opportunities.

First, patterns of emotional engagement and responsiveness in everyday marital interactions are important predictors of relationship stability and happiness (Gottman et al., 1998; Kiecolt-Glaser et al., 2003). The physiological correlates of these processes play a critical role in these interactions. Specifically, the negative emotions experienced during a conflict are physiologically arousing for both men and women, but because of men's higher sensitivity to their internal bodily state compared to women (Roberts & Pennebaker, 1995), men and women have different reactions to conflict in the moment. Men tend to withdraw emotionally from the conflict to avoid the physical discomfort of arousal. Although women are less immediately affected by their physiological reactions, they remain vulnerable to the long-term health consequences of physiological arousal. During the conflict, couples who use positive emotions such as interest, humor, and affection to deescalate the physiological as well as emotional tension are most likely to remain married and report higher levels of satisfaction over the long term.

Although there are important differences between marital and organizational relationships (Duck, chap. 9, this volume), this example points toward several ways that physiological mechanisms may be implicated in conflicts experienced in organizational relationships. First, physiological arousal may prompt emotional withdrawal during a conflict, particularly among men. Second, the physiological processes prompted by relationship conflicts can be deescalated by positive emotions (Fredrickson, 1998). Both of these mechanisms can be used to better understand how physiological mechanisms contribute to relationship processes.

For example, the physiological lens may help explain why people have difficulty recovering from a relationship conflict (Sias, Heath, Perry, Silva, & Fix, 2004). When conflicts occur in work relationships, people respond in many different ways, from reconnecting and building a stronger relationship to remaining distant and having feelings of disconnection that intensify over time (Kanov, 2005). How people respond to relationship conflict may be affected by how well they are able to physiologically soothe themselves and others, a form of physiological and relational competence overlooked in organizations. It also suggests that the interactions between people during a conflict can be analyzed for how successful they are at deescalating physiological processes. For example, researchers can study the conditions under which humor at work ameliorates detrimental physiological processes associated with relationship conflict.

A second finding from this literature that can be used to understand relational dynamics is that when people recall and discuss social relationships, it can invoke the physiological processes associated with that person or with a particular interaction (Bloor, Uchino, Hicks, & Smith, 2004; Uvnäs-Moberg, 1998). If the physiological effects of positive social interactions can be evoked through recall and memory, this may help explain why positive organizational relationships, such as developmental relationships, can be generative for the protégé over long periods of time and in spite of infrequent contact. For example, protégés in developmental relationships sometimes report that they recall a mentor as "always there, in the back [of my mind]," even as they have entered the next stage of their career and are no longer in the same organization (Gersick, Bartunek, & Dutton, 2000, p. 1026). The process of recalling the positive relationship may be the catalyst for a physiological reaction that prompts feelings of calm and openness and even generous behavior toward others (Kosfeld, Heinrichs, Zak, Fischbach-er, & Fehr, 2005; Uvnäs-Moberg, 1998; Zak et al., 2004).

The Social Mechanisms of Relationships' Physiological Effects

Existing research on the physiology of work relationships presents us with a puzzle. Studies that take general measures of work relationships (e.g., "I am getting on well with my coworkers"; there is a pleasant atmosphere at my work.) find significant results. Yet more fine-grained studies that measure specific relationships reveal that some but not all work relationships are associated with cardiovascular and immune outcomes. For example, a study of traffic enforcement agents in New York City found that different relationships were consequential for women and men, with women benefiting from immediate supervisor support and men benefiting from coworker support (Karlin, Brondolo, & Schwartz, 2003). However, positive relationships with unit supervisors never had cardiovascular effects on agents.

This raises an important question: Which work relationships have consequential physiological effects and why? Answering this question is important for understanding the potential physiological and health benefits of positive organizational relationships. It also responds to a call to better understand how social context affects the physiology of social relationships, a necessary step for integrating physiology into the social sciences (Granger & Shirtcliffe, 2005; Uchino, 2004).

At present, there are only a handful of studies that can suggest answers to this question. For example, Kiecolt-Glaser and Newton (2001) argued that people have longer physiological responses to those relationships that they view as important to the self. In their review of the literature on U.S. marital relationships, they argued that women are more likely to have self-construals characterized by relational interdependence compared to men, which they used to explain women's greater physiological reactivity to marital relationships. In an example from medical anthropology, Dressler, Balieiro, and Dos Santos (1997) found that having a "culturally consonant" social support, or social support that is similar to the cultural ideal, is a better predictor of blood pressure when compared to general availability of social support. Based on these studies, one could hypothesize that individuals are physiologically affected by relationships that are socially and culturally constructed as meaningful to the self. This explanation would be consistent with a study of breast cancer patients that found that perceptions of relationship quality with doctors, but not nurses, strengthened the immune system (Levy et al., 1990). Breast cancer patients may see emotional support from their doctors as particularly diagnostic of their ability to recover from surgery because of doctors' status and training.

In seeking to understand which work relationships and connections are likely to benefit health, organizational scholars can turn to familiar theories, such as social identity theory (Tajfel & Turner, 1986), and both qualitative and quantitative research methods to try to understand what makes a relationship meaningful to the self in organizations, and how much this varies across organizations, industries, and cultural contexts. For those who work outside of formal organizations, such as independent contractors or temporary employees (Barley & Kunda, 2004; Blatt & Camden, chap. 13, this volume), the constellation of people who compose one's relational context may be especially consequential if they have fewer relationships overall. Addressing these issues can contribute to the study of positive organizational relationships as well as the broader, interdisciplinary issue of how and why social contexts, such as organizations, shape physiological reactions to relationships.

Physical Health

Conducting research on physical health is important because it is a basic resource all of us need to accomplish our work. Organizations care about physical health because they rely on employees to be physically able to perform their jobs. Although organizational researchers have long known that relationships at work affect physical health and mortality (Broadhead et al., 1983; Cohen & Syme, 1984), we have paid less attention to how organizations systematically affect physical health through how they affect the quality of relationships. The physiology lens brings this possibility into focus. The robust finding that positive relationships strengthen health through their effects on physiology allows us to step back a level and consider how organization-level variables influence the occurrence of these consequential relational processes.

Most researchers who have studied social relationships and physiology typically use Karasek's job demand-control model (Karasek, 1979; Karasek & Theorell, 1990). This model considers the effects of job demand, job discretion, decision latitude, and more recently social support, on psychological strain and poor physical health, with mixed results (Fletcher & Jones, 1993). However, organizational scholars have a wealth of group- and organization-level constructs that can be used to better understand how organizations affect physical health, through how they affect relationship quality. Organizational culture, structure, selection processes, and physical space all influence the quality of relationships employees have in organizations (Dutton, 2003).

To illustrate this idea, I compare two ways that organizations structure feedback among employees. Many organizations use 360° feedback to review the performance of their employees (Ghorpade, 2000). Typically, negative and positive feedback are solicited from peers, subordinates, and managers about a person's work performance, which is then delivered anonymously to the feedback recipient. The anonymity of the feedback process promotes social distance between people, sending the implicit message that the feedback recipient and feedback giver are not capable of talking honestly to one another about their performance. In fact, organizations sometimes resist instituting 360º feedback because of concerns that it will jeopardize work relationships (Lepsinger & Lucia, 1997). This organizational practice seems likely to inhibit employees from feeling emotionally supported by their colleagues, reducing the opportunities for them to reap the physical health benefits associated with positive organizational relationships.

Contrast the 360° feedback model with the Reflected Best Self (RBS) exercise (Roberts et al., 2005), in which people solicit stories from others about situations in which these friends, colleagues, and family members saw them at their best. Individuals request the feedback personally and the stories are delivered with the identity of the story provider intact. In addition, the feedback includes only the positive stories, not critical ones that illustrate "areas to improve." The instruction to share stories about what the person does well often prompts feedback givers to share information that comes as a complete surprise to the recipient. This process often deepens and improves the quality of the relationship because it provides an opportunity for the pair to grow closer. This feedback process is likely to increase employees' opportunities to feel emotionally supported by their colleagues. This strengthened relationship lasts beyond the feedback exercise, and becomes a lasting social resource (Fredrickson, 1998).

Although there are clearly a number of important differences between 360° feedback and the RBS exercise (e.g., 360° feedback is used as a form of performance evaluation, whereas the RBS is not), both are organizational feedback practices that have an impact on the quality of relationships at work. This is just one illustration of how we can generate hypotheses about how organizational structures and practices influence physical health through the mechanism of relationship quality. Researchers can also consider how social networks, organizational culture, and selection routines such as hiring and firing, affect physical health through the mechanism of relationship quality.

Measurement of Physiological Data

The broader availability, increased quality, and decreased intrusiveness of physiological measures makes the time ripe for integrating physiology into organizational research (Granger et al., 2006). However, using physiological data is unfamiliar to many organizational researchers. Although a complete discussion of this issue is beyond the scope of the chapter (but see Semmer, Grebner, & Elfering, 2004), much of the excellent research that has developed over the last 20 years has been done through collaborations, such as Ohio State's Institute for Behavioral Medicine Research, and by the graduates of their training programs. Finding collaborators in psychology and health-related departments interested in organizations as social contexts and willing to collaborate on such projects is likely to be a good first step.

Summary

By viewing the body as a physiological system, we can gain insight into the dynamics of organizational relationships, raise the important question of which organizational relationships have beneficial physiological effects and why, and consider how organizational structures and practices affect physical health through the mechanism of relationship quality. Through this lens, we can begin to see positive organizational relationships as critical resources that help us not only socially, emotionally, and psychologically, but physiologically as well. This lens contributes to organizational research more broadly because it points toward how physiological measures can be useful outside of their traditional organizational domains of stress and social support research (see Table 3.1 for a summary).

LENS 2: SUBJECTIVE EXPERIENCE OF ONE'S OWN BODY: BODILY CUES, SENSEMAKING AND MEANING MAKING

Subjective experience of one's own body refers to individuals' perceptions, feelings, and beliefs about their own body (Pennebaker, 1983). Feeling sleepy or energetic, a racing heart or constricted throat, crying or blushing—these are all physical, bodily sensations that people experience at work. Although rarely a topic of study, individuals' subjective experience of their own body, in the form of *bodily cues,* contributes to the meaning people make of their work. Thus, the subjective experience lens uncovers an important contribution to meaning making at work.

We can understand bodily cues from the theoretical perspectives of sensemaking and meaning making at work. Sensemaking is the process through which people make sense of ambiguous cues at work and place them into existing or emerging frameworks (Weick, 1995). Not all cues are attended equally. Cues vary in the degree to which they are considered diagnostic; therefore, some bodily cues people notice and attend to as signifi-

TABLE 3.1

Summary of Physiological and Subjective Experience Lenses

Lens	Focus of the Lens	Body-Positive Organizational Relationship (POR) Linkage	Examples of Opportunities for Future Research
Body as a physiological system	Physiological responsiveness to PORs	Physiology as a *mechanism* of relationship dynamics, including: • Emotional withdrawal in relationships as a result of physiological arousal • Deescalation of physiological arousal by positive emotions • Memory of social relationships prompts beneficial physiological reactions Social *mechanisms* of physiological reactivity PORs and associated physiology as *mechanism* between organization's and individual's physical health	• Recovery from relationship conflict • Physiological soothing after relationship conflict as relational competence • Individual and dyadic effectiveness at physiological soothing (e.g., humor) • Long-term benefits of mentoring enhanced through physiology Why different constellations of relationships have physiological effects on, for example, men versus women, organizational employees versus independent contractors Organizational structures and processes (e.g., feedback processes and hiring routines), influencing individuals' physical health through their effect on relationship quality
Subjective experience of one's own body	Bodily cues	Bodily cues as *indicators* and *mechanisms* of PORs PORs as *microsocial contexts* to make sense of bodily cues Attunement to body during interactions as a *form of competence*	• Strongly positive or negative relationships generate bodily cues, whereas neutral ones do not • Recalled bodily cues associated with positive relationship as motivator • During transition periods, relationships help people interpret bodily cues • Relationship quality with supervisor influences work-related injury • Bodily attunement as a source of agency in jobs with high relational content (e.g., patient advocate, ombuds)

cant, whereas others pass by unnoticed (Dutton, Ashford, Lawrence, & Miner-Rubino, 2002). Bodily cues are felt. This is consistent with definitions of feeling, which is often considered a bodily manifestation of emotional experience (Hochschild, 1983; Sandelands, 2003).

Meaning making is one type of sensemaking (Pratt & Ashforth, 2003). A specific type of meaning making, work meaning is employees' understanding of what they do and the significance of what they do (Wrzesniewski, Dutton, & Debebe, 2003). Work meaning, in turn, is consequential because it provides a framework that shapes how people act to shape their work tasks and relationships (Wrzesniewski & Dutton, 2001). I argue that people use sensemaking to interpret their felt bodily cues, which in turn they use to make meaning about their relationships at work, as well as themselves and their social context.

Explaining the Power of Bodily Cues at Work

There are two reasons why bodily cues may play a particularly important role in meaning making at work. First, people often relate to their bodies in emotionally charged ways (Joas, 1996), in part because people often view the body as an integral part of their self and identity (Casey, 2000). Therefore, when bodily cues do grab our attention, they may be particularly salient. Second, in many U.S. organizations, successful performance at work is associated with control over the body (Bordo, 1988; Goffman, 1959; Meyerson, 1998). Therefore, when people experience bodily cues, it may make the situation stand out as particularly evocative. An example comes from my own work on understanding how patient advocates use their bodies to competently perform their work (Heaphy, 2005):

> Whenever I tell the story about that patient and the hospital's inability to help him and his family, simply because we were unable to get an interpreter in time, I start tearing up. He was in so much pain, and it was just excruciating for his family. It's not often that I cry, but his experience was so painful. . . . My tears remind me that I want to work hard to change the organization. How can you work for an organization you don't respect? It prompted me to get a study started of non-English speaking patients, so now we can at least talk about this as an issue. The study has been an excuse to foster conversations with the right people.

Just as we rely on grammatical punctuation to clarify meaning in written communication, the patient advocate's tears served as social punctuation, marking the non-English-speaking patient's experience as particularly meaningful. This bodily reaction, in turn, shaped how he crafted his job and built relationships to change the organization.

Dimensions of Bodily Cues

Bodily cues vary in the degree to which they are public or private. Public bodily cues, such as crying, laughing, and blushing, are evident to other people, as well as the individual experiencing them. Private bodily cues—such as feelings of energy and tension—are evident primarily to the individual experiencing them. For example, a manager describes what it feels like to work successfully: "Oh, I feel light when things are going well, and when things aren't going well, I feel heavy. The office feels lighter. The paperwork seems lighter. I probably walk with a lighter step" (Lennie, 2000, p. 142). This manager experiences a bodily cue that is not explicitly evident to the people around her. Other people may notice some difference in her gestures or mood, but the subjective bodily experience is her own. No matter how private or public, bodily cues are always part of individuals' subjective experience.

At the same time, bodily cues reflect individuals' perceptions of their social environment (Gregg, 1993). Research on feeling points out that people often experience feelings as a result of, or in reaction to, social situations (Lennie, 2000), such as our feelings of unity or division from a group (Sandelands, 2003). A person experiencing a division from a group may experience objectification, or "whenever people's bodies, body parts, or sexual functions are separated out from their identity, reduced to the status of mere instruments or regarded as if they were capable of representing them (Bartky, 1990)" (Fredrickson & Roberts, 1997, p. 269). Thus, an individual's subjective experience of his or her own body is shaped by the interpersonal context and the social setting.

Theoretical Contributions

The subjective experience lens on the body makes two theoretical contributions. First, this lens provides us with a theoretical justification for attending to a dimension of human experience in organizations that often goes completely unnoticed. Our bodies provide a wealth of information in the form of sensations, but we often underestimate their effects on our lives (Loewenstein, 1996). Our subjective experience of our own body goes unremarked for a number of reasons, and the Cartesian mind–body split is a critical one. It posits that the mind must control and discipline the body less it spiral out of control, threatening a smooth performance (Goffman, 1959; Joas, 1996; Meyerson, 1998; Plessner, 1970). This often results in researchers and the people we study devaluing these signals. Thus, the second theoretical contribution of considering the role of bodily cues in organizational life is that it provides us with a way of conceptualizing the body not as a threat to performance, but as a source of competence.

There are three ways that the subjective experience lens can help us understand positive organizational relationships. First, we can consider bodily cues as indicators of the quality of relationships. Baker, Cross and Wooten's (2003) study of energizing relationships is suggestive. Asked to describe an energizing relationship, each of their 63 informants described physical sensations as an important marker of an energizing interaction. This example implies that individuals make attributions about the quality of their relationship based in part on the bodily cues they experience during the interaction.

There are several ways to apply this in future research. First, it may be that strongly positive (or strongly negative) relationships evoke potent bodily cues, whereas more neutral relationships never grab our attention with bodily cues. Bodily cues experienced in positive organizational relationships may be one mechanism through which relationships evoke such powerful meaning and attachment to other people in organizations. It would be particularly interesting to discover if the bodily cues associated with a particular relationship partner can be evoked even in that person's absence. When people are cued to think about a particular energizing relationship, do they experience those same bodily cues in the moment?

Second, positive organizational relationships may function as microsocial contexts in which people make sense of bodily cues experienced in organizations, especially disorienting or jarring ones. For example, an experienced teacher in a teaching group may help a first-timer reinterpret her sweaty-palmed nervous energy before class. Instead of the first-timer fearing that her students will detect her discomfort, with the help of the more experienced teacher, the newcomer may use it constructively as a way of animating and energizing the class. Positive organizational relationships may be critical contexts for people to make sense of bodily cues, especially in socialization processes, such as the one described previously. Transitions are full of evocative and sometimes uncomfortable moments, and one function of relationships may be to help people develop new interpretive frameworks for their bodily cues.

The bodily sensemaking that occurs in relationships may have very concrete consequences when the cues are health related. For example, a common problem among nurses is work-related injuries (Trossman, 2004). Nurses often ignore small signs of pain to accomplish their demanding work, although they could interpret these bodily cues as meaningful information that some aspect of their work is harmful. Interestingly, nurses' relationships with their supervisors are a critical predictor of how they interpret bodily cues at work (Brown et al., 2005). A nurse may ignore these bodily cues because she does not believe her supervisor will take them seriously or will view talk of pain as a sign of incompetence. This example reveals how organizational relationships, both positive and negative, have the potential to both heal sick and injured bodies as well as cause injury and harm.

Finally, skillfully using bodily cues during interactions with others may be a form of competence at work. Relational attunement, for example, involves using one's subjective awareness of one's body as a tool for gauging how to interact from moment to moment (Grebow, 2004; Smith, 2004). Physically felt sensations become a source of subjective, bodily knowledge instead of a performance threat (Casey, 2000). A patient advocate, for example, might use relational attunement to sense how to engage in a conversation with a patient about a sensitive, emotional issue:

> When dealing with people who are so upset, I have to walk a fine line so as to not upset them any more than they already are. It's hard to know where that line is, but I turn on all my senses in those moments to intuit how to react, or figure out what to say next. My body is like an extra sense, an instrument. It's a lot of work; I often have to take a short walk once they are taken care of to calm down.

Qualitative researchers also consider subjective bodily experiences a valuable research tool. Yanow (2006) wrote that researchers commonly use their own bodily responses, as well as affective and behavioral ones, as a proxy for others' experiences when conducting inductive research on a topic involving organization members' tacit knowledge. Because tacit knowledge is difficult to access directly, researchers' felt bodily experiences help to construct provisional inferences about the topic. Similarly, experts advise interviewers to monitor their own subjective bodily experiences as information about the quality of the relationship with the interviewee (Weiss, 1994).

Summary

Individuals' subjective experiences of their body are felt cues that contribute to sensemaking and meaning making at work. We underestimate the importance of bodily cues in organizational life. This lens suggests three ways in which they are important. First, bodily cues are indicators of positive relationships. Second, relationships are microsocial contexts in which people make meaning of bodily cues. This reveals relationships' potential to heal the cue interpreter (as well as harm them). Finally, the skillful use of bodily cues is a form of interpersonal competence. In contrast to most perspectives on the body, this allows us to see the body not as a threat to an individual's performance at work, but as a source of competence. (See Table 3.1 for a summary.)

LENS 3: CULTURAL INTERPRETATIONS
OF BODILY SYMBOLS

Cultures provide toolkits that people draw on to make sense of their own and others' bodies, as well as the relationship between bodies (Martin, 2002; Swidler, 1986). These, in turn, shape the interactions and relationships individuals do or do not form at work (Acker, 1990). Symbols of the body may be particularly powerful in generating meaning in work organizations, beyond the reasons presented in the subjective experience lens. Human bodies occupy a dangerous place in many U.S. organizational cultures because they have the potential to represent the irrationality, passion, and sexuality that organizations, at least in many of our theories, try to keep at bay in the name of efficiency, productivity, and depersonalization (Martin, 2002; Schultz, 2003; Shawver, 1996; Thomas, 1989).

We can see evidence of this in a number of settings. Physicians develop strategies to desexualize their interactions with patients (Giuffre & Williams, 2000; Riordan, 2004). Many U.S. organizations have rules about the kinds of relationships that are permitted as a way of institutionalizing appropriate physical and sexual contact within organizational relationships (Schultz, 2003; Williams, Giuffre, & Dellinger, 1999). In the United States, when workers with different kinds of bodies (e.g., in the 1970s, women in organizations populated by men; Neugarten & Shafritz, 1980) or sexual desires about bodies (e.g., in the 1990s, homosexuals in the military; Herek, Jobe, & Carney, 1996) enter organizations, social debates ensue as people worry that the potential for sexual relations between new and incumbent workers could derail the organization and potentially victimize both new and incumbent workers.

Most of our knowledge about how cultural interpretations of bodies affect organizational relationships comes from research on gender, race, and sexual orientation, perhaps because they require researchers to acknowledge that the people actually doing the work are neither universally alike nor disembodied (Acker, 1990). This research shows us, for example, that the cultural meaning associated with particular identity groups influences how members of that group prepare their bodies for interactions with others through various forms of impression management (e.g., Dellinger & Williams, 1997). Members of nondominant identity groups, who may have to work harder to construct a professional image to overcome negative stereotypes (Roberts, 2005), tend to have more complex schemas regarding bodily forms of impression management, such as personal grooming and dress (Rafaeli, Dutton, Harquail, & Mackie-Lewis, 1997).

Cultural norms and beliefs about group members' sexuality affects relationship processes, such as self-disclosure (Herek, 1996; Ragins, 2004; Thomas, 1989). These, in turn, may be one mechanism that explains the patterns of relationships, such as social networks (e.g., Ibarra, 1992, 1995), that develop in organizations. Organizational relationships can also form in resistance to harmful cultural meanings about bodies. For example, intragroup relationships may form in part as a way to resist harmful stereotypes that objectify bodies (Collins, 1991; Fredrickson & Roberts, 1997). In these cases, relationships become social contexts in which external pressures are eased and alternative discourse can sometimes be launched and sustained. How outsiders view these relationships depends on the cultural context. For example, women are more likely to experience their common gender identity as a positive basis for identification and friendship only when women are well represented in organizations' upper echelons. When they are not, women view one another as competitors (Ely, 1994, 1995).

I extend the culture lens by discussing two additional research opportunities. First, building on the subjective experience lens, I discuss how culture shapes individuals' access to and interpretation of their subjective experiences of their own bodies. Second, physical touch is an important building block of positive relationships, and therefore is an area ripe for future research on positive organizational relationships. However, the cultural meanings associated with physical touch shape whether it is interpreted as beneficial or harmful to relationship quality.

Interpretation of Subjective Experience of One's Own Body

In the previous lens, I argued that people interpret their bodily cues. Cultural contexts influence how people make sense of the wealth of information that bodily cues provide by providing interpretive frameworks. This happens not only at the dyad level, which we saw in the previous section. Indeed, interpretive frameworks originate from many different levels, including organizational, institutional, societal, and even historical. Each of these cultural layers provides symbolic forms, such as language, goals, beliefs, or mission, to help people use the information that bodily cues provide.

A fascinating example of how the institutional level of culture can affect the interpretation of bodily cues comes from Meyerson's (1994, 1998) study of hospital social workers. She found that social workers employed by hospitals with a medical ideology interpreted experiences of stress and burnout as personal failings, weaknesses, and indicative of poor personal performance. In contrast, in a hospital with a social work ideology, social workers interpreted these same experiences as meaningful signals of one's experience of work, perhaps indicating that they needed a break. By comparing the same type of work (social work) in the same type of organizations (hospitals), this example allows us to see the powerful influence that cultural ideology can have in shaping our interpretations and the meaning we make of bodily cues.

In some circumstances, culture may be helpful to people who are ill by providing a distraction from the body. A study of chronic pain patients from different generations illustrates this possibility (Del Vecchio Good, 1992). Older patients viewed work as a domain in which they had control over their bodies, and that enabled them to contribute positively to society. This meant that at work, they could focus on a positive aspect of themselves and temporarily alleviate the physical pain from which they suffered. In contrast, chronic pain sufferers a generation younger grew up with a model of work that associated work with stress. These younger patients were less likely to experience work as a haven from pain. Here, individuals' subjective experience of their pain varied as a result of their generational perspective on work.

These two examples illustrate that culture, as well as relationships with others, shapes people's interpretations of their bodily cues. In some circumstances, an enhanced sensitivity to the subjective experiences of one's body is beneficial, whereas in others cases it may have negative consequences. Understanding the contours of how culture influences subjective experience of the body and the outcomes associated with it is an important topic for future research.

Cultural Interpretation of Physical Touch

Physical touch is a bodily symbol ripe with meaning relevant for positive organizational relationships. Interpersonal physical touch, defined as physical contact between two or more people, is inherently relational (Merleau-Ponty, 1962; Stack, 2001), making it particularly appropriate for relationship research. However, the meaning of physical touch depends on the cultural context and personal meaning associated with it (Weiss & Campos, 1999, cited in Hertenstein, 2002), so it is especially important to understand the cultural meanings associated with physical touch.

Our current knowledge in this area focuses on situations in which strong organizational or cultural norms about touch exist. We know, for example, that strong societal norms about the appropriate physical distance to maintain and the amount of physical contact that should occur during interpersonal interactions constitute important and largely unspoken criteria for successful interactions (Field, 2001; Hall, 1966). In cross-cultural interactions, these differences sometimes cause tension (Early & Ang, 2003). In the United States, organizational policies often restrict or even prohibit physical contact in an effort to prohibit inappropriate sexuality within organizations. For example, day care centers regulate the amount of physical contact between its employees and the children they care for as a way of guarding against parents' claims of sexual abuse (Field, 2001). Finally, flirtatious physical contact can be viewed as a source of camaraderie, depending on the organizational and cultural context. Medical professionals working on surgical teams, for example, sometimes view this kind of behavior as not only fun, but an important way of coping with the stress of the job (Williams et al., 1999).

It seems likely that physical touch is an important way in which people convey closeness and intimacy to others in nonsexual ways. This is consistent with attachment-based theories of relationships, which are based on infants and caregivers (Bowlby, 1969; Winnicott, 1965) but have also been used in the study of organizational relationships (e.g., Joplin, Nelson, & Quick, 1999; Kahn, 2001). For example, people in positive organizational relationships may physically touch one another as a form of reward (e.g., a charismatic leader sending social cues of affection to subordinates), to reinforce reciprocity (e.g., a handshake to close a mutually agreed on business deal), or to signal safety and soothing (e.g., offering a hug to a colleague overwhelmed by anxiety or trauma at work). Here, the symbolic meaning of physical touch can contribute to building closeness and intimacy. Although these and other meanings of physical touch have been identified in the infant–caregiver relationship (Hertenstein, 2002), we have yet to attend to these relationship-building functions of touch in work relationships.

We need to know much more about the organizational contexts in which physical touch enhances organizational relationships. Is physical touch only culturally interpreted as relationship building when it is initiated by a higher status person, such as when a leader shows affection with a subordinate (Major, Schmidlin, & Williams, 1990)? Are the social rules of physical touch different in private interactions, compared to public ones? Do organizations provide culturally sanctioned rituals and practices that bring people into physical contact with one another as a way of institutionally building relationships? The answers to these and other questions can help us understand how the cultural interpretation of physical touch can build organizational relationships.

Summary

Bodies evoke meaning in organizations. Currently, research on race, gender, and sexual orientation offers the most insight into how cultural interpretations of bodily symbols affect individuals, relationships, and patterns of relationships. Building on this research, I suggest two areas for future research. First, I propose that culture shapes individuals' interpretations of their subjective experience of their bodies. Second, I offer physical touch as an important bodily symbol because of its potential for building relationships. Physi-

TABLE 3.2
Summary of Cultural Interpretation Lens

Lens	Focus of the lens	Body-Positive Organizational Relationship (POR) Linkage	Examples of Opportunities for Future Research
Culture interpretation of bodily symbols	Cultural meaning and interpretation of body-related symbols	*Cultural interpretation* of differences between bodies (e.g., race, gender, sexual orientation) as *antecedent, mechanism,* and *outcome* of relationship processes, relationship patterns, schema development	• Self-disclosure processes across race, gender, and sexual orientation • PORs developing in resistance to negative stereotypes about one's social identity group
		Culture as *toolkit for interpretation* of bodily cues	• Cultures' potential for healing (or harming) through tools it provides for interpretation of bodily cues • Institutional enhancing or obscuring sensitivity to bodily cues
		Physical touch as a form of *interpersonal reward, reinforcement of reciprocity, signal of safety and soothing*	• Organizational rituals that encourage physical touch as a means of building relationships • Leaders use of touch as way of conveying affection to subordinates

cal touch can evoke meanings of nonsexual love, caring, concern, interest, and other dynamics that are hallmarks of positive organizational relationships. However, it must be understood through the cultural lens because depending on its cultural meaning, physical touch can damage and undermine organizational relationships (see Table 3.2 for a summary).

CONCLUSION

The purpose of this chapter is to present three ways of conceptualizing the body to generate insight and research on positive organizational relationships and, more broadly, organizations. We have considered the physiology, subjective experience, and cultural meanings of the body. Each lens has been applied to the study of organizational relationships by linking it to existing organizational constructs and presenting applications to organizational research (see Tables 3.1 and 3.2 for a summary). In the process, I have demonstrated a number of ways in which bodies help us see individuals, relationships, and organizations differently, which I argue merits them a more prominent place in organizational studies.

Although I have presented them as separate views of the body, the lenses clearly overlap in important ways. For example, some of the subjective bodily cues people feel may be associated physiological reactions. That marital research finds a subjective, felt component of physiological arousal suggests a link between the physiology and subjective experience lenses. At the same time, our subjective experience of our bodies is shaped by our cultural milieu. Cultural environments can enhance or obscure sensitivity to bodily cues. Finally, physical touch can be viewed not only through the cultural lens, but through the physiological one. A small but growing literature is beginning to reveal the physiological mechanisms of touch (Uvnäs-Moberg, 1998) and its beneficial psychological and social effects at work, such as massage (Field et al., 1996).

Human bodies are an integral part of human relationships. The lenses we have inherited to see embodiment—lenses that view bodies as machines and instruments (Marx, 1977; Taylor, 1911) or as personal and sexual (Weber, 1948/1991)—are far from obsolete. I believe they do, however, have limited resonance with two theoretical calls central to the study of positive organizational relationships: the call for relational research (Emirbayer, 1997; Baron & Pfeffer, 1994; Bradbury & Bergmann Lichtenstein, 2000), and positive organizational scholarship, which seeks to understand "positive outcomes, processes and attributes of organizations and their members" (Cameron, Dutton, & Quinn, 2003, p. 4). To reintegrate the body into organizational scholarship in ways that will animate and further ongoing scholarly debates, and to help us see the importance of bodies to individuals, organizational relationships, and organizations, we need lenses that allow us to envision these possibilities. I hope that this chapter is one step toward that end.

ACKNOWLEDGMENTS

Thanks to Belle Rose Ragins, Jane Dutton, Ruth Blatt and Jason Kanov, as well as the other contributors to this volume, for their insightful feedback and suggestions on earlier versions of this chapter.

REFERENCES

Acker, J. (1990). Hierarchies, jobs and bodies: A theory of gendered organizations. *Gender and Society, 42,* 139–158.

Adam, E. K. (2005). Momentary emotions and physiological stress levels in the everyday lives of working parents. In B. Schneider & L. J. Waite (Eds.), *Being together, working apart: Dual-*

career families and the work-life balance (pp. 105–133). New York: Cambridge University Press.

Adam, E., & Gunnar, M. (2001). Relationship functioning and home and work demands predict individual differences in diurnal cortisol patterns in women. *Psychoneuroendocrinology, 26,* 189–208.

Baker, W., Cross, R. & Wooten, M. (2003). Positive organizational network analysis. In K. E. Cameron, J. E. Dutton & R. E. Quinn (Eds.), *Positive organizational scholarship* (pp. 328–342). San Francisco: Berrett Koehler.

Barley, S. R., & Kunda, G. (2004). *Gurus, hired guns, and warm bodies: Itinerant experts in a knowledge economy.* Princeton, NJ: Princeton University Press.

Baron, J. N., & Pfeffer, J. (1994). The social psychology of organizations and inequality. *Social Psychology Quarterly, 57,* 190–209.

Barsade, S. (2002). The ripple effect: Emotional contagion and its influence on group behavior. *Administrative Science Quarterly, 47,* 644–675.

Bartky, S. L. (1990). *Femininity and domination: Studies in the phenomenology of oppression.* New York: Routledge.

Bloor, L. E., Uchino, B. N., Hicks, A., & Smith, T. W. (2004). Social relationships and physiological function: The effects of recalling social relationships on cardiovascular reactivity. *Annals of Behavioral Medicine, 28,* 29–38.

Bordo, S. (1988). Anorexia nervosa: Psychopathology as the crystallization of culture. In I. Diamond & L. Quinby (Eds.), *Feminism and Foucault* (pp. 87–118). Boston: Northeastern University Press.

Bowlby, J. (1969). *Attachment and loss: Vol. 1. Attachment.* New York: Basic Books.

Bradbury, H., & Bergmann Lichtenstein, B. M. (2000). Relationality in organizational research: Exploring the space between. *Organization Science, 11,* 551–564.

Broadhead, E. W., Kaplan, B. H., James, S. A., Wagner, E. H., Schoenbach, V. J., Grimson, R., et al. (1983). The epidemiological evidence for a relationship between social support and health. *American Journal of Epidemiology, 117,* 521–537.

Brondolo, E., Rieppi, R., Erickson, S. A., Bagiella, E., Shapiro, P. A., McKinley, P., et al. (2003). Hostility, interpersonal interactions, and ambulatory blood pressure. *Psychosomatic Medicine, 65,* 1003–1011.

Brown, J. G., Trinkoff, A., Rempher, K., McPhaul, K., Brady, B., Lipscomb, J., et al. (2005). Nurses' inclination to report work-related injuries: Organizational, work-group, and individual factors associated with reporting. *AAOHN Journal, 53,* 213–217.

Cameron, K. S., Dutton, J. E., & Quinn, R. E. (2003). Foundations of positive organizational scholarship. In K. E. Cameron, J. E. Dutton & R. E. Quinn (Eds.), *Positive organizational scholarship* (pp. 3–13). San Francisco: Berrett Koehler.

Casey, C. (2000). Sociology sensing the body: Revitalizing a disassociate discourse. In J. Hassard, R. Holliday, & H. Wilmott (Eds.), *Body and organization* (pp. 52–70). London: Sage.

Cohen, S., & Syme, S. L. (1984). *Social support and health.* Orlando, FL: Academic.

Collins, P. H. (1991). *Black feminist thought: Knowledge, consciousness, and the politics of empowerment.* New York: Routledge.

Dellinger, K., & Williams, C. L. (1997). Makeup at work: Negotiating appearance rules in the workplace. *Gender & Society, 11,* 155–177.

Del Vecchio Good, M. (1992). Work as a haven from pain. In M. Del Vecchio Good, P. E. Brodwin, B. J. Good, & A. Kleinman (Eds.), *Pain as a human experience* (pp. 49–76). Berkeley: University of California Press.

Douglas, M. (1996). *Natural symbols: Exploration in cosmology* (2nd ed.). New York: Routledge.

Dressler, W. W., Balieiro, M. C., & Dos Santos, J. E. (1997). The cultural construction of social support in Brazil: Associations with health outcomes. *Culture, Medicine, Psychiatry, 21,* 303–335.

Dutton, J. E. (2003). *Energize your workplace: How to create and sustain high-quality connections at work.* San Francisco: Jossey-Bass.

Dutton, J. E., Ashford, S., Lawrence, K. A., & Miner-Rubino, K. (2002). Red light, green light: Making sense of the organizational context for issue-selling. *Organization Science, 13,* 355–369.

Dutton, J. E., & Heaphy, E. D. (2003). The power of high-quality connections. In K. E. Cameron, J. E. Dutton, & R. E. Quinn (Eds.), *Positive organizational scholarship* (pp. 263–278). San Francisco: Berrett Koehler.

Early, P. C., & Ang, S. (2003). *Cultural intelligence: Individual interactions across cultures.* Stanford, CA: Stanford Business Books.

Ely, R. (1994). The effects of organizational demographics and social identity on relationships among professional women. *Administrative Science Quarterly, 39,* 203–238.

Ely, R. (1995). The power in demography: Women's social constructions of gender identity at work. *Academy of Management Journal, 38,* 589–634.

Emirbayer, M. (1997). Manifesto for a relational psychology. *American Journal of Sociology, 103,* 281–317.

Epel, E., McEwen, B. S., & Ickovics, J. R. (1998). Embodying psychological thriving: Physical thriving in response to stress. *Journal of Social Issues, 54,* 301–322.

Field, T. (2001). *Touch.* Cambridge, MA: MIT Press.

Field, T., Ironson, G., Scafidi, F., Nawrocki, T., Goncalves, A., Burman, I., et al. (1996). Massage therapy reduces anxiety and enhances EEG pattern of alertness and math computations. *International Journal of Neuroscience, 86,* 197–205.

Fletcher, B. C., & Jones, F. (1993). A refutation of Karasek's demand-discretion model of occupational stress with a range of dependent measures. *Journal of Organizational Behavior, 14,* 319–300.

Fredrickson, B. L. (1998). What good are positive emotions? *Review of General Psychology, 2,* 300–319.

Fredrickson, B.L., & Roberts, T. (1997). Objectification theory: Toward understanding women's lived experiences and mental health risks. *Psychology of Women Quarterly, 21,* 173–206.

Gersick, C. J. G., Bartunek, J., & Dutton, J. E. (2000). Learning from academia: The importance of relationships in professional life. *Academy of Management Journal, 43,* 1026–1044.

Ghorpade, J. (2000). Managing five paradoxes of 360-degree feedback. *Academy of Management Executive, 14,* 140–154.

Giuffre, P. A., & Williams, C. L. (2000). Not just bodies: Strategies for desexualizing the physical examination of patients. *Gender & Society, 14,* 457–482.

Goffman, E. (1959). *The presentation of self in everyday life.* New York: Doubleday.

Gottman, J. M. (1998). Psychology and the study of marital processes. *Annual Review of Psychology, 49,* 169–197.

Gottman, J. M., Coan, J., Carrere, S., & Swanson, C. (1998). Predicting marital happiness and stability from newlywed interactions. *Journal of Marriage and the Family, 60,* 5–22.

Granger, D. A., Kivlighan, K. T., Blair, C., El-Sheikh, M., Mize, J., Lisonbee, J. A., et al. (2006). Integrating the measurement of salivary A-amylase into studies of child health, development, and social relationships. *Journal of Personal and Social Relationships, 23,* 267–290.

Granger, D. A., & Shirtcliffe, E. A. (2005). Commentary. In B. Schneider & L. J. Waite (Eds.), *Being together, working apart: Dual-career families and the work-life balance* (pp. 134–137). New York: Cambridge University Press.

Grebow, H. (2004, November). *Seeing with our senses.* Paper presented at the 27th annual conference on the Psychology of the Self, Los Angeles.

Gregg, N. (1993). "Trying to put first things first": Negotiating subjectivities in a workplace organizing campaign. In S. Fisher & K. Davis (Eds.), *Negotiating at the margins: The gendered discourses of power and resistance* (pp. 172–204). New Brunswick, NJ: Rutgers University Press.

Hall, E. T. (1966). *The hidden dimension.* Garden City, NY: Doubleday.

Heaphy, E. D., & Dutton, J. E. (2006). *Positive social interactions and the human body at work: Linking organizations and physiology* (Working paper). Ann Arbor: University of Michigan.

Heaphy, E. D. (2005, August). *Enriching the construct of engagement: Physiological correlates and sensory awareness of the body.* Paper presented at the 2005 National Academy of Management meetings, Honolulu, HI.

Herek, G. M. (1996). Why tell if you're not asked? Self-disclosure, intergroup contact, and heterosexuals' attitude toward lesbians and gay men. In G. M. Herek, J. B. Jobe, & R. M. Carney (Eds.), *Out in force: Sexual orientation in the military* (pp. 197–225). Chicago: University of Chicago Press.

Herek, G. M., Jobe, J. B., & Carney, R. M. (1996). *Out in force: Sexual orientation in the military.* Chicago: University of Chicago Press.

Hertenstein, M. J. (2002). Touch: Its communicative functions in infancy. *Human Development, 45,* 70–94.

Hochschild, A. R. (1983). *Managed heart: Commercialization of human feeling.* Berkeley: University of California Press.

House, J. S., Landis, K. R., & Umberson, D. (1988). Social relationships and health. *Science, 241,* 540–545.

Ibarra, H. (1992). Homophily and differential returns: Sex differences in network structure and access in an advertising firm. *Administrative Science Quarterly, 37,* 422–447.

Ibarra, H. (1995). Race, opportunity and diversity of social circles in managerial networks. *Academy of Management Journal, 38,* 673–703.

Joas, H. (1996). *The creativity of action.* Chicago: University of Chicago Press.

Joplin, J. R. W., Nelson, D. L., & Quick, J. C. (1999). Attachment behavior and health: Relationships at work and home. *Journal of Organizational Behavior, 20,* 783–196.

Kahn, W. A. (2001). Holding environments at work. *Journal of Applied Behavioral Science, 37,* 260–279.

Kanov, J. (2005). *Re-envisioning feeling and relating at work: An inductive study of interpersonal disconnection in organizational life.* Unpublished doctoral dissertation, University of Michigan, Ann Arbor.

Karasek, R. (1979). Job demands, job decision latitude, and mental strain: Implications for job redesign. *Administrative Science Quarterly, 24,* 285–308.

Karasek, R., & Theorell, T. (1990). *Healthy work: Stress, productivity, and the reconstruction of working life.* New York: Basic Books.

Karlin, W. A., Brondolo, E., & Schwartz, J. (2003). Workplace social support and ambulatory cardiovascular activity in New York City traffic agents. *Psychosomatic Medicine, 65,* 167–176.

Kasulis, T. P., Ames, R. T., & Dissanayake, W. (1993). *Self as body in Asian theory and practice.* Albany: State University of New York Press.

Kiecolt-Glaser, J. K, Bane, C., Glaser, R., & Malarkey, W. B. (2003). Love, marriage, and divorce: Newlyweds' stress hormones foreshadow relationship changes. *Journal of Counseling and Clinical Psychology, 71,* 176–188.

Kiecolt-Glaser, J. K., & Newton, T. L. (2001). Marriage and health: His and hers. *Psychological Bulletin, 127,* 472–503.

Kosfeld, M., Heinrichs, M., Zak, P. J., Fischbacher, U., & Fehr, E. (2005). Oxytocin increases trust in humans. *Nature, 435*(7042), 673–676.

Lennie, I. (2000). Embodying management. In J. Hassard, R. Holliday, & H. Wilmott (Eds.), *Body and organization* (pp. 130–146). London: Sage.

Lepsinger, R., & Lucia, A. D. (1997). *The art and science of 360° feedback.* San Francisco: Pfeiffer.

Levy, S. M., Herberman, R. B., Whiteside, T., Sanzo, K., Lee, J., & Kirkwood, J. (1990). Perceived social support and tumor estrogen/progesterone receptor status as predictors of natural killer cell activity in breast cancer patients. *Psychosomatic Medicine, 52,* 73–85.

Loewenstein, G. (1996). Out of control: Visceral influences on the body. *Organizational Behavior and Human Decision Processes, 65,* 272–292.

Major, B., Schmidlin, A. M., & Williams, L. (1990). Gender patterns in social touch: The impact of setting and age. *Journal of Personality and Social Psychology, 58,* 634–643.

Martin, J. (2002). *Organizational culture: Mapping the terrain.* Thousand Oaks, CA: Sage.

Marx, K. (1977). *Capital: Vol. 1.* (B. Fowkes, Trans.). New York: Vintage.

Mehrabian, A. (1972). *Nonverbal communication.* Chicago: Aldine.

Merleau-Ponty, M. (1962). *Phenomenology of perception* (C. Smith, Trans.). New York: Humanities Press.

Meyerson, D. E. (1994). Interpretation of stress in institutions: The cultural production of ambiguity and burnout. *Administrative Science Quarterly, 39,* 628–653.

Meyerson, D. E. (1998). Feeling stressed and burned out: A feminist reading and re-visioning of stress-based emotions within medicine and organization science. *Organization Science, 9,* 103–118.

Neugarten, D. A., & Shafritz, J. M. (1980). *Sexuality in organizations: Romantic and coercive behaviors at work.* Oak Park, IL: Moore.

Pennebaker, J. W. (1983). Physical symptoms and sensations: Causes and correlates. In J. Cacioppo & R. E. Petty (Eds.), *Social psychophysiology* (pp. 543–564). New York: Guilford Press.

Plessner, H. (1970). *Laughing and crying: A study of the limits of human behavior.* Evanston, IL: Northwestern University Press.

Pratt, M., & Ashforth, B. E. (2003). Fostering meaningfulness in working and at work. In K. E. Cameron, J. E. Dutton, & R. E. Quinn (Eds.), *Positive organizational scholarship* (pp. 309–327). San Francisco: Berrett Koehler.

Rafaeli, A., Dutton, J., Harquail, C. V., & Mackie-Lewis, S. (1997). Navigating by attire: The use of dress by female administrative employees. *Academy of Management Journal, 40,* 9–45.

Ragins, B. R. (2004). Sexual orientation in the workplace: The unique work and career experiences of gay, lesbian and bisexual workers. *Research in Personnel and Human Resources Management, 23,* 35–120.

Riordan, D. C. (2004). Interaction strategies of lesbian, gay, and bisexual healthcare practitioners in the clinical examination of patients: Qualitative study. *British Medical Journal, 328,* 1227–1229.

Roberts, L. M. (2005). Changing faces: Professional image construction in diverse organizations. *Academy of Management Review, 30,* 685–711.

Roberts, L. M., Spreitzer, G., Dutton, J. E., Quinn, R., Heaphy, E. D., & Barker, B. (2005). How to play to your strengths. *Harvard Business Review,* 74–80.

Roberts, T. A., & Pennebaker, J. W. (1995). Women's and men's strategies in perceiving internal state. In M. Zanna (Ed.), *Advances in experimental social psychology* (Vol. 27, pp. 143–176). New York: Academic.

Sandelands, L. E. (2003). *Thinking about social life.* Lanham, MD: University Press of America.

Schultz, V. (2003). The sanitized workplace. *The Yale Law Journal, 112,* 2061–2193.

Seeman, T. (2001). How do others get under our skin?: Social relationships and health. In C. D. Ryff & B. Singer (Eds.), *Emotion, social relationships and health* (pp. 189–210). New York: Oxford University.

Semmer, N. K., Grebner, S., & Elfering, A. (2004). Beyond self-report: Using observational, physiological, and situation-based measures in research on occupational stress. In P. L. Perrewe & D. C. Ganster (Eds.), *Emotional and physiological processes and positive intervention strategies: Research in occupational stress and well-being* (pp. 205–263). Boston: JAI.

Shawver, L. (1996). Sexual modesty, the etiquette of disregard, and the question of gays and lesbians in the military. In G. M. Herek, J. B. Jobe, & R. M. Carney (Eds.), *Out in force: Sexual orientation in the military* (pp. 226–244). Chicago: University of Chicago Press.

Sias, P. M., Heath, R. G., Perry, T., Silva, D., & Fix, B. (2004). Narratives of workplace friendship deterioration. *Journal of Social and Personal Relationships, 21,* 321–340.

Smith, C. (2004). Relational attunement: Internal and external reflections on harmonizing with clients. In D. A. Paré & G. Larner (Eds.), *Collaborative practice in psychology and therapy* (pp. 85–96). Binghampton, NY: Haworth Clinical Practice Press.

Stack, D. M. (2001). The salience of touch and physical contact during infancy: Unraveling some of the mysteries of the somaesthetic sense. In G. Bremner & A. Fogel (Eds.), *Blackwell handbook of infant development: Part II. Social, emotional and communicative development* (pp. 351–378). Oxford, England: Blackwell.

Swidler, A. (1986). Culture in action: Symbols and strategies. *American Sociological Review, 51,* 273–286.

Tajfel, H., & Turner, J. (1986). The social identity theory of intergroup behaviour. In S. Worchel & W. G. Austin (Eds.), *Psychology of intergroup relations* (pp. 7–24). Chicago: Nelson.

Taylor, F. W. (1911). *The principles of scientific management.* New York: Harper & Brothers.

Thomas, D. A. (1989). Mentoring and irrationality: The role of racial taboos. *Human Resource Management, 28,* 279–290.

Trossman, S. (2004). Handle with care: The ANA launches a multifaceted campaign to prevent workplace injuries. *American Journal of Nursing, 104,* 73–75.

Uchino, B. (2004). *Social support and physical health: Understanding the consequences of relationships.* New Haven, CT: Yale University Press.

Uchino, B., Cacioppo, J., & Kiecolt-Glaser, J. (1996). The relationship between social support and physiological processes: A review with emphasis on underlying mechanisms and implications for health. *Psychological Bulletin, 199,* 488–531.

Uvnäs-Moberg, K. (1998). Oxytocin may mediate the benefits of positive social interaction and emotions. *Psychoneuroendocrinology, 23,* 819–835.

Weber, M. (1991). *Max Weber: Essays in sociology.* (H. H. Gerth & C. Wright Mills, Ed. & Trans). London: Routledge. (Original work published 1948)

Weick, K. (1995). *Sensemaking in organizations.* Thousand Oaks, CA: Sage.

Weiss, R. S. (1994). *Learning from strangers: The art and method of qualitative interview studies.* New York: The Free Press.

Weiss, S. J., & Campos, R. (1999). Touch. In C. A. Lindeman & M. McAthie (Eds.), *Fundamentals of contemporary nursing practice* (pp. 941–962). Philadelphia: Saunders.

Williams, C. L., Giuffre, P. A., & Dellinger, K. (1999). Sexuality in the workplace: Organizational control, sexual harassment, and the pursuit of pleasure. *Annual Review of Sociology, 25,* 73–93.

Winnicott, D. W. (1965). *The maturational processes and the facilitating environment.* New York: International University Press.

Wrzesniewski, A., & Dutton, J. E. (2001). Crafting a job: Revisioning employees as active crafters of their work. *Academy of Management Review, 26,* 179–201.

Wrzesniewski, A., Dutton, J. E., & Debebe, G. (2003). Interpersonal sensemaking and meaning at work. *Research in Organizational Behavior, 25,* 93–135.

Yanow, D. (2006). How built spaces mean: A semiotics of space. In D. Yanow & P. Schwarz-Shea (Eds.), *Interpretation and method: Empirical research methods and the interpretive turn.* Armonk, NY: Sharpe.

Zak, P.J., Kurzban, R., & Matzner, W.T. (in press). The Neurobiology of Trust. *Annals of the New York Academy of Sciences, 358*(1451), 1737–1748.

4

Energizing Others
in Work Connections

Ryan W. Quinn

A book on positive relationships at work could not be complete without a chapter on energy. Energy—also referred to as subjective energy (Marks, 1977), emotional energy (Collins, 1993), energetic arousal (Thayer, 1989), positive affect (Watson & Tellegen, 1985), vitality (Ryan & Frederick, 1997), or zest (Miller & Stiver, 1997)—is a dimension of affective experience in which a person feels eager to act and capable of action (Quinn & Dutton, 2005). Affect is a label for subjective physiological experiences people have, including short-term, targeted emotions; longer-term, less targeted moods; and enduring dispositions. Affective experiences can be categorized along two dimensions: energy and tension (Thayer, 1989; also referred to as positive affect and negative affect; see Watson & Tellegen, 1985). People use affective experience to discriminate positive from negative to form dispositions toward others (Zajonc, 1998). Therefore, people discern the degree to which their interactions with other people are positive based largely on the energy (positive affect) they feel as they relate with those people, and people build positive relationships, in part, as they repeatedly experience energy in their interactions with other people (Collins, 1981). Positive relationships are more than energy, but without energy there could not be positive relationships.

The claim that energy is necessary for positive relationships highlights a gap in our research on the role of energy in work relationships. Scholars who study work relationships suggest that people generate and respond to changes in energy as they coordinate (Quinn & Dutton, 2005), that people who energize others in their social networks outperform people who do not energize others or who deplete others' energy (Baker, Cross, & Wooten, 2003), and that the higher the quality of the connection between two people is (where "connection" is an evolving pattern of mutual awareness and social interaction between two people; Berscheid & Lopes, 1997) the more energy those people will feel (Dutton & Heaphy, 2003). The focus of this research, then, has been on how high-quality connections can generate energy in people who interact with each other, and on how this energy can have positive organizational outcomes.

The recognition that energy can also affect the quality of the connection itself, and that this feedback helps define the dynamics of positive work relationships, is largely missing. If we include this feedback in our models of energy and work relationships, we see more clearly how people create, evolve, and sustain, or let die the connections that this volume suggests are so critical to individual and organizational functioning. In other words, by examining the energy dynamics of work relationships, we see sources of transformation and change in relationships that are endogenous to the relationships themselves. These endogenous sources of change include the creation of resources and feedback that structure work connections, the attachment that motivates the creation and preservation of connections, the possibility of virtuous and vicious cycles in the way people connect at work, and the interplay of conversational skill and affective experience within the evolving social structure of an organizational setting.

We can see the reciprocal influence of energy and connection in the story of an interaction at work. I once observed two professors who were working together to design a new executive education course. These two professors worked together often, and sometimes engaged in social activities outside of work. As they spoke, the strategy professor, who I call Jose, described a possible design for the course and made suggestions about how they could execute that design. The organizational behavior professor, who I call Peter, mostly listened, but occasionally spoke and seemed to be energized by the conversation. As Jose described a module that involved some financial theory and analysis, however, he stopped, looked at Peter, and said, "Okay, I can see that we'll have to change that module—your energy just dropped like rock." Jose then proposed some alternative methods for designing and implementing that module. Peter appreciated Jose's suggestions, worked with him until they agreed on a design, and both of them felt increasingly energized as they developed the new design. Jose and Peter implemented the new module, improved the program over time, and developed other successful programs together.

The story of Jose and Peter illustrates how the energy of interaction partners varies according to the quality of the connection. Jose and Peter began their conversation with high energy because of their existing connection, Peter's energy decreased when an issue arose that suggested that there might be a problem with their ability to collaborate on the project (or at least on part of the project), and his energy increased again as they addressed that problem in a constructive fashion. The story also illustrates ways in which energy affects connection. It shows, for example, how people build new, valuable resources (e.g., Jose and Peter's improved module) when they are energized (Fredrickson, 1998), how attachment develops when parties to an interaction both feel energy about the focus of their interaction (Collins, 1993), and how people use their energy or perceptions of others' energy to infer information about both their interaction and the topic of their interaction (Quinn & Dutton, 2005)—sometimes even using words like *energy* to identify the feeling and to imply the information the feeling suggests.[1] I introduce these ideas as ways to explain how energy affects the creation and development of work connections, using the example of the two professors throughout. I begin, however, by reviewing the existing research on energy and connection.

A REVIEW OF ENERGY AND CONNECTIONS AT WORK

Energy

Energy is the feeling that one is eager to act and capable of acting (Quinn & Dutton, 2005). It is similar to efficacy, which is "the conviction that one can successfully execute the behavior required to produce particular outcomes" (Bandura, 1977, p. 193). However, efficacy is a cognitive evaluation and energy is an affective experience. As an affective experience, energy not only involves the feeling of being eager to act and capable of action, but also involves an appraisal of a situation (usually unconscious), changes in body language, and affective arousal—the activation of physiological subsystems (Thoits, 1989). Energy can take the form of emotions, moods, or dispositions. It is a positive feeling, distinct from tension (i.e., negative affect [Watson, Clark, & Tellegen, 1988] or tense arousal [Thayer, 1989]), which is a feeling of worry or anxiety. Energy's positivity, however, is limited to the way a person feels. A person can, for example, engage in nega-

---

[1]The interaction between Jose and Peter is a face-to-face interaction. Some scholars, such as Collins (1981), claim that physical copresence is necessary for many of the relationships I describe in this chapter. As I discuss each of the mechanisms through which energy and connection influence each other, I note when copresence is important, and I also assume that the richer the medium of communication is (Daft & Lengel, 1986)—where face-to-face conversation is maximally rich and communication printed on paper is minimally rich—the more powerful the causal effects proposed in this chapter should be.

tive actions (e.g., lying, insults) and feel energized about those actions. The feeling is positive even if the activity is not.

Energy as I use it here is also distinct from but related to physical energy.[2] Physical energy (which is neither positive nor negative) is the capacity to do work. It can take the form of either potential energy or kinetic energy. The human body stores potential energy in the chemical bonds of adenosine triphosphate (ATP), produced from glucose in food. As long as people eat adequately and are not overburdened with stress, the potential energy (ATP) that people have for an activity at any given moment is abundant rather than scarce (Marks, 1977). The degree to which people act consciously in ways that convert their potential energy into kinetic energy (i.e., devote effort to a particular activity—a motivational construct) depends largely on how much energy they feel for that activity (Marks, 1977). People can, of course, expend effort on activities that they do not feel energized about, but the less energy they feel for these activities, the more physical energy they expend on distractions, such as complaining, thinking of ways to get out of the situation, devising shortcuts, and so forth. The effect of this is for people to feel depleted, worn out, or tired from the work—the opposite experience from energy (Thayer, 1989).

Organizational scholars are interested in energy in part because of this relationship between felt energy and physical energy (effort). These scholars use energy to explain people's motivation for the formation, maintenance (Collins, 1981), and change (Jansen, 2004) of organizational structures; the ways in which energized employees energize external constituents (Feldman & Khademian, 2003); or the coordinating of interaction and work activities (Quinn & Dutton, 2005). Many factors, such as health habits (Loehr & Schwartz, 2003) or circadian rhythms (Thayer, 1989) influence a person's energy. However, organizational scholars tend to focus on the impact that interpersonal connections have on energy (Dutton & Heaphy, 2003), as connections appear to have a particularly powerful influence on the energy people have for day-to-day work activities (Baker et al., 2003; Dutton & Heaphy, 2003; Quinn & Dutton, 2005).

Connection

A connection is "the dynamic, living tissue (Berscheid & Lopes, 1997) that exists between two people when there is some contact between them involving mutual awareness and social interaction" (Dutton & Heaphy, 2003,

---

[2]Following Marks (1977), I propose that the feeling of energy is related to physical energy. I am not, however, discussing spiritualistic or paranormal "energies." Such energies may or may not exist, and may or may not be related to felt energy or physiological energy, but the existence and relationship of these concepts need to clear significant hurdles (Saravi, 1999) before they can be accepted by the scientific community.

p. 264). The word *connection* includes both momentary encounters and recurring patterns of social encounters over time. It is more inclusive than
the word *relationship,* acknowledging the potential significance of even momentary encounters. The word *tissue* connotes that connections are or-
ganic: They can live, grow, and change over time. The tissue is not a property of a person, but of the interaction—or of the evolving pattern of
interacting (Berscheid & Lopes, 1997). A connection, then, is any pattern of
social interaction that occurs between two people who are aware of each
other. The quality of a connection is a feature of the evolving pattern of social interaction. Three characteristics define the quality of an interaction
pattern: (a) its carrying capacity (the intensity and range of emotion that a
connection can handle), (b) its tensility (the degree of adverse experience
that the connection can handle), and (c) its connectivity (the degree of
openness to new ideas or influences and generativity people find in the connection; Dutton & Heaphy, 2003). Mutual awareness and social interaction
are both necessary for connection. People who are aware of each other but
do not interact are not connected. If only one person is aware, then that
person may feel connected, but this felt connection lies beyond the scope
of what I discuss here.

Energy From Connection

Research on energy and connection to date focuses almost exclusively on
the proposition that the quality of a connection has a positive effect on the
energy of people who interact with each other. Some scholars, such as Collins (1993) and Miller and Stiver (1997), describe the effect of relationships
on energy. Other scholars (Dutton & Heaphy, 2003; Quinn & Dutton, 2005)
also seek to explain why relationships affect energy. I briefly review this
work, identifying the mechanisms through which these scholars explain the
effect of relationships on energy and noting cases where they make claims
about energy affecting relationships in return. Also, using the earlier example of the two professors, I focus my discussion on work connections—connections that exist for the purpose of accomplishing work. People in work
connections may or may not consider a connection to be intrinsically valuable or desirable, but the connection must be necessary or useful to get the
work done for me to consider it to be a work connection.

Descriptive Accounts. Psychologists and sociologists claim that the
quality of a relational connection affects people's energy. For example,
Miller and Stiver (1997) described how people who engaged in empathetic
interaction generated energy, or "zest," in their interaction partners, and
Collins (1993) described the conditions under which people who interact
feel increased solidarity and energy. Miller and Stiver's zest, however, is

somewhat epiphenomenal in their description of the connection process—an outcome that is simply part of a broader phenomenon—and as such, they do not really articulate mechanisms for the effect of connection on energy. Collins (1981), on the other hand, gave a more complete description by drawing on Goffman's (1967) interaction rituals. Interaction rituals, which occur when people are physically copresent, share common emotions and a common focus for their attention, and have social boundaries to their interaction, are common occurrences in everyday life. The more intensely people focus and the more common their emotions are, the more solidarity the interacting parties will feel toward one another, and the more energy and commonly understood symbols they will have when they leave the interaction (Collins, 1993). Jose and Peter, for example, both focused their attention on the same items throughout the course of their conversation. However, when Peter's energy dropped, their emotions and moods were no longer common between them. This was a signal that, at least with regards to the module they were discussing, their solidarity had decreased. If they had not addressed this issue, they may have lost their common base of understanding and the energy they both felt toward the project as a whole.

The advantages of Collins's (1981) model include an understanding of less intense interactions, interactions between people of different status, and the ways in which interaction rituals develop into "chains" that create social organization. Collins also discussed power differentials and social organization, which make his work particularly relevant to work relationships. However, because his focus was on explaining more macroscopic phenomena, Collins treated entire interaction chains as single units of analysis. For him, energy was an output of the interaction, and its effects were on the desire it creates for subsequent interaction and on the energy that people bring with them to subsequent interactions. As such, he provided little discussion of the mechanisms through which connections increase or decrease people's energy during a single interaction, which leaves us little theoretical leverage for understanding how Peter's energy changed over time, or what that meant for their evolving connection overall.

Explanatory Accounts. A more explicit focus on the effect of connection on energy comes from Dutton and Heaphy (2003), who identified energy as an outcome of high-quality connections. Dutton and Heaphy discussed possible explanations for why high-quality connections generate energy when they described four lenses (exchange, identity, growth, and learning) for examining how connections enliven people. Thus, from an exchange perspective, high-quality connections generate energy because people derive utility or receive valued goods through the connection. For example, Jose and Peter may have been energized because they provided each other the resources that they needed to design and execute the program, making them feel more eager to act and capable of acting. From an identity perspective, high-quality connections generate energy because people use them to construct identities that give them a sense of meaning and self-worth. Thus, Jose and Peter could find energy in their interaction because they confirmed each other's identity as competent professional educators, necessary to teach this particular program. From a growth perspective, high-quality connections generate energy because they provide people with a sense of empowerment, attachment, and belonging. Thus, Jose and Peter may have been energized because of the mutual feelings that they had for each other, and the sense of capability they derive from their relationship. Finally, from a learning perspective, high-quality connections generate energy because they are effective ways to transfer knowledge or because the effective interaction of people constitutes their mutual knowledge. Thus, Jose and Peter may be energized because the improvement in themselves and in the program that they perceive themselves to be making makes them feel more eager to act and capable of acting. Each of these lenses is a provocative way to look at how connections can enliven people. However, most of these explanations need further explication.

One theory that explicates mechanisms further in the relationship between connection and energy is Quinn and Dutton's (2005) theory of coordination as the interplay of speech acts and energy. In this theory, Quinn and Dutton argued that conversational acts (where conversation can be considered as a primary means for connection) increase energy when they increase a person's perceived belongingness, competence, and autonomy. If the connection that people create in conversation is the kind of high-quality connection that Dutton and Heaphy (2003) described, it will increase their perceived belongingness by conveying worthiness to the participants, it will increase their perceived competence because of the additional resources relationships bring to a person, and it will increase their perceived autonomy because mutual respect includes respect for another's agency—a person's ability to "choose to do otherwise" (Giddens, 1984). According to Ryan and Deci (2000), belongingness (Baumeister & Leary, 1995), competence (White, 1963), and autonomy (deCharms, 1968) are fundamental needs. Presumably, it is adaptive to have a positive affective experience like energy when people meet their needs, so as to reinforce the continued meeting of these needs. The degree to which a person belongs, is competent, or is autonomous is also a perception, however. Both the perceptions and the energy felt can change dramatically as people in conversation frame and reframe their personal status and circumstances. Thus, we can now see that Peter's energy dropped in his conversation with Jose because he thought he might be constrained to participate in a program module that he was neither interested in nor capable of executing well (low autonomy and competence). We can also see how Jose worked with Peter to alter the form of their connection with respect to that module so that both he and Peter would be sufficiently interested in and competent at performing the module so that they would both willingly choose to participate in its execution (high competence and autonomy). This extensive reconstruction of their proposed reality could have failed: The acts of articulating and interpreting a proposed reality are rife with opportunities for misunderstanding, with unintentional impacts on people's energy. People can be impressive in their ability to rely on the context (i.e., the other relevant "texts") of an interaction to minimize misinterpretation. However, the potential for misinterpretation is always there, and people can never be certain they truly understand another's intent (Axley, 1984).

Quinn and Dutton (2005) did not discuss connection as a distinct construct. They did, however, examine the ways in which the energy felt in a conversation affects the conversation, which is the substance of a connection. When people experience a change in their energy, that change serves as a cue, or a text, that can be interpreted by both the person who experiences the change and the person who perceives it (e.g., through body language). Jose's recognition of Peter's drop in energy is an example of this. If people interpret the perceived change to contribute to their own belongingness, competence, or autonomy, they should be more disposed to respond in ways that will affirm or increase the competence, belongingness, or autonomy of others. If they perceive the change to detract from their belongingness, competence, or autonomy, then they will be disposed to try to change the situation, to submit unenergetically, or to escape from the interaction, depending on the context in which the interaction is occurring. In the case of Jose and Peter, Jose chose to try to change the situation. Thus, energy can affect the quality of the connection, signaling possible advantages and disadvantages to people in the interaction and guiding people's decisions about how to shape that interaction.

Summary. The quality of a connection has a positive impact on participants' energy. Theory and observations confirm this descriptive fact. Less work has been done on why connection tends to generate energy in the people who connect, but the work that exists on this topic suggests that as people use their connections to exchange, create, and maintain identities, grow, and learn, they fulfill their needs for belonging, competence, and autonomy—need fulfillment that is reinforced by felt energy. This work also hints at the possibility that energy may help the development of positive connections. I now explore the question, "How?"

CONNECTION FROM ENERGY

People develop preferences, moral judgments, and dispositions to view the world in particular normative ways through affective experiences (Zajonc, 1998), and energy motivates people to create, repeat, or change patterns of interaction (Collins, 1981). Connection, then, could have no "quality," and may not have any consistent pattern to it, if there were no energy. Research and personal experience give us reason to believe that energy plays a role in developing our interpersonal connections, but little has been written about how.

Energy is not the only factor that affects the quality of a connection. It may not even be the most important factor. However, it does appear to be necessary. Also, it can be possible for energy to reduce the quality of a connection. For example, if people are energized about performing unkind or immoral actions, the energy is likely to reduce the quality of the connection. The effect of energy on connection quality is usually positive, however, and it can also be powerful.

Mechanisms

Energy influences connection quality through three mechanisms—mutual resource creation, feedback, and attachment. Mutual resources and feedback structure connections, and attachment motivates the creation, preservation, or improvement of connections. I discuss each of these, including the role of agency in the effect of energy on connection.

Mutual Resource Creation. Energy affects connection quality in part through the creation of mutual resources. Resources are means that people can use to get things done, such as physical or symbolic assets (Feldman, 2004). People who feel energy tend to build resources because energy is a positive affective experience, and positive affective experiences broaden people's thought/action repertoires in ways that enable them to approach the world in different ways (e.g., through playfulness, curiosity, or love; Fredrickson, 1998). As people approach the world in new and different ways, they learn and develop new ways of getting things done (i.e., resources). When people feel energy as they interact, they can use their broadened thought and action repertoires to discover or create new means for getting work done. Because they do this in an energized interaction, the resources they create often require the participation of both parties to be of use, and are often mutually beneficial. This happened to Jose and Peter. After Peter's energy dropped, Jose made suggestions about how to change the module. Peter was energized by the changes that Jose was proposing for the design of the program module. Reinvigorated, Peter then joined Jose in making suggestions for redesign. They came up with and refined new ideas until they created a module that would accomplish their goals more effectively and that they were both energized about. These changes affected how they taught the module, their interactions about the program, and their interactions about future programs.

The newly designed module and its constituent parts were mutual resources for Jose and Peter. A *mutual resource,* such as Jose and Peter's new module, is a resource that two or more parties consider to be valuable in getting things done, and that requires the participation of each of the parties to an interaction for its use. In other words, the use of a mutual resource is an interdependent activity. If people desire to continue using a mutual resource, that resource has the effect of binding participants together until the resource is adapted or another person can be made interchangeable for one of the original people in using the resource.

Mutual resources—as long as they remain valuable to both parties—should affect connection quality. For example, if two people such as Jose and Peter find mutual resources to be valuable, they will want to use those resources again. Because they find those resources to be valuable, they will be willing to tolerate more emotion and more variance in emotion (carrying capacity) and adversity in the relationship (tensility) to continue benefiting from those resources. Mutual resources should improve connection quality by giving people more options for responding to the situations they encounter than if they did not have those resources—making the connection more open and generative (connectivity).

Mutual resources must be valued to have this effect. The value that people perceive in mutual resources—actual or potential—moderates the effect of mutual resources on connection quality. For example, one of the reasons that Jose was interested in maintaining a high-quality connection with Peter is because they already had mutual resources that Jose valued, and Jose believed in the potential that he and Peter had to create more valuable mutual resources. Had Jose had neither an existing valued mutual resource, nor a belief in his potential to create future valued mutual resources with Peter, he may have cared much less about connection quality, and thus may have paid much less attention to the drop that occurred in Peter's energy.

People may have access to mutual resources even after they cease to find those resources valuable. In such cases, if left to their own devices, these people will probably stop using the resources, even though the resource may still exist. For example, after teaching the executive education course that they designed together for a few years, Jose and Peter may grow bored with the course, or feel like it is less relevant to the current business environment. However, if other people (e.g., the associate dean of executive education or potential executive education clients) find these re-sources to be valuable even after Jose and Peter cease to find the resource to be valuable, Jose and Peter may still be constrained to continue using the resource together. As a result, the resource may come to be viewed negatively. Under some circumstances, this could reduce or even impair the quality of their connection.

Feedback. A second mechanism through which energy can influence the quality of a connection is as a text that provides feedback to others in-volved in an interaction. As I mentioned previously, energy is a physiologi-cal text to people who feel energy (I can "read" how I feel), and an expres-sive text to people who observe changes in others' energy (I can "read" his or her body language; Quinn & Dutton, 2005). Jose's comment about Peter's energy dropping is an example of reading another person's body language. Because people often feel energy in response to things that are said or done in an interaction, these physiological and expressive texts can be in-terpreted as forms of feedback. If the energy feedback is a response to something that the interpreter believes is desirable, the quality of the con-nection should improve because affirmation for things that people believe to be important also provides affirmation for the people themselves (for be-lieving it to be important in the first place), and also for the relationship that affirms that importance (see Brewer & Gardner, 1996). For example, when Jose saw that Peter was excited about the modules he was proposing, it affirmed to him that he was a valuable person for generating these mod-ules, and that their relationship was valuable, because Peter could also en-vision executing these modules with Jose. Such affirmation should increase the carrying capacity and tensility of the connection because people will endure negative emotion, extreme emotion, or adversity for a relationship that adds worth to their identity. Further, positive feedback tends to make the people who receive it feel positive, which should increase the openness and generativity of the connection because of the broadened thought and action repertoires of the participants (Fredrickson & Losada, 2004).

Attachment. Energy may also have a direct emotional effect on connec-tion quality, particularly when both people in an interaction feel energy. This is because people who feel the same emotion in the same place, and perceive that the other person is feeling the same emotion in the same place, tend to feel increased solidarity (Collins, 1993) through the rhythmic interaction of their copresent physiological reactions (Field, 1985; Kimberly, 1970). (This could be an issue in long-distance work relationships—see Blatt and Camden [chap. 13, this volume] on cultivating community—but in the absence of copresence, people can at least come to trust each other through communication media of increasing richness [Bos, Olson, Gergle,

Olson, & Wright, 2002], so research should consider the moderating effect of copresence and media richness in examining this effect.) This type of experience can take on deep, although sometimes unconscious, meaning for people increasing their felt attachment toward one another. People will often endure more emotion, more variance in emotion, and more adversity when they feel this attachment (e.g., Kram & Isabella's [1985] "special peers"). Further, the positivity of attachment (i.e., love) should increase the openness and generativity of the connection because of the broadened thought and action repertoires of the participants (Fredrickson, 1998). Although I do not have "evidence" of attachment between Jose and Peter, there are some indicators of an affective bond, manifested in behaviors such as social interactions with spouses outside of work and the exchange of holiday and birthday gifts.

Summary. Figure 4.1 is an illustration of the reciprocal influence between energy and connection. The box at the top of the figure contains the three mechanisms through which the quality of a connection generates energy in its participants, and the boxes at the bottom of the figure contain the mechanisms through which energy affects the quality of a connection. These constructs, generally speaking, should influence each other positively. Thus, if connection quality is high, energy should increase, which should improve connection quality, each construct reinforcing the other in

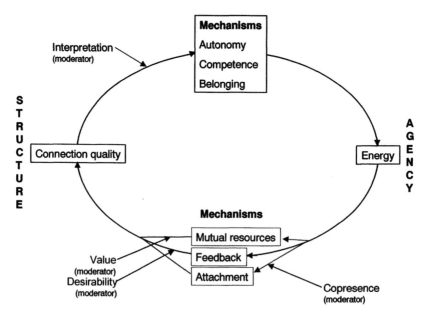

FIG. 4.1. The reciprocal influence of energy and the quality of a connection.

a virtuous cycle. However, exogenous factors, such as the constructs that are not encased in boxes, could change the nature of these relationships. For example, one person can misinterpret another person's comments or actions, changing his or her perceived autonomy, competence, or relatedness in ways that were not intended by the other participant. A mutual resource could lose its value, and then have a negative effect on connection quality. A person could perceive an interaction partner as being energized about an undesirable issue, which could damage connection quality. People could be energized by an interaction, but not become more attached because they are not copresent. Thus, the relationship between energy and connection could be disrupted, and if that disruption is not mitigated, then energy could be depleted, connection quality could be reduced, and a virtuous cycle of increasing energy and connection quality could become a vicious cycle of decreasing energy and connection quality.

Agency and Structure

I depict the relationship between energy and connection as a reinforcing feedback loop. However, if the model contained only the feedback loop, it would be incomplete. It would not only be incomplete because other variables and interactions remain to be proposed and tested, but also because agency, depicted on the right side of the model, prevents the connecting process from ever being fully determined. We can see this in the interaction between Jose and Peter.

Jose and Peter were engaged in an interaction in which their energy and the quality of their connection were reinforcing each other positively when Peter interpreted a proposed arrangement (the program module) to affect his autonomy and competence adversely. This led to a drop in his energy, which limited Jose and Peter's ability to produce mutual resources, reduced their attachment, and was perceived by Jose as negative feedback. According to the model, this should have reduced the quality of the connection between Jose and Peter. Instead, Jose chose to change his course of action and sought to preserve the quality of his connection with Peter.

This capacity to "choose to do otherwise," according to Giddens (1984), is what constitutes agency. Jose could have continued pursuing the agenda that he had when he began his conversation with Peter—a course of action that is not uncommon in organizations—and could have changed the structure of his relationship with Peter (thus, the word *structure* on the left side of the model). Instead, he saw Peter's energy as important. Perhaps he thought Peter's energy was important for its own sake, because he cared about Peter. Or perhaps he believed that Peter's energy was important for successfully executing the program. Whatever the reason, he used his agency to institute a personal change in an attempt to preserve the connection as it was currently structured, raise Peter's energy, and willingly alter his design for the course for the sake of Peter's energy. This exercise of his personal agency not only preserved the relationship, but also altered the organizational structure of the executive education program and its execution.

When one person uses his or her agency to change the approach to an interaction with another person, we can say that this person is attempting to engage in skilled conversational practice (see Fletcher [chap. 19, this volume] for a similar perspective). A practice, like a conversation, is a "situated, recurring activit[y]" (Orlikowski, 2002, p. 253), which is "done on the basis of what members learn from others, and is capable of being done well or badly, correctly or incorrectly" (Barnes, 2001, p. 19). Because conversational practice can be done well or badly, people can become skilled conversationalists. For example, Ancona and Isaacs (chap. 12, this volume), advocate a particular set of skills that people can develop and use in conversation. The skill that Jose illustrates is an ability to see and "read" the energy of another person—Peter. Jose's contribution goes beyond skill, however. He also cares about Peter's energy. Peter can tell that Jose cares from the changes that Jose makes in his own agenda and from the effort that Jose puts into raising Peter's energy. Some scholars (e.g., Warner, 2001) would argue that the subsequent change in Peter is more likely to be a result of Jose's concern for Peter's personal affective experience than of any action that Jose may have taken. To the extent that this is true, researchers who study conversational practice and the interplay between structure and agency that occurs in such practice, should pay as much attention to the affective experience of participants as they do to the skills the participants have or the actions they take. Energy can structure—through the resources it generates and the texts (i.e., feedback) it preserves or creates—and motivate—through feelings of attachment—the connections with which and in which people work.

AN INVITATION TO ENERGY AND CONNECTION

My purpose thus far has been to complete a model of the reciprocal influence of energy and connection in organizational interactions. I did this by reviewing the mechanisms through which connection quality affects energy and by introducing mechanisms that explain how energy affects the quality of relational connections. I also discussed the limits of this model, primarily by identifying the role of agency in the conversational practice of seeking to enhance the energy of another person. The conceptual model, when coupled with the concept of agency, suggests that paying attention to, caring about, and responding to the subjective state of another person—and in particular, that person's energy—may be a significant factor in assessing the effectiveness of a person's conversational practice. Further, the conceptual model and the practice perspective suggest two ways in which we need to advance our understanding of energy and connection at work. First, we need to continue to add to, refine, and test the model and its components. Second, we need to understand more fully what it means for people to care about energy (and perhaps other subjective experiences as well) in their conversational practices at work.

There are at least four ways in which we can continue to improve the theoretical model presented here. First, we can test relationships within the model that have not been tested. For example, do mutual resources increase the carrying capacity, tensility, and connectivity of a work connection as proposed? Is this relationship moderated by the perceived value of the mutual resources? Second, we can add to the model in ways that help us understand theoretical conundrums. For example, what role does tension (i.e., negative affect or tense arousal) play in determining connection quality? What factors have the most significant impact on the sustaining of employees' energy during particular organizational initiatives? Third, as we continue to refine the model, it would be useful to examine how well we can use the model as a whole as a way to explain the dynamics of energy and connection. Fourth, we could extend the model across social situations. For example, it would be useful to examine the interplay of energy and connection as three or more people interact over time. In such a scenario, one of the key questions we would need to address is what is left behind when an individual interaction is over. Collins (1981) offered useful insight into this question, but we have only begun to explore how ephemeral or enduring energy and connectedness tend to be over time.

We can also improve our understanding of how energy and connection affect work organizations by examining how affective experiences (like energy) and concern for the affective experiences of others affect conversational practice. Research suggests that improvisation and knowledgeable practice alters organizational structures (e.g., Orlikowski, 1996, 2002). However, stories like the interaction between Jose and Peter suggest that the transformation could have as much to do with the affective experience of organizational participants as it does with knowledge and skills. For example, Peter's drop in energy and Jose's concern for Peter's energy ended up affecting the design of their executive education program. Are there boundary conditions in conversations like Jose and Peter's that make affective experience such a significant factor? Are there conditions that make particular affective states more or less likely? Do different types of affective experiences have particular effects on the change or maintenance of organizational structures? (See Baker & Quinn [2006] for an examination of how the energy in interactions aggregates to affect organizational networks.)

The theoretical territory covered by considering energy and connection quality in relationships at work is vast, and we have only begun to map the territory. What we have learned is that energy and connection affect each other in a dynamic feedback relationship, suggesting that employee energy and the quality of work connections can evolve endogenously over time. This helps us see not only how people can endogenously create, sustain, change, or let die the work relationships, but also—through mutual resources, feedback, and attachment—how the dynamics of work relationships affect the creation, maintenance, and change of the organization around these relationships. The opportunity is ripe for discovery. If it is true that managers spend more of their time engaged in talk than in any other activity (Mintzberg, 1973), then researchers as well as managers should show more concern for others' affective states and their potential impact on how we live and work with each other.

REFERENCES

Axley, S. R. (1984). Managerial and organizational communication in terms of the conduit metaphor. *Academy of Management Review, 9,* 428–437.

Baker, W., Cross, R., & Wooten, M. (2003). Positive organizational network analysis and energizing relationships. In K. S. Cameron, J. E. Dutton, & R. E. Quinn (Eds.), *Positive organizational scholarship: Foundations of a new discipline* (pp. 328–342). San Francisco: Berrett-Koehler.

Baker, W., & Quinn, R. W. (2006). *Energy networks and information loss.* Working paper, University of Michigan.

Bandura, A. (1977). Self-efficacy: Toward a unifying theory of behavior change. *Psychological Review, 84,* 191–215.

Barnes, B. (2001). Practice as collective action. In T. R. Schatzki, K. K. Cetina, & E. von Savigny (Eds.), *The practice turn in contemporary theory* (pp. 17–28). London: Routledge.

Baumeister, R. F., & Leary, M. R. (1995). The need to belong: Desire for interpersonal attachments as a fundamental human motivation. *Psychological Bulletin, 117,* 497–529.

Berscheid, E., & Lopes, J. (1997). A temporal model of relationship satisfaction and stability. In R. J. Sternberg & M. Hojjat (Eds.), *Satisfaction in close relationships* (pp. 129–159). New York: Guilford.

Bos, N., Olson, J., Gergle, D., Olson, G., & Wright, Z. (2002). *Effects of four computer-mediated communications channels on trust development.* In *Proceedings of CHI 2002* (pp. 135–140). New York: ACM Press.

Brewer, M. B., & Gardner, W. (1996). Who is this "we"? Levels of collective identity and self-representations. *Journal of Personality and Social Psychology, 71,* 83–93.

Collins, R. (1981). On the micro-foundations of macro-sociology. *American Journal of Sociology, 86,* 984–1014.

Collins, R. (1993). Emotional energy as the common denominator of rational action. *Rationality and Society, 5,* 203–230.

Daft, R. L., & Lengel, R. H. (1986). Organizational information requirements, media richness, and structural design. *Management Science, 32,* 554–571.

deCharms, R. (1968). *Personal causation.* New York: Academic.

Dutton, J. E., & Heaphy, E. D. (2003). The power of high quality connections. In K. S. Cameron, J. E. Dutton, & R. E. Quinn (Eds.), *Positive organizational scholarship: Foundations of a new discipline* (pp. 263–278). San Francisco: Berrett-Koehler.

Feldman, M. S. (2004). Resources in emerging structures and processes of change. *Organization Science, 15,* 295–309.

Feldman, M. S., & Khademian, A. M. (2003). Empowerment and cascading vitality. In K. S. Cameron, J. E. Dutton, & R. E. Quinn (Eds.), *Positive organizational scholarship: Foundations of a new discipline* (pp. 343–358). San Francisco: Berrett-Koehler.

Field, T. (1985). Attachment as psychobiological attunement: Being on the same wavelength. In M. Reite & T. Field (Eds.), *The psychobiology of attachment and separation* (pp. 415–454). Orlando, FL: Academic.

Fredrickson, B. (1998). What good are positive emotions? *Review of General Psychology, 2,* 300–319.

Fredrickson, B. L., & Losada, M. (2005). Positive affect and the complex dynamics of human flourishing. *American Psychologist, 60,* 678–686.

Giddens, A. (1984). *The constitution of society.* Berkeley: University of California Press.

Goffman, E. (1967). *Interaction ritual: Essays in face-to-face behavior.* Garden City, NY: Doubleday/ Anchor.

Jansen, K. (2004). From persistence to pursuit: A longitudinal examination of momentum during the early stages of strategic change. *Organization Science, 15,* 276–294.

Kimberly, R. P. (1970). Rhythmic patterns in human interaction. *Nature, 228*(5266), 88–90.

Kram, K. E., & Isabella, L. A. (1985). Mentoring alternatives: The role of peer relationships in career development. *Academy of Management Journal, 28,* 110–132.

Marks, S. R. (1977). Multiple roles and role strain: Some notes on human energy, time, and commitment. *American Sociological Review, 42,* 921–936.

Miller, J. B., & Stiver, I. (1997). *The healing connection.* Boston: Beacon Press.

Mintzberg, H. (1973). *The nature of managerial work.* New York: Harper & Row.

Orlikowski, W. J. (1996). Improvising organizational transformation over time: A situated change perspective. *Information Systems Research, 7,* 63–92.

Orlikowski, W. J. (2002). Knowing in practice: Enacting a collective capability in distributed organizing. *Organization Science, 13,* 249–273.

Quinn, R. W., & Dutton, J. E. (2005). Coordination as energy-in-conversation. *Academy of Management Review.*

Ryan, R. M., & Deci, E. L. (2000). Self-determination theory and the facilitation of intrinsic motivation, social development, and well-being. *American Psychologist, 55,* 68–78.

Ryan, R. M., & Frederick, C. (1997). On energy, personality, and health: Subjective vitality as a dynamic reflection of well-being. *Journal of Personality, 65,* 529–566.

Saravi, F. D. (1999). Energy and the brain: Facts and fantasies. In S. D. Sala (Ed.), *Mind myths: Exploring popular assumptions about the mind and brain* (pp. 43–58). West Sussex, England: Wiley.

Thayer, R. E. (1989). *The biopsychology of mood and arousal.* New York: Oxford University Press.

Thoits, P. A. (1989). The sociology of emotions. In W. R. Scott & J. Blake (Eds.), *Annual review of sociology* (Vol. 15, pp. 317–342). Palo Alto, CA: Annual Reviews.

Warner, C. T. (2001). *Bonds that make us free: Healing our relationships, coming to ourselves.* Salt Lake City, UT: Shadow Mountain.

Watson, D., Clark, L. A., & Tellegen, A. (1988). Development and validation of brief measures of positive and negative affect: The PANAS scales. *Journal of Personality and Social Psychology, 54,* 1063–1070.

Watson, D., & Tellegen, A. (1985). Toward a consensual structure of mood. *Psychological Bulletin, 98,* 219–235.

White, R. W. (1963). *Ego and reality in psychoanalytic theory.* New York: International Universities Press.

Zajonc, R. B. (1998). Emotions. In D. T. Gilbert, S. T. Fiske, & G. Lindzey (Eds.), *The handbook of social psychology* (Vol. 1, 4th ed., pp. 591–632). Boston: McGraw-Hill.

5

Positive Relationships in Action: Relational Mentoring and Mentoring Schemas in the Workplace

Belle Rose Ragins
Amy Klemm Verbos

At its best, mentoring exemplifies a positive relationship at work in action. Although mentoring can inform the blossoming field of positive relationships at work, not all mentoring relationships are positive; they fall along a continuum ranging from high quality to marginal or even dysfunctional (cf. Eby, McManus, Simon, & Russell, 2000; Ragins, Cotton, & Miller, 2000; Scandura, 1998). Although effective mentoring processes may parallel processes underlying other positive work relationships, there has been little theoretical progress in this aspect of the mentoring field. Most empirical mentoring research in the past 20 years is based on Kram's (1985) rich theoretical work that explains what protégés receive from the relationship. Mentoring theory has yet to fully explain the underlying cognitive, affective, and behavioral processes through which mentoring relationships develop and to explain mentoring from both the protégé's and the mentor's perspective. Consequently, we believe that relationship theory and research is uniquely suited to both inform, and be informed by, mentoring research.

This chapter advances our understanding of positive relationships at work by examining the processes underlying effective mentoring relationships. Our specific objectives are to explore (a) how mentoring research may inform positive relationships at work, and (b) the potential for expanding the scope of mentoring theory by linking relational and social cognitive theory to mentoring. Toward these goals, we start by examining four insights that mentoring offers to the positive relationships arena. Next, we outline three limitations in the mentoring field and build a case for relational perspectives on mentoring. We envision relational mentoring as the most positive mentoring state (Ragins, 2005). Then, we break new ground by developing a theoretical model of "mentoring schemas" that applies relational schema theory (Baldwin, 1992; Planalp, 1985) to mentoring relationships. Last, we offer an invitation for future research into the cognitive and relational aspects of mentoring.

HOW MENTORING MAY INFORM POSITIVE RELATIONSHIPS AT WORK

What Is Mentoring?

Traditionally, mentoring has been defined as a relationship between an older, more experienced mentor and a younger, less experienced protégé for the purpose of developing and helping the protégé's career (Hunt & Michael, 1983; Kram, 1985; Ragins, 1989). Although early perspectives on mentoring focused on career benefits for protégés, evolving views point to the importance of defining mentoring as a mutually beneficial developmental relationship (cf. Kram, 1996; see also reviews by Noe, Greenberger, & Wang, 2002; Wanberg, Welsh, & Hezlett, 2003). As defined here, relational perspectives in mentoring relationships refer to the mutually interdependent, empathic, and empowering processes that create personal growth, development, and enrichment for mentors and protégés (Ragins, 2005). Relational perspectives incorporate the idea that the concept of self is nested within and defined by relationships (cf. Brewer & Gardner, 1996; Cross & Madson, 1997; Ogilivie & Ashmore, 1991; Surrey, 1985) and that relationships have the potential to increase the generative capacity of individuals (see Baker & Dutton, chap. 18, this volume) by providing new knowledge, resources, identities, and forms of psychological growth (Dutton & Heaphy, 2003; see also Fletcher, 1998; Miller, 1976; Miller & Stiver, 1997). Accordingly, we use a relational perspective to define mentoring as a developmental relationship that involves mutual growth, learning, and development in personal, professional, and career domains. Mentors may or may not be employed in the same organization as their protégés, or be in the protégé's chain of command (Ragins, 1997). Some mentoring relationships may be informal and develop spontaneously, whereas other relationships are formal relationships assigned through formal mentoring programs (Chao, Walz, & Gardner, 1992; Ragins & Cotton, 1999).

According to Kram's (1985) mentoring theory, mentors help their protégés through providing career functions (i.e., sponsorship, exposure and visibility, coaching, protection, and challenging assignments) and psychosocial support (i.e., role modeling, acceptance and confirmation, counseling, and friendship). Mentors may provide some or all of these functions and the functions provided vary over time and by relationship. There is extensive empirical evidence that protégés experience an array of desirable work and career outcomes, including job and career satisfaction, organizational commitment, reduced turnover intentions, increased compensation, power, and advancement (cf. reviews by Allen, Eby, Poteet, Lentz, & Lima, 2004; Noe et al., 2002; Ragins, 1999; Wanberg et al., 2003). The limited findings on outcomes for mentors include reports of career success and revitalization, social recognition, and a sense of personal fulfillment and satisfaction (Allen, Poteet, & Burroughs, 1997; Bozionelos, 2004; Mullen & Noe, 1999; Ragins & Scandura, 1999).

Insights From Mentoring

Mentoring can be an exemplar of a positive work relationship, and we offer four insights gleaned from 20 years of mentoring research that may help us understand positive relationships at work.

The first insight is that *positive relationships at work may transcend organizational boundaries.* As positive work relationships, many mentoring relationships are "external relationships" that are not confined to one organization (Eby, 1997; Ragins, 1997). Some relationships develop through external networks (deJanasz, Sullivan, & Whiting, 2003; Higgins & Kram, 2001), while others operate electronically as "virtual mentoring" (Ensher, Heun, & Blanchard, 2003; Hamilton & Scandura, 2003). Even when initiated within an organization, protégés and mentors who leave to pursue their protean careers often maintain their old mentoring relationships in their new organizational settings (Ragins & Scandura, 1997). Mentoring research offers the possibility that positive relationships at work are not bounded by physical proximity or organizational boundaries, suggesting that the concept of positive relationships could be expanded to include positive career and professional relationships that involve work.

Second, recent advances in mentoring theory suggest that *positive relationships are nested within and are influenced by a constellation of other relationships* (cf. Higgins & Kram, 2001; Higgins & Thomas, 2001; Kram, 1996; van Emmerik, 2004). Under this perspective, mentoring extends beyond the dyad to a constellation of developmental relationships that supply career assistance and psychosocial support to the protégé. This perspective can be extended to include relationships that support mentors, as well as nonwork relationships (e.g., friends, family) whose support spills over into the workplace. The constellation perspective recognizes that the needs of members within a given relationship are affected by the resources obtained from other relationships. It is therefore useful to study positive relationships at work within a constellation of work and nonwork relationships that occur within and outside the organization.

The third insight is that *positive relationships may evolve through life cycles*. Mentoring relationships usually involve four distinct stages: initiation, cultivation, separation, and redefinition (Chao, 1997; Kram, 1985). Each stage involves different roles, functions, and expectations. Of particular interest is that mentoring involves separation and redefinition stages that either end the relationship or redefine it as a peer relationship (Chao, 1997; Kram, 1985). It is reasonable to expect that positive relationships at work also change and transform over time. The study of positive relationships could therefore benefit from a longitudinal approach that examines relationship patterns, life cycles, and transformations.

Finally, *positive relationships involve a "need-based" fit between members of the relationship*. Need-based fit reflects the ability of the members of the mentoring relationship to meet each others' personal, career, and developmental needs. The capacity to meet each other's needs is a key concept in relational mentoring (Ragins, 2005) and is prevalent in the relationship field (cf. Duck, 1994). A needs-based perspective offers the view that relationships are vehicles that provide instrumental and relational functions, such as sensemaking, purpose, or meaning, information and resources critical for task accomplishment, career assistance, and personal support (cf. Kahn chap. 10, this volume). Existing mentoring research supports a need-based perspective on positive relationships; members that believe the mentoring relationship meets their needs are more likely to report their relationship as effective than members who do not have such beliefs (Wanberg et al., 2003; Young & Perrewé, 2000a, 2004). Moreover, needs in mentoring relationships change over the course of a career and are influenced by individual differences and diversity (cf. Ragins, 1997). This suggests that positive relationship scholars may find the changing and evolving needs of the members to be an enlightening area of inquiry.

Now that we have suggested how mentoring may inform the study of positive relationships at work, let us turn the table and use a relational lens to explore how relational perspectives can address limitations in the mentoring field.

THE CASE FOR RELATIONAL PERSPECTIVES ON MENTORING

In this section we first identify three aspects of the mentoring literature that limit its scope and explanatory potential. We next offer relational mentoring as a positive mentoring state, which can expand the scope of mentoring research to the positive end of the mentoring spectrum (Ragins,

2005). Then, we explain how relational mentoring fits into the continuum of mentoring quality.

The Three Limitations

The first limitation of mentoring is that it is often viewed as a one-sided relationship leading to instrumental outcomes. This view of mentoring is analogous to a "Godfather approach" in which a patriarchal mentor doles out favors, protects the protégé, and expects allegiance in return for these favors. As an example of this ideology, research on mentoring functions provided by the mentor to the protégé proliferates (cf. reviews by Noe et al., 2002; Wanberg et al., 2003), but we lack theory and research that addresses the functions provided by the protégé to the mentor or perspectives that view the relationship as a source of mutual growth and development for *both* mentor and protégé. Even the psychosocial functions provided to the protégé do not encompass relational dynamics such as thriving, flourishing, and resiliency (Cameron, Dutton, & Quinn, 2003). The Godfather approach conceptualizes mentoring as instrumental rather than relational. The relationship is valued for *what it can do*, rather than for *what it can be*. This ideology advises protégés to use their mentors as a career resource, and "trade them in" when a better mentor comes along. Mentors are viewed as fostering independence and individuation (measured through advancement) rather than interdependence and mutual growth (measured through personal growth and self-knowledge). This view ignores the reciprocal nature of mentoring relationships, and takes a hierarchical and perhaps stereotypically masculine approach to the relationship (cf. Fletcher, 1998; Kolb, 1992; Kram, 1996).

The second limitation of mentoring is that a narrow lens has been used to assess mentoring outcomes. This "show me the money" approach assesses the effectiveness of mentoring using a narrow range of available outcome measures. For example, most mentoring research focuses on work and career outcomes received by the protégé (e.g., career advancement, promotion, compensation, and work attitudes; Noe et al., 2002; Wanberg et al., 2003). This is problematic for two reasons. First, with a few exceptions (Allen & Eby, 2003; Allen, Poteet, & Burroughs, 1997; Bozionelos, 2004; Ragins & Scandura, 1999), the benefits for mentors have not been clearly articulated or studied. Second, instrumental outcome measures shape our perception of the relationship, leading us to view mentoring in economic rather than relational terms.

The third limitation faced in the mentoring literature is that the dynamic cognitive, and affective processes underlying effective mentoring relationships have not been explicated. Whereas the mentoring literature explains mentor behaviors and protégé outcomes, it does not address mutual relational behaviors and relational outcomes. Exchange theory offers some insights into traditional mentoring (Young & Perrewé, 2000b, 2004), although its roots in economic theory do not capture the relational aspects of mentoring. Economic behavioral models view self-interest as a primary motivator for behavior (Ferraro, Pfeffer, & Sutton, 2005; Jensen & Meckling, 1994), but self-interest does not explain the motivation to become a mentor (cf. Allen, 2003; Aryee, Chay, & Chew, 1996; McManus & Russell, 1997; Ragins & Scandura, 1994) and does not capture the cognitive and affective processes underlying effective mentoring relationships. In addition, although mentoring scholars have examined characteristics leading to the dysfunctional end of the mentoring spectrum (cf. Eby & Allen, 2002; Eby, Butts, Lockwood, & Simon, 2004; Eby et al., 2000; Scandura, 1998), the highest quality mentoring relationships have yet to be explored.

From Limiting to Revisioning: Relational Mentoring as a Mentoring State

In contrast to traditional, one-sided approaches to mentoring that model behavior using exchange norms to predict instrumental outcomes, a relational approach widens the lens of mentoring to include mutual and interdependent relationships that function using communal norms to predict growth, learning, and personal and professional development (Ragins, 2005). Communal norms are present when benefits are given in response to the needs of the other in the relationship without expecting a reciprocal benefit (Clark & Mills, 1979, 1993), as would be the case in a relationship functioning under exchange norms. Relational mentoring draws on relational approaches to career development (cf. Fletcher, 1996; Kram, 1996) and relational practice (Fletcher, 1998, 1999; see also Miller, 1976; Miller & Stiver, 1997), which view work relationships as opportunities for personal growth. Relational mentoring is a form of anchoring relationship (Kahn, 1998) in that it involves emotional attachment, care giving, and care receiving. Relational mentoring incorporates processes found in effective mentoring relationships, such as mutual learning (Allen & Eby, 2003; Godshalk & Sosik, 2003; Lankau & Scandura, 2002), information exchange (Mullen, 1994; Mullen & Noe, 1999) and transformational leadership behaviors (Godshalk & Sosik, 2000; Sosik & Godshalk, 2000; Sosik, Godshalk, & Yammarino, 2004).

Relational mentoring is defined as an interdependent and generative developmental relationship that promotes mutual growth, learning, and development within the career context (Ragins, 2005). Building on positive organizational scholarship perspectives (cf. Cameron et al., 2003), relational mentoring is a flourishing, life-sustaining relationship (Reis & Gable, 2003) that can lead to positive psychological capital outcomes of hope, self-confidence, optimism, and resiliency (Luthans & Youssef, 2004), as well as vitality, meaningfulness, authenticity, and exhilaration (Cameron et al., 2003). Relational mentoring therefore extends beyond the limits of psychosocial and career development functions and instrumental outcomes to include relational processes (i.e., reciprocity, mutual learning, and empathetic teaching), relational behaviors (i.e., empathy, disclosure, sensitivity and empowerment), and relational outcomes that are unique to relational mentoring and reinforce the development of future relationships (i.e., life satisfaction, role integration and balance, relational competence, meaningfulness, vitality, and resilience; e.g., Cameron et al., 2003; Fletcher, 1998), overcoming the first two limitations of mentoring research.

We call the highest quality dyadic affective outcome of relational mentoring a *close mentoring bond,* which is a kind of high-quality connection (Dutton & Heaphy, 2003). According to Dutton and Heaphy (2003), high-quality connections reflect emotional capacity, openness, generativity, and tensility, or the ability to withstand strain. High-quality connections lead to subjective experiences of vitality, positive regard, and mutuality, as well as physiological outcomes associated with reduced anxiety and stress. As an affective outcome of relational mentoring, close mentoring bonds should be reciprocally related to high levels of commitment to the relationship. In addition, the identity salience (cf. Stryker & Serpe, 1982) associated with the role of mentor or protégé is expected to be strengthened in relationships that experience close mentoring bonds.

A key characteristic of relational mentoring is that the relationship relies on communal, rather than exchange norms. Clark and Mills (1979, 1993) theorized that relationships use communal or exchange norms to govern the giving and receiving of benefits in a relationship. When exchange norms are used, benefits are given in exchange for a debt, coupled with the expectation that a comparable benefit will be returned by the partner. In contrast, when communal norms are used, benefits are given in response to the needs of others or to demonstrate a general concern for the other without creating a repayment obligation. Like other relationships, mentoring relationships may rely on communal or exchange norms, but we believe that communal norms are critical for relational mentoring and developing close mentoring bonds.

Mentoring relationships are dynamic and can transform through various states of quality. We identify three basic relationship states: dysfunctional, traditional, and relational. These states represent the low, medium, and high end of the quality continuum. The behaviors, prevailing norms, and outcomes associated with these states are depicted in Figure 5.1; the bell-shaped curve reflects their frequency of occurrence. Most mentoring relationships exist in the traditional state, using exchange norms (cf. Young & Perrewé, 2000b), and producing desirable career development and psychosocial support for the protégé. Relational mentoring relies on communal norms and

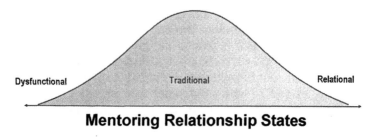

Mentoring Relationship States

	Dysfunctional	Traditional	Relational
Perceived Quality:	Low	Medium	High
Behaviors:	Negative or Dysfunctional	Career Development & Psychosocial Support for Protégé	Career Development, Psychosocial Support for Protégé & Relational Behaviors
Prevailing Norms:	Violated or Exploitative	Exchange	Communal
Outcomes:	Negative	One-sided; Instrumental	Close Mentoring Bonds Mutual learning/growth

FIG. 5.1. Continuum of quality in mentoring.

builds on traditional mentoring outcomes by adding relational outcomes for both members. Dysfunctional states violate exchange or communal norms and may rely on exploitative norms in which members gain benefits for themselves without regard for their partner's interest or needs (Mills, Clark, Ford, & Johnson, 2004). Dysfunctional mentoring states can lead to negative or even harmful outcomes (cf. Eby et al., 2004). Two points about mentoring states need to be made. First, mentoring relationships may transition both up and down the continuum. For example, a traditional relationship may improve by moving to a relational state or may backslide to a dysfunctional state. Second, although we identify three primary states, many other states exist on the continuum. For example, the state of marginal mentoring (Ragins et al., 2000) could be found between traditional and dysfunctional states. Marginal mentoring relationships vacillate between positive and negative states, producing a marginal sense of satisfaction with the relationship. Marginal relationships are barely adequate but not quite dysfunctional. For example, a marginal mentor may provide support to his or her protégé only when it is convenient, thus being an undependable source of career support. In contrast, a dysfunctional mentor may actively undermine his or her protégé's career for political or personal reasons.

In sum, a relational perspective extends our lens on mentoring from a one-sided, exchange-based relationship focused on protégé career outcomes to a dyadic communal relationship with cognitive and affective processes that lead to mutual learning, growth, and development. Let us now examine some cognitive processes that lead to different perceptions of quality and mentoring states.

RELATIONAL SCHEMAS IN MENTORING RELATIONSHIPS

In this section of the chapter we apply relational cognition theory to the mentoring arena to both enrich mentoring theory and increase our understanding of the cognitive aspects of positive relationships at work. We briefly review major constructs and theories of social cognition relevant to cognitive processes in relationships. These social cognition theories are the foundation for our theoretical model of mentoring schemas. We posit that mentoring schemas serve as fluid cognitive maps that guide members' expectations and behaviors and their subsequent evaluation of the quality and effectiveness of their relationship. We propose that mentoring schemas are developed from accumulated sources of relational knowledge and are influenced by individual differences in how people approach relationships. We examine the conditions under which mentoring schemas lead to effective mentoring relationships and propose a positive cycle of mentoring that incorporates a norm congruency effect.

Relational Cognition Theory

Social Cognitions and Schemas. Relational cognition theory offers a theoretically rich lens for uncovering the complex cognitive processes involved with mentoring and other positive relationships at work. Relational cognition theory extends social cognition theory to relationships for the purpose of understanding the cognitive processes underlying social interactions (cf. Berscheid, 1994; Fiske, 2004; Haslam, 2004).

Social cognition theory examines how people mentally organize and represent information about themselves and others (Fiske, 1992). The building block of social cognition theory is schemas (Markus & Zajonc, 1985). Schemas are mental knowledge structures that guide an individual's behaviors in social interactions (Berscheid, 1994; Fiske & Taylor, 1984; Schneider, 1973). Schemas are developed through past experiences and affect our expectations about our own behavior, the behavior of others, and the nature and outcomes of our future social interactions (Markus & Zajonc, 1985). Schemas influence the kinds of social information that we attend to, the categorization and interpretation of new information, and the storage and retrieval of the information from our memory (Berscheid, 1994; Markus & Zajonc, 1985). In essence, schemas are organized structures of tacit knowledge that serve to construct, construe, and evaluate the behavior of self, others, and the relationship (Baldwin, 1992; Planalp, 1987).

Relational Schemas. Planalp (1985, 1987) introduced relational schemas as "coherent frameworks of relational knowledge that are used to derive relational implications of messages and are modified in accord with ongoing experience with relationships. They provide the cognitive equivalent of 'definitions of relationships' that guide message interpretation and production" (Planalp, 1985, p. 9).

Baldwin's framework of relational schemas (Baldwin, 1992, 1997, 1999) integrates and extends Planalp's ideas by drawing from symbolic interactionist theory (Cooley, 1902; Mead, 1934), social-cognitive models of personality (Schneider, 1973), relational models theory (Fiske, 1992), interpersonal theory (Safran, 1990), attachment theory (Bowlby, 1969), script theory (Tomkins, 1987), and relational-self theory (Horowitz, 1989; Ogilvie & Ashmore, 1991).

Baldwin (1992) defined relational schemas as "cognitive structures representing regularities in patterns of interpersonal relatedness" (p. 461) with three interrelated components: a self-schema, an other-schema, and an interpersonal script that guides patterns of interactions in the relationship. Self-schemas denote mental representations about one's self in a given relationship. This idea is grounded in the view that individuals have multiple selves and that a particular subset of the self, the working self-concept, is activated in a given relational context (Markus & Kunda, 1986).

Ogilvie and Ashmore's (1991) model of relational self elaborates the process of internalizing relationships into the working model of the self: "We not only internalize and mentally represent our selves and others; *we also form images of what we are like and how we feel when we are with specific other people in our lives*" (p. 286). They observed that self-schemas of "who I am when I'm with you" are influenced by past experiences and affect future behavior (Ogilvie, Fleming, & Pennell, 1998). Finally, they offered the provocative idea that individuals develop constellations of self with other structures that reflect more generalized patterns of experiences across similar types of relationships (Ogilvie & Ashmore, 1991). In essence, self-schemas encompass both cognitive structures envisioning "who I am when I'm with you" and, more generally, "who I am when I'm with someone like you." Individuals therefore use both specific relationships and generic prototypes in their self-schemas.

In addition to self and other schemas, relational schemas also include interpersonal scripts that guide roles and behaviors in the relationship (Baldwin, 1992). Drawing on script theory (Tomkins, 1987) and other models of interpersonal scripts (Abelson, 1981; Anderson, 1983; Schank & Abelson, 1977), Baldwin (1992) defined interpersonal scripts as "a cognitive structure representing a sequence of actions and events that defines a stereotyped relational pattern" (p. 468). Interpersonal scripts develop from past experiences and interactions (Tomkins, 1987) and reflect culturally shared systems of meaning (Stryker & Statham, 1985). Now that we have reviewed relational schema theory, let us apply this theory to a prototypical positive relationship at work: mentoring.

A Theory of Mentoring Schemas

A theory of mentoring schemas is developed in this section. Integrating related theory on social cognition, we examine the components of and the processes by which mentoring schemas are shaped by relational knowledge and individual differences. We then explore the impact of mentoring schemas on the expectations, behaviors, and evaluation of the relationship. The final portion of the theory involves examining the cognitive behavioral cycle and the conditions under which high-quality mentoring relationships develop. A model depicting key relationships in mentoring schema theory is displayed in Figure 5.2.

Components of Mentoring Schemas. As defined here, *mentoring schemas* are fluid cognitive maps derived from past experiences and relationships that guide mentor's and protégé's perceptions, expectations, and behaviors in mentoring relationships. These mental maps of mentoring are visions that frame our experiences, shape our expectations, and motivate our behaviors in mentoring relationships. By extending and integrating relational schema theory (Baldwin, 1992; Planalp, 1987) and relational self-theory (Ogilvie & Ashmore, 1991) to mentoring relationships, mentoring schemas are held to involve cognitive representations of the role of mentor, the role of protégé, and *mentoring scripts* that guide the pattern of interaction in the relationship.

Drawing on Ogilvie and Ashmore's (1991) model of relational self, we propose that mentoring schemas include *generic* mental representations about the general roles of mentors and protégés as well as *particularistic* mental representations reflecting mentor and protégé roles in their specific relationship. For example, a protégé in a mentoring relationship holds a self-schema that reflects generic knowledge of what protégés do in mentoring relationships (i.e., "Protégés follow their mentor's advice"), as well as a particularistic cognition of what his or her role is in this specific mentoring relationship ("I play the devil's advocate and question my mentor"), and who he or she becomes in this particular relationship ("I become an independent critical thinker"). The protégé also holds an other-schema that reflects cognitive structures about who the mentor is in the relationship. This other-schema involves both generic knowledge about what mentors gener-

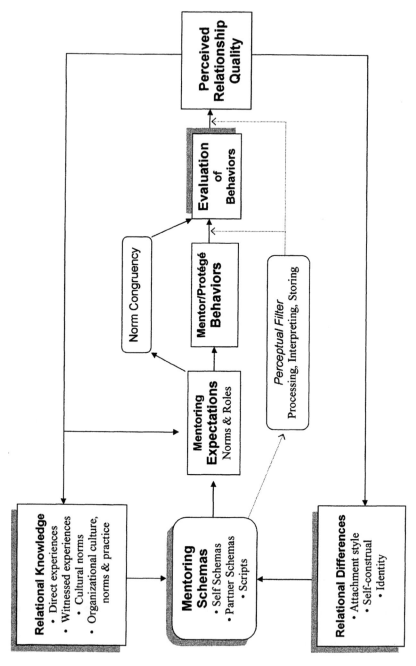

FIG. 5.2. The mentoring schema model.

ally are ("Mentors help their protégés"), as well as particularistic knowledge about what his or her mentor does in this particular relationship ("My mentor helps me to help myself"). At the same time, the mentor has a self-schema that involves general knowledge of what mentors do in mentoring relationships as well as specific knowledge about his or her role and emerging self in that particular relationship. The mentor also holds other-schema representations of what protégés do in mentoring relationships. As indicated in Figure 5.3, a given mentoring relationship can yield eight potential schemas involving generic and particularistic representations of mentor and protégé schemas from both the mentor's and the protégé's perspective. Moreover, these schemas can reflect relationships ranging from relational to dysfunctional mentoring relationships.

Mentoring schemas include not only self-schemas and other schemas, but also interpersonal scripts generated from self and other schemas, which in turn reinforce these cognitive structures (cf. Baldwin, 1992). Scripts are "predetermined, stereotyped sequence of actions that defines a well-known situation" (Schank & Abelson, 1977, p. 41). Scripts represent rules that are used in interpreting, evaluating, predicting, and controlling interactions (Tomkins, 1987). Accordingly, *mentoring scripts* are the "rules of the road" for specific sequences of interactions in mentoring relationships. An example of a mentoring script is when a protégé asks for help, the mentor helps the protégé discover the solution rather than fixing the problem for the protégé. This example illustrates that as part of the mentoring schema, mentoring scripts should be congruent with the self and other schemas held by members of the relationship.

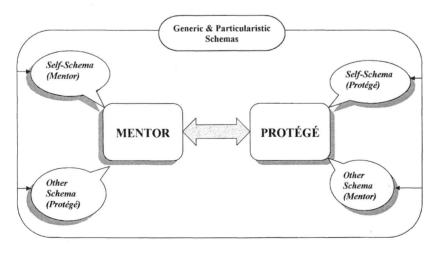

FIG. 5.3. Components of mentoring schema.

Although schema congruence is optimal, the mentoring schemas guiding mentors and protégés often diverge. For example, a mentor may hold a generic mentoring schema that good mentors are those who help their protégés help themselves, but his or her protégé's schema may be that good mentors "open doors" for their protégés. It is reasonable to expect some divergence in the mentoring schemas held by the members of the relationship, but we expect congruent schemas are more likely than incongruent schemas to result in reports of effective mentoring relationships.

Finally, as discussed later, mentoring schemas adapt and evolve as a consequence of changing antecedents and behavioral feedback from the relationship. Time therefore becomes an important factor to consider when examining schema congruency. It is reasonable to expect that although many relationships begin with incongruent mentoring schemas, over time schemas will converge as members modify their schemas in response to the realities of the relationship.

Although our discussion of mentoring schemas often implies role expectations in the relationship (cf. Young & Perrewé, 2000b, 2004), social cognition theory distinguishes between these constructs (Berscheid, 1994). Mentoring schemas are knowledge structures or visions of what a real or ideal mentoring relationship "looks like." In contrast, role expectations are evaluative standards about what individuals should do, be, think, or believe in their role in a relationship (Katz & Kahn, 1978). In essence, this represents the difference between "what is" and "what should be," a distinction that is important conceptually but often blurred in reality. In reality, relationship expectations are driven by cognitive schema, and because cognitive schema represent a "black box" for measurement, we often measure expectations as a surrogate for schemas. Nevertheless, from a theoretical perspective, it is important to keep these constructs distinct; schemas are the underlying mechanism that creates expectations and these mental maps of mentoring help us understand how mentoring expectations are created. Let us now examine some factors that shape these mental maps of mentoring.

Antecedents of Mentoring Schemas. Relational schemas develop from past experiences or events that provide relational knowledge (Baldwin, 1992; Planalp, 1987). In his review of the literature, Andersen (1993) identified a number of sources of relational knowledge. Our model incorporates three of these sources and adds a fourth source that is relevant to work relationships.

The first and perhaps most potent source of relational knowledge is the direct experience of being in a mentoring relationship. Information gleaned from past experiences crafts mentoring schemas that guide future relationships. This perspective is consistent with the findings that prior experience in mentoring relationships influences the mentor's expectations about the outcomes of the relationship (Ragins & Scandura, 1999), as well as the decision to enter a mentoring relationship again as a mentor (Allen, 2003; Allen, Poteet, Russell, & Dobbins, 1997; Ragins & Cotton, 1993; Ragins & Scandura, 1999) or as a protégé (Ragins & McFarlin, 1990). Mentoring schemas may range from very positive to very negative and past experiences with positive, negative, or marginal relationships play a key role in shaping these schemas. Although high-quality mentoring experiences result in mentoring schemas that reflect positive relationships, negative relationships do not automatically consign individuals to negative mentoring schemas; individuals can choose to not assimilate their negative experience into their mentoring schemas. In fact, illustrating what a mentor is not can crystallize the components of good mentoring.

The second source of relational knowledge is witnessed mentoring; that is, developing mentoring schema based on observing others' relationships. It is reasonable to expect that relationships witnessed firsthand should yield more detailed and explicit mentoring schemas than relationships witnessed at a distance. As with firsthand experiences, witnessed mentoring may fall along a continuum of positive to negative experiences, and individuals may transform negative experiences to positive schemas through conscious intervention. In addition, some mentoring relationships may be neither clearly positive nor negative to observers, and these ambiguous situations may lead to less detailed and explicit mentoring schemas.

The third source of relational knowledge is cultural norms related to mentoring. Culture may play a strong role in the development of mentoring schemas (cf. Clutterbuck & Ragins, 2002). For example, the sponsorship of a protégé's advancement is viewed as an appropriate mentoring function in the United States, but Europeans view this as favoritism. Europeans tend to view mentoring as a vehicle for personal development and mutual growth, whereas Americans usually envision mentoring as a relationship focused on a protégé's career advancement.

Finally, the organization is an important source of relational knowledge about mentoring. Mentoring is ingrained into the lexicon of language, values, and practice in organizations; we witness formal mentoring programs, executive coaching, and performance appraisal systems that include mentoring as a core managerial competency. Although mentoring has moved into the mainstream, there is tremendous variation in how organizations frame mentoring. Some frame it as an informal relationship aimed at professional development, learning, and growth. Others actively "manage" mentoring through formal mentoring programs aimed at orienting new employees, increasing diversity, or building apprenticeship models. Still others envision mentoring as a form of job coaching that is part of the manager–employee relationship. These frames influence the mentoring schema held by organizational members. As an example of explicit schemas, participants in formal programs are often given guidelines that define the expected behaviors, roles, frequency of meetings, length, and outcomes of the relationship (cf. Murray, 2001; Ragins et al., 2000). This practice distinguishes formal from informal relationships and reduces the potential for incongruent mentoring schemas.

Organizations also vary in the degree to which mentoring is incorporated into their cultures; some organizations actively promulgate mentoring as a key cultural value whereas others barely acknowledge it. Organizations with mentoring cultures increase the prevalence of mentoring, and thereby provide more opportunities for developing mentoring schemas. Organizations with mentoring cultures also offer greater depth and clarity to mentoring schemas, and it is reasonable to expect that their employees should have more detailed, precise, and positive mentoring schemas than employees who work in organizations that lack mentoring cultures. For example, mentoring relationships are visible and valued in organizations with mentoring cultures. Managers in these organizations are expected to provide mentoring and may be evaluated, and rewarded, on the degree to which they develop others. Management training programs may explicitly include coaching and mentoring as core managerial skills, thus providing concrete mentoring schemas about what constitutes an effective mentoring relationship.

In sum, relational knowledge gleaned from personal or witnessed mentoring relationships, cultural norms in society, and organizational cultures combines to shape, define, and articulate the mentoring schemas held by mentors and protégés. The clarity, salience, and strength of relational knowledge should influence the degree of detail, specificity, and the quality of the mentoring schema. We also expect that even as these various sources of relational knowledge combine to shape mentoring schemas, some sources are more potent than others, depending on the situation and the individual. In addition, individuals can take an active role in developing their schemas by consciously choosing to accept or reject different forms of relational knowledge.

Relational Difference Variables. There are individual differences in how people approach relationships (cf. review by Aron, 2003). We identify three relational difference variables that may be particularly relevant for shaping mentoring schema.

First, an individual's attachment style should directly impact mentoring schemas. Attachment styles are stable patterns of emotion and behaviors that are exhibited in close relationships (Bartholomew & Horowitz, 1991; Bowlby, 1969; see also Pietromonaco & Barrett, 2000). According to attachment theory, individuals develop attachment styles from their early childhood experiences (Bowlby, 1969). These experiences influence internal working models that guide future relationships. Some attachment styles allow individuals to feel secure in their relationships with others, whereas other styles result in anxiety, ambivalence, insecurity, or the avoidance of emotional intimacy (Bartholomew & Horowitz, 1991). It is reasonable to expect that attachment styles affect mentoring relationships (cf. Noe et al 2002) and that individuals with secure attachment styles will be more likely to develop relational mentoring schema than individuals who have insecure, anxious, or avoidant styles.

Self-construal, or how the self is viewed in relation to others, is the second variable that may influence mentoring schemas. Markus and Kitayama (1991) theorized that some individuals hold independent self-construals, defining themselves in terms of the things that make them unique, separate and independent from others, whereas others hold interdependent self-construals and define themselves based on their relationships with others. Extending this idea, Cross and her colleagues offered the idea of relational-interdependent self-construal (Cross, Bacon et al., 2000; Cross & Madson, 1997), or the tendency to define oneself in terms of relationships: "For individuals with this self-construal, representations of important relationships and roles share the self-space with abstract traits, abilities and preferences. To maintain and enhance this interdependent view of the self, individuals will tend to think and behave in ways that emphasize their connectedness to others and that strengthen existing relationships" (Cross et al., 2000, p. 791). It is reasonable to expect that self-construals shape mentoring schemas, and that individuals with interdependent self-construals will be more likely to develop relational mentoring schemas than those with independent self-construals.

The third variable that may influence mentoring schemas is the individual's relational identity. Like those with interdependent self-construals, individuals with relational identities define themselves in terms of their relationships with others (Brewer & Gardner, 1996). Relational identity may also motivate behavior and self-evaluations:

> The motivation to promote the other's welfare emerges when a relational orientation is made salient. This may take the form of caring and concern (in close relationships) or obligation and responsibility (as in role relationships). In either case, because self-evaluation depends on one's ability to succor another individual's welfare through one's role performance, it implies a form of cooperative interdependence between individuals whereby the other's well-being enhances one's own. (Brickson & Brewer, 2001, pp. 53–54)

Relational identity may underlie pro-social personality variables and altruism, which are related to mentors' decisions to enter a relationship and the functions they provide in the relationship (Allen, 2003; Aryee et al., 1996). We expect that the presence of relational identity will be associated with the development of relational mentoring schemas.

In addition to the three individual difference variables, we expect that gender, race, and culture should also affect mentoring schemas. Women are more likely than men to have interdependent self-construals (Cross & Madson, 1997) and engage in relational practices in organizations (Fletcher, 1998). Race, ethnicity, and culture also influence whether individuals employ independent or interdependent self-construals (Markus & Kitayama, 1991) and the type of relational schemas employed in work groups (Sanchez-Burks, Nisbett, & Ybarra, 2000). It is therefore reasonable to expect that the three cognitive processes identified here not only have a direct effect on mentoring schema, but also mediate the relation between demographic differences and mentoring schemas.

Outcomes of Mentoring Schemas. Mentoring schemas influence members' expectations and behaviors in the relationship, their satisfaction with the relationship, and their overall evaluation of the relationship's quality and effectiveness. As illustrated in Figure 5.2, these schemas shape the role expectations and norms that are used in the mentoring relationship. These expectations in turn guide mentors' and protégés' behaviors and are used to evaluate these behaviors (cf. Hassebrauck, 1997; Hassebrauck & Aron, 2001; Young & Perrewé, 2000a, 2000b). Ultimately this process determines whether or not members describe their mentoring relationships as relational, traditional, or dysfunctional. The evaluation of behaviors in a relationship is influenced by the degree to which members agree on the norms governing the relationship (Katz & Kahn, 1978). Accordingly, we expect that mentors and protégés who share norms should perceive the relationship as more satisfactory than members who hold conflicting norms. This *norm congruency effect* is particularly important when members apply communal and exchange norms to mentoring relationships (e.g., Clark & Mills, 1979). We expect that congruency in the use of either communal or exchange norms will lead to positive evaluations of the behaviors and the relationship. Relational mentoring is most likely to occur when both members apply communal norms in which benefits are given in response to partners' needs without the expectation of receiving comparable benefits in exchange. Congruency in the use of exchange norms may also lead to positive evaluations of the relationship; formal mentoring represents an example of this transactional approach to mentoring. In contrast, the use of incongruent norms can lead to frustration or even dysfunctional mentoring relationships.

Like other types of relational schemas (cf. Planalp, 1987), mentoring schemas create a perceptual filter influencing how information about the relationship is processed and interpreted. Mentoring schemas direct our attention to specific types of information, and influence the way we store and retrieve information from our memory. This perceptual filter is also used to evaluate the behaviors in the relationship, which Planalp (1987) called the *assimilation effect.*

Our theoretical model includes two feedback loops. First, members' evaluation of the effectiveness of their relationship should influence their future role expectations and their relational knowledge about mentoring. Planalp (1987) called this feedback loop the *accommodation effect.* Other scholars refer to this as a cognitive-behavioral cycle in which cognitions lead to behaviors that in turn confirm or modify initial cognitions (cf. Baldwin, 1992; Baldwin & Fergusson, 2001; Safran & Segal, 1990). Second, the perceived quality of the relationship should influence members' perceptions of themselves in relation to others. This idea stems directly from relational-self theory, which holds that self-perceptions are influenced by evaluations of relationships (Ogilvie & Ashmore, 1991). High-quality relationships should reinforce interconnected views of self and allow members to feel more secure in relationships. High-quality mentoring relationships should therefore bolster and fortify secure attachment styles, interdependent self-construals, and relational identities.

These feedback loops suggest that mentors and protégés can enter a *cycle of relational mentoring.* The experience of being in a close mentoring relationship should reinforce interdependent self-construals, relational identities, and secure attachment styles. This experience also creates and clarifies knowledge about relational mentoring. These perceptions reinforce and solidify relational mentoring schema, which perpetuates the cycle. This theory of mentoring schemas offers substantial guidance for future research on relational mentoring and social cognitive processes in mentoring relationships. Let us now explore some additional areas for future research.

FUTURE RESEARCH: AN INVITATION FOR A RELATIONAL APPROACH TO MENTORING

A relational perspective on mentoring offers an array of exciting research opportunities for positive relationship and mentoring scholars. First, we need typologies that define the underlying dimensions of mentoring schemas that are associated with formal and informal relationships, virtual relationships, supervisory mentoring relationships, and diverse mentoring relationships. We need to understand how mentoring schemas map onto schemas associated with transformational and authentic leadership (Godshalk & Sosik, 2000; Luthans & Aviolo, 2003; cf. Fletcher, chap. 19, this volume) and other high-quality connections in organizations (Dutton & Heaphy, 2003). What are the similarities and differences in the visions, expectations and roles of these positive work relationships? What are the generic and particularistic schemas of these relationships and what forms of relational knowledge prevail in their development? How do these schemas evolve independently and in relation to one another? What processes and environmental factors are involved with schema development and change?

Second, future research could also explore the process by which mentoring relationships create positive self-identities (cf. Roberts, chap. 2, this volume). By integrating self in relation to other theory (Aron, Aron, & Norman, 2001; Ogilvie & Ashmore, 1991) with emerging theory on positive self-identities in organizational contexts (Roberts, Dutton, Sprietzer, Heaphy, & Quinn, 2005), we can assess how positive self-identities emerge from mentoring relationships. Relational mentoring may also offer positive relationship scholars the opportunity to observe the "self at its best" within a relationship context.

Third, we need to have a better understanding of the antecedents and outcomes associated with relational mentoring. Under what conditions is relational mentoring created and optimized in organizational settings? What types of organizational, team, and individual outcomes are associated with relational mentoring? How do we create close mentoring bonds in these settings? Along similar lines, we need to understand the processes by which mentoring relationships transition across the relationship states discussed in the first part of this chapter and illustrated in Figure 5.1.

Finally, a social cognitive perspective offers methodological guidance for future mentoring research. Specifically, the common practice of asking protégés to recall their mentor's behaviors is problematic in that it may reflect particularistic mentoring schemas rather than actual mentoring behaviors. Schemas, expectations, behaviors, and evaluations constitute different aspects of the relationship and these effects can be assessed directly with questions to both mentor and protégé such as: (a) What constitutes a good mentor, a good protégé, and a good mentoring relationship? (b) What do members expect from their partner, themselves, and their relationship? (c) What behaviors are typically exhibited in the relationship? and (d) What are their evaluations of the behaviors and quality of the relationship? This dyadic approach allows for the assessment of congruency in perceptions, cognitive structures, and expectations (cf. Duck, 1990) and has been applied effectively in mentoring research (cf. Armstrong, Allinson, & Hayes, 2002; Sosik & Godshalk, 2004; Waters, 2004).

Measurement methods that have been used in social cognition research can be applied to the study of mentoring schemas. Hassebrauck (1997) provided an example of how to measure relationship prototypes. Ogilvie and colleagues operationalized the self-with-other construct and offered examples of its measurement (Ogilvie & Ashmore, 1991; Ogilvie et al., 1998). Rose (2003, 2005) recently developed the Ideal Mentoring Scale, which measures prototypes of effective mentoring.

In summary, our chapter examined the interface between mentoring and positive relationships at work. We explored how these areas can enrich and inform one another and developed a theory of mentoring schemas based on relationship and social cognition theory. By using a relational lens to examine the interface between mentoring and positive relationships we attempted to extend both areas of inquiry and offer a foundation for future theory and research.

ACKNOWLEDGMENTS

We would like to thank the other contributors to this volume for their insightful feedback and suggestions during the University of Michigan Positive Relationships at Work Book-Building Conference. We would also like to thank Joseph A. Gerard for his artistic help designing Figure 5.1.

REFERENCES

Abelson, R. P. (1981). Psychological status of the script concept. *American Psychologist, 36,* 715–729.

Allen, T. D. (2003). Mentoring others: A dispositional and motivational approach. *Journal of Vocational Behavior, 62,* 134–154.

Allen, T. D. & Eby, L. T. (2003). Relationship effectiveness for mentors: Factors associated with learning and quality. *Journal of Management, 29,* 469–486.

Allen, T. D., Eby, L. T., Poteet, M. L., Lentz, E., & Lima, L. (2004). Career benefits associated with mentoring for protégés: A meta analysis. *Journal of Applied Psychology, 89,*127–136.

Allen, T. D., Poteet, M. L., & Burroughs, S. M. (1997). The mentor's perspective: A qualitative inquiry and future research agenda. *Journal of Vocational Behavior, 51,* 70–89.

Allen, T. D., Poteet, M. L., Russell, J. E. A., & Dobbins, G. H. (1997). A field study of factors related to supervisors' willingness to mentor others. *Journal of Vocational Behavior, 50,* 1–22.

Andersen, P. A. (1993). Cognitive schemata in personal relationships. In S. Duck (Ed.), *Individuals in relationships: Vol. 1. Understanding relationship processes series* (pp. 1–29). Thousand Oaks, CA: Sage.

Anderson, J. R. (1983). *The architecture of cognition.* Cambridge, MA: Harvard University Press.

Armstrong, S. J., Allinson, C. W., & Hayes, J. (2002). Formal mentoring systems: An examination of the effects of mentor/protégé cognitive styles on the mentoring process. *Journal of Management Studies, 39,* 1111–1137.

Aron, A. (2003). Self and close relationships. In M. R. Leary & J. P. Tangney (Eds.), *Handbook of self and identity* (pp. 442–461). New York: Guilford.

Aron, A., Aron, E. N., & Norman, C. (2001). Self-expansion model of motivation and cognition in close relationships and beyond. In M. Clark & G. Fletcher (Eds.), *Blackwell handbook of social psychology: Vol. 2. Interpersonal processes* (pp. 478–501). Oxford, England: Blackwell.

Aryee, S., Chay, Y. W., & Chew, J. (1996). The motivation to mentor among managerial employees: An interactionist approach. *Group and Organization Management, 21,* 261–277.

Baldwin, M. W. (1992). Relational schemas and the processing of social information. *Psychological Bulletin, 112,* 461–484.

Baldwin, M. W. (1997). Relational schemas as a source of if–then self-inference procedures. *Review of General Psychology, 1,* 326–335.

Baldwin, M. W. (1999). Relational schemas: Research into social-cognitive aspects of interpersonal experience. In D. Cervone & Y. Shoda (Eds.), *The coherence of personality: Social cognitive bases of consistency, variability, and organizations* (pp. 127–154). New York: Guilford.

Baldwin, M. W., & Fergusson, P. (2001). Relational schemas: The activation of interpersonal knowledge structures in social anxiety. In W. R. Crozier & L. E. Alden (Eds.), *International handbook of social anxiety: Concepts, research and interventions relating to the self and shyness* (pp. 235–257). New York: Wiley.

Bartholomew, K., & Horowitz, L. M. (1991). Attachment styles among young adults: A test of a four-category model. *Journal of Personality and Social Psychology, 61,* 226–244.

Berscheid, E. (1994). Interpersonal relationships. *Annual Review of Psychology, 45,* 79–129.

Bowlby, J. (1969). *Attachment and loss: Vol. 1. Attachment.* New York: Basic Books.

Bozionelos, N. (2004). Mentoring provided: Relation to mentor's career success, personality, and mentoring received. *Journal of Vocational Behavior, 64,* 24–46.

Brewer, M. B., & Gardner, W. (1996). Who is this "we"? Levels of collective identity and self representations. *Journal of Personality and Social Psychology, 71,* 83–93.

Brickson, S., & Brewer, M. (2001). Identity orientation and intergroup relations in organizations. In M. A. Hogg & D. J. Terry (Eds.), *Social identity processes in organizational contexts* (pp. 49–66). Philadelphia: Psychology Press.

Cameron, K. S., Dutton, J. E., & Quinn, R. E. (2003). Foundations of positive organizational scholarship. In K. S. Cameron, J. E. Dutton, & R. E. Quinn, (Eds.), *Positive organizational scholarship: Foundations of a new discipline* (pp. 3–13). San Francisco: Berrett-Koehler.

Chao, G. T. (1997). Mentoring phases and outcomes. *Journal of Vocational Behavior, 51,* 15–28.

Chao, G. T., Walz, P. M., & Gardner, P. D. (1992). Formal and informal mentorships: A comparison on mentoring functions and contrast with nonmentored counterparts. *Personnel Psychology, 45,* 619–636.

Clark, M., & Mills, J. (1979). Interpersonal attraction in exchange and communal relationships. *Journal of Personality and Social Psychology, 37,* 12–24.

Clark, M., & Mills, J. (1993). The difference between communal and exchange relationships. *Personality and Social Psychological Bulletin, 19,* 684–691.

Clutterbuck, D., & Ragins, B. R. (2002). *Mentoring and diversity: An international perspective.* Oxford, England: Butterworth-Heinemann.

Cooley, C. H. (1902). *Human nature and the social order.* New York: Scribner's.

Cross, S. E., Bacon, P. L., & Morris, M. L. (2000). The relational-interdependent self-construal and relationships. *Journal of Personality and Social Psychology, 78,* 791–808.

Cross, S. E., & Madson, L. (1997). Models of the self: Self-construals and gender. *Psychological Bulletin, 122,* 5–37.

deJanasz, S. C., Sullivan, S. E., & Whiting, V. (2003). Mentor networks and career success: Lessons for turbulent times. *Academy of Management Executive, 17*(4), 78–93.

Duck, S. (1990). Relationships as unfinished business: Out of the frying pan and into the 1990's. *Journal of Social and Personal Relationships, 7,* 5–28.

Duck, S. (1994). *Meaningful relationships: Talking, sense, and relating.* Thousand Oaks, CA: Sage.

Dutton, J. E., & Heaphy, E. D. (2003). The power of high-quality connections. In K. S. Cameron, J. E. Dutton, & R. E. Quinn (Eds.), *Positive organizational scholarship: Foundations of a new discipline* (pp. 263–278). San Francisco: Berrett-Koehler.

Eby, L. T. (1997). Alternative forms of mentoring in changing organizational environments: A conceptual extension of the mentoring literature. *Journal of Vocational Behavior, 51,* 125–144.

Eby, L. T., & Allen, T. D. (2002). Further investigation of protégés' negative mentoring experiences: Patterns and outcomes. *Group and Organization Management, 27,* 456–479.

Eby, L. T., Butts, M., Lockwood, A., & Simon, S. A. (2004). Protégés' negative mentoring experiences: Construct development and nomological validation. *Personnel Psychology, 57,* 411–447.

Eby, L. T., McManus, S. E., Simon, S. A., & Russell, J. E. A. (2000). The protégé's perspective regarding negative mentoring experiences: The development of a taxonomy. *Journal of Vocational Behavior, 57,* 1–21.

Ensher, E., Heun, C., & Blanchard, A. (2003). On-line mentoring and computer mediated communication: New directions in research. *Journal of Vocational Behavior, 63,* 264–288.

Ferraro, F., Pfeffer, J., & Sutton, R. I. (2005). Economics language and assumptions: How theories can become self-fulfilling. *Academy of Management Review, 30,* 8–24.

Fiske, A. P. (1992). The four elementary forms of sociality: Framework for a unified theory of social relations. *Psychological Review, 99,* 689–723.

Fiske, A. P. (2004). Relational models theory 2.0. In N. Haslam (Ed.), *Relational models theory: A contemporary overview* (pp. 3–25). Mahwah, NJ: Lawrence Erlbaum Associates.

Fiske, S. T., & Taylor, S. E. (1984). *Social cognition.* New York: Random House.

Fletcher, J. K. (1996). A relational approach to developing the protean worker. In D. T. Hall & Associates (Eds.), *The career is dead—Long live the career* (pp. 105–131). San Francisco: Jossey-Bass.

Fletcher, J. K. (1998). Relational practice: A feminist reconstruction of work. *Journal of Management Inquiry, 7,* 163–186.

Fletcher, J. K. (1999). *Disappearing acts: Gender, power, and relational practice at work.* Cambridge, MA: MIT Press.

Godshalk, V. M., & Sosik, J. J. (2000). Does mentor–protégé agreement on mentor leadership behavior influence the quality of a mentoring relationship? *Group and Organization Management, 25,* 291–317.

Godshalk, V. M., & Sosik, J. J. (2003). Aiming for career success: The role of learning goal orientation in mentoring relationships. *Journal of Vocational Behavior, 63,* 417–437.

Hamilton, B. A., & Scandura, T. A. (2003). E-mentoring: Implications for organizational learning and development in a wired world. *Organizational Dynamics, 31,* 388–403.

Haslam, N. N. (Ed.). (2004). *Relational models theory: A contemporary overview.* Mahwah, NJ: Lawrence Erlbaum Associates.

Hassebrauck, M. (1997). Cognitions of relationship quality: A prototype analysis of their structure and consequences. *Personal Relationships, 4,* 163–185.

Hassebrauck, M., & Aron, A. (2001). Prototype matching in close relationships. *Personality and Social Psychology Bulletin, 27,* 1111–1122.

Higgins, M. C., & Kram, K. E. (2001). Reconceptualizing mentoring at work: A developmental network perspective. *Academy of Management Review, 26,* 264–288.

Higgins, M. C., & Thomas, D. A. (2001). Constellations and careers: Toward understanding the effects of multiple developmental relationships. *Journal of Organizational Behavior, 22,* 223–247.

Horowitz, M. J. (1989). Relationship schema formulation: Role-relationship models and intrapsychic conflict. *Psychiatry, 52,* 260–274.

Hunt, D. M., & Michael, C. (1983). Mentorship: A career training and development tool. *Academy of Management Review, 8,* 475–485.

Jensen, M. C., & Meckling, W. H.(1994, Summer). The nature of man. *Journal of Applied Corporate Finance,* 4–19.

Kahn, W. A. (1998). Relational systems at work. In B. Staw & L. L. Cummings (Eds.), *Research in organizational behavior* (Vol. 20, pp. 39–76). Greenwich, CT: JAI.

Katz, D., & Kahn, R. L. (1978). *The social psychology of organizations* (2nd ed.). New York: Wiley.

Kolb, D. M. (1992). Women's work: Peacemaking in organizations. In D. M. Kolb & J. Bartunek (Eds.), *Hidden conflict in organizations: Uncovering behind the scenes disputes* (pp. 63–91). Newbury Park, CA: Sage.

Kram, K. (1985). *Mentoring at work: Developmental relationships in organizational life.* Glenview, IL: Scott, Foresman.

Kram, K. (1996). A relational approach to career development. In D. T. Hall (Ed.), *The career is dead—Long live the career: A relational approach to careers* (pp. 132–157). San Francisco: Jossey-Bass.

Lankau, M. J., & Scandura, T. A. (2002). An investigation of personal learning in mentoring relationships: Content, antecedents, and consequences. *Academy of Management Journal, 45,* 779–790.

Luthans, F., & Avolio, B. (2003). Authentic leadership development. In K. S. Cameron, J. E. Dutton, & R. E. Quinn (Eds.), *Positive organizational scholarship: Foundations of a new discipline* (pp. 241–258). San Francisco: Berrett-Koehler.

Luthans, F., & Youssef, C. M. (2004). Human, social, and now positive psychological capital management: Investing in people for competitive advantage. *Organizational Dynamics, 33,* 143–160.

Markus, H. R., & Kitayama, S. (1991). Culture and the self: Implications for cognition, emotion, and motivation. *Psychological Review, 98,* 224–253.

Markus, H., & Kunda, Z. (1986). Stability and malleability of the self-concept. *Journal of Personality and Social Psychology, 51,* 858–866.

Markus, H., & Zajonc, R. B. (1985). The cognitive perspective in social psychology. In G. Lindzey & E. Aronson (Eds.), *Handbook of social psychology* (3rd ed., Vol. 1, pp. 137–230). New York: Random House.

McManus, S. E., & Russell, J. E. A. (1997). New directions for mentoring research: An examination of related constructs. *Journal of Vocational Behavior, 51,* 145–161.

Mead, G. H. (1934). *Mind, self and society.* Chicago, IL: University of Chicago Press.

Miller, J. B. (1976). *Toward a new psychology of women.* Boston: Beacon Press.

Miller, J. B., & Stiver, I. (1997). *The healing connection.* Boston: Beacon Press.

Mills, J., Clark, M. S., Ford, T. E., & Johnson, M. (2004). Measurement of communal strength. *Personal Relationships, 11,* 213–230.

Mullen, E. J. (1994). Framing the mentoring relationship as an information exchange. *Human Resource Management Review, 4,* 257–281.

Mullen, E. J., & Noe, R. A. (1999). The mentoring information exchange: When do mentors seek information from their protégés? *Journal of Organizational Behavior, 20,* 233–242.

Murray, M. (2001). *Beyond the myths and magic of mentoring: How to facilitate an effective mentoring process.* San Francisco: Jossey-Bass.

Noe, R. A., Greenberger, D. B., & Wang, S. (2002). Mentoring: What we know and where we might go. *Research in Personnel and Human Resources Management, 21,* 129–173.

Ogilvie, D. M., & Ashmore, R. D. (1991). Self-with-other representation as a unit of analysis in self-concept research. In R. C. Curtis (Ed.), *The relational self: Theoretical convergences in psychoanalysis and social psychology* (pp. 282–314). New York: Guildford.

Ogilvie, D. M., Fleming, C. J., & Pennell, G. E. (1998). Self-with-other representations. In D. F. Barone, M. Hersen, & V. B. van Hasselt (Eds.), *Advanced personality* (pp. 353–375). New York: Plenum.

Pietromonaco, P. R., & Barrett, L. F. (2000). The internal working models concept: What do we really know about the self in relation to others? *Review of General Psychology, 4,* 155–175.

Planalp, S. (1985). Relational schemata: A test of alternative forms of relational knowledge as guides to communication. *Human Communication Research, 12,* 3–29.

Planalp, S. (1987). Interplay between relational knowledge and events. In R. Burnett, P. McGhee, & D. Clarke (Eds.), *Accounting for relationships: Explanation, representation, & knowledge* (pp. 175–191). New York: Methuen.

Ragins, B. R. (1989). Barriers to mentoring: The female manager's dilemma. *Human Relations, 42,* 1–22.

Ragins, B. R. (1997). Diversified mentoring relationships in organizations: A power perspective. *Academy of Management Review, 22,* 482–521.

Ragins, B. R. (1999). Gender and mentoring relationships: A review and research agenda for the next decade. In G. N. Powell (Ed.), *Handbook of gender and work* (pp. 347–370). Thousand Oaks, CA: Sage.

Ragins, B. R. (2005). *Towards a theory of relational mentoring.* Unpublished manuscript, University of Wisconsin–Milwaukee, Milwaukee.

Ragins, B. R., & Cotton, J. L. (1993). Gender and willingness to mentor in organizations. *Journal of Management, 19,* 97–111.

Ragins, B. R., & Cotton, J. L. (1999). Mentor functions and outcomes: A comparison of men and women in formal and informal mentoring relationships. *Journal of Applied Psychology, 84,* 529–550.

Ragins, B. R., Cotton, J. L., & Miller, J. S. (2000). Marginal mentoring: The effects of type of mentor, quality of relationship, and program design on work and career attitudes. *Academy of Management Journal, 43,* 1177–1194.

Ragins, B. R., & McFarlin, D. B. (1990). Perceptions of mentor roles in cross-gender mentoring relationships. *Journal of Vocational Behavior, 37,* 321–339.

Ragins, B. R., & Scandura, T. A. (1994). Gender differences in expected outcomes of mentoring relationships. *Academy of Management Journal, 37,* 957–971.

Ragins, B. R., & Scandura, T. A. (1997). The way we were: Gender and the termination of mentoring relationships. *Journal of Applied Psychology, 82,* 945–953.

Ragins, B. R., & Scandura, T. A. (1999). Burden or blessing? Expected costs and benefits of being a mentor. *Journal of Organizational Behavior, 20,* 493–509.

Reis, H. T., & Gable, S. L. (2003). Toward a positive psychology of relationships. In C. L. M. Keyes & J. Haidt (Eds.), *Flourishing: Positive psychology and the life well-lived* (pp. 129–159). Washington, DC: American Psychological Association.

Roberts, L. M., Dutton, J. E., Sprietzer, G. M., Heaphy, E. D., & Quinn, R. E. (2005). Composing the reflected best self-portrait: Building pathways for becoming extraordinary in work organizations. *Academy of Management Review, 30,* 712–736.

Rose, G. L. (2003). Enhancement of mentor selection using the ideal mentor scale. *Research in Higher Education, 44,* 473–494.

Rose, G. L. (2005). Group differences in graduate students' concepts of the ideal mentor. *Research in Higher Education, 46,* 53–81.

Safran, J. D. (1990). Towards a refinement of cognitive therapy in light of interpersonal theory: I. Theory. *Clinical Psychology Review, 10,* 87–105.

Safran, J. D., & Segal, Z. V. (1990). *Interpersonal process in cognitive therapy.* New York: Basic Books.

Sanchez-Burks, J., Nisbett, R. E., & Ybarra, O. (2000). Cultural styles, relational schemas, and prejudice against out-groups. *Journal of Personality and Social Psychology, 79,* 174–189.

Scandura, T. A. (1998). Dysfunctional mentoring relationships and outcomes. *Journal of Management, 24,* 449–467.

Schank, R. C., & Abelson, R. P. (1977). *Scripts, plans, goals, and understanding: An inquiry into human knowledge structures.* Hillsdale, NJ: Lawrence Erlbaum Associates.

Schneider, D. J. (1973). Implicit personality theory: A review. *Psychological Bulletin, 79,* 294–309.

Sosik, J. J., & Godshalk, V. M. (2000). Leadership styles, mentoring functions received, and job-related stress: A conceptual model and preliminary study. *Journal of Organizational Behavior, 21,* 365–390.

Sosik, J. J., & Godshalk, V. M. (2004). Self–other rating agreement in mentoring: Meeting protégé expectations for development and career advancement. *Group and Organization Management, 29,* 442–469.

Sosik, J. J., Godshalk, V. M., & Yammarino, F. J. (2004). Transformational leadership, learning goal orientation, and expectations for career success in mentor–protégé relationships: A multiple levels of analysis perspective. *The Leadership Quarterly, 15,* 241–261.

Stryker, S., & Serpe, R. T. (1982). Commitment, identity salience, and role behavior: Theory and research example. In W. Ickes & E. S. Knowles (Eds.), *Personality, roles, and social behavior* (pp. 199–218). New York: Springer-Verlag.

Stryker, S., & Statham, A. (1985). Symbolic interaction and role therapy. In G. Lindzey & E. Aronson (Eds.), *Handbook of social psychology* (3rd ed., pp. 311–378) New York: Random House.

Surrey, J. (1985). *The self in relation.* Working paper #13 Centers for Women, Wellesley College, Wellesley, MA. http://www.wcwonline.org

Tomkins, S. S. (1987). Script theory. In J. Aronoff, A. I. Rabin, & R. A. Zucker (Eds.), *The emergence of personality* (pp. 147–216). New York: Springer.

van Emmerik, I. J. H. (2004). The more you can get the better: Mentoring constellations and intrinsic career success. *Career Development International, 9,* 578–594.

Wanberg, C. R., Welsh, E. T., & Hezlett, S. A. (2003). Mentoring research: A review and dynamic process model. *Research in Personnel and Human Resources Management, 22,* 39–124.

Waters, L. (2004). Protégé–mentor agreement about the provision of psychosocial support: The mentoring relationship, personality, and workload. *Journal of Vocational Behavior, 65,* 519–532.

Young, A. M., & Perrewé, P. L. (2000a). The exchange relationship between mentors and protégés: The development of a framework. *Human Resources Management Review, 10,* 177–209.

Young, A. M., & Perrewé, P. L. (2000b). What did you expect? An examination of career-related support among mentors and protégés. *Journal of Management, 26,* 611–632.

Young, A. M., & Perrewé, P. L. (2004). The role of expectations in the mentoring exchange: An analysis of mentor and protégé expectations in relation to perceived support. *Journal of Managerial Issues, 16,* 103–126.

6

Rebuilding Trust and Restoring Positive Relationships: A Commitment-Based View of Trust

Michael G. Pratt
Kurt T. Dirks

In prosperity our friends know us; in adversity we know our friends.
—John Churton Collins (2006)

Positive relationships, like friendships in our epigraph, are not without adversity and periods of struggle. Whereas some may argue about what constitutes the heart and soul of these positive relationships, we argue that trust serves as the "bones" that allow positive relationships to stand tall, move forward, and endure injury. We argue that trust is central to all positive relationships. However, we further suggest that our current views of trust—those based on a social exchange perspective—are insufficient for understanding trust in these relationships. Additionally, we believe that positive relationships—those that are resilient and generative—must also involve an understanding of how trust is repaired. We believe that positive relationships, by definition, not only describe the beneficial functioning of dyads and larger groups when times are good, they also provide support and strength when relationships are tested.

We focus on trust, which is commonly defined as a psychological state whereby individuals in a relationship accept vulnerability based on positive expectations of the intentions or behavior of another (Rousseau, Sitkin, Burt, & Camerer, 1998), as we believe that it is a benefit for a variety of relationships, including positive relationships. Researchers have documented that trust in a work partner is associated with more positive attitudes toward the partner, more willingness to provide assistance to the partner, more effective communication processes, and the ability to more effectively address conflict in the relationship, among other benefits (for a review, see Dirks & Ferrin, 2001). Existing research on trust has also begun to provide insight into the process by which trust is built in work relationships (e.g., Whitener, Brodt, Korsgaard, & Werner, 1998). We argue, however, that existing perspectives on trust are likely to provide incomplete insight into how trust operates in relationships that are deemed to be positive relationships. If positive relationships are both generative and resilient, then we must have a model of trust that allows for both personal growth and relational toughness. We argue that conceptualizations of trust based on social exchange, the most common view of workplace trust, do not account for the robustness of positive relationships.

As noted, positive relationships, like all relationships, are inevitably subject to episodes of challenge. For example, Driver, Tabares, Shapiro, Nahm, and Gottman (2003) observed that even close relationships involve not only positive events, but also negative events or conflict in which the relationship is threatened. Their work also implies the difference between whether a relationship is generally positive or negative is contingent on how individuals respond following challenges. In work contexts, similar relationship challenges can occur among coworkers. How coworkers respond to these challenges, especially when they involve broken trust, is critical. Consequently, to ensure that the relationship remains positive following such challenges, it is important to understand how trust can be rebuilt and the relationship restored.

The insight that a key test of a positive relationship is not only how it functions when times are good, but also when there are challenges, leads us to the ironic conclusion that one of the best ways to gain insight into the role of trust in positive relationships is to understand the breaking and repair of trust. To date, however, only a handful of studies have explored how trust might be repaired and the relationship restored in any type of work relationship. We address this gap by focusing on how trust in positive relationships is broken and restored. Returning to our bone metaphor, trust reparation in positive relationships can be illustrated using the physiology of a broken bone. After a break occurs, several outcomes are possible. If the break is set properly, the bone may be as strong, or stronger, than ever. Alternatively, if the bone is not well set, it may cause ongoing pain and may become brittle and prone to further breaks. Similarly, relationships that are not well set after a break in trust occurs may die or, if they survive, cause ongoing pain for those who remain. We believe that in positive relationships, breaks in trust are properly reset so that relationships can become stronger and continue to thrive.

RECONCEPTUALIZING TRUST
FROM AN EXCHANGE-BASED
TO A COMMITMENT-BASED CONCEPT

Before considering the processes by which trust may be repaired, we give some consideration to the nature of trust and the processes by which it operates. Our interest in the role of trust in positive relationships has implications for considering which theoretical lens may be most helpful for understanding the process of trust repair: exchange based versus commitment based.

Many extant conceptualizations of trust view trust from a social exchange perspective. More specifically, trust is often posed as a key mechanism in social exchange as it represents the expectation that one's contributions to another will be equitably paid back (Blau, 1964; Konovsky & Pugh, 1994). Likewise, trust is described as evolving through an exchange process in which individuals start with small exchanges and gradually increase them over time (Whitener et al., 1998). Such social exchange is also implicit in some definitions of trust as "a psychological state comprising the intention to accept vulnerability based on positive expectations of the intentions or behavior of another" (Rousseau et al., 1998; see Mayer, Davis, & Schoorman, 1995, for a similar conceptualization). A component of these definitions of trust involves accepting some degree of vulnerability in the hope or expectation of obtaining a benefit at the discretion of another person. This is consistent with Blau's (1964) formulation, in which individuals are willing to provide a resource or service at the present (make themselves vulnerable) with expectation of a future benefit, based on what they believe about the other party.

Little attention has been given to the possible deficiencies of solely using a social exchange perspective to understand the role of trust in organizations. For example, a social exchange perspective has proven elusive to actually verify in empirical research. In addition, an individual's vulnerability is not exchanged in the traditional sense—that is, it is not given away. Rather, vulnerability on the part of both participants in a trust relationship is an ongoing aspect of the relationship. It cannot be easily separated from the benefits of a trusting relationship. Thus, it would be useful to more effectively recognize the ongoing coexistence of positive and negative elements that are inherent in the conceptualization of trust—as well as the interplay of these elements. Third, although social exchange may represent one archetype that governs a relationship, Fiske's (1992) work highlights that there are numerous other archetypes that govern relationships, some of which may also be associated with positive, trusting relationships (e.g., communal sharing).[1] A form of trust that is elastic enough to capture differ-

---

[1]Other scholars make closely related distinctions between different archetypes of relationships, including Clark and Mills (1979) and Sahlins (1972).

ent archetypes and processes may be valuable for understanding positive relationships. Last and specifically related to the purposes of this chapter, a social exchange perspective provides limited theoretical leverage for understanding how trust can be rebuilt, beyond the observation that trust occurs—and by extrapolation, might possibly be rebuilt—over a series of exchanges. However, an exchange perspective might even suggest that once trust is broken, the exchange relationship would likely terminate. Indeed, if trust is needed to facilitate social exchange, its absence should lead to the cessation of social exchange. Such a perspective says little, then, about how trust is regained, or about the role of vulnerability in this process.

Viewing Trust as Commitment Based Rather Than Exchange Based

In searching for an alternative lens for viewing trust, we looked for concepts that could explain how trust can add resiliency and strength to a relationship. That is, we needed a perspective that explains not only how trust is formed, but also how it can be repaired. We argue that commitment, especially as conceptualized by Brickman and colleagues (1987), offers a more fruitful lens than social exchange when viewing the role of trust in positive relationships. According to Brickman et al. (1987):

> Commitment is about the relationship between "want to" and "have to." Commitment involves three elements: a positive element, a negative element, and the bond between the two. We have already seen that there are negative elements in the most totally absorbing of commitments. Surgeons, mountain climbers, and chess players make heavy sacrifices for their skills and run risks—both material and psychological—in the exercise of these skills. . . . On the other hand, we have also seen that there is a positive element in even the most alienated commitment. People who stay with a job or marriage after the life has gone out of it may no longer have the reason that initially drew them, but they still have reasons, they still have something of value that they do not wish to lose. . . . It is the connection between the positive and negative element . . . the nature of their connection or their bonding that determines the nature of the commitment. (pp. 5–6)

We argue that the nature and development of trust may be better understood by considering its similarities to this type of commitment. Following Pratt and Rosa (2003), we refer to Brickman's conceptualization of the concept as *relationship-based commitment* to differentiate it from other types of commitment such as affective, continuance, normative, and behavioral commitment (Becker, 1960; Kiesler, 1971; Meyer & Allen, 1997). In our view, relationship-based commitment is the binding together of positive and negative elements in a relationship. Such commitment is more holistic than these other conceptualizations of commitment as it involves both attitudes and behaviors. Moreover, it is referred to as relationship-based because the target of commitment is an interpersonal relationship, rather than the organization (e.g., affective or normative organizational commitment) or a pattern of activity (e.g., behavioral commitment or escalation of commitment).

Relationship-based commitment and trust appear to have much in common. First, like relationship-based commitment, trust involves the simultaneous existence of both positive and negative elements. With regard to commitment in a work relationship with one's boss, the feelings of support and direction one gets may be inexorably linked to the vulnerability one feels because the boss also has power over you and will evaluate your performance. Inherently, trust also has both positive and negative elements as well. On the one hand, when trust exists, individuals are privy to potential benefits that the relationship may bring. On the other, trust also involves exposing one's self to risks. Because both positive and negative elements exist simultaneously, they both can influence how commitment and trust are experienced. For example, sometimes a commitment is experienced as a joy (I want to) and sometimes an obligation (I have to). Similarly, trust can be experienced as both a boon and as a burden as it can facilitate both rewards and vulnerabilities in a relationship. In the commitment literature, these different experiences are sometimes referred to as different *faces*.

These two faces of commitment and trust may be tied up in emotions (Pratt & Rosa, 2003). Relationship-based commitment may be characterized by love and guilt, or excitement and fear. For trust, the positive face may result in feelings of comfort and safety (with another individual) or a sense of excitement (about potential benefits). The negative face, in turn, may be associated with anxiety. Consider these two uses of trust we use: In this chapter, Kurt is the "trust expert" and Mike is the "commitment expert." Given this arrangement, Mike can comment, "I feel great about working with Kurt, I can trust him to come through with his part of the chapter." Kurt, alternatively, can express feelings of trust that have a less positive tone: "I don't know anything about commitment, so I will have to trust Mike to talk about this part of the chapter."

Mike's excitement and Kurt's anxiety may not (and hopefully will not in the case of Kurt) stay constant as the relationship evolves. This illustrates a second commonality between trust and relationship-based commitment: Different faces may be more salient at different points in a relationship. Taking the example further, Kurt and Mike may experience more of the positive face of trust 6 months before the chapter is to be delivered to the editor, but the negative face 1 week before their deadline. Throughout the relationship, however, trust exists. Like our analysis, Lewicki, McAllister, and Bies (1998) discussed how relationships tend to involve both positive and negative elements (they equate these with trust and distrust) and recognized that these elements are dynamic across a relationship.

This dynamic interplay between positive and negative elements in the relationship suggests that in the presence of trust and commitment, individuals will be drawn toward some aspects of the relationship, and away from others. As we have argued, trust involves more than the simple exchange of resources. In fact, the power of the trust concept is that it can operate in the absence of obvious external incentives—it persists without a guarantee that one will receive anything of value. Because trust inherently involves a sense of vulnerability and the possibility of being hurt (a negative element) that is inexorably fused with the anticipation of positive intentions or outcomes on behalf of the other person (a positive element), then trust—by its nature—involves ambivalence. How these competing elements are resolved, however, differs by theoretical perspective.

Social exchange relationships appear to involve more of a hedonistic calculus with the net result either a "net positive" or a "net negative" assessment of the relationship. In a commitment-based view, by contrast, these positive and negative elements associated with trust do not "cancel out" to reveal either a positive or a negative relationship; rather both positive and negative elements are simultaneously present in all trust relationships. It is the resolution of this ambivalence that gives relationships their energy and resilience. Ambivalence becomes the fuel for trust, and the ability to manage positive and negative elements that allow relationships to survive in the face of adversity.

A third and related point of similarity between relationship-based commitment and our conceptualization of trust is that both involve choice. In Brickman's theory, the transformation of positive and negative elements of a relationship into commitment can only occur when members enter a relationship of their own free will (Pratt & Rosa, 2003). One cannot be forced to commit to someone. Likewise, one cannot be forced to trust someone. Choice creates the need for a justification to explain how both positive and negative elements can coexist in the relationship in a manner that leads to the perpetuation rather than the destruction of the relationship (Kiesler, 1971; Salancik, 1977; Weick, 1995).

The transformation of ambivalence into commitment through volition and justification differentiates relationship-based commitment from broader reinforcement perspectives, such as social exchange. Commitment is necessary to act in the face of ambivalence: to persevere in a relationship that is not 100% positive or 100% negative. We believe that trust can play a similar role in positive relationships. Trust that is viewed primarily as social exchange may be more fragile, and thus characteristic of other types (i.e., nonpositive) of relationships. In other words, when positive and negative elements are not bound together, then reactions to ambivalence may not result in the maintenance of the relationship. As noted in their review of the concept (Pratt & Doucet, 2000), ambivalence can, and often does, lead to more negative outcomes. For example, ambivalence in a relationship can lead to paralysis, vacillation, or retreat—outcomes that are not likely to lead to either growth or even maintenance of the relationship. From a social exchange perspective, trust should only lead to the continuing of a relationship when benefits outweigh costs. However, this is only one possible outcome: When the cost and benefit calculations come out even, an individual may experience paralysis; when the cost–benefit ratio is in flux an individual may vacillate; and when costs outweigh benefits, an individual may retreat from the relationship. We argue that the perseverance in a relationship brought on by the presence of trust in a positive relationship is relatively robust against minor (and sometimes major) violations—an outcome that would not be predicted by an exchange-focused conceptualization of trust. For example, rationalizations might protect the violated party from experiencing a breakdown of trust. Examples might include Martha Stewart supporters in the face of criminal allegations. As noted, rationalizations may not just be key in the formation of trust, they may also play a role in its protection and reestablishment.

To summarize, taking a relationship-based commitment view of trust involves recognizing how trust involves a volitional acceptance of the simultaneous existence of both the vulnerability and the benefits associated with being in a relationship with another individual. As such, it involves justifications that might not be necessary from a more extrinsic, social exchange view. Moreover, unlike a social exchange perspective, we see trust as relatively robust and potentially difficult to damage. This is because trust is dynamic. In the face of challenges, sometimes trust is experienced in a more positive light, and sometimes in a more negative light. However, each of these challenges creates opportunities for trust to be transformed. Thus to the extent that the parties consciously recognize and accept not only the positive elements, but also the negative elements, we expect trust to be more robust. Finally, it is this dynamic and robust nature of trust that follows from a commitment-based view that makes it uniquely appropriate when talking about how trust operates in positive relationships. We now turn to the implications of such a commitment-based perspective on trust dynamics.

Implications of a Commitment Perspective on Trust

Viewing trust as being like relationship-based commitment suggests new ways that trust can be formed. As noted earlier, we believe that trust involves the noncoerced acceptance and justification of both personal vulnerability and potential benefit in a relationship with another. However, the notion that trust is a tripartite concept—involving a positive element, a negative element, and a bond between the two—also provides new insights into how trust can be broken down and restored.

Breaking Down Trust

Although we argue that trust in a relationship makes the relationship more robust and resilient, this does not mean that the relationship is impervious to harm. In fact, we have already argued that trust involves a dynamic coherence in a relationship—one where either the positive or negative face is more salient—rather than a static consistency. A commitment view of trust suggests at least three ways that this dynamic coherence can become "broken down" as it becomes imbalanced, violated, or destroyed. Specifically, we suggest that trust may break down when negative elements overwhelm positive elements in the relationship, when ambivalence disappears, and when ambivalence cannot be transformed.

When Negative Elements Overwhelm Positive Elements. Over the course of a relationship, the balance of the positive and negative elements may change so that the negative elements consistently overwhelm the positive ones (Pratt & Rosa, 2003). This may be due to the introduction of a dramatic negative event in the relationship. For example, the sudden discovery that a trusted coworker has been stealing your ideas and spreading negative rumors about you might intensify the negative elements in the relationship enough that they can no longer become integrated into the positive aspects of the relationship. However, negative elements in a relationship may also accrue more slowly over time, causing the relationship to slowly dissolve. Similar to the story about the frog who did not notice that the water in the pot was getting progressively warmer before becoming boiled to death, negative elements can accrue slowly enough that one does not notice how badly a relationship has been damaged until a need to draw on the trusting relationship results in a reevaluation of that relationship. This increase in the negative aspects of a relationship is a primary means of damaging trust, as psychology has documented how negative elements and events (e.g., being harmed) tend to be highly salient and can inordinately influence one's perception of another (Skrowronski & Carlston, 1989).

The balance between the negative and positive elements of a relationship may also become imbalanced due to a reduction of the positive elements. For example, a coworker may endure the idiosyncrasies (e.g., brusque manner) of a mentor who provides guidance and support. As the protégé develops over time, he or she may find that the formerly positive element of advice giving is either no longer necessary (i.e., has a less positive valence) or has taken on a negative valence. Once again, negative elements threaten to overwhelm the positive. Although the trust in a positive relationship can sometimes show a negative face, we believe that if this face becomes the dominant one (as it might in some abusive relationships), the relationship can become negative and trust can erode.

The addition of overwhelming negative elements in a relationship is also—and some might argue the only—means of destroying trust from a social exchange perspective. However, there are key differences here with the commitment-based perspective. To begin, from a commitment-based view, we believe that the dissolution of trust due to the addition of negative elements would normally[2] occur much more slowly than would be expected from a social exchange perspective—which might dissolve after one or two negative exchanges. Moreover, because commitment-based trust involves the creation of justifications, elements in a relationship may become negative for reasons that do not involve the actions of the "trusted" (as one would expect from a social exchange perspective). For example, pretend that you have similar trust relationships with two coworkers. A serious betrayal by one of them may essentially poison the relationship with the other if your anxiety toward all work-related relationships increases. Such anxiety may make the burden of vulnerability too much to bear even in relationships with people who have never betrayed your trust.

When Ambivalence Disappears. Extrapolating from Pratt and Rosa's (2003) arguments about the breakdown of commitment, we suggest that trust may break down when ambivalence disappears. Although it is easy to see how trust might erode if all positive elements of the relationship disappeared, we argue that trust would also become meaningless if all of the negative elements of the relationship disappeared as well. At this point, trust is not necessary—the relationship has essentially become a reinforcement or exchange relationship in which individuals pursue positive outcomes but take on little risk. Without any relational costs (i.e., no need for vulnerability), the issue of trust becomes moot. The end result is a relationship that may continue, but is fragile. As noted earlier, relationships based strictly on social exchange are at high risk for dissolution when any "bad exchanges"—which are likely to happen in any relationship—occur.

When Ambivalence Cannot Be Transformed. Pratt and Rosa (2003) further argued that individuals dislike being in an ambivalent state (see also Festinger, 1957). Individuals need release from their "dissonance." Thus, if one's justification or rationale for integrating the positive and negative elements of trust no longer serves in this capacity, trust may fail. This may oc-

---

[2]Of course, in extreme circumstances (where violations are highly severe), both social exchange and commitment-based perspectives might predict a rapid dissolution of the relationship.

cur as individual experiences change, and the elements of the relationship take on new meaning. Thus, even though no additional negative or positive elements are added to the relationship, ambivalence increases and cannot be transformed. Without such transformation, negative relational outcomes ensue: paralysis, vacillation, and retreat.

One reason that justifications might fail would be if members' beliefs about the volitional nature of being in the relationship failed as well. Thus, a breakdown in trust should also occur when one believes that he or she was tricked into a relationship and really did not have all of the information needed to make an informed choice. Trust, like commitment, involves a volitional entry into the relationship: It involves the noncoerced and simultaneous acceptance of both vulnerability and benefit. Again, in the absence of such volition, justification becomes unnecessary because relationships involve little more than a hedonistic calculus of costs and benefits. If coercion continues, an individual might stay in the relationship to avoid sanction. Alternatively, he or she may choose to remain to accrue benefits. In either case, the relationship would not require trust.

Restoring Trust

A relationship-based commitment conceptualization of trust has some useful implications for understanding how trust can be restored. More specifically, such a perspective can serve to reevaluate extant research on trust by suggesting why some strategies for restoring trust work better than others. It can also provide new insights into how trust can be restored. In laying out the following framework, we emphasize how rebuilding the relationship requires actions by both parties in which some concession is both offered and accepted. Although it is obvious that the violator must play a prominent role in trying to provide redress for his or her actions, Tomlinson, Dineen, and Lewicki (2004) suggested that it is also necessary for the violated to be willing to reconcile lest the relationship terminate. Wilson (1988) argued that reconciliation and the repair of trust requires steps by both parties, because a relationship involves an implicit set of agreements to which both parties must assent. Last, summarizing their work on close relationships, Driver et al. (2003) reported that an important component of relationship repair is each partner's ability and willingness to respond when repair is attempted. For each step, we begin with the actions taken by the violator, as we believe that each step is more likely to happen—and is more likely to be effective—when initiated by that party.

We now discuss the implications of using a relationship-based commitment perspective for restoring trust. Specifically, critical elements of trust restoration strategies—which are derived from this perspective—are summarized in Table 6.1. The examples provided here serve as illustrations of

TABLE 6.1
Repairing Trust From a Commitment-Based Perspective

	Party in the Relationship	
Strategy for Repair	Violator	Violated
Reestablishing link between positive and negative elements	• Renewal of vulnerability • Allow the other person "space" •	• Perception that re-entry is voluntary
Managing positive and negative elements	• Framing of violation • Apologize or demonstrate repentance • Emphasize positives • Hope and optimism	• Empathy • Belief in violator's sincerity • Forgiveness • Evaluating positives or rationalization • Hope and optimism

these strategies and the principles that underlie them, and are not intended to be exhaustive. Moreover, given that paucity of research on both positive relationships and trust restoration, and given that we are introducing a commitment-based perspective on trust, we have tended to be somewhat conservative in our discussion. Thus, it is not our intention to suggest that the strategies described here fit only a commitment-based perspective on trust, and by extension are only applicable to positive relationships. We consider the principles to be applicable across both exchange and commitment-based perspectives, although some processes may be especially applicable to the former perspective or they may manifest themselves in different ways in that perspective. We identify these instances throughout the following discussion.

Reestablishing the Link Between Positive and Negative Elements. Building on a commitment-based perspective, one avenue of repairing a relationship is to reestablish the link between positive and negative elements of trust so that individuals are willing to accept both vulnerability and benefit. According to Brickman's model, a principle means of leveraging this route is to ensure that the violated party recognizes that reentry into the relationship is volitional. Each party has a role to play in ensuring that this occurs.

The violator can help facilitate this process by taking the first step of making oneself vulnerable by asking for the forgiveness of the violated. In their study of relationship repair, Bottom, Gibson, Daniels, and Murnighan (2002) proposed that forgiveness often can be most effectively obtained by providing open offers of "substantive penance" (in their study, an open offer to make reparations) that make the violator completely vulnerable to the violated. They suggest that the violated party may then feel they directed or determined the process and thus are controlling their fate in the relationship. The important issue here was not the fact that the individual offered to make reparation, but how he or she did so. The open offer clearly signals that the choice lies with the violated party, that is, the choice of what happens to the violator, and the choice of whether he or she chooses to proceed in the relationship. Thus, whereas an exchange perspective on trust may suggest that these effects derive from reparation (and thus the amount of reparation is a key concern), a commitment-based perspective would suggest that the choice is of key concern to the violated party. This suggests that the process of reparation making may be as critical as the reparations themselves.

Of course, the violated party can take steps to ensure that they perceive that they are voluntarily reentering the relationship. In the process of choosing, they may need to consciously weigh the decision and consciously recognize that they will need to accept both the benefits and vulnerabilities. Choosing may also necessitate creating newer, and perhaps more resilient, justifications for taking on these positive and negative elements in the relationships. Failing to use this opportunity to volitionally reestablish trust may result in regret when future challenges arise—and may ultimately result in a reseparation. To facilitate this process among the violated, the violator may give the party the opportunity to freely make the decision. In practice, this may mean giving them space or time, or more generally avoiding exerting pressure on the other party.

Managing Positive and Negative Elements. According to a commitment-based perspective, a second avenue for repairing the relationship is to manage the positive and negative elements in trust. As noted earlier, when trust is broken, the negative elements of the relationship may have overwhelmed the positive elements. Consequently, there are at least three ways of addressing this problem: (a) minimizing the perceived magnitude of the negative events, (b) removing some of the negative elements from the violated party, or (c) reevaluating the positive elements the violator brings, relative to the negative. Examples of each are provided here. In several cases, the approaches work in conjunction with each other.

A promising means of beginning to manage the positive and negative is through the framing of the basis of the violation. Doing so may help to minimize the perceived magnitude of the violation. Kim, Ferrin, Cooper, and Dirks (2004) suggested that the framing of the violation as based on competence (e.g., due to lack of knowledge) as opposed to integrity (e.g., due to one's moral character) has important implications for the repair of trust. Their theory draws on findings from psychology that demonstrate that individuals evaluate positive and negative information asymmetrically when it comes to issues related to competence as opposed to integrity. More specifically, when it comes to assessments of competence, individuals weigh positive information more heavily than negative information, but in assessments of integrity, greater weight is placed on negative information than positive information. According to Reeder and Brewer (1979), the factor behind the asymmetry is the structure of schemas that individuals use to assess individual attributes. A result of the asymmetry is that competence may be more fixable than integrity (Reeder & Coovert, 1986). Thus, for our purposes, framing the violation as one of competence allows the violator to keep a primary element (integrity) whole, while weakening a fixable element (competence). This serves several related purposes. First, the perception that a violation was intentional or malicious, as opposed to an accident or the result of a lack of competence, is likely to lead to a desire for revenge as opposed to reconciliation (Bies & Tripp, 1996) and thus should be avoided. Another related purpose is to allow an apology or signal of repentance to effectively repair trust and signal that learning has occurred and that a violation will not occur again (see next point). A final purpose of framing the violation is that it opens the door for the violated to feel empathy (e.g., I've made mistakes, too).

Another, perhaps complementary step, would involve the violator assuming a greater burden of the negative elements of the relationship. To do this, he or she might apologize or demonstrate repentance. Kim et al. (2004) found that apologizing for a transgression perceived to result from competence was successful in repairing trust, because it signaled remorse and a commitment to avoiding future transgressions. Likewise, Bottom et al., (2002) found that a victim was more willing to cooperate in the future when the transgressor offered repayment of the loss that was suffered and interpreted the results as deriving from the signal of "substantive penance" (i.e., absorbing a substantive loss as a signal of repentance). As noted, the sincere offer of an apology or penance can signal the remorse to the victim and provide hope for a more positive relationship in the future. In addition, whereas a social exchange perspective would focus solely on how taking ownership of a violation would reduce the likelihood of future violations because of repentance (Kim, Dirks, Cooper, & Ferrin, 2006), a commitment-based perspective might further highlight how taking ownership could also ensure that the violated party does not feel partly to blame for the incident (and thus removes a negative element). Both of these examples demonstrate how a relationship might be repaired when the violator is willing to take on extra negative elements to maintain the relationship.

Obviously, from the perspective of the violated party, he or she must see the commitment to taking on the negative elements to be sincere, and therefore must see the apology or the demonstration of repentance as sincere. An intriguing issue on the role of the victim is whether he or she should try to extract (initiate) reparation from the violator to rebalance the positive and negative elements in the relationship. Although Lewicki and Bunker (1996) offered this as a potential solution, North (1987) argued that doing so is inherently in conflict with the notion of forgiveness. From our perspective, this approach seems to shift the relationship more toward social exchange perspective, which is based on equity, instead of a commitment-based approach, which is based on rebalancing and rejustifying positives and negatives.

A third possible tactic is to minimize the violation by reemphasizing the positive elements of the relationship. Put differently, although the positive and negative elements of the relationship remain, the violator might ensure that the violated party recognizes both. There are numerous ways that the violator can make salient the value of the positives they bring to the relationship. For example, individuals might demonstrate how, despite the fact that they hurt the other party in one domain, they help them in other domains of the relationship by providing resources or support that they value. To illustrate, in professional sports, a team member who has been accused of a crime (e.g., rape) may still be trusted by teammates due to his or her ability to contribute to team goals. Likewise, following the Monica Lewinsky scandal, President Clinton emphasized his ability to effectively run the country to help offset his personal failings—and keep the trust of his aides and supporters. Although these illustrations occur in distinctive types of relationships, similar dynamics frequently occur in personal and work relationships. Obviously, the success of these approaches is contingent on a number of factors such as the seriousness of the violation, the importance of different domains of the relationships, the ability of the violated party to obtain the positive elements in other relationships, and so on.

Exploring the approach of reemphasizing the positive elements can be functional in that research suggests that there is a natural tendency for individuals to attend to negative events (Baumeister, Bratslavsky, Finkenauer, & Vohs, 2001). Consequently ensuring that the violated party recognizes both positives and negatives is important for avoiding a cognitive bias. The fact that positive relationships are generative (i.e., create growth and development) means that they may have the advantage taking those positives into account. That is, the relationship may confer a positive bias on the interpretation of events. Given that these factors are intangible and distal, they can be easy to overlook (and do not seem to be a concern from a social exchange perspective). This strategy can become problematic, however, when it turns into self-destructive rationalization by the violated party, that is, the violated party is searching for any reason to stay in the relationship. Looking at the downside of focusing on the generative aspects of a relationship, because factors such as growth and development are intangible and distal, it may also be easy to overestimate them if one is searching for a reason to stay in the relationship. A second concern about this resolution strategy is that it moves the relationship closer to an exchange relationship, and thus makes it less robust to future violations.

Finally, we believe each of these trust-restoring strategies will substantially benefit from the existence of hope and optimism within both parties (e.g., see Luthans, 2002). From an appraisal theory perspective, hope "is a positively valenced emotion evoked in response to an uncertain but possible goal-congruent outcome" (MacInnis & de Mello, 2005, p. 2). In terms of hope for the violator, he or she must not only be determined to repair the relationship, he or she must also envision "that successful plans can be formulated and pathways identified in order to attain goals" (Luthans, 2002, p. 62). That is, the trust violator must feel that trust can be repaired. Hope also provides the violator the motivation to continue the repair efforts even in the face of initial failure. Optimism serves the similar function.

This sense of hope that trust is restorable and the relationship is repairable must also be kindled in the violated. From a commitment perspective, this means that even in the face of overwhelming and salient negative aspects of the relationship, some positive emotion must survive, even if such positive emotion is based more on future potential than current realizations in a relationship. There must also be a belief that the violated not only is willing and able to restore the relationship, but that the "goal" of both parties in the relationship is aligned: that both parties in the relationship want the trust to be maintained. If the violated believes that the violator is going for a "quick fix" and will likely betray trust again, then there is little hope for the long-term aspects of this relationship. Clearly, we would expect hope and optimism to be particularly applicable to positive relationships.

DISCUSSION

In sum, we have argued that understanding positive relationships entails understanding how they are maintained during adversity. We suggest that considering trust from a commitment-based perspective helps to provide insight into this process.

Clearly, our analysis is only an initial step toward understanding the repair of trust in positive (as well as other types of) relationships. At the individual level of analysis, there are several issues for future consideration. Our analysis focused on how trust can begin to be repaired and relationships restored. As noted, our analysis was intended to provide illustrations of how the principles of a commitment-based perspective on trust might serve to help repair trust. The extent to which these rudimentary examples work, and the conditions under which they might work, need to be considered.

Although our analysis examined the repair of the relationship, the ultimate goal is typically to create a sustainable positive relationship. How can this objective be achieved? A commitment-based perspective would point toward understanding how positive and negative elements, such as vulnerability and safety, may be kept in balance or equilibrium. However, equilibrium does not mean that there exist equal parts of each element. Recent theorizing suggests that flourishing relationships may need to maintain a particular ratio of positive to negative actions to be generative and positive. The model of Frederickson and Losada (2004) suggests that the ratio of positive to negative acts needs to be approximately three to one. In his study of marriages, Gottman (1994) observed that the ratio of positive to negative was approximately five to one.

That there might exist an optimal ratio of positive and negative elements in trusting relationships has some intriguing implications. To begin, it raises the issue of how different elements contribute to the ratio. Research suggests that not all positive elements—and not all negative elements—are weighed equally. To illustrate, some prior research has suggested that it is particularly difficult to overcome violations of trust that are based on integrity (Reeder & Coovert, 1986). Indeed, research has yet to demonstrate how such violations can be addressed aside from denying them (Kim et al., 2004). Thus, some violations may be of a quality that no mixing of positive elements is possible to create the right ratio.

In other circumstances (or with regard to other trust violations), the fact that it may be possible to overcome a trust violation by engaging in a certain number of positive acts of similar magnitude or diagnosticity is an interesting idea warranting more attention. How far can this idea be taken? Is it possible—or even desirable—to attempt to gauge the effectiveness of certain positive and negative elements (e.g., two reparations make up for one competency violation)? Alternatively, might it be that these "ratios" simply reflect the fact that negative information is often more salient than positive (Baumeister et al., 2001), and that individuals have different thresholds for recognizing positive information? Finally, from a commitment-based view of trust, it may not be the sheer number of acts at all, but the justification of these acts in light of negative relationship acts that may be most important in the restoration of trust. Future research should examine these competing claims.

Related to the preceding point, our chapter may also have other implications for research on trust. As noted earlier, the majority of existing research has tended to utilize a social exchange perspective to understand trust and how it is created. In providing a commitment-based perspective, we have attempted to provide a different lens through which trust and its development and repair can be understood. Each perspective appears to make salient different issues, but the approaches do not necessarily appear to be in direct conflict with each other. Future research might further explore how the commitment-based approach provides new insight into trust research. Our work might also have implications for literatures in which trust and relationships are essential elements (e.g., psychological contracts).

Our research may also have implications on trust in different types of relationships. Our focus in this chapter has been primarily on personal dyadic relationships. However, we know that trust may also become violated in impersonal relationships. For example, in the early years of the 21st century, employees and other constituencies (e.g., consumers) felt betrayed by the actions of the CEOs at Martha Stewart Living Omnimedia, Enron, and Tyco. Here, trust was broken despite the fact that many of the people who felt betrayed did not have a personal relationship with these corporate leaders. To what degree is the restoration of trust in impersonal relationships between leader and follower similar to and different from the violation of trust among individuals with personal relationships? With the possible exception of allowing each of the violated a chance to have their own unique "personal space," there do not seem any restoration techniques that we propose that appear—on the face of it—to be closed to leaders. More generally, these examples also beg the question about whether it is even possible to have generative and resilient relationships with people you do not know personally. Thus, future research may explore the similarities and differences in the development, maintenance, and restoration of trust in positive relationships with people with whom you have personal versus more impersonal ties.

Including leaders and others into the conversation about trust violation and reparation begs the question of how organizations might foster trust within and among their own people. Pratt and Rosa (2003) argued that organizations can and do affect the positive and negative elements of relationships, as well as the binding together of these elements. However, there is little work that has been done in the area of trust on similar issues (for an exception, see Whitener et al., 1998). In his chapter on positive organizational justice, Greenberg (chap. 8, this volume) discusses how individuals may engage in positive organizational justice acts as a way of creating trust. More specifically, he suggests that managers might provide "over the top" (i.e., beyond normative expectations) displays of sensitivity and respect in their communications regarding decisions, particularly in adverse situations. Illustrating the idea, Greenberg provides an example of how a manager might go beyond normal expectations when an employee has lost a loved one by not only expressing sensitivity verbally, but also through behaviors that are costly to the supervisor, such as giving the employee time off and allowing a flexible work schedule for a period of time. From a commitment-based trust perspective, such positively radical behaviors may highlight the positive face of trust and facilitate justifications to remain in the relationship.

In Conclusion: Trust and Positive Relationships

We began this chapter by stating that trust is an integral part of positive relationships. We have also argued that positive relationships are robust and generative. How does trust lead to relationships that foster such attributes as personal growth, positive "cycles" of relating, and communal sharing? First, if we were to posit an "orthopedics" of trust, we would argue that restored trust might be stronger than untested trust—just as a broken bone that is properly set can be stronger than an unbroken bone. Thus, relationships that have successfully restored trust may have a stronger basis from which to build. Ideally, they will have learned the skills necessary to restore the bond that binds together the positive and negative elements inherent in trust, and can apply them when adversity arises again.

Second, the various elements associated with trust, such as vulnerability and safety, may also facilitate generative relationships. Vulnerability may help prevent the growth of aggressiveness and ego, two barriers to generative relationships. Second, the sense of safety that accompanies trust (McAllister, 1995) may allow for interpersonal openness, personal risk taking, and exploration, conditions we feel are integral to fostering generative relationships.

Finally, the general "lessons" learned from trust, that relationships have both positive and negative elements—and that the integration of the two can make relationships more robust and stable over time—reminds us that positive (e.g., resilient and generative) relationships are not uniformly positive. They are ongoing works in progress that strive for a beneficial, dynamic coherence rather than the once-and-for-all attainment of an ideal and static goal.

REFERENCES

Baumeister, R. F., Bratslavsky, E., Finkenauer, C., & Vohs, K. D. (2001). Bad is stronger than good. *Review of General Psychology, 5,* 323–370.

Becker, H. (1960). Notes on the concept of commitment. *American Journal of Sociology, 66,* 32–40.

Bies, R. J., & Tripp, T. M. (1996). Beyond distrust: Getting even and the need for revenge. In R. M. Kramer & T. R. Tyler (Eds.), *Trust in organizations: Frontiers of theory and research* (pp. 246–260). Thousand Oaks, CA: Sage

Blau, P. (1964). *Exchange and power in social life.* New York: Wiley.

Bottom, W. P., Gibson, K., Daniels, S., & Murnighan, J. K. (2002). When talk is not cheap: Substantive penance and expressions of intent in rebuilding cooperation. *Organization Science, 13,* 497–513.

Brickman, P., et al. (1987). Commitment, conflict, and caring. In C. B. Wortman & R. Sorrentino (Eds.), Englewood Cliffs, NJ: Prentice-Hall.

Clark, M. S., & Mills, J. R. (1979). Interpersonal attraction in exchange and communal relationships. *Journal of Personality and Social Psychology, 37,* 12–24.

Collins, J. C. (2006). ThinkExist.com Quotations Online, June 1, 2006, and July 19, 2006. Available online @ http://einstein/quotes/johnchurchton

Dirks, K. T., & Ferrin, D. L. (2001). The role of trust in organizational settings. *Organization Science, 12,* 450–467.

Driver, J., Tabares, A., Shapiro, A., Nahm, E. Y., & Gottman, J. (2003). Interactional patterns in marital success or failure: Gottman laboratory studies. In F. Walsh (Ed.), *Normal family processes: Growing diversity and complexity* (pp. 493–513). New York: Guilford.

Festinger, L. (1957). *A theory of cognitive dissonance.* Stanford, CA: Stanford University Press.

Fiske, A. P. (1992). The four elementary forms of sociality: Framework for a unified theory of social relations. *Psychological Bulletin, 99,* 689–723.

Frederickson, B., & Losada, M. (2004). *The complex dynamics of human flourishing: Toward a general theory of positivity* (Working paper). Ann Arbor: University of Michigan.

Gottman, J. M. (1994). *What predicts divorce: The relationship between marital processes and marital outcomes.* Hillsdale, NJ: Lawrence Erlbaum Associates.

Kiesler, C. (1971). *The psychology of commitment.* New York: Academic.

Kim, P. H., Dirks, K. T., Cooper, C. D., & Ferrin, D. L. (2006). When more blame is better than less: The implications of internal vs. external attributions for the repair of trust after a competence- vs. integrity-based trust violation. *Organizational Behavior and Human Decision Processes, 99,* 49–65.

Kim, P., Ferrin, D. L., Cooper, C., & Dirks, K. T. (2004). Removing the shadow of suspicion: The effects of apology vs. denial for repairing competence- vs. integrity-based trust violations. *Journal of Applied Psychology, 89,* 104–118.

Konovsky, M., & Pugh, D. (1994). Citizenship behavior and social exchange. *Academy of Management Journal, 37,* 656–669.

Lewicki, R. J., & Bunker, B. B. (1996). Developing and maintaining trust in work relationships. In R. M. Kramer & T. R. Tyler (Eds.), *Trust in organizations: Frontiers of theory and research* (pp. 114–139). Thousand Oaks, CA: Sage.

Lewicki, R. J., McAllister, D. J., & Bies, R. J. (1998). Trust and distrust: New relationships and realities. *Academy of Management Review, 23,* 438–458.

Luthans, F. (2002). Positive organizational behavior: Developing and managing psychological strengths. *Academy of Management Executive, 16,* 57–72.

MacInnis, D., & de Mello, G. (2005). The concept of hope and its relevance to product evaluation and choice. *Journal of Marketing, 69,* 1–14.

Mayer, R. C., Davis, J. H., & Schoorman, F. D. (1995). An integrative model of organizational trust. *Academy of Management Review, 20,* 709–734.

McAllister, D. J. (1995). Affect- and cognition-based trust as foundations for interpersonal cooperation in organizations. *Academy of Management Journal, 38,* 24–59.

Meyer, J. P., & Allen, N. J. (1997). *Commitment in the workplace: Theory, research and application.* Thousand Oaks, CA: Sage.

North, J. (1987). Wrongdoing and forgiveness. *Philosophy, 62,* 499–508.

Pratt, M. G., & Doucet, L. (2000). Ambivalent feelings in organizational relationships. In S. Fineman (Ed.), *Emotions in organizations* (Vol. 2, pp. 204–226). Thousands Oaks, CA: Sage.

Pratt, M. G., & Rosa, J. A. (2003). Transforming work–family conflict into commitment in network marketing organizations. *Academy of Management Journal, 46,* 395–418.

Reeder, G. D., & Brewer, M. B. (1979). A schematic model of dispositional attribution in interpersonal perception. *Psychological Review, 86,* 61–79.

Reeder, G. D., & Coovert, M. (1986). Revising an impression of morality. *Social Cognition, 4,* 1–17

Rousseau, D. M., Sitkin, S. B., Burt, R. S., & Camerer, C. (1998). Not so different after all: A cross-discipline view of trust. *Academy of Management Review, 23,* 393–404.

Sahlins, M. (1972). *Stone age economics.* Chicago: Aldine & Atherton.

Salancik, G. (1977). Commitment and the control of organizational behavior and belief. In B. M. Staw & G. R. Salancik (Eds.), *New directions in organizational behavior* (pp. 1–54). Chicago: St. Clair.

Skowronski, J. J., & Carlston, D. E. (1989). Negativity and extremity biases in impression formation: A review of explanations. *Psychological Bulletin, 105,* 131–142.

Tomlinson, E. C., Dineen, B. R., & Lewicki, R. J. (2004). The road to reconciliation: Antecedents of victim willingness to reconcile following a broken promise. *Journal of Management, 30,* 165–187.

Weick, K. (1995). *Sensemaking in organizations.* Thousand Oaks, CA: Sage.

Whitener, E., Brodt, S., Korsgaard, M. A., & Werner, J. (1998). Managers as initiators of trust: An exchange relationship for understanding managerial trustworthy behavior. *Academy of Management Journal, 23,* 513–553.

Wilson, J. (1988). Why forgiveness requires repentance. *Philosophy, 63,* 534–535.

7

The Engines of Positive Relationships Across Difference: Conflict and Learning

Martin N. Davidson
Erika Hayes James

Human experience is replete with examples of how challenging it is to build mutually supportive, enduring, and resilient relationships in organizations comprised of individuals who differ in background, perspective, and life experience. People in organizations are constantly dealing with difficult relationships as so many dimensions of difference become increasingly salient in organizational life (e.g., Lubensky, Holland, Wiethoff, & Crosby, 2004; Ragins, 1997; Thomas & Gabarro, 1999). Fortunately, there are also many examples of high-quality energizing relationships across difference and common sense converges with a good deal of research to suggest that such relationships promote more effective work outcomes: They foster collaboration to complete organizational tasks (Ancona & Caldwell, 1992); encourage sharing of information (Gersick, Bartunek, & Dutton, 2000; Ibarra, 1992); create career developmental support (Kram, 1988; Ragins, 1997; Thomas & Gabarro, 1999); and provide mental, physical, and emotional well-being (DeLongis, Folkman, & Lazarus, 1988; Kirmeyer & Lin, 1987; Krackhardt & Kilduff, 1990; Totterdell, Spelten, Smith, & Barton, 1995). How can individuals transform cross-difference relationships steeped in cynicism, mistrust, and enmity into relationships that are energizing, nurturing, and productive?

The critical element contributing to this transformation is the way individuals navigate the journey from relying on stereotypes and predisposing expectations about others who are different, to adopting a learning approach with the other in the relationship. It is this attitude of learning about the other that is critical in building strong and sustained positive relationships across difference. The path from expectation to learning is challenging because socially salient identity differences between people are often accompanied by expectations that heighten the likelihood that conflict will be felt and manifested in the relationship (Pondy, 1969). However, that conflict is not a bad thing. Indeed, we submit that the opportunity to transform such conflict into learning is the only means by which high-quality relationships across difference are fostered.

HIGH-QUALITY RELATIONSHIPS ACROSS DIFFERENCE

High-quality relationships across difference are sustained relationships between individuals of different contextually salient social identities that are characterized by a sense of well-being between the individuals and a resilience or tensility in the relationship (Dutton & Heaphy, 2003). By contextually salient social identities, we mean social identity group membership in which the individuals are members of different social groups, and that being a member of either group carries significance because of cultural, historical, and political power dynamics associated with the groups within the society. For example, in a U.S. context, race (Black and White), ethnicity (Asian, African, Hispanic, Native American, or European descent), gender (male and female), or region (Southeast and Northeast) exemplifiy such differences; in contrast, in a South African context, race (Black, White, colored), tribe (Xhosa, Bantu, Zulu), or ethnicity (Afrikaans, British, Indian, Black African, etc.) would illustrate the differences.

High-quality relationships across difference in organizations have five specific core characteristics. First, they engender positive affect and rapport between the individuals in the relationship; the individuals involved have authentic affection and positive regard for one another. Second, they promote mindsets and behaviors that encourage ongoing learning in the relationship. Because relationships across difference are characterized by differing social, cultural, and historical perspectives, the method by which individuals share these perspectives (and evolve as a result) is a critical characteristic of these high-quality relationships. Third, high-quality relationships across difference have longevity. These relationships manifest over time and following Dutton and Heaphy's conception of high-quality connection (Dutton & Heaphy, 2003), we suggest that there are very few high-quality relationships across difference that are short-lived. Fourth, high-quality relationships across difference are resilient. Individuals engaged in such a relationship feel compelled to remain engaged with one another despite personal or situational factors that would foster separation. Finally, high-quality relationships across difference create the rapport and capacity for individuals to engage, challenge, and support one another with clarity and confidence in a professional context in ways that lead to effective work, career, and developmental outcomes.

CREATING RELATIONSHIPS ACROSS DIFFERENCE

"Some of my best friends are . . ." People often mistake interpersonal connections across difference for high-quality relationships across difference when, in fact, the former often lack all but the first characteristic of high-quality relationships—positive affect. Creating genuine high-quality relationships across difference requires intentional and sustained effort. The process for achieving such relationships, however, has not been clearly articulated and is thus both poorly understood and poorly practiced. In this section, we present a model in which learning plays a critical role as a precursor to and outcome of high-quality relationships across difference. As an antecedent, learning occurs when one interacts with another who is different and is faced with the novel worldview—perspective, thought processes, values—that the other person presents. The way in which one engages that difference will, as we will see, determine the quality of the ongoing relationship. However, in addition, learning continues as the relationship continues. High-quality relationships across difference foster more learning about difference and in this way, experience with others who are different continually deepens the understanding and appreciation of both self and others. Thus, it is in seeking and gaining knowledge about others that one sets the foundation for strong relationships across difference. Without this learning, relationships will likely be based on a set of assumptions or biases that can impede the authenticity of the relationship.

Our model uses social identity theory to depict the formation of relationships and how the strength of relationships across difference is a function, at least in part, of personal experiences with others. Those experiences, in turn, lead to strongly held expectations about others, and it is the extent to which those expectations are confirmed or violated that produces tension or experienced conflict in the relationship. That experienced conflict fuels one of three behavioral paths: (a) engaging in conflict behaviors that make the tension manifest into behavioral conflict (Jehn, 1995; Pondy, 1967), (b) severing the relationship by actively or passively disengaging, or (c) transforming the experienced conflict into learning about the identity-related differences in the relationship. This learning approach is the direct antecedent to a strengthened high-quality relationship across difference. Experienced conflict shifts to learning when an individual is sufficiently invested in the relationship to engage the conflict, and when the individual is capable of adopting a learning approach. Moreover, whereas disengaging virtually eliminates the chance of strengthening the relationship, engaging in manifest conflict can foster learning if the manifest conflict is handled constructively. That learning then strengthens the relationship. In contrast, when the manifest conflict is poorly handled, the relationship is likely to be damaged and the chance of a strengthened relationship across difference all but eliminated. This process is illustrated in Figure 7.1.

Experience With "Others" in Creating Expectations

What factors contribute to forming strong relationships across difference is, at some level, affected by the personal set of experiences, beliefs, and expectations about dissimilar others. Said differently, the quality of the relationships we develop (and the people with whom we develop them) is a product of long-held assumptions about people based on meaningful identity characteristics (e.g., race and gender). When those assumptions are based on faulty or inflexible generalizations, as, for example, the prejudice described by Allport (1954), the quality of the relationship suffers.

Self-categorization and social identity theories help explain how the assumptions and consequences of similarity and dissimilarity come to be. Self-categorization theory suggests that people seek to develop and maintain positive social identities (Tajfel & Turner, 1985). This is achieved through a process of classifying oneself and others into salient social categories such as race, ethnicity, or gender (Turner, Hogg, Oakes, Reicher, & Wetherell, 1987). People then ascribe meaning or value to the various categories that, in turn, shape the way we interact with others from similar and dissimilar identity groups (Tajfel, 1978, 1982). In short, social identity is a perception of oneness or sameness with a group of individuals based primarily on shared and valued characteristics.

However, the lenses through which we perceive those characteristics are not always crystal clear. Biases and prejudice, and the discrimination that manifests from them, have played a substantial and enduring role in social psychological and related literatures. As early as the 1950s, Allport (1954) characterized prejudice as "an antipathy based upon a faulty and inflexible generalization" (p. 9). Prejudice was and continues to be largely embedded in a social structure or context and as a result takes a form that is consistent with that context. At the time of Allport's writing, the majority population in the United States was White. White men in particular occupied a position of privilege and high status, and the psyche of the dominant group was associated with a type of blatant or aversive discrimination against outgroup members, including women and people belonging to a different racial or ethnic group (Myrdal, Sterner, & Rose, 1944; Sniderman & Tetlock, 1986). The racial climate, in particular, was tense, so relationships

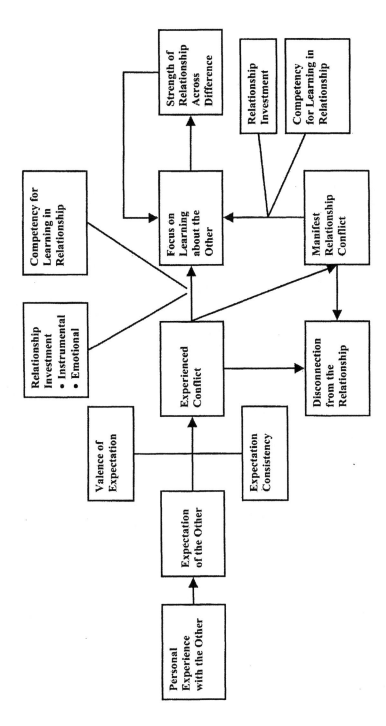

FIG. 7.1. Factors that create strong relationships across difference.

across difference were generally strained. The passage of time and civil rights legislation, however, has tempered that tension as well as the blatant manifestation of prejudice.

In recent years scholars have described a new, subtle, and indirect form of prejudice against racial minorities and women (e.g., Crosby, Bromley, & Saxe, 1980). The empirical investigations of this type of complex and indirect prejudice suggest that negative attitudes persist, but are less obvious than in earlier times (James, Brief, Dietz, & Cohen, 2001; Swim & Miller, 1999). Nonetheless, like their more blatant predecessor, modern-day prejudices can hinder one's desire or ability to learn about difference, and in turn obstruct the potential for high-quality relationships across difference to occur.

Shared identities lead to activities that are congruent with the relevant identity and to stereotypical perceptions of self and others (Ashforth & Mael, 1989). Particularly relevant is the formation of relationships according to ingroup (shared characteristics) or outgroup (dissimilar characteristics) status (Brewer, 1991, 1993; Hogg, 2003; Hogg & Terry, 2000; Roccas & Brewer, 2002). In fact, consistent with social identity theory is the similarity-attraction paradigm (Byrne, 1971) that espouses that individuals prefer to interact more often with those with whom they are similar than dissimilar. These preferences play out in various contexts, including organizational settings, and lead to behaviors and consequences that serve to advantage ingroup members and disadvantage outgroup members. For example, leader–subordinate relationships that share demographic characteristics are reported as being more positive than dyads that are demographically dissimilar (Tsui & O'Reilly, 1989). Dissimilar dyads report more tension resulting from misunderstandings, misperceptions, and conflicts of interest (Riordan, 2000); higher levels of mistrust (Jeanquart-Barone, 1993); and reduced support and liking (Ensher & Murphy, 1997). As a consequence of the quality of relationship experienced in the workplace, research has found that subordinates who are demographically dissimilar from supervisors or others in high-power positions report receiving less career guidance and a slower promotion rate (James, 2000).

A fundamental assumption of social identity theory is that people differentiate others by identity groups to achieve or maintain a personal level of self-esteem (Riordan, 2000) as well as perceptions of superiority over dissimilar others (Tajfel & Turner, 1985). Both claiming membership in a highly valued, high-status ingroup and denigrating outgroup members serve to enhance self-esteem and perceptions of superiority over others. Yet, in addition to self-esteem enhancement, relationship ease, and other manifestations of interacting with similar others, we argue that social identity theory and the similarity-attraction paradigm serve another purpose. Namely, they help to establish a set of expectations about how people should or will act. When we encounter someone who is similar to us a schema is automatically enacted (Fiske & Taylor, 1991). That schema is based on the assumption that people from the same demographic group share attitudes, experiences, beliefs, and values. From that assumption, we believe we are better able to predict behavior. We further believe that our expectations about the ingroup member's behavior will be validated in our interactions with him or her (Geddes & Konrad, 2003). When these expectations are not met during the encounter cognitive dissonance may be evoked (Cooper & Stone, 2000). In contrast, when we encounter someone who is demographically dissimilar—an outgroup member—a schema is enacted that is often based on negative stereotypes. This is especially true if we have limited personal experience with other representatives of the outgroup, or if that prior experience confirms our existing stereotype.

In short, regardless of whether we are interacting with similar or dissimilar others, schemas serve to establish a set of expectations about how others will behave. It is when those expectations are violated that the potential for cognitive dissonance and tension arises that, in turn, can manifest as conflict behavior, learning behavior, or separation. The relation between expectations of others and potential tension, however, may be contingent on the valence of the expectations (e.g., positive or negative) and expectation consistency.

The Impact of Expectations of Others

Experienced conflict—the discord or tension that is experienced by individuals prior to engaging in conflict behaviors—can emerge when two diverse individuals' prior expectations of how the other will behave are tested in the actual interaction. The extent to which that conflict emerges depends on two factors: the valence of the expectation and the consistency between one party's expectation and the behavior he or she encounters on engaging the other party (Maass, Milesi, Zabbini, & Stahlberg, 1995). Experienced conflict results from the interaction of expectation valence and expectation consistency two ways. First, if Person A has an expectation of some positive behavior when interacting with Person B (say people of Person B's identity group are likely to be industrious), then tensions may mount when that expectation is violated— when Person B is bored and unproductive. Person A may be surprised, even shocked, and ultimately annoyed, frustrated, or angry. This is an example of a positive (+) expectation that is met with inconsistency. Conversely, Person A may expect Person B to be unproductive and when Person B is in fact, unproductive, discord tension may again arise. This would be an example of a negative (−) expectation being met with consistency. These two conditions create a high-level experienced conflict.

The interaction of expectation consistency and valence may not always lead to experienced conflict. If each of the preceding conditions are reversed, feelings of harmony and ease come to characterize the relationship. For example, a positive expectation met with consistency is all good: Person A expects Person B to be industrious and Person B is. Similarly, negative expectations that are disconfirmed generate harmonious climates: Person A expects Person B to be lazy, and finds Person B to be industrious, thus creating a positive affect in the relationship. Paradoxically, such outcomes may actually impede the path toward high-quality relationships across difference because they do not provide the opportunity for experienced conflict to catalyze learning, and hence stronger relationships. We would not argue that this kind of harmony is bad or unproductive. Rather, we reinforce our proposition that conflict in the relationship is necessary if the desire is to build high-quality relationships across difference.

CONFLICT IN RELATIONSHIPS ACROSS DIFFERENCE

If conflict is necessary to build strong relationships, what is the nature of that conflict? Indeed, there are numerous examples of the ways in which diversity-related conflict damages or destroys relationships across difference (Chan & Goto, 2003; Davidson, 2001; Garcia-Prieto, Bellard, Schneider, & Garcia-Prieto, 2003; Jehn, Northcraft, & Neale, 1999; Pelled, Eisenhardt, & Xin, 1999). So if we are suggesting that conflict is essential in the relationship, under what conditions does that conflict trigger learning instead of disengagement?

The conflict we explore has two key characteristics. First the experience of conflict is distinguishable from the behavioral manifestation of the conflict. Conflict process theorists have meticulously outlined the means by which conflict arises and is managed (e.g., Blake & Mouton, 1964; Pondy, 1967; Pruitt & Rubin, 1986; Putnam & Poole, 1987; Thomas, 1992). Many have posited that a critical aspect of the conflict process is the emergent awareness that discord exists (e.g., Pondy, 1967). In Pondy's (1967, 1969) model of organizational conflict, the tension we discuss is an amalgam of what he termed *perceived conflict*—the awareness or knowledge that conflicting interests are present—and *felt conflict*—the emotional experiences of anger, frustration, fear, and so on, that accompany conflict. Consistent with emotion appraisal theory (Lazarus, 1991, 1995), we suggest that it is more parsimonious to theorize that emotion and thought combine to create tension or what we label *experienced conflict* in these relationships across difference (Davidson & Greenhalgh, 1999). This experienced conflict is the direct consequence of the violated expectations as we previously discussed.

Second the content of the conflict that is critical for our model is difference-related conflict; that is, conflict experienced about identity differences such as culture, gender, race, age, and other factors that are relevant within the relationship. Thus, if one individual in the relationship is gay, and the other straight, the two individuals must come to terms with the discord that will arise regarding their difference in sexual orientation for the relationship to strengthen. Individuals from diverse identity groups are likely to confront experienced conflict related to their difference (Brewer, 2001), and the importance of engaging that difference head-on surfaces as we map the path from experienced conflict to high-quality relationships across difference.

The Consequences of Experienced Conflict

Experienced conflict can lead to any of three outcomes. A common option in relationships across difference is to exit the relationship. Such disengagement is so ubiquitous that it has been highlighted in the literature as an obvious barrier to bridging differences as far back as Allport's (1954) contact hypothesis. Indeed, predisposition to mistrust as well as many structural barriers that divide groups make it all the more likely that individuals would frequently see disengagement as the only reasonable option in the face of experienced conflict (Alderfer, 1977; Brewer & Brown, 1998; Sidanius & Pratto, 1999; Wong, 1995).

However, there are other options, the most obvious of which is that the experienced conflict leads to conflict behavior; in Pondy's language, manifest conflict. There has been a voluminous literature on the variety of ways in which conflict is expressed, as well as the positive or negative outcomes that result from that expression (e.g., Blake & Mouton, 1964; De Dreu, Weingart, & Kwon, 2000; Kilmann & Thomas, 1978). With regard to generating positive and negative outcomes in relationships across difference, the literature on manifest conflict in diverse teams has established that task conflict—surfaced disagreements about the work at hand—improves performance, but that relationship or emotional conflict—surfaced disagreements in dealing with differences as they manifest in the relationship—diminishes performance (Jehn, 1995; Pelled et al., 1999). Such relationship conflict "causes members to be negative, irritable, suspicious, and resentful" and in sum, "there has been no evidence of a positive effect of relationship conflict on either performance or satisfaction" (Jehn, 1997, pp. 531–532). More recent meta-analyses of research on task and relationship conflict in teams suggest an even bleaker scenario in which both task and relationship conflict diminish performance (De Dreu & Weingart, 2003). Although focused on team dynamics, these results leave us with a tentative understanding of how to improve task performance when individuals are different, but not for how to create high-quality relationships between those individuals. This supports the all-too-familiar path in Figure 7.1 that illustrates the movement from manifest conflict to disconnection from the relationship: In the presence of expressed conflict about the relationship, particularly about the differences in the relationship, one option is to disconnect from the relationship.

However, there is also evidence that relationship conflict can have a positive impact. For example, teams performing well were characterized by low but increasing levels of process conflict, low levels of relationship conflict (with a rise near project deadlines), and moderate levels of task conflict at the midpoint of group interaction (Jehn & Mannix, 2001). Also, even though some types of diversity such as race and tenure create heated emotional conflict, they did not impair performance on the team (Pelled et al., 1999). Finally, identity diversity has been found to create relationship conflict while increasing the morale of the individuals engaged in the conflict (Jehn et al., 1999).

It is likely that open engagement of conflict in relationships across difference is sometimes counterproductive because individuals do not have the competence to transform the conflict into something more productive. The third option for reframing experienced conflict in the relationship is to adopt a learning approach.

LEARNING IN RELATIONSHIPS
ACROSS DIFFERENCE

Simply put, a learning approach is a set of behaviors that reflect curiosity and inquisitiveness and result in gaining new knowledge about a given context, person, or relationship. As advanced by the traditional discipline of psychology, learning refers to a process in which people engage that results in a relatively long-term change in attitude, knowledge, and behavior (Bandura, 1977; Skinner, 1969). Rotter's (1966) social learning theory and Bandura's (1977, 1986) social cognition theory have been identified as two of the most relevant and comprehensive approaches to adult learning (Merriam, 1983). Briefly, social learning theory uses behavior, cognitive, and personality theory to predict individual behavior. In its most basic form, it suggests that for a behavior to persist, one must expect that the behavior will be reinforced (either positively or negatively), and one must assign value to the reinforcement (Rotter, 1982). Social cognition theory extends social learning theory with a much greater emphasis on the cognitive influence in the learning process. Bandura's concept of self-efficacy (Bandura, 1977, 1986) is a cognitive variable that has been accorded an important role in the learning process. It is the belief that one can succeed despite challenges and refers to one's judgments as to how effective he or she is likely to be in a given situation. According to Lefrancois (1987), the cognitive aspect of learning highlights our ability to determine cause-effect relationships, and anticipate the outcomes of behavior.

Taken together, and in the context of learning across difference, social learning and social cognition theory apply and perhaps extend Vroom's (1964) expectancy theory. In particular, they emphasize learning as a product of (a) a desire to change one's attitudes and behaviors (valence), (b) an expectation that change will be reinforced (expectancy), and (c) a belief that one can change (self-efficacy). Implicit in these theories is the notion that the change in attitudes and behaviors that results from learning is indicative of one's willingness to be open and receptive to new information, ideas, perspectives, or people—being open to difference.

Gaertner, Dovidio, and colleagues noted that "interaction provides members the opportunity to work together, to communicate, to express values, to argue, to compromise, to reach agreement, and to gain information about in-group and out-group members" (Gaertner et al., 1999, p. 388). We add to this assertion that interaction, such as that occurring among peers or in boss–subordinate dyads in work settings, allows for learning about others across the disparate category memberships to which people ascribe. Learning is particularly relevant in the development of relationships across differences, because without it people will likely persist in thinking about and acting toward others in potentially naive ways. That is, in the absence of a true understanding about the other, attitudes and behaviors will likely reflect stereotypes or generalizations that can be suspect in their accuracy. To counteract the natural proclivity to use such generalizations as a basis for interacting positively with ingroup members or denigrating outgroup members we must genuinely want to learn about the other in a way that goes beyond superficial exchanges. When people enter relationships with information and understanding of others that, through its richness, modifies stereotypes and refutes inaccurate perceptions of the other person, the potential for conflict is lessened, and the potential for mutually supportive relationships heightens. Developing a learning approach fosters such outcomes.

This enhanced capacity to connect across difference in relationships also translates into greater work team and organizational effectiveness. A learning approach within a set of relationships in an organization quickly positions the organization to operate from an "integration and learning" paradigm in which activities and processes within the organization are fundamentally changed as a result of the knowledge that is shared and captured from relationships among its diverse members (Ely & Thomas, 2001, 2005).

Getting to Learning

Although adopting a learning approach holds the promise of generating high-quality relationships across difference (which, in turn, may translate into team and organizational effectiveness), the journey from experienced conflict to learning can be arduous. Once experienced conflict emerges in the relationship, at least two factors influence the extent to which a learning approach can be adopted: the investment by an individual in the relationship and the individual's relationship competency to adopt learning.

Relationship Investment. For an individual to be motivated to remain engaged in the relationship in the midst of experienced conflict, the relationship must be experienced as valuable to the individual. Otherwise, there would be no benefit to exerting the effort to move toward learning across difference. This value is assessed in two ways: instrumentally and emotionally. Instrumental value is simply the political or functional importance of remaining connected in the relationship. For example, if the relationship is a manager–subordinate relationship or a team member relationship, then the relationship is more interdependent than a relationship between hierarchical peers who function in disparate silos of the organization. In the former situation, one's career progression depends on engagement and cooperation; in the latter situation, disengaging is not likely to affect one's career options in any meaningful way (Adams, 1965; Cole, Schaninger, & Harris, 2002).

However, the value of a relationship cannot be measured by instrumental gains alone. The individual's emotional investment in the relationship will also influence her or his willingness to put in the effort to take a learning approach in the face of experienced conflict. This emotional investment can come in two forms. First, the individuals in the relationship may simply like each other because they have built a relationship around common interests or perspectives as would be predicted by similarity-attraction theory (Byrne, 1971). In essence, this basic attraction would motivate individuals to want to stay connected even in the midst of the experienced conflict.

However, in the same way that commonality produces an emotional investment in the relationship across difference, so too may the difference itself. For example, when the individuals in the relationship are members of identity groups that have traditionally been antagonistic toward one another, the opportunity to cultivate a high-quality relationship across those group differences can be understood as rare and hence, experienced as extremely important. At the most superficial level, individuals may be invested in pushing through the experienced conflict because it enhances their self-image as a person who is capable of resolving potentially intractable conflict (Carver, Glass, & Katz, 1978; Friedman & Davidson, 2001). At a deeper psychological level, one or both individuals may even feel that working constructively through the experienced conflict as members of these groups holds hope that long-standing enmity can be overcome. In either case, the more these forces are present, the more likely individuals will remain engaged despite the experienced conflict.

Competency for Learning in Relationship. The motivation to seek a learning approach in the relationship is necessary but insufficient to achieve the learning that will lead to a high-quality relationship across difference. Individuals must also possess the skill set to learn in the relationship. We suggest that five core skills contribute to this competency, with level of mastery of each skill contributing to overall level of competency. A number of researchers have begun to map the competencies that are critical in navigating multicultural systems and in cultivating learning. However, few have explicitly charted the skill set necessary for stepping into and out of conflict and transforming that conflict into learning across difference (Adler & Bartholomew, 1992; Joplin & Daus, 1997; Ramsey & Latting, 2005; Tung, 1993)

First, individuals must process the emergent emotions associated with the perceived conflict. As we noted earlier, experienced conflict subsumes felt conflict—the emotion associated with the conflict (Pondy, 1969). As such, the common conflict emotions—annoyance, fear, anger, embarrassment, and so on—are inextricably linked to experienced conflict. Left unexamined, these emotions interfere with the capacity to learn in a number of ways. For example, negative emotions, whether conscious or unconscious, constrain one's capacity to seek out new and innovative solutions to problems, or simply to see new possibilities (Fredrickson & Branigan, 2001). When suppressed or repressed, negative emotions and the resulting stress diminish one's capacity to receive and provide effective feedback (Weinberger, 1995). Moreover, short-term memory, cognitive processing, and empathic ability are all attenuated by unexamined negative emotion (Gross, 2001). Several methods for gaining awareness of the emotions associated with the conflict are possible including rational-emotive reflection and "self-talk" (Girodo, 1977), writing about the experience (Pennebaker, 1997), and even mindfulness practice.

A second skill in this learning competency is the capacity to reframe the conflict by acknowledging a superordinate goal or purpose in the relationship. This goal may be concrete, as in the desire to complete a task efficiently, or it may be more principled, as in the desire to maintain positive relations with the people in one's life (Thomas, 1992). In any event, this capacity to transcend the competitive dynamic in the relationship by appealing to a larger common goal is a cornerstone of a variety of conflict resolution and negotiation models (e.g., Boulding, 1961; Thomas, 1992). This skill is similar to the intergroup competency skill of "committing to personal change" that Ramsey and Latting described (Ramsey & Latting, 2005). Such a commitment is a kind of superordinate goal that can reorient an individual within the relationship.

Whereas these first two skills are self-focused, the remaining three are social skills. The third core skill is to foster openness to the other. One fosters openness to the other in two ways. First, one must be able to take the initiative in self-disclosing relevant information to the other (Dindia, 2000). Relevant information in this context is information pertaining to the identity differences that stimulate the experienced conflict. In other words, one must be able offer information and insight about one's own experience of the difference in question. This can be done through description or, more powerfully, through personal narratives or stories about one's own experiences involving the differences. For example in the midst of an experienced conflict about race in the United States, a White individual might tell a story about what it means for her or him to be White (Hill, 1997).

However, self-disclosure is also a dynamic process in which personal information and truths shift as two individuals are engaged in a relationship (Dindia, 2000). To that end, it is also important to disclose responsively, to share one's reactions with the other as they emerge in the relationship. For example, if an individual experiences annoyance at something the other person says, to tell the person about the annoyance is an act of self-disclosure. These types of real-time disclosures are an essential aspect of openness in relationships across difference because these relationships are so often shrouded in misunderstanding and mistrust. This kind of disclosure promotes transparency in the relationship and counteracts the common experiences of silence and subversion that frequently characterize these relationships (Morrison & Milliken, 2000).

The fourth skill is inquiry. In this way, an individual is positioned to understand the perspective of the other person and acquire knowledge about the other person, including knowledge about the other's relevant differences (Senge, 1990). Inquiry occurs primarily through asking questions, but the depth of this skill goes deeper than simply acquiring information verbally. The inquiry extends to asking about rationales that lead to the other's conclusions, exploring assumptions about the other's goals and interests (Ramsey & Latting, 2005).

The fifth and final skill is giving and receiving feedback. Many researchers have written on the importance of having access to accurate feedback as a mechanism for improving performance (Ashford, 1986; Baron & Ganz, 1972; Brockner, 1979). However, a lack of comfort and competence in building relationships (personal and professional) across many differences (e.g., race, gender, sexual orientation, etc.) can make it difficult to engage in honest communication. This lack of feedback competence can manifest in two ways—feedback givers may be possessed by bias and may give feedback that is simply inaccurate (Thomas & Gabarro, 1999). Alternatively, constructive feedback may be withheld in the relationship for fear (a) that it will demotivate or dishearten the other, or (b) it will make the feedback giver seem unsupportive, biased, or prejudiced. In either instance, the ability of the individuals in the relationship to learn from one another is compromised. To effectively create learning in the relationship, there must be open channels through which individuals can exchange feedback.

A recent stream of research into the conditions under which diversity in teams produces positive results has demonstrated that interpersonal congruence—the degree to which group members see others in the group as others see themselves—serves as a moderator of the relationship between diversity and group effectiveness. For example, in one study, diversity tended to improve creative task performance in groups with high interpersonal congruence, whereas diversity undermined the performance of groups with low interpersonal congruence (Polzer, Milton, & Swann, 2002). This interaction effect also emerged on measures of relationship conflict. The interpersonal congruence approach suggests that group members can achieve harmonious and effective work processes by expressing rather than suppressing the characteristics that make them unique. Congruence is created by exchanges of feedback that, of necessity, explicitly transmit information about one's differences (Ely & Thomas, 2005).

From Manifest Conflict to Learning Relationships Across Difference

Although we have mapped the path from experienced conflict to learning in relationships across difference, an even more visible and seemingly ubiquitous outcome of experienced conflict is manifest conflict, the behavioral reaction to experienced conflict (e.g., Thomas, 1992). We established earlier that manifest conflict can lead to disengagement from the relationship; but manifest conflict can also generate learning in the relationship. In colloquial terms, it is not uncommon to have a fight with a colleague or loved one after which one feels that the "air has been cleared" and that one feels emotionally closer to the other person. The factors contributing to the shift from experienced conflict to learning are also evident in shifting from manifest conflict to learning: relationship investment and competency for learning in a relationship. However, moving from an internal (and presumably private) sense of tension in a relationship to learning is somewhat different from moving from a more public display of discord, at least initially. To move from manifest conflict to learning, an individual must first be motivated to stop fighting.

The motivation to cease hostilities in a relationship across difference can stem from external or internal forces. External pressure may come from stakeholders who experience the conflict as too disruptive to the organization or community. Interventions ranging from third-party involvement to forcible restraint may serve the goal of stopping the manifest conflict from proceeding further (Rubin, 1994). In addition, one or both individuals may choose to stop the conflict simply because they tire from engaging in it. A characteristic of intractable conflict is that it is sustained and often repetitive in the continuing lack of resolution (e.g., Friedman & Davidson, 1999). This repetition may result in the continuing inability of individuals in the relationship to complete tasks (if task achievement matters) as well as persistent stress from ongoing negative feelings within the relationship.

Why Learning Matters in Relationships Across Difference

In sum, we argue that high-quality relationships across difference are extremely rare. They are not simply positive relationships between individuals of different backgrounds, skin colors, or genders. There are many relationships across difference that endure for long periods of time that are characterized by warmth and caring. This is not necessarily a bad thing. However, far too often the individuals in those relationships discover that the ties that connect them are not especially strong and that when they are tested by the tensions that inevitably arise around diversity, those ties often break apart. Moreover, the excessive carefulness and lack of confidence that can arise in individuals in these relationships when their differences become salient can make both individuals ineffective (or even counterproductive) in dealing with professional situations where differences must be skillfully addressed.

To realize the breadth of benefits that high-quality relationships across difference can produce, individuals must confidently and fearlessly remain present and engaged when difference-related conflict tests the resiliency of the relationship. We submit the source of that resiliency is the individuals' commitment to learn from their difference.

A RESEARCH AGENDA

The model we introduce and the insights accompanying it suggest a number of important research questions that need to be addressed. First, we submit that a learning approach is a necessary prerequisite to create a high-quality relationship across difference. Are such relationships fostered in other ways? For example, familiarity alone could be the antecedent to a high-quality relationship. Individuals who have experience with the difference embodied in another individual could have learned how to interact effectively in past relationships and, because that person is culturally competent, can create a high-quality relationship. Moreover, even if learning in the relationship is a prerequisite for a high-quality relationship with a person who is different, does that learning have to be done in the context of the difference that is salient in the relationship? It is possible that task-relevant learning is all that is needed to build the relationship. Indeed, recall that the conflict literature suggests that task conflict creates more positive outcomes than relationship conflict (e.g., Jehn, 1995). Analogously, task-related learning, not relationship learning, could be sufficient to forge strong relationships across difference.

Our argument that conflict is essential in creating high-quality relationships across difference also poses several important research questions. Is conflict really essential to stimulate learning? This presupposes a model of change in which people only shift toward a new paradigm when a traumatic event throws them into disequilibrium: experienced manifest conflict is that trauma. However, it is possible that other phenomena could foster a learning approach such as simple proximity. An abundance of research demonstrates that contact and proximity can enhance attitudes about members of other groups (Dovidio, Gaertner, & Kawakami, 2003). Perhaps a process can be mapped in which those more positive attitudes translate into high-quality relationships that endure and are resilient.

Finally, it would be intriguing to explore the impact that having a high-quality relationship across difference has on the development of future relationships across difference. We posited early in the chapter that a high-quality relationship across difference produces positive outcomes. What outcomes, precisely, would result? We argue that high-quality relationships produce better work and better career outcomes and that can be tested. On the flip side, our model presents multiple ways of exiting the relationship: in reaction to conflict, perceived or manifest. What impact does exiting a relationship across difference have on the likelihood of future attempts to build relationship? Such disconnections could, for example, reinforce or create stereotypes about people who are members of the severed group. Alternatively, such disconnection could spur an individual to redouble efforts to build a successful relationship.

CONCLUSION

Relationships in society and in organizations come in many forms. Those that are the easiest to develop, maintain, and gain comfort from are those in which the members share common identity characteristics. Our goal for this chapter was to present a model for creating high-quality relationships that cross social identities; relationships characterized by a sense of well-being, positive regard, and resiliency in the face of adversity. As the world continues to become smaller and as organizations increasingly operate in a global context, the need to develop the competency for creating relationships across difference is enhanced. Central to our model for creating such relationships is a willingness and ability to learn about others and skill in managing difference. Furthermore, as a result of having worked through and learned from the experienced and manifest conflict that difference can produce, it is possible that one becomes even more receptive to future relationships across difference.

Although the ideas behind adult learning and conflict management are not new, we articulate how they can be powerful levers for creating strong relationships across difference. In so doing, our chapter contributes to the burgeoning body of work on positive organizational relationships in the following ways. First, it presumes that relationships across difference can be positive. On the surface this may seem a trivial point, but given that so much theoretical and empirical attention has been given to the adversities of difference relationships, it would be a mistake to take the notion of positive relationships across difference for granted. Second, our ideas are theoretically grounded and we provide practical guidance for implementing them. In this way, developing relationships across difference can be a vehicle for bridging the knowing–doing gap or the theory–practice divide. Third, it articulates the underlying mechanisms, or engines (learning and conflict) linking the expectations associated with identity differences and strong relationships across those differences.

REFERENCES

Adams, J. S. (1965). Inequity in social exchange. In L. Berkowitz (Ed.), *Advances in experimental social psychology* (Vol. 2, pp. 267–299). New York: Academic.

Adler, N. J., & Bartholomew, S. (1992). Managing globally competent people. *Academy of Management Executive, 6*(3), 52–65.

Alderfer, C. P. (1977). Group and intergroup relations. In J. R. Hackman & J. L. Shuttle (Eds.), *Improving life at work: Behavioral sciences approaches to organizational change:* (pp. 227–296). Santa Monica, CA: Goodyear.

Allport, G. W. (1954). *The nature of prejudice.* Cambridge, MA: Addison-Wesley.

Ancona, D. G., & Caldwell, D. F. (1992). Bridging the boundary: External activity and performance in organizational teams. *Administrative Science Quarterly, 37,* 634–665.

Ashford, S. J. (1986). Feedback-seeking in individual adaptation: A resource perspective. *Academy of Management Journal, 29,* 465–487.

Ashforth, B. E., & Mael, F. (1989). Social identity theory and the organization. *Academy of Management Review, 14,* 20–39.

Bandura, A. (1977). *Social learning theory.* Englewood Cliffs, NJ: Prentice-Hall.

Bandura, A. (1986). *Social foundations of thought and action: A social cognitive theory.* Englewood Cliffs, NJ: Prentice-Hall.

Baron, R. M., & Ganz, R. L. (1972). Effects of locus of control and type of feedback on the task performance of lower-class Black children. *Journal of Personality and Social Psychology, 21,* 124–130.

Blake, R. R., & Mouton, J. S. (1964). *The managerial grid.* Houston, TX: Gulf.

Boulding, E. (1961). *Conflict management in organizations.* Ann Arbor, MI: Foundation for Research on Human Behavior.

Brewer, M. B. (1991). The social self: On being the same and different at the same time. *Personality and Social Psychology Bulletin, 17,* 475–482.

Brewer, M. B. (1993). Social identity, distinctiveness, and in-group homogeneity. *Social Cognition, 11,* 150–164.

Brewer, M. B. (2001). Ingroup identification and intergroup conflict: When does ingroup love become outgroup hate? In R. D. Ashmore & L. Jussim (Eds.), *Social identity, intergroup conflict, and conflict reduction* (pp. 17–41). London: Oxford University Press.

Brewer, M. B., & Brown, R. J. (1998). Intergroup relations. In D. T. Gilbert & S. T. Fiske (Eds.), *Handbook of social psychology* (4th ed., Vol 2, pp. 554–594). New York: McGraw-Hill.

Brockner, J. (1979). The effects of self-esteem, success-failure, and self-consciousness on task performance. *Journal of Personality and Social Psychology, 37,* 1732–1741.

Byrne, D. (1971). *The attraction paradigm.* New York: Academic.

Carver, C. S., Glass, D. C., & Katz, I. (1978). Favorable evaluations of Blacks and the handicapped: Positive prejudice, unconscious denial, or social desirability? *Journal of Applied Social Psychology, 8,* 97–106.

Chan, D. K. S., & Goto, S. G. (2003). Conflict resolution in the culturally diverse workplace: Some data from Hong Kong employees. *Applied Psychology: An International Review, 52,* 441–460.

Cole, M. S., Schaninger, W. S., & Harris, S. G. (2002). The workplace social exchange network: A multilevel, conceptual examination. *Group and Organization Management, 27,* 142–167.

Cooper, J., & Stone, J. (2000). Cognitive dissonance and the social group. In D. J. Terry & M. A. Hogg (Eds.), *Attitudes, behavior, and social context: The role of norms and group membership* (pp. 227–244). Mahwah, NJ: Lawrence Erlbaum Associates.

Crosby, F., Bromley, S., & Saxe, L. (1980). Recent unobtrusive studies of Black and White discrimination and prejudice: A literature review. *Psychological Bulletin, 87,* 546–563.

Davidson, M. N. (2001). Know thine adversary: The impact of race on styles of dealing with conflict. *Sex Roles, 45,* 259–276.

Davidson, M. N., & Greenhalgh, L. (1999). The role of emotion in negotiation: The impact of anger and race. In R. J. Bies, R. L. Lewicki, & B. H. Sheppard (Eds.), *Research in negotiation in organizations* (Vol. 7, pp. 3–26). Stamford, CT: JAI.

De Dreu, C. K. W. & Weingart, L. R. (2003). Task versus relationship conflict, team performance, and team member satisfaction: A meta-analysis. *Journal of Applied Psychology, 88,* 741–749.

De Dreu, C. K. W., Weingart, L. R., & Kwon, S. (2000). Influence of social motives on integrative negotiation: A meta-analytic review and test of two theories. *Journal of Personality and Social Psychology, 78,* 889–905.

DeLongis, A., Folkman, S., & Lazarus, R. S. (1988). The impact of daily stress on health and mood: Psychological and social resources as mediators. *Journal of Personality and Social Psychology, 54,* 486–495.

Dindia, K. (2000). Self-disclosure, identity, and relationship development: A dialectical perspective. In K. Dindia & S. Duck (Eds.), *Communication and personal relationships* (pp. 147–162). Chichester, England: Wiley.

Dovidio, J. F., Gaertner, S. L., & Kawakami, K. (2003). Intergroup contact: The past, present, and the future. *Group Processes and Intergroup Relations, 6,* 5–20.

Dutton, J., & Heaphy, E. (2003). The power of high quality connections. In K. Cameron, J. Dutton, & R. Quinn (Eds.), *Positive organizational scholarship* (pp. 263–278). San Francisco: Berrett-Koehler.

Ely, R. J., & Thomas, D. A. (2001). Cultural diversity at work: The effects of diversity perspectives on work group processes and outcomes. *Administrative Science Quarterly, 46,* 229–273.

Ely, R. J., & Thomas, D. A. (2005). *Team learning and the link between racial diversity and performance.* Cambridge, MA: Harvard Business School.

Ensher, E. A., & Murphy, S. E. (1997). Effects of race, gender, perceived similarity, and contact on mentor relationships. *Journal of Vocational Behavior, 50,* 460–481.

Fiske, S. T., & Taylor, S. E. (1991). *Social cognition* (2nd ed.). New York: McGraw-Hill.

Fredrickson, B. L., & Branigan, C. (2001). Positive emotions. In T. J. Mayne & G. A. Bonanno (Eds.), *Emotions: Currrent issues and future directions* (pp. 123–151). New York: Guilford.

Friedman, R., & Davidson, M. N. (1999). The Black–White gap in perceptions of discrimination: Its causes and consequences. In R. J. Bies, R. L. Lewicki, & B. H. Sheppard (Eds.), *Research on negotiation in organizations* (Vol. 7, pp. 203–228). Stamford, CT: JAI.

Friedman, R. A., & Davidson, M. N. (2001). Managing diversity and second-order conflict. *International Journal of Conflict Management, 12,* 132–153.

Gaertner, S. L., Dovidio, J. F., Rust, M. C., Nier, J. A., Banker, B. S., Ward, C. M., et al. (1999). Reducing intergroup bias: Elements of intergroup cooperation. *Journal of Personality and Social Psychology, 76,* 388–402.

Garcia-Prieto, P., Bellard, E., Schneider, S. C., & Garcia-Prieto, P. P. G. (2003). Experiencing diversity, conflict, and emotions in teams. *Applied Psychology: An International Review, 52,* 413–440.

Geddes, D., & Konrad, A. M. (2003). Demographic differences and reactions to performance feedback. *Human Relations, 56,* 1485–1513.

Gersick, C. J. G., Bartunek, J. M., & Dutton, J. E. (2000). Learning from academia: The importance of relationships in professional life. *Academy of Management Journal, 43,* 1026–1044.

Girodo, M. (1977). Self-talk: Mechanisms in anxiety and stress management. In C. D. Spielberger & I. G. Sarason (Eds.), *Stress and anxiety* (pp. 229–250). New York: Hemisphere.

Gross, J. J. (2001). Emotion regulation in adulthood: Timing is everything. *Current Directions in Psychological Science, 10,* 214–219.

Hill, M. (1997). *Whiteness: A critical reader.* New York: New York University Press.

Hogg, M. A. (2003). Social identity. In M. R. Leary & J. P. Tangney (Eds.), *Handbook of self and identity* (pp. 462–479). New York: Guilford.

Hogg, M. A., & Terry, D. J. (2000). Social identity and self-categorization processes in organizational contexts. *Academy of Management Review, 25,* 121–140.

Ibarra, H. (1992). Homophily and differential returns: Sex differences in network structure and access in an advertising firm. *Administrative Science Quarterly, 37,* 422–447.

James, E. H. (2000). Race-related differences in promotions and support: Underlying effects of human and social capital. *Organization Science, 11,* 493–508.

James, E. H., Brief, A. P., Dietz, J., & Cohen, R. R. (2001). Prejudice matters: Understanding the reactions of Whites to affirmative action programs targeted to benefit Blacks. *Journal of Applied Psychology, 86,* 1120–1128.

Jeanquart-Barone, S. (1993). Trust differences between supervisors and subordinates: Examining the role of race and gender. *Sex Roles, 29,* 1–11.

Jehn, K. A. (1995). A multimethod examination of the benefits and detriments of intragroup conflict. *Administrative Science Quarterly, 40,* 256–282.

Jehn, K. A. (1997). A qualitative analysis of conflict types and dimensions in organizational groups. *Administrative Science Quarterly, 42,* 530–557.

Jehn, K. A., & Mannix, E. A. (2001). The dynamic nature of conflict: A longitudinal study of intragroup conflict and group performance. *Academy of Management Journal, 44,* 238–251.

Jehn, K. A., Northcraft, G. B., & Neale, M. A. (1999). Why differences make a difference: A field study of diversity, conflict, and performance in workgroups. *Administrative Science Quarterly, 44,* 741–763.

Joplin, J. R. W., & Daus, C. S. (1997). Challenges of leading a diverse workforce. *Academy of Management Executive, 11*(3), 32–47.

Kilmann, R. H., & Thomas, K. W. (1978). Four perspectives on conflict management: An attributional framework for organizing descriptive and normative theory. *Academy of Management Review, 3,* 58–68.

Kirmeyer, S. L., & Lin, T. R. (1987). Social support: Its relationship to observed communication with peers and superiors. *Academy of Management Journal, 30,* 138–151.

Krackhardt, D., & Kilduff, M. (1990). Friendship patterns and culture: The control of organizational diversity. *American Anthropologist, 92,* 142–154.

Kram, K. E. (1988). *Mentoring at work: Developmental relationships in organizational life.* Lanham, MD: University Press of America.

Lazarus, R. S. (1991). *Emotion and adaptation.* New York: Oxford University Press.

Lazarus, R. S. (1995). Vexing research problems inherent in cognitive-mediational theories of emotion—and some solutions. *Psychological Inquiry, 6,* 183–196.

Lefrancois, G. R. (1987). *The lifespan* (2nd ed.). Belmont, CA: Wadsworth/Thomson Learning.

Lubensky, M. E., Holland, S. L., Wiethoff, C., & Crosby, F. J. (2004). Diversity and sexual orientation: Including and valuing sexual minorities in the workplace. In M. S. Stockdale & F. J. Crosby (Eds.), *The psychology and management of workplace diversity* (pp. 206–223). Malden, MA: Blackwell.

Maass, A., Milesi, A., Zabbini, S., & Stahlberg, D. (1995). Linguistic intergroup bias: Differential expectancies or in-group protection? *Journal of Personality and Social Psychology, 68,* 116–126.

Merriam, S. (1983). Mentors and proteges: A critical review of the literature. *Adult Education Quarterly, 33,* 161–173.

Morrison, E. W., & Milliken, F. J. (2000). Organizational silence: A barrier to change and development in a pluralistic world. *Academy of Management Review, 25,* 706–725.

Myrdal, G., Sterner, R. M. E., & Rose, A. M. (1944). *An American dilemma: The Negro problem and modern democracy.* New York: Harper & Brothers.

Pelled, L. H., Eisenhardt, K. M., & Xin, K. R. (1999). Exploring the black box: An analysis of work group diversity, conflict, and performance. *Administrative Science Quarterly, 44,* 1–28.

Pennebaker, J. W. (1997). Writing about emotional experiences as a therapeutic process. *Psychological Science, 8,* 162–166.

Polzer, J. T., Milton, L. P., & Swann, W. B., Jr. (2002). Capitalizing on diversity: Interpersonal congruence in small work groups. *Administrative Science Quarterly, 47,* 296–324.

Pondy, L. R. (1967). Organizational conflict: Concepts and models. *Administrative Science Quarterly, 12,* 295–320.

Pondy, L. R. (1969). Varieties of organizational conflict. *Administrative Science Quarterly, 14,* 499–506.

Pruitt, D. G., & Rubin, J. Z. (1986). *Social conflict: Escalation, stalemate, and settlement.* New York: Random House.

Putnam, L. L., & Poole, M. S. (1987). Conflict and negotiation. In F. M. Jablin, L. L. Putnam, K. H. Roberts, & L. W. Porter (Eds.), *Handbook of organizational communication: An interdisciplinary perspective* (pp. 549–599). Newbury Park, CA: Sage.

Ragins, B. R. (1997). Diversified mentoring relationships in organizations: A power perspective. *Academy of Management Review, 22,* 482–521.

Ramsey, V. J., & Latting, J. K. (2005). A typology of intergroup competencies. *Journal of Applied Behavioral Science, 41,* 265–284.

Riordan, C. M. (2000). Relational demography within groups: Past developments, contradictions, and new directions. *Research in Personnel and Human Resources Management, 19,* 131–173.

Roccas, S., & Brewer, M. (2002). Social identity complexity. *Personality and Social Psychology Review, 6,* 88–106.

Rotter, J. B. (1966). Generalized expectancies for internal versus external control of reinforcement. *Psychological Monographs, 80,* 1–28.

Rotter, J. B. (1982). Social learning theory. In N. T. Feather (Ed.), *Expectation and actions: Expectancy-value models in psychology* (pp. 241–260). Hillsdale, NJ: Lawrence Erlbaum Associates.

Rubin, J. Z. (1994). Models of conflict management. Special issue: Constructive conflict management: An answer to critical social problems? *Journal of Social Issues, 50,* 33–45.

Senge, P. M. (1990). *The fifth discipline: The art and practice of the learning organization.* New York: Doubleday.

Sidanius, J., & Pratto, F.(1999). *Social dominance: An intergroup theory of social hierarchy and oppression.* Cambridge, England: Cambridge University Press.

Skinner, B. F. (1969). *Contingencies of reinforcement.* New York: Appleton-Century-Crofts.

Sniderman, P. M., & Tetlock, P. E. (1986). Symbolic racism: Problems of motive attribution in political analysis. *Journal of Social Issues, 42,* 129–150.

Swim, J. K., & Miller, D. L. (1999). White guilt: Its antecedents and consequences for attitudes toward affirmative action. *Personality and Social Psychology Bulletin, 25,* 500–514.

Tajfel, H. (1978). *Differentiation between social groups: Studies in the social psychology of intergroup relations.* New York: Academic.

Tajfel, H. (1982). Social psychology of intergroup relations. *Annual Review of Psychology, 33,* 1–39.

Tajfel, H., & Turner, J. C. (1985). The social identity theory of intergroup behavior. In S. Worchel & W. G. Austin (Eds.), *Psychology of intergroup relations* (2nd ed., pp. 7–24). Chicago: Nelson-Hall.

Thomas, D. A., & Gabarro, J. J. (1999). *Breaking through: The making of minority executives in corporate America.* Boston: Harvard Business School Press.

Thomas, K. (1992). Conflict and conflict management: Reflections and update. *Journal of Organizational Behavior, 13,* 263–274.

Totterdell, P., Spelten, E., Smith, L., & Barton, J. (1995). Recovery from work shifts: How long does it take? *Journal of Applied Psychology, 80,* 43–57.

Tsui, A. S., & O'Reilly, C. A. (1989). Beyond simple demographic effects: The importance of relational demography in superior–subordinate dyads. *Academy of Management Journal, 32,* 402–423.

Tung, R. L. (1993). Managing cross-national and intra-national diversity. *Human Resource Management, 32,* 461–477.

Turner, J. C., Hogg, M. A., Oakes, P. J., Reicher, S. D., & Wetherell, M. S. (1987). *Rediscovering the social group: A self-categorization theory.* Cambridge, MA: Basil Blackwell.

Vroom, V. H. (1964). *Work and motivation.* New York: Wiley.

Weinberger, D. A. (1995). The construct validity of the repressive coping style. In J. L. Singer (Ed.), *Repression and dissociation: Implications for personality theory, psychopathology, and health* (pp. 337–386). Chicago: University of Chicago Press.

Wong, R. R. (1995). Divorce mediation among Asian Americans: Bargaining in the shadow of diversity. *Family and Conciliation Courts Review, 33,* 110–128.

8

Positive Organizational Justice: From Fair to Fairer—and Beyond

Jerald Greenberg

Over the past two decades, organizational scientists have devoted considerable attention to studying people's perceptions of fairness in organizations—a concept known as *organizational justice* (Greenberg, 1987; Greenberg & Colquitt, 2005). Historically, researchers and theorists have focused attention on three major forms of organizational justice (Colquitt, Greenberg, & Zapata-Phelan, 2005). Specifically, these are:

- *Distributive justice*—The perceived fairness of the distribution of rewards and resources between parties.
- *Procedural justice*—The perceived fairness of the methods and procedures used as the basis for making decisions.
- *Interactional justice*—The perceived fairness of the interpersonal treatment accorded others in the course of communicating with them.

Despite the moniker, it may be observed that the field of organizational justice has emphasized not the attainment of justice per se, but the avoidance of injustice by managers and responses to injustice by subordinates. We see this with respect to all three types of justice. For example, scientists have studied responses to distributive injustices in such forms as reductions in performance (e.g., Greenberg, 1996) and increases in employee theft (e.g., Greenberg, 1990a) following inequitably low levels of desired rewards. Researchers also have studied job dissatisfaction (e.g., McFarlin &

Sweeney, 1992), turnover intentions (e.g., Simons & Roberson, 2003), and noncompliance with tax laws (e.g., Wenzel, 2002) stemming from procedurally unfair work policies. Additionally, studies have assessed how violations of interactional justice in the form of rude and uncaring supervision discourages workers from following company policies (e.g., Greenberg, 1994) and encourages them to engage in various forms of retaliation against their bosses (Skarlicki & Folger, 1997), including the initiation of lawsuits against former employers (e.g., Lind, Greenberg, Scott, & Welchans, 2000). These are just a few of many examples of attention to the negative side of justice that may be found in the literature (for overviews, see Colquitt & Greenberg, 2003; Greenberg & Colquitt, 2005).

This attention to injustice as opposed to justice contrasts with philosophical conceptualizations of justice that focus on such positive notions as morality and virtue (e.g., Buchanan & Mathieu, 1986) as well as lay rhetoric equating justice with what is right and good (Finkel, 2000). In light of these far more positive orientations, why do social scientists highlight injustice? One answer is that this is in keeping with the fact that fairness is normative, expected as the status quo, and therefore most salient whenever it is violated. As such, this may be considered a manifestation of the general tendency for unexpected or negative information to be more informative and to be given greater attention than expected, or positive information—the so-called negativity bias (Ito, Larsen, Smith, & Cacioppo, 1998). A key implication of this is that organizational scientists find it more informative to examine variations from the norm (i.e., injustice) than behavior consistent with the norm (i.e., justice).

Interestingly, even when social scientists make an effort to promote justice, they tend to focus primarily on being proactive about avoiding sources of injustice—that is, behaving in a less unfair manner (e.g., Greenberg & Wiethoff, 2001). Thus, if one views organizational phenomena along a continuum from negative at one pole to positive at the other, with a neutral point falling between these two extremes, as some have done (e.g., Cameron, Dutton, & Quinn, 2003), then the study of organizational justice appears to be anchored firmly at the negative end.

That this state of affairs may pose a limitation to our understanding of organizational justice is suggested by the movement toward positive organizational scholarship that has gained popularity in recent years (e.g., Cameron & Caza, 2004; Luthans, 2002; Wright, 2003). Specifically, this orientation has emphasized a commitment to the well-being of employees beyond the traditional, utilitarian, profit-driven concerns of managers and organizations (Wright & Wright, 2002). It also eschews the "repair shop" perspective (Keyes & Haidt, 2003) or the disease model (Wright & Cropanzano, 2000), embracing such positive emotions as joy, interest, and happiness, resulting in the capacity of individuals to grow and flourish (Frederickson, 2001). Importantly, to the extent that there are benefits to be derived from efforts to understand and promote the positive side of justice—including that it is an end in itself—it is clear that the field's present orientation will inhibit these from developing.

Acknowledging this limitation, I intend to bring balance to the study of organizational justice by refocusing attention from degrees of negative reactions to injustice to the less studied, positive side of the spectrum. To accomplish this I examine the conceptual peculiarities of the various forms of organizational justice with respect to ways in which prevailing expectations of fairness can be exceeded—what colloquially is called being "more than fair." I refer to this as *positive organizational justice* (POJ), which may be defined as deliberate efforts to promote, enhance, and sustain perceived fairness in the workplace in a manner that develops the positive capacities of individuals and organizations.

I envision POJ not as a distinct form of justice beyond the three major forms already described, but instead as an orientation to studying forms of justice that focuses on promoting vitality and thriving, and that encourages people to flourish. In this regard, POJ is built on positive relationships in organizations, those in which workers are given opportunities to prosper emotionally and to enjoy personally fulfilling experiences. In developing this theme, this chapter promises both to expand present thinking about organizational behavior and to introduce a new intellectual domain to the burgeoning field of positive organizational behavior (e.g., Luthans, 2002).

The organizing heuristic I am using in this chapter may be referred to as the *self-regenerating cycle of positive organizational justice*. This conceptualization, summarized in Figure 8.1, claims the following. (a) Certain individual acts promote POJ. (b) These behaviors, in turn, create certain positive psychological states in individuals. (c) Cumulatively, people experiencing these states contribute to a POJ culture, which promotes still more acts of POJ. This contributes to the continuation of the cycle. I consider this process to be self-regenerating insofar as each complete cycle strengthens the

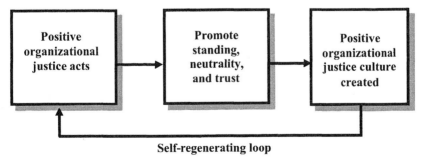

FIG. 8.1. Self-regenerating cycle of positive organizational justice.

next one, ultimately creating a self-sustaining positive culture. The following sections of the chapter ARE devoted to each step in the cycle.

FORMS OF POSITIVE ORGANIZATIONAL JUSTICE

The self-regenerating perspective begins by identifying acts of POJ. In keeping with general notions of positive organizational behavior, these are behaviors that promote fairness in a manner that incorporates such elements as compassion, dignity, respectful encounters, and integrity (Luthans, 2002). Extrapolating from the three forms of organizational justice, it is possible to consider ways in which each form of justice may lend itself to a more positive orientation. As will become evident, however, the positive orientation is a far better fit with some forms of justice than others.

Distributive Justice: Too Much of a Good Thing Is a Bad Thing

Earlier, I noted that *distributive justice* refers to people's perceptions of the fairness of the resources distributed between parties. The conceptualization of distributive justice of greatest familiarity to organizational scholars is Adams's (1965) theory of inequity. This approach specifies that: (a) when people receive outcomes that are lower than those received by comparable others, they are underpaid, leading to feelings of anger; and (b) when people receive outcomes that are higher than those received by comparable others, they are overpaid, leading to feelings of guilt. These negative emotional reactions motivate people to redress these negative states behaviorally or psychologically by turning them into equitable states, which result in feelings of satisfaction (for a review, see Greenberg, 1982).

Given this theory's dominance from the mid-1960s through the late 1980s, it is understandable why attention to matters of justice focused solely on negative perceptions. After all, satisfaction, the emotion associated with equity, is a neutral one, implying a state of quiescence. It is not a positive emotion like happiness or joy that results from equitable payment, but an affective state that is simply not negative. Put differently, distributive justice can be characterized as a narrow point, above which and below which negative reactions occur. Thus, strictly speaking, there can be no such thing as high amounts of distributive justice in any absolute sense, just different degrees of distributive injustice—that is, negative emotional deviation from the neutral point. In other words, achieving distributive justice is defined as a point along a continuum, where higher or lower levels are considered unfair (i.e., being overbenefited or underbenefited).

The implication of this is that the possibility of "positive distributive justice" has no basis in reality. As such, distributive justice does not lend itself to the creation of positive organizational justice in the sense just described. Given that distributive justice prevailed as an orientation in the justice literature before researchers conceived of other forms of justice, it is not surprising that theorists have not viewed it as a candidate for incorporation into the positive psychology movement (Seligman & Csikszentmihalyi, 2000).

Positive Procedural Justice: Following Exceptionally Fair Practices

As noted earlier, *procedural justice* refers to the perceived fairness of the policies and procedures followed in the course of distributing resources. Whereas distributive justice focuses on what is distributed to whom, procedural justice focuses on how the distribution decision is made. Unlike distributive justice, which does not lend itself to extension in the form of POJ, procedural justice does precisely this. Specifically, procedural justice takes several forms that, with appropriate qualifications, may be magnified to promote positive experiences of justice.

Promoting Transparency. Following Leventhal (1980), one way of enhancing procedural justice is by ensuring that evaluation procedures are transparent in nature—that is, accurate and open to verification. Often, companies implementing such policies make it possible for procedures to be monitored by those who wish to do so, but only via awkward, sometimes coercive means (e.g., in a state agency by filing a request under its Freedom of Information law). Strictly speaking, although a mechanism may be in place to ensure that the decision is made accurately and in verifiable fashion sometimes, the procedure is sufficiently unfriendly and Draconian as to be a barrier to true openness—what Weaver and Conlon (2003) referred to as "the façade of choice."

However, leaders who sincerely wish to promote justice should go out of their way to ensure that everyone is readily and fully aware of the decisions made. For this to occur, high levels of transparency are key. For example, salaries may be published in the company's newsletter, as may information about performance appraisals. Although the traditionally private nature of this information may make some feel uneasy, the company's openness to sharing it sends a strong message about its commitment to "getting it right." By providing public monitoring opportunities, organizations are building glass houses, so to speak, that ensure residents that stones will not be thrown. The resulting perceptions of procedural fairness are likely to be exceptionally high.

An important caveat must be noted. For this practice to be effective, of course, it is necessary for the decision rules to be clearly spelled out and explained so that even those who do not like the outcomes can be convinced of the fairness of the procedure by which they were determined. This is indeed possible. Notably, research has shown that even litigants found guilty of crimes accept those verdicts as fair to the extent that they believe the legal procedures were fair (for a review, see Lind & Tyler, 1988).

The more extreme a company's measures are—in the sense that its leaders bend over backwards to be open—the more positive perceptions of procedural justice are likely to be. Based on Kelley's (1972) augmentation principle of attribution, these acts must be "above and beyond" standard expectations of openness to be perceived as indicative of the actor's true commitment to justice. Given the benefits of positive perceptions of procedural justice (as chronicled by Greenberg, 1990b), the more advantageous these practices are expected to be.

Granting Voice. Following Thibaut and Walker's (1975) research on the role of voice in sociolegal settings, it is widely acknowledged that providing voice in decision-making procedures enhances people's perceptions of the fairness of those procedures (for a review, see Greenberg & Folger, 1983). Typically, people expect to have only limited voice in the decisions affecting them on the job, leading them to believe that those voice-granting procedures are especially fair. If no voice is expected, then some voice constitutes an improvement, suggesting that going beyond expectations promotes fairness.

With this in mind, leaders of companies who wish to promote justice should go out of their way to ensure that employees are given a voice in decision making that they did not expect to have. These opportunities should be plentiful in number and rich in nature. A great deal of research has established that the effectiveness of voice results not only from the belief that it will improve the chance of receiving desirable outcomes, but also from the message sent that one's input is valued, which enhances perceptions of fairness (Lind & Tyler, 1988; Tyler & Lind, 1992).

Some Caveats. Successful application of this practice requires attention to three important caveats. First, research has shown that there is an important limitation to the voice effect (for a review, see Greenberg, 2000). Specifically, although workers are more satisfied with having some voice as opposed to no voice in decisions affecting them, giving workers too much voice tends to be perceived as unfair insofar as it is considered to be relinquishing one's supervisory obligations inappropriately. Indeed, Peterson (1999) found that the relation between voice and perceived fairness took the form of an inverted U. Thus, higher voice was perceived as higher in fairness until a moderate level of voice was attained. At that point, however, additional amounts of voice lowered perceptions of fairness. In other words, although some voice raises perceptions of justice, too much voice lowers it. The implication for POJ is that with respect to this particular form of procedural justice, it is possible to have too much of a good thing.

A second caveat also is in order. Specifically, is not sufficient to give employees voice; they also must believe that their voice is listened to and considered with great care. Although not all suggestions can be implemented, of course, certainly all decisions can be—and should be—considered carefully. With this in mind, managers should carefully explain the procedures by which input is considered and also explain the basis for any decisions contingent on this input. This is a way in which POJ may be enhanced. Specifically, although there may be a limit to the amount of voice that is effective in promoting, there appears to be no limit to the effectiveness of explanations that are accurate, thorough, genuine, and sincere (Shapiro, Buttner, & Barry, 1994).

A third caveat follows from these first two. Specifically, there is reason to believe that managers who exceed prevailing norms of procedural justice may find themselves bumping up against workers' rising expectations. After all, the more transparent an organization's policies are and the more voice is given, the more transparency and voice will be expected in the future. Following from Helson's (1964) adaptation level theory, this makes each successive encounter with fair procedures less contributory to fairness perceptions. As a result, a climate of procedural fairness (Liao & Rupp, 2005) is likely to emerge in which the incremental improvements required to promote POJ become more challenging to achieve. That is, when POJ becomes normative, sustaining the resulting culture by exceeding expectations incrementally is not easy to do, given that the utility value of successive expressions of POJ is reduced. In such instances, managers may have to resort to finding novel forms of procedural justice that have not yet been identified.

Positive Interactional Justice: Communicating in a Fair Manner

Interactional justice refers to the fairness of the manner in which information is communicated to people in organizations (Bies, 2001). It consists primarily of two major components: (a) the interpersonal treatment given—that is, the degree of dignity and respect shown, and (b) the nature of the information shared—that is, the thoroughness and quality of explanations and other information presented to employees. Research has painted a compelling picture that giving people high-quality information about outcomes while treating them in a highly dignified and respectful manner helps them accept, and respond less negatively to, adverse outcomes, such as pay cuts, layoffs, terminations, and undesirable work policies (Greenberg, 1993).

In addition to helping people accept negative outcomes, on which existing research has focused, I believe that showing high degrees of interactional justice also will promote fairness perceptions when behaving this way is not instigated by the need to mitigate negative reactions. In fact, displays of interactional justice that have no apparent trigger (e.g., the need to explain a pay cut) may be seen as particularly genuine as a result—a "gift without an occasion," so to speak. This encourages the acts to be attributed to internal motives from which the actor—typically, a manager—will be seen as especially fair (Greenberg, 2003). Unlike distributive justice, in which positive acts of justice are not possible, and procedural justice, in which positive acts of justice face a myriad of limitations and qualifications, the nature of interactional justice is such that more of it is, in fact, better. Thus, when it comes to promoting interactional justice, the manager's mission is to exceed prevailing expectations regarding dignity and respect as well as sensitivity and thoroughness of the explanations of events. This is in keeping with the notion that a healthy company can be created by actively showing respect for others.

This "over the top" approach to dignity, sensitivity, and information richness requires that managers go out of their way to explain the decisions they make, and in a manner that shows considerable respect for their subordinates. Although many managers already may be inclined to do this when dealing with "sensitive" issues such as layoffs (Spreitzer & Mishra, 2002) and pay cuts (Greenberg, 2006), it is important to note that the positive benefits of engaging in interactional justice may be most likely to accrue when such behavior is followed in a routine encounter, when it is unexpected, a pleasant surprise. Under such circumstances, the fact that the superior is willing to make such an ostensible display of sensitivity and respect is more likely to be taken as a sign of the superior's interest in being fair, thereby resulting in more positive reactions than if the same behavior occurs under conditions in which it is expected. In attribution theory terms, it is the unusual nature of the situation that encourages the internal attribution to be made (Jones & Davis, 1965)—in this case, the attribution that the supervisor is a fair individual. Thus, promoting positive interactional justice requires exceeding expectations with respect to dignity, respect, and information thoroughness, which may be accomplished most readily when such behavior is unexpected.

Although it is indeed possible to exceed normative expectations regarding interactional justice when such behavior is expected (e.g., demonstrating sensitivity in a crisis situation, or in response to a personal tragedy), doing so is likely to require deeds that go beyond words. For example, because any supervisor would be expected to be kind and sensitive to a worker who has lost a loved one, the supervisor in this situation will have to exceed normative expectations for sensitivity to demonstrate positive interactional justice effectively. Doing this verbally is limited, of course, because there are only so many times and so many ways in which he or she can express condolences. Furthermore, one runs the risk of being excessively solicitous, which, under such circumstances may come across as ingenuine, leading to negative reactions instead of the positive ones intended. Under such circumstances, it may be most appropriate for the manager to demonstrate sensitivity to the employee's needs behaviorally, such as by proposing an idiosyncratic work arrangement that allows him or her to satisfy some other non-work-related need (Greenberg, Roberge, Ho, & Rousseau, 2004). In this case, for example, an arrangement may be made that enables the employee to get time off the job temporarily or to have flexible working hours while making necessary family arrangements. Although typically not considered as such, arrangements of this nature may be considered behavioral operationalizations of interpersonal sensitivity— one whose action speaks louder than its words.

Summary

As summarized in Table 8.1, behavior that promotes POJ may take many forms that distinguish it from acts that traditionally are advocated in the name of justice. Typically, these involve exceeding standards of procedural justice (albeit within certain prescribed limits), and interactional justice.

TABLE 8.1
Key Distinctions Between Traditional Organizational Justice and Positive
Organizational Justice for Each Form of Justice

Form of Justice	Traditional Organizational Justice	Positive Organizational Justice
Distributive justice	Outcomes are fair when allocated in proportion to work contributions. Justice is a specific point; outcomes that are too high or too low are unfair.	Not possible because distributive standards cannot be exceeded without causing unfairness.
Procedural justice	Procedures are fair when employees have a voice in determining outcomes and when these are based on accurate, thorough, and unbiased information.	Excessive levels of voice may be seen as inappropriate, but exceeding expected levels of attention to transparent procedures enhances justice perceptions.
Interactional justice	Fairness is enhanced by sharing information about the making of decisions in a manner that emphasizes dignity and respect for the individuals involved.	Extremely high levels of information presented in an exceptionally dignified and respectful manner stand to enhance justice perceptions beyond typical levels.

Such acts of POJ, as I explain next, are effective in promoting various positive psychological states and conditions.

RESPONSES TO POJ: UNDERLYING PSYCHOLOGICAL STATES AND CONDITIONS

In keeping with Luthans's (2002) conceptualization of positive organizational behavior, the second part of the self-regenerative conceptualization focuses on the underlying psychological states and conditions triggered by positive acts. In the case of POJ, three of the most relevant states and conditions are identified by Tyler and Lind's (1992) relational model of justice. Specifically, research bearing on this theory suggests that three factors—standing, neutrality, and trust—are responsible for positive reactions to interactional justice. Each of these, as I note, is associated with specific acts that may be performed to enhance POJ.

In general terms, the relational model of justice purports that people are sensitive to the procedures used by authority figures insofar as these stimulate their beliefs that their group or organization is functioning properly and that they are worthwhile individuals. The possibility that this conceptualization may be extended from structural procedures to interpersonal procedures (i.e., interactional justice) is suggested by the fact that information about standing, neutrality, and trust is communicated not just by the procedures used by authorities, but also the manner in which this information is communicated to subordinates. The essential underlying notion is that people desire to strengthen their social bonds to others in their work groups insofar as these connections provide an important source of self-valuation. This, in turn, gives individuals important information about their own status relative to others. Of course, given that people's fundamental needs for affiliation make the strengthening of social bonds desirable itself (Baumeister & Leary, 1995), such efforts contribute to the positive experiences of employees. I now turn attention to how each of these three elements of relational identity contribute to interactional justice in ways that may promote POJ.

Standing

The concept of *standing* refers to recognition of one's status in a group—that is, one's position relative to others along key dimensions of organizational hierarchy. A great deal of information about standing is communicated with respect to the politeness and dignity one is accorded in the course of communication. Typically, high status others are accorded respect—so-called dignitary treatment—whereas lower status others generally do not receive as much sensitive treatment. Accordingly, following Kelley's (1972) augmentation principle, high-status people may be able to cultivate feelings of inclusion and acceptance among lower status others by treating them with levels of dignity and respect that exceed expectations (Greenberg, Eskew, & Miles, 1991). Again, the fact that it is not expected makes it mean that much more. Such actions may be taken as an indication of a low-status person's "special" status given that the treatment—although an episode of status incongruence (Adams, 1953)—represents a surprisingly pleasant deviation from normative expectations. This, in turn, may signal the superior's concern for his or her status as a fully valued member of the group. The resulting boost to the subordinate's feelings of self-worth as a desired member of the organization may be considerable, and, of course, feeling that one is valued and recognized as an individual may be expected to be taken as expressing a proactive commitment to one's well-being (Baumeister & Leary, 1995).

There are several ways of doing this that represent good examples of POJ in action. For example, this may involve saying things that reflect one's sensitivity to the interests of others and being highly polite to them. It also may take such behavioral forms as allowing others ahead of oneself in line and giving another high priority in scheduling time, or in not permitting interruptions. Such acts have been found to promote perceptions of dignity and politeness (Tyler & Lind, 1992), which enhances feelings of social inclusion, thereby boosting one's apparent standing in a work group (van Prooijen, van den Bos, & Wilke, 2004). It is important to note that promoting POJ requires performing such acts under circumstances in which they are not expected by virtue of prevailing norms. For example, a subordinate who is acting especially polite to his or her superior is merely behaving as expected, precluding the possibility that he or she will be perceived to be especially interactionally fair. However, because a superior generally is not expected to engage in such demonstrable displays of politeness toward his or her subordinates, such actions are likely to be taken as signs of his or her commitment to fair treatment. This is in keeping with Jones and Davis's (1965) classic theory of correspondent inferences, which notes that behavior that is unusual and unexpected is more likely to be used as the basis for making internal attributions than behavior that is normatively expected (in large part because there are fewer plausible explanations for it).

Neutrality

POJ also may be promoted by adherence to the *neutrality* criterion of justice—that is, the belief that an authority figure is unbiased and committed unwaveringly to the even-handed treatment of all. Although this may be accomplished structurally by the use of unbiased procedures (Greenberg,

Bies, & Eskew, 1991), it also may be accomplished interpersonally by deliberately and ostensibly communicating information that is factual in nature and clear in articulation (Shapiro et al., 1994). In other words, fairness may be communicated not only by the application of unbiased procedures, but by demonstrative efforts to ensure that these are acknowledged by the individuals affected by them. To the extent that such communicative efforts are atypical, if not extraordinary in some respects, actors who engage in them are likely to be perceived as being especially fair by exceeding normative standards for demonstrating concerns about doing the right thing, and for ensuring that those affected by their actions are attuned to this propriety. Again, this may be taken as a means of promoting POJ.

Supervisors can demonstrate neutrality by providing extensive information that assures direct reports that they are unbiased and factual in collecting information on which decisions are made. This involves not only gathering and using valid and even-handed information but also establishing this in the eyes of others. In this connection, timing is key. Consider, for example, the way in which a manager may communicate information about performance evaluations in his or her department. A high level of positive interactional justice would be demonstrated by ensuring that all concerned parties are given thorough explanations regarding the accuracy of the information on which decisions are made in advance of the decisions. When an explanation of procedures used to determine outcomes is presented in advance of the outcomes, recipients are assured that the decision maker is operating behind what Rawls (1999) referred to as "a veil of ignorance." That is, fairness is promoted by the fact that the procedure, as explained, cannot be biased by knowledge of the outcomes.

Importantly, procedural justice is promoted by the fact that such a procedure is used, but interactional justice is promoted by providing an advance explanation that lays to rest any thoughts of impropriety. The same explanation offered after the fact, such as in response to an outcome being challenged by an employee, may be taken as a sign that the supervisor had something to hide, lowering the degree to which he or she would be judged to be fair. In sum, ostensible acts that promote a superior's commitment to a subordinate's well-being may be considered acts of positive interactional justice.

Trust

A third state or condition created by acts of POJ is *trust*—that is, the extent to which an authority figure can be counted on to behave in an ethical fashion. Thus, a supervisor who is perceived as trustworthy is one on whom others can depend to do the right thing, whatever that may be, across a broad spectrum of situations. In this sense, Person A's willingness to attribute trustworthiness to Person B is established over time by Person B not letting Person A down. This makes it possible for Person A to be less vigilant about monitoring Person B's behavior.

Consider a specific example. Suppose a supervisor is asked to represent the interests of a certain worker in making a case to management about the worker's request for special work hours. To the extent that the supervisor is believed to represent the interests of that worker in an accurate and sensitive fashion, he or she may be considered trustworthy in this respect. Trustworthiness is an important consideration for attaining justice (and the smooth functioning of organizations) insofar as it discourages conflict and promotes nonhostile, friendly interactions. As Pratt and Dirks (chap. 6, this volume) tell us, trust also plays a key role in the development of positive relationships. Trust takes time to develop, of course, but efforts to build trust (and to repair trust that has been broken) have been shown to contribute greatly to perceptions of justice (Lewicki, Wiethoff, & Tomlinson, 2005). From a POJ perspective, trust is an essential state insofar as it contributes to feelings of hope for a positive and fulfilling future, which as Luthans (2002) explained, is an important but neglected aspect of positive organizational behavior.

Although several mechanisms may be available for promoting one's trustworthiness to be fair, all such efforts appear to begin with an ostensible effort to explain one's own attention to fairness. Like the proverbial tree that nobody can hear because it falls in a vacant forest, the manager who engages in fair acts about which others may be unaware may be missing an opportunity to "make a sound"—that is, to demonstrate their commitment to justice. It is with this in mind that I once advocated the wisdom of a bit of modest self-promotion of one's commitment to fairness, such as by explaining the manner in which concerns about fairness were taken into account when making key decisions (Greenberg, 1990b). Thus, it may be said that promoting POJ requires, at the very least, convincing subordinates that one's actions are driven by a commitment to justice. Again, explanations appear to be key. Indeed, the sharing of thorough information about how decisions are made enhances one's trustworthiness in the eyes of others (similarly, see Pratt & Dirks's discussion of the role of apologizing and repentance in repairing trust, chap. 6, this volume).

POSITIVE ORGANIZATIONAL JUSTICE CULTURE—AND ITS RENEWAL

Thus far, I have been focusing on individual managerial acts that promote POJ. However, the greatest benefits of POJ are likely to accrue when such acts become normative, incorporated into the organization's culture, or institutionalized in keeping with formal organizational practices. Drawing from research and theory on organizational culture (e.g., Martin, 1992, 2001), when this occurs, social conditions are created in which we may expect both the number of people engaging in POJ and the magnitude of acts of POJ to be extraordinarily high. In large part, this results from sensemaking processes through which individuals socially construct perceptions of fairness as influenced by others (Lamertz, 2002). Moreover, those who may be disinclined to engage in POJ themselves will be pressured into doing otherwise, further strengthening the norm (Ott, 1989). Likewise, newcomers to the organization will be socialized into the POJ ways of the individuals who work there (Schein, 1999), such as through storytelling that reinforces the centrality of fairness concerns (Neuhauser, 1993).

Cumulatively, individual acts of POJ—especially positive interactional justice—may have several important beneficial effects that are likely to promote positive aspects of organizational culture. Beneficial criterion outcomes take several forms, including such organizational benefits as enhanced job satisfaction, organizational commitment, and organizational citizenship behavior, and such individual outcomes as feeling valued, welcomed, and respected as a member of the organization (for reviews, see Colquitt & Greenberg, 2003; Lind & Tyler, 1988). Again, the key is that being far more dignified and respectful to people than they expect cannot help but result in positive reactions. This pleasant surprise may stand out as especially positive in a world in which incivility is becoming all too common (Pearson & Porath, 2003), even among children (Vincent, 2004) and athletes (Robbins, 2004). Importantly, these reactions are likely to be "contagious" insofar as they contribute to a culture in which such positive acts are openly encouraged and in which violations are actively discouraged. Indeed, evidence suggests that work groups in which ethical concerns are incorporated into the culture tend to be maintained because of the high degrees of cohesion and morale that result (Dickson & Smith, 2001). Thus, when POJ is well integrated into the prevailing culture, its impact on a wide variety of positive behaviors is likely to be profound. This is in keeping with the findings of several recent studies showing that organizational cultures and climates that support fairness and ethics tend to thrive (Liao & Rupp, 2005; Naumann & Bennett, 2002), particularly with respect to such positive factors as enactment of organizational citizenship behavior (Erhart, 2004) and individual well-being (Schwepker, 2001).

By virtue of the strong behavior-directing nature of organizational culture, it is reasonable to claim that strong POJ cultures promote even more acts of POJ, and so the cycle goes. With each successive iteration, the cycle may strengthen as it reinforces itself. For this reason, I conceive of it as self-regenerating.

CONCLUSION: THE POSITIVE ORGANIZATIONAL JUSTICE AGENDA

In concluding this chapter, it is important to acknowledge that my discussion of POJ has focused exclusively on subordinates' impressions of the fairness of their superiors. This restriction reflects an existing bias in the study of organizational justice, which has focused primarily on top-down, hierarchical relationships (Colquitt & Greenberg, 2003). However, now that we are beginning to see attention to matters of justice among peers in the literature (e.g., Colquitt, Zapata-Phelan, & Roberson, 2005), it is reasonable for researchers to examine the attainment of POJ within such relationships. To assume that the same factors that promote POJ, or that interfere with its attainment in top-down relationships, also operate in the case of peers would be imprudent in view of differences in the context-embedded nature of these relationships.

This raises a more general issue. Namely, although the propositions presented here are derived from the literature logically, they beg to be tested empirically. Doing so will help promote the positive organizational science agenda while also expanding our knowledge of organizational justice, bringing it from the realm of the negative to the positive. One particularly promising avenue to consider in developing this area is with respect to the often elusive positive effects of stress, known as *eustress* (Nelson & Simmons, 2004). In this regard, recent theorizing on the use of executives as "engines for positive stress" is particularly promising (Quick, Mack, Gavin, Cooper, & Quick, 2004). Although prevailing research has focused on stressful reactions to injustice (e.g., Elovainio, Kivimäki, & Helkama, 2001; Vermunt & Steensma, 2005), research is called for that examines the health-related benefits of fair workplace experiences.

Although in its infancy, indications of such connections are beginning to appear in the literature (e.g., Theorell, 2004). Consider, for example, a recent study (Greenberg, 2006). In a field experiment, I found that nurses who were underpaid suffered higher levels of insomnia than those who were fairly paid. I then trained the supervisors of these nurses in ways of promoting interactional justice and found that the insomnia levels of their direct reports dropped significantly as a result—and that they remained at low levels 6 months later. Given that insomnia is a well-established response to stress (in this case, the stress of underpayment), these findings suggest that promoting interactional justice was an effective means of lowering stress, thereby contributing to a physically and mentally healthier workforce.

The Greenberg (2006) study, although traditional in its effort to mitigate responses to an injustice rather than to promote justice, has important implications for the study of POJ. Specifically, it suggests that workers can enjoy healthier lives as a result of being treated fairly by their supervisors. Moreover, the study also reveals that supervisors can be trained in techniques that promote feelings of fairness, and that its healthy effects are relatively long-lasting. This notion is in keeping with Luthans's (2002) idea, which I have embraced here, that because positive acts trigger certain psychological states, they are open to change via training programs. Indeed, Greenberg (2006) enhanced the healthiness of his research participants by training their supervisors in techniques to promote fairness. Although such training efforts are relatively new (for a review, see Skarlicki & Latham, 2005), it appears that managerial training in interactional justice is a promising tool for promoting POJ—and hence, the health and happiness of employees.

This research illustrates well my concluding point, and the central idea behind this chapter: Given the inherently positive nature of the concept of justice, it is ironic that organizational scientists have focused almost exclusively on its "dark side." Fully understanding the notion of justice requires studying more than only injustice. By analyzing the positive nature of organizational justice, along with ways of promoting this ideal, I have attempted to promote our understanding of this important notion. Hopefully, the impact of my efforts will be as positive as the behavior I am attempting to promote.

ACKNOWLEDGMENTS

I acknowledge the encouragement and helpful suggestions of Kirk Dirks, Jane Dutton, Belle Ragins, and members of the University of Michigan's Positive Organizational Scholarship community, who aided in the development of this work.

REFERENCES

Adams, J. S. (1965). Inequity in social exchange. In L. Berkowitz (Ed.), *Advances in experimental social psychology* (Vol. 2, pp. 267–299). New York: Academic Press.

Adams, S. (1953). Status congruency as a variable in small group performance. *Social Forces, 32,* 16–22.

Baumeister, R. F., & Leary, M. R. (1995). The need to belong: Desire for interpersonal attachments as a fundamental human motive. *Psychological Bulletin, 117,* 497–529.

Bies, R. J. (2001). Interactional (in)justice: The sacred and the profane. In J. Greenberg & R. Cropanzano (Eds.), *Advances in organizational justice* (pp. 85–108), Stanford, CA: Stanford University Press.

Buchanan, A., & Mathieu, D. (1986). Philosophy and justice. In R. L. Cohen (Ed.), *Justice: Views from the social sciences* (pp. 11–46). New York: Plenum.

Cameron, K. S., & Caza, A. (2004). Contributions to positive organizational scholarship. *American Behavioral Scientist, 47,* 731–739.

Cameron, K. S., Dutton, J. E., & Quinn, R. E. (2003). Foundations of positive organizational scholarship. In K. S. Cameron, J. E. Dutton, & R. E. Quinn (Eds.), *Positive organizational scholarship: Foundations of a new discipline* (pp. 3–23). San Francisco: Berrett-Koehler.

Colquitt, J. A., & Greenberg, J. (2003). Organizational justice: A fair assessment of the state of the literature. In J. Greenberg (Ed.), *Organizational behavior: The state of the science* (2nd ed., pp. 165–210). Mahwah, NJ: Lawrence Erlbaum Associates.

Colquitt, J. A., Greenberg, J., & Zapata-Phelan, C. P. (2005). What is organizational justice? An historical overview of the field. In J. Greenberg & J. A. Colquitt (Eds.), *Handbook of organizational justice* (pp. 3–56). Mahwah, NJ: Lawrence Erlbaum Associates.

Colquitt, J. A., Zapata-Phelan, C. P., & Roberson, Q. M. (2005). Justice in teams: A review of fairness effects in collective contexts. In J. Martocchio (Ed.), *Research in personnel and human resources management* (Vol. 24, pp. 53–94). San Diego, CA: Elsevier.

Dickson, M. W., & Smith, D. B. (2001). An organizational climate regarding ethics: The outcome of leader values and the practices that reflect them. *Leadership Quarterly, 12,* 197–217.

Elovainio, M., Kivimäki, M., & Helkama, K. (2001). Organizational justice evaluations, job control, and occupational strain. *Journal of Applied Psychology, 86,* 418–424.

Erhart, M. (2004). Leadership and procedural justice climate as antecedents of unit-level organizational citizenship behavior. *Personnel Psychology, 57,* 61–95.

Finkel, N. J. (2000). But it's not fair! Commonsense notions of unfairness. *Psychology, Public Policy, and Law, 6,* 898–952.

Fredrickson, B. L. (2001). The role of positive emotions in positive psychology: The broaden-and-build theory of positive emotions. *American Psychologist, 56,* 219–226.

Greenberg, J. (1982). Approaching equity and avoiding inequity in groups and organizations. In J. Greenberg & R. L. Cohen (Eds.), *Equity and justice in social behavior* (pp. 389–435). New York: Academic.

Greenberg, J. (1987). A taxonomy of organizational justice theories. *Academy of Management Review, 12,* 9–22.

Greenberg, J. (1990a). Employee theft as a reaction to underpayment inequity: The hidden cost of pay cuts. *Journal of Applied Psychology, 75,* 561–568.

Greenberg, J. (1990b). Looking fair vs. being fair: Managing impressions of organizational justice. In B. M. Staw & L. L. Cummings (Eds.), *Research in organizational behavior* (Vol. 12, pp. 111–157). Greenwich, CT: JAI.

Greenberg, J. (1993). The social side of fairness: Interpersonal and informational classes of organizational justice. In R. Cropanzano (Ed.), *Justice in the workplace: Approaching fairness in human resources management* (pp. 79–103). Hillsdale, NJ: Lawrence Erlbaum Associates.

Greenberg, J. (1994). Using socially fair procedures to promote acceptance of a work site smoking ban. *Journal of Applied Psychology, 79,* 288–297.

Greenberg, J. (1996). *The quest for justice the job: Essays and experiments.* Thousand Oaks, CA: Sage.

Greenberg, J. (2000). Promote procedural justice to enhance acceptance of work outcomes. In E. A. Locke (Ed.), *Handbook of principles of organizational behavior* (pp. 181–195). Malden, MA: Blackwell.

Greenberg, J. (2003). Creating unfairness by mandating fair procedures: The hidden hazards of a pay-for-performance plan. *Human Resource Management Review, 13,* 41–57.

Greenberg, J. (2006). Losing sleep over organizational injustice: Attenuating insomniac reactions to underpayment inequity with supervisory training in interactional justice. *Journal of Applied Psychology, 91,* 9–20.

Greenberg, J., Bies, R. J., & Eskew, D. E. (1991). Establishing fairness in the eye of the beholder: Managing impressions of organizational justice. In R. Giacalone & P. Rosenfeld (Eds.), *Applied impression management: How image making affects managerial decisions* (pp. 111–132). Newbury Park, CA: Sage.

Greenberg, J., & Colquitt, J. A. (2005). *Handbook of organizational justice.* Mahwah, NJ: Lawrence Erlbaum Associates.

Greenberg, J., Eskew, D. E., & Miles, J. (1991, August). *Adherence to participatory norms as a moderator of the fair process effect: When voice does not enhance procedural justice.* Paper presented at the meeting of the Academy of Management, Miami Beach, FL.

Greenberg, J., & Folger, R. (1983). Procedural justice, participation, and the fair process effect in groups and organizations. In P. B. Paulus (Ed.), *Basic group processes* (pp. 235–256). New York: Springer-Verlag.

Greenberg, J., Roberge, M. E., Ho, V. T., & Rousseau, D. (2004). Fairness as an "i-deal": Justice in under-the-table employment arrangements. In J. Martocchio (Ed.), *Research in personnel and human resources management* (Vol. 23, pp. 1–34). San Diego, CA: Elsevier.

Greenberg, J., & Wiethoff, C. (2001). Organizational justice as proaction and reaction: Implications for research and application. In R. Cropanzano (Ed.), *Justice in the workplace: Vol. 2. From theory to practice* (pp. 271–301). Mahwah, NJ: Lawrence Erlbaum Associates.

Helson, H. (1964). *Adaptation level theory.* New York: Harper & Row.

Ito, T. A., Larsen, J. T., Smith, N. K., & Cacioppo, J. T. (1998). Negative information weighs more heavily on the brain: The negativity bias in evaluative categorizations. *Journal of Personality and Social Psychology, 75,* 887–900.

Jones, E. E., & Davis, K. E. (1965). Form acts to dispositions: The attribution process in person perception. In L. Berkowitz (Ed.), *Advances in experimental social psychology* (Vol. 2, pp. 219–266). New York: Academic.

Kelley, H. H. (1972). The process of causal attribution. *American Psychologist, 28,* 107–128.

Keyes, C. L. M., & Haidt, J. (2003). Introduction: Human flourishing—The study of that which makes life worthwhile. In C. L. M. Keyes & J. Hadit (Eds.), *Flourishing: Positive psychology and the life well-lived* (pp. 3–22). Washington, DC: American Psychological Association.

Lamertz, K. (2002). Social construction of fairness: Social influence and sense making in organizations. *Journal of Organizational Behavior, 23,* 19–37.

Leventhal, G. S. (1980). What should be done with equity theory? New approaches to the study of fairness in social relationships. In K. Gergen, M. Greenberg, & R. Willis (Eds.), *Social exchange: Advances in theory and research* (pp. 27–55). New York: Plenum.

Lewicki, R. J., Wiethoff, C., & Tomlinson, E. C. (2005). What is the role of trust in organizational justice? In J. Greenberg & J. A. Colquitt (Eds.), *Handbook of organizational justice* (pp. 247–272). Mahwah, NJ: Lawrence Erlbaum Associates.

Liao, H., & Rupp, D. E. (2005). The impact of justice climate, climate strength, and justice orientation on work outcomes: A multilevel-multifoci framework. *Journal of Applied Psychology, 90,* 242–256.

Lind, E. A., Greenberg, J., Scott, K. S., & Welchans, T. D. (2000). The winding road from employee to complainant: Situational and psychological determinants of wrongful termination claims. *Administrative Science Quarterly, 45,* 557–590.

Lind, E. A., & Tyler, T. R. (1988). *The social psychology of procedural justice.* New York: Plenum.

Luthans, F. (2002). The need for and meaning of positive organizational behavior. *Journal of Organizational Behavior, 23,* 695–706.

Martin, J. (1992). *Cultures in organizations: Three perspectives.* New York: Oxford University Press.

Martin, J. (2001). *Organizational culture: Mapping the terrain.* Newbury Park, CA: Sage.

McFarlin, D. B., & Sweeney, P. D. (1992). Distributive and procedural justice as predictors of satisfaction with personal and organizational outcomes. *Academy of Management Journal, 35,* 626–637.

Naumann, S. E., & Bennett, N. (2002). The effects of procedural justice climate on work group performance. *Small Group Research, 33,* 361–377.

Nelson, D. L., & Simmons, B. L. (2004). Eustress: An elusive construct, an engaging pursuit. In P. L. Perrewe & D. C. Ganster (Eds.), *Research in occupational stress and well being* (Vol. 3, pp. 265–322). San Diego, CA: Elsevier.

Neuhauser, P. C. (1993). *Corporate legends and lore: The power of storytelling as a management tool.* New York: McGraw-Hill.

Ott, J. S. (1989). *The organizational culture perspective.* Chicago: Dorsey.

Pearson, C. M., & Porath C. L. (2003). On incivility, its impact and directions for future research. In R. Griffin & A. O'Leary-Kelly (Eds.), *The dark side of organizations* (pp. 403–425). San Francisco: Jossey-Bass.

Peterson, R. S. (1999). Can you have too much of a good thing? The limits of voice for improving satisfaction with leaders. *Personality and Social Psychology Bulletin, 25,* 315–324.

Quick, J. C., Mack, D., Gavin, J. J., Cooper, C. L., & Quick, J. D. (2004). Organizational Stress. In P. L. Perrewe & D. C. Ganster (Eds.), *Research in occupational stress and well being* (Vol. 3, pp. 359–405). San Diego, CA: Elsevier.

Rawls, J. (1999). *A theory of justice* (Rev. ed.). Cambridge, MA: Harvard University Press.

Robbins, L. (2004, November 22). One player barred for season as N.B.A. responds to brawl. *New York Times,* pp. C1, C3.

Schein, E. H. (1999). *The corporate culture survival guide.* San Francisco: Jossey-Bass.

Schwepker, C. H., Jr. (2001). Ethical climate's relationship to job satisfaction, organizational commitment, and turnover intentions in the salesforce. *Journal of Business Research, 54,* 39–52.

Seligman, M., & Csikszentmihalyi, M. (2000). Positive psychology. *American Psychologist, 55,* 5–14.

Shapiro, D. L., Buttner, E. H., & Barry, B. (1994). Explanations: What factors enhance their perceived adequacy? *Organizational Behavior and Human Decision Processes, 58,* 346–368.

Simons, T., & Roberson, Q. (2003). Why managers should care about fairness: The effects of aggregate justice perceptions on organizational outcomes. *Journal of Applied Psychology, 88,* 432–443.

Skarlicki, D. P., & Folger, P. (1997). Retaliation in the workplace: The roles of distributive, procedural, and interactional justice. *Journal of Applied Psychology, 82,* 434–443.

Skarlicki, D. P., & Latham, G. P. (2005). How can training be used to foster organizational justice. In J. Greenberg & J. A. Colquitt (Eds.), *Handbook of organizational justice* (pp. 499–522). Mahwah, NJ: Lawrence Erlbaum Associates.

Spreitzer, G. M., & Mishra, A. K. (2002). To stay or to go: Voluntary survivor turnover following an organizational downsizing. *Journal of Organizational Behavior, 23,* 707–729.

Theorell, T. (2004). Democracy at work and its relationship to health. In P. L. Perrewe & D. C. Ganster (Eds.), *Research in occupational stress and well being* (Vol. 3, pp. 323–357). San Diego, CA: Elsevier.

Thibaut, J., & Walker, L. (1975). *Procedural justice: A psychological analysis.* Hillsdale, NJ: Lawrence Erlbaum Associates.

Tyler, T. R., & Lind, E. A. (1992). A relational model of authority in groups. In M. P. Zanna (Ed.), *Advances in experimental social psychology* (Vol. 25, pp. 115–191). San Diego, CA: Academic.

van Prooijen, J.-W., van den Bos, K., & Wilke, H. A. M. (2004). Group belongingness and procedural justice: Social inclusion and exclusion by peers affects the psychology of voice. *Journal of Personality and Social Psychology, 87,* 66–79.

Vermunt, R., & Steensma, H. (2005). How can justice be used to manage stress in organizations? In J. Greenberg & J. A. Colquitt (Eds.), *Handbook of organizational justice* (pp. 343–367). Mahwah, NJ: Lawrence Erlbaum Associates.

Vincent, P. F. (2004). *Restoring school civility.* Chapel Hill, NC: Character Development Group.

Weaver, G. R., & Conlon, D. E. (2003). Explaining façades of choice: Timing, justice effects and behavioral outcomes. *Journal of Applied Social Psychology, 33,* 2217–2243.

Wenzel, M. (2002). The impact of outcome orientation and justice concerns on tax compliance: The role of taxpayers' identity. *Journal of Applied Psychology, 87,* 629–645.

Wright, T. A. (2003). Positive organizational behavior: An idea whose time has truly come. *Journal of Organizational Behavior, 24,* 437–442.

Wright, T. A., & Cropanzano, R. S. (2000). The role of organizational behavior in occupational health psychology: A view as we approach the millennium. *Journal of Occupational Health Psychology, 5,* 5–10.

Wright, T. A., & Wright, V. P. (2002). Organizational researcher values, ethical responsibility, and the committed-to-participant research perspective. *Journal of Management Inquiry, 11,* 173–185.

9

Commentary: Finding Connections at the Individual/Dyadic Level

Steve Duck

Although this part of the book focuses on individual and dyadic elements of positive relationships at work, this is done for analytic reasons rather than from naiveté. Ever since Simmel noted in the 1890s (Simmel, 1950) that any relationship is essentially a *social* concept that involves both dyads and society at large, it has been recognized that the only decisive influence that one individual per se can have on a relationship is to end it! One theme here is that all aspects of relationships require cooperation or interdependence with an Other and with various social norms. Both individual and dyadic levels of analysis are therefore embedded in a complex interplay of other levels of analysis also represented in this book. For example, an analysis of bodily appearance (Heaphy, chap. 3, this volume) implies not only a body, but also a viewer, and because *trust* (Pratt & Dirks, chap. 6, this volume) is a transitive verb, it necessarily implies an object, a person in whom someone confides.

Second, just as any relationship is essentially a social entity with individual and dyadic components, so too positivity is a socially grounded concept, rather than an absolute. It derives definition largely from the society in which it is embedded even when individuals or dispassionate researchers appear to be making the judgments. Individually and collectively, the chapters in this part make this point in subtle ways. For example, Quinn's (chap. 4, this volume) notion that energy is a good thing—rather than something self-centered and destructively personal—is implicitly embedded in a set of norms that regard it positively from an individualistic—rather than a collectivist—perspective. Likewise, fairness (Greenberg, chap. 8, this volume) is judged differently in a profit-maximizing capitalist organization that compares outcomes to efforts and in a socialist society that compares means to needs, so that positive organizational justice is nested within existing frameworks of justice.

In addition to the theme of interdependence, and the socially grounded nature of positivity, a third theme running through the chapters in this part is that relationships are open-ended enterprises, rather than final states: Any assessment of positivity is necessarily incomplete at any point in time. Any individual assessments of the positivity or negativity of a relationship are fluid, continuous, dynamic, and processual, a point implicit in all chapters but made explicit by Pratt and Dirks (chap. 6), Greenberg (chap. 8), and Quinn (chap. 4). The continuous interplay between different elements is thus a paradigmatic feature of experiences of relationships both positive and negative, whether at work or elsewhere.

This chapter focuses on these three themes as manifested in the separate chapters in this part. Because the same points are true at other levels (the groups, communities, and organizational levels), however, the commentary also connects these chapters to the rest of the volume by way of these points.

Positive relationships at work obviously have many components embodied at the individual and dyadic level. Individual identity can be analyzed at the psychological level as personality. Roberts's (chap. 2, this volume) emphasis on the social forces impinging on individual personality, however, forces us to recognize the links between individual and social levels of analysis: Relationships are intricately implicated in many other social processes such that identity, justice, and energy have other roots beyond the individual.

Positive relationships at work rely not only on individual judgment, but also on accounts, criteria, and standards in the organizations where they occur. Davidson and James (chap. 7, this volume) recognize this theme through their insistence that we acknowledge the learning stance necessary as prerequisites to blending organizational needs positively with individual experiences. Their emphasis on self-disclosure and negotiation recognizes the interplay of individual psychology with social embeddedness.

Likewise Roberts (chap. 2) clearly connects individual identity with broader social processes in ways that centralize the role of relationships as an identity-constructing medium. Her chapter also serves to note that individuals are affected by the positive relationships at work at least as much as they contribute to them and gain a large part of their identity from their experiences in the workplace. Organizations that create positive relationships at work thereby nourish and sustain the personal identities of individuals.

A related theme in the foregoing chapters is the inherently social nature of positivity in relationships at work; that is to say, they are based on social comprehension of what is good. Ragins and Verbos (chap. 5, this volume) offer some good examples of this point in relation to mentoring. Researchers can determine the individual and dyadic qualities of a good mentor, and our current understanding comes largely from the power-down position based on the identification of those aspects of mentoring behavior that are identified as positive by (or for) the recipient. The positive benefits of mentoring are qualified by the society and organization within which it is accessed, nevertheless, an individualist society tends to count it as a positive relationship when there is individual self–other improvement. A collectivist culture would stress that the mentor should encourage team spirit over individual accomplishment and thereby create requisite social and personal obligations in the recipient. Mentoring is also a helpful two-way dyadic professional process that does not carry the power relationship implied by a simple mentor–protégé depiction (Hecht & Warren, 2006). Likewise, Pratt and Dirks (chap. 6) emphasize the social nature of individual trust in that commitment and safety are both denoted individually—that is to say, are described in terms of their effects on a person—even though they are dependent not only on dyadic exchange and commitment, but also on a particular organization's or society's view of what may be safely entrusted to another person or expected from them. Societies differ in their beliefs about what is trustworthy behavior (La Gaipa, 1982), so any definition of trust in relationships implicitly adopts a set of assumptions about the aspects of self and other that represent trust and vulnerability—a point implicitly made by such TV series as *The Sopranos,* a social subgroup where trust centers around protection of honor as much as it involves protection of personal secrets. Discussions about trust can therefore be specified and localized to a particular organization or group. Although trust is a valued asset in most Western social judgments about a relationship, there are some cultures in which trust is essentially irrelevant or less salient to judgments about relationships (La Gaipa, 1982).

Similarly, Greenberg's (chap. 8) discussion of justice in positive relationships and work also represent a new "strain" of justice, tied to other forms but also capturing new experiences. Although it invokes the quintessential prerequisite of fairness in all positive relationships, it is clear that justice and the standard by which justice is assessed depend on a particular group's view of what is "just" (La Gaipa, 1977). Such judgments range from strict *equality* (everyone in the relationship gets the same thing), through *equity* (the person who works the hardest gets the most back), to *Marxist justice* (those people with the most need receive the most, "from each according to his means, to each according to his needs"). As our society on the whole tends to value equity over the other two forms of justice, then it is equity assessment that will be brought to the question of whether a relationship is positive or negative. In societies where hierarchy is expected to be rigidly respected, the notion of fairness may take a different form from the one that it takes in any society based on equity (e.g., the Japanese relationship of *amae* is based on long-term implied mutual respect and obligation between unequals). In North American culture, great weight is given to openness, honesty, and the frank declaration of feelings, but in Japan such openness, honesty, and declaration would be regarded with great suspicion—and certainly would not count as an example of positive behavior. On the other hand, the assertive form of honesty represented by the Israeli *dugri* forms of speech (Katriel, 1986) is regarded in the United States as uncivil and overly aggressive. Equally, American culture values independence and individuality in a way that is not always regarded in the same positive light in collectivist cultures. Finally, Heaphy (chap. 3) implicitly makes a similar point in her discussion of bodies and the material nature of agency, as it is applied to men and women. The very fact of differences of application of this concept underlines the point about social relativity about judgments of what is positive.

Therefore there are no such things as inherently positive or inherently negative relationships (Duck, Foley, & Kirkpatrick, 2006), but only qualities as assessed by a particular society or organization that sets its own standards for such judgments (Montgomery, 1988). Whenever we describe a relationship as "positive" there is always an implicit reference to such a relative set of bounded criteria in every case.

Given that positive relationships at work are continuously open-ended ventures contextualized by the embedding society's or organization's assumptions about the nature of positivity, these chapters also make clear the inextricable interconnectedness of individual, group, network, and organizational or community influences, even when they focus on outcomes at the individual level of satisfaction and sense of positivity.

It is evident also that a perpetual re-creation of positive relationships runs through discussion of justice, equity, trust, and energy, because no permanence—and certainly no end state—of positivity is presumed by any of the authors here. Clearly the continuous creation of positivity in relationships at work is one of the major outcomes to which this book is directed and the emphasis on continuity (and the effort necessary to provide it) is paramount in the analysis. Indeed, Heaphy's (chap. 3) careful rendering of the role of bodily materiality in interactions (plural) mirrors the emphasis on sequences of trust creation (Pratt & Dirks, chap. 6) and the maintenance of justice (Greenberg, chap. 8) insofar as it emphasizes the essentially transitory nature of positive experiences at work and the consequent importance of repeated energetic management and accumulation of such experiences (Quinn, chap. 4), whether in the individual's head or in the organization's connective structures. Indeed, Pratt and Dirks (chap. 6) conclude that even positive relationships at work are not uniformly positive but represent a work in progress. In the independently flourishing social and personal relationships field, a similar recognition that relationships themselves are always unfinished business has long been made (Duck, 1990). In the context of any discussion of positive relationships at work, therefore, it is important to recognize that positivity is not a perpetual state, but merely a predominant form of relationship. One cannot expect individuals to view all positive relationships as positive all the time.

Key voluntary relationships are unusual in that they develop in intimacy, when most of the relationships that we experience in life—especially at work—are involuntary consequences of organizational membership. They cannot therefore be presumed to be inherently developmental, in the sense that they do not normally develop in intimacy (Delia, 1980). When considering positivity in relationships, it is important to decide whether "positivity" is intended to promote or to successfully prevent intimacy growth. A number of chapters here do not appear to include intimacy as a relevant issue in assessments of positivity in relationships at work when other work does (e.g., Prager, 1995). However, we must be careful in describing the nature of intimacy at work, and also place such intimacy in cultural context. For example, intimacy at work may involve self-disclosure only about limited (work-relevant) domains, or could connect trust to task-related performance alone, rather than to general trustworthiness in other domains. Roberts (chap. 2) indicates the value of a satisfactory sense of identity in the definition of relationships as positive; Heaphy (chap. 3) identifies bodies as material resources with which people actuate their relationships, in particular their interaction with notions of agency; and Pratt and Dirks (chap. 6) on the one hand and Greenberg (chap. 8) on the other indicate the importance of trust and a sense of justice and indeed a sense of mutual respect. All of these concepts are normally associated with intimacy in the social and personal relationships literature, but intimacy at work may be different from intimacy elsewhere—it requires supportive teamwork, rather than self-disclosure—although the basic idea is still that positive relationships at work are richer than mere procedural mechanics of management and so they require imitation of relational forms in other spheres of life.

Second, many workplace transactions are brief and not geared toward intimacy growth except in terms of teamwork in regular workplace activity or special, intense, T-groups. Thus although some workplaces encourage friendship among coworkers, it is often specific to the development of cooperation in the workplace rather than outside of it. Quinn (chap. 4) discusses the role of energy in the improvisation and knowledgeable practices of organizational structures, and it is clear that the sense of energy is an affective experience that creates motivation rather than intimacy. Energy, however, as Quinn points out, is an important resource specifically in relationships that have short-term objectives. The importance of energy therefore lies in its ability to point people toward particular goals at particular times, while also creating a general environment where individuals feel motivated by something other than intimacy needs.

Third, relationships that result from voluntary exercise of choice by both parties for their development are different from involuntary ones that characterize the workplace. Ragins and Verbos (chap. 5) indicate the ways in which mentoring can create a sense of reliable alliance and a friendship between a superior and the subordinate. Mentoring relationships very often represent positive relationships for the "underdog" but they may not necessarily be like voluntary relationships, because the protégé is most often required to be guided by the mentor. Although positive relationships at work may include genuine concern for the welfare and personal development of the other, a sense of obligation is specific to success in the workplace even if the relationship employs communal norms.

Fourth, issues of trust and fairness take on a different compass when the relationships are voluntary, as compared to involuntary. When a person is treated unfairly in a voluntary relationship he or she may leave. In the workplace, those persons who perceive themselves to be treated unfairly do not have such a range of choice. Therefore issues of trust and fairness are bounded by different judgments, standards, and outcomes in the case of voluntary and involuntary relationships.

An additional observation current in the independent field of social and personal relationships is a large emphasis on the *praxis* of relationships, or the daily practices by which they are enacted (Wood & Duck, 2006). We not only experience a sense of intimacy in relationships, but we talk intimately; we not only feel collegial, but we do favors; we not only feel, but may also make, love. Abstract emotions are not all there is to relationships, then. Furthermore, relationships occur in a context where there are always competing forces simultaneously present (Baxter & Montgomery, 1996). The most frequent and arresting example of the force of such dialectics in relationship performance is that of autonomy and connection. Individuals like to be themselves and to have a certain amount of individual freedom (autonomy); it is in the nature of things, however, that in relationships people become interdependently connected and therefore must give up some of this autonomy. However, nobody wants to be connected to another person at the expense of all their autonomy and even when they are willing to make some concessions to connectedness, there are also times when they wish to reassert their autonomy. Therefore, many relationship behaviors are generated by the struggle between the competing desires for autonomy and connection. This tension is consistently present in the operation of people's decisions about relationship management. In the context of positivity in relationships at work, it must be recognized that positivity must result from a balance between different competing forces, as well as being a desirable goal in itself. In addition, there can be a need for balance within the dyad—one partner wants more connection than another—and this can lead to strained work relationships.

It is also important to recognize that relationships do things for people rather than simply representing emotional or organizational states between them. Carl and Duck (2004) indicated the ways in which relationships act as implicit persuaders in many interactions and social life. People are often able to achieve things through their relational connections that they cannot do alone, but it is also through relational membership that people acquire and evaluate knowledge or attitudes. Such forces are also present in positive relationships in the workplace, and one of the major outcomes of relationships with other people is *epistemic,* or related to knowledge. People gain a large sense of their identity, of the nature of the world, of all sorts of experiences, of things that can be expected in the world and the general views of how things should be done from their relationships with other people at work.

Given all this, the study of positive relationships at work represents an enormous opportunity for researchers to make the organizational, group, dyadic, and individual levels of analysis come into useful play. To detach the individual from these other factors that are generative of positive relationships at work is useful only at the analytic level and one must be ever alert to the need for eventual recombination of the original analytic separations. We can usefully analyze individual processes only to the extent that we actively hold in mind that they are also socially situated and perpetually open-ended.

REFERENCES

Baxter, L. A., & Montgomery, B. M. (1996). *Relating: Dialogs and dialectics.* New York: Guilford.

Carl, W. J., & Duck, S. W. (2004). How to do things with relationships. In P. Kalbfleisch (Ed.), *Communication yearbook* (Vol. 28, pp. 1–35). Thousand Oaks, CA: Sage.

Delia, J. G. (1980). Some tentative thoughts concerning the study of interpersonal relationships and their development. *Western Journal of Speech Communication, 44,* 97–103.

Duck, S. W. (1990). Relationships as unfinished business: Out of the frying pan and into the 1990s. *Journal of Social and Personal Relationships, 7,* 5–29.

Duck, S. W., Foley, M. K., & Kirkpatrick, C. D. (2006). Relating difficulty in a triangular world. In C. D. Kirkpatrick, S. W. Duck, & M. K. Foley (Eds.), *Relating difficulty: The processes of constructing and managing difficult interaction* (pp. 225–232). Mahwah, NJ: Lawrence Erlbaum Associates.

Duck, S. W., Foley, M. K., & Kirkpatrick, C. D. (in press). Uncovering the complex roles behind the "difficult" co-worker. In J. F. Harden & B. Omdahl (Eds.), *Working with difficult people.* New York: Peter Lang.

Hecht, M., & Warren, J. R. (2006). Helpful professional relating: constructing the mentoring relationship through everyday talk. In J. T. Wood & S. W. Duck (Eds.), *Composing relationships: Communication in everyday life* (pp. 156–165). Belmont, CA: Thomson Wadsworth.

Katriel, T. (1986). *Talking straight: "Dugri" speech in Israeli sabra culture.* New York: Cambridge University Press.

La Gaipa, J. J. (1977). Interpersonal attraction and social exchange. In S. W. Duck (Ed.), *Theory and practice in interpersonal attraction* (pp. 129–164). London: Academic.

La Gaipa, J. J. (1982). Rules and rituals in disengaging from relationships. In S. W. Duck (Ed.), *Personal relationships 4: Dissolving personal relationships* (pp. 189–209). London: Academic.

Montgomery, B. M. (1988). Quality communication in personal relationships. In S. W. Duck (Ed.), *Handbook of personal relationships* (pp. 343–362). Chichester, England: Wiley.

Prager, K. J. (1995). *The psychology of intimacy.* New York: Guilford.

Simmel, G. (1950). *The sociology of Georg Simmel.* New York: The Free Press.

Wood, J. T., & Duck, S. W. (Eds.). (2006). *Composing relationships: Communication in everyday life.* Belmont, CA: Thomson Wadsworth.

POSITIVE RELATIONSHIPS: GROUPS AND COMMUNITIES

10

Meaningful Connections: Positive Relationships and Attachments at Work

William A. Kahn

Relationships among organization members are a significant part of their lived experiences at work. They shape how people think, how they feel, and what they do. This seems axiomatic, a basic tenet of organizational behavior that predates the oft-cited Hawthorne studies. Since those studies, researchers have routinely included coworker and hierarchical relationships as variables in their studies of satisfaction and commitment, performance, and turnover and have generally found that the quality of work relationships does make some difference in such outcomes (see Hom & Griffeth, 1995). This is unsurprising. It matches our intuitive understanding of what makes a difference to people in their work lives. What is surprising is the extent to which work relationships by and large appear in organizational theory as part of the background; that is, as one variable among many that influence organizational life and outcomes, rather than as a central figure. Work relationships are central enough in organizational life to deserve consideration in their own right as a primary factor in people's attitudes and behaviors.

Such consideration means developing models or theories about work relationships that are reasonably comprehensive. Concepts involving work relationships are generally scattered across different literatures. They are split into different categories of relationship that include, for example, coworkers and team members (Hackman, 1987), leaders and subordinates (Bass, 1981), group members (Smith & Berg, 1987), and mentors (Kram,

1985). They are also split into different models of organizational behavior, used as variables to help explain the variance of members' attitudes (job satisfaction, organizational commitment or attachment) and behaviors (performance, absenteeism, turnover). In each of these categories or models, research has led to the construction of useful theory. Yet the various splits have also led to a fragmented understanding of the nature, meaning, and impact of work relationships more generally. We lose a sense of the whole, nuanced, complicated, and occasionally paradoxical individual, who moves toward and away from aspects of work, identity, and self based on the relationships that he or she creates. We are thus left with bounded theories that account for organization members in some roles and not others, with implications for some attitudes or behaviors and not others. We cannot examine the totality of people's relationships at work and the implications of that totality for their experiences and actions.

I argue in this chapter that placing relationships at the center rather than at the periphery of people's experiences of work—as the figure, not the ground—throws into sharp relief the significance of positive relationships. I define positive relationships as those that enable individuals to personally engage in their work—that is, to be authentic, present, and intellectually and emotionally available as they go about their work (Kahn, 1992). This formulation is based on the premise that personal engagement is more likely to occur when people feel meaningfully connected to others. Such connections are a matter of feeling supported, helped, understood, and worked with in nonsuperficial ways. The depth of such connections enables people to bring themselves more authentically into their work—to say what they think and feel, to display their true gifts and capabilities, to react honestly to what they see and experience. Moreover, positive relationships help attach people to their organizations. When people feel meaningfully connected to others, they are more likely to feel connected as well to what they are doing and the group and organizational contexts in which they are doing it.

In this chapter I unpack these formulations. I begin by articulating the dimensions of meaningful connections among people at work. There are five such dimensions, drawn from various literatures across organizational studies. Individuals vary in terms of how much they each value these particular dimensions, have access to others who can and will provide these dimensions, and are able to themselves seek out and make use of others along these dimensions. As a result, people vary in terms of the particular constellations of positive relationships that they have access to and help create at work. I explore these variations, and the resulting implications for people's engagements at work and the attachments they form to their work and to their group, and organizational contexts.

DIMENSIONS OF MEANINGFUL CONNECTIONS

There are various ways in which we can understand what types of connections are meaningful to people at work. Indeed, social network researchers have narrowed in on five types of social networks—communication, advice, support, friendship, and influence (Ibarra, 1993)—that serve particular functions for organization members. This offers a useful starting point for conceptualizing the dimensions of what I refer to as meaningful connections, which need to range from instrumental to expressive to accommodate different types of people. From this point, we can also look more broadly across the expanse of organizational behavior theory and research to include what social network theorists do not. A review of the literature suggests five primary dimensions, taken across form (e.g., hierarchical, peer) and context (e.g., formal, informal). I review here the five dimensions: task accomplishment, career development, sense making, provision of meaning, and personal support. Table 10.1 lists the primary concepts and research areas that define each of these dimensions.

Task Accomplishment

Work relationships, at their most instrumental, are the vehicles by which most organizational tasks are accomplished. Individuals develop, employ, and respond to relationships in the service of their organizational roles and the completion of given tasks. Various types of relationships are important, at different times, for task accomplishment. In hierarchical relationships, subordinates are provided with goals, direction, and resources (Tsai & Ghoshal, 1998). In peer relationships, organization members exchange information and knowledge (Ibarra, 1992), join together in coalitions and task forces that enable problem solving, creativity and innovation, and influence (Brass & Burkhardt, 1992), and span boundaries (Ancona & Caldwell, 1992). Across these and other forms of work relationships, individuals tap into relational webs that influence the formal and informal workings of their organizations on behalf of moving their projects ahead.

Career Development

Work relationships also serve instrumental functions at the individual level, in terms of enhancing organization members' careers (see also Higgins, chap. 11, this volume). Relationships with hierarchical superiors offer opportunities for visibility, significant challenge, and promotion (Burt, 1992; Podolny & Baron, 1997). They are also the vehicles through which coaching, mentoring, and training can help develop the skills and perspectives re-

TABLE 10.1
Dimensions of Meaningful Connections at Work

Task accomplishment: Relationships that enhance people's abilities to perform their tasks effectively	• Information and knowledge (Granovetter, 1973; Ibarra, 1992; Lincoln & Miller, 1979) • Resources (Tsai & Ghoshal, 1998) • Power and influence (Brass, 1984; Brass & Burkhardt, 1992; Ibarra, 1993) • Coalitions and upward influence (Brass & Burkhardt, 1993; Stevenson & Greenberg, 2000) • Task direction (Bass, 1981) • Creativity and innovation (Ibarra, 1993) • Decision making and problem solving (Alper, Tjosvold, & Law, 1998) • Boundary spanning and management (Ancona & Caldwell, 1992) • Adoption of innovations (Burkhardt, 1994); goal setting (Locke, 2000)
Career development: Relationships that offer individuals access and opportunity to advance their careers	• Career mobility and opportunities (Ibarra, 1992; Podolny & Baron, 1997; Tsai & Ghoshal, 1998) • Promotions (Burt, 1992) • Visibility and reputation (Kilduff & Krackhardt, 1994; Sparrowe & Liden, 1997) • Longevity (Krackhardt & Porter, 1986) • Instrumental support (Gersick, Bartunek & Dutton, 2000; Ibarra, 1993; Thomas, 1993) • Mentoring (Kram, 1985; Ragins, 1994; Thomas, 1993) • Coaching (Evered & Selman, 1990) • Personal skill development (Hall, 1996)
Sense making: Relationships that help people make sense of events, experiences, and shifting organizational and environmental contexts	• Socialization (Louis, 1980; Van Maanen & Schein, 1979) • Reduction of uncertainty (Krackhardt & Porter, 1986) • Adaptation to change (Burkhardt, 1994) • Crisis management (Mitroff, 1993) • Communication networks and social information processing (Lincoln & Miller, 1979; Stevenson & Gilly, 1993) • Social construction of organizational reality (Weick, 1995)
Provision of meaning (purpose): Relationships that enable people to feel validated and valued, connected to larger purposes, and reinforced in a meaningful identity	• Relatedness and connection to coworkers (Alderfer, 1972) and leaders (Kahn, 2005) • Construction of preferred identity (Somers, 1994) • Relational practice (Miller, 1987) • Sense of being valued and cared for (Kahn, 1993) • Social exchange and citizenship behavior (Konovsky & Pugh, 1994) • Enjoyment (Baldwin, Bedell, & Johnson, 1997) • Shared ethical stance (Brass, Butterfield, & Skaggs, 1998) • Community of practice (Wenger, 1998)

(Continued)

TABLE 10.1
(Continued)

Personal support: Relationships that provide help with potential and real sources of stress and anxiety	• Buffering against job stress and burnout (Cohen & Wills, 1985; Cordes & Doughtery, 1993) • Coping resources (Heaney, House, Israel & Mero, 1995) • Mentoring (Kram, 1985; Thomas, 1993) • Friendship (Krackhardt & Porter, 1986; Lincoln & Miller, 1979) • Relational ties and attachments (Josselson, 1996; Kahn, 1998; Lawler & Yoon, 1998) • Anxiety management (Frost, 2002; Kahn, 2001) • Caregiving and compassion (Kahn, 1993; Kanov et al., 2004) • Feedback and personal development (Rogers, 1958)

quired for advancement (Hall, 1996; Kram, 1985). Relationships with peers also provide opportunities for career advancement and skill development (Ibarra, 1993). Across these and other forms of formal and informal work relationships, individuals may develop the access and opportunity to advance their careers along traditional (i.e., hierarchical advancement within their organizations) or self-managing (i.e., increasingly challenging roles in different organizations) paths.

Sense Making

Organization members also depend on others to help them cognitively understand and make sense of events, experiences, and shifting organizational and environmental contexts. People routinely seek out others in the practice of socially constructing organizational life (Weick, 1995) and in the special practice of making sense of new situations (Louis, 1980), significant changes (Burkhardt, 1994), or organizational crises (Mitroff, 1993) that leave them uncertain about how to frame and integrate unfamiliar or upsetting information and experiences. It is likely that the more unfamiliar, upsetting, or dissonant the events and experiences, the more crucial it is for organization members to have access to significant relationships for cognitive sense-making purposes. Sense making occurs across various forms of hierarchical and nonhierarchical work relationships, and through various formal and informal communication mechanisms.

Provision of Meaning

People at work also enable others to experience a sense of meaning and purpose. This occurs in a myriad of ways. Organization members turn to others for validation in relation to the specific tasks they perform and the roles they assume. Such validation provides a sense of being valued (Kahn,

1993). Individuals also turn to others to help them construct or reinforce an identity that they find meaningful, through their sense of belonging to a group, organization, project team, or other social system that feels personally important (Albert & Whetten, 1985). Indeed, effective leaders—both formal and informal—are those who are able to frame stories that link individuals to some larger purpose, engaging them in situations, settings, and social systems through which their lives will be enlarged and made meaningful (Mitroff, 1993). Work relationships are instrumental in enabling organization members to satisfy their needs for relatedness and growth (Alderfer, 1972), to join some larger "project," in concert with others, that provides the sense that one's life has meaning.

Personal Support

Work relationships are also a valuable source of personal support. Organization members give and receive help with potential and real sources of stress at work or elsewhere (Cordes & Doughtery, 1993), situations that trigger anxiety and uncertainty (Frost, 2002), and emotionally difficult or complicated tasks (Kahn, 1993). At such times, people at work may use work relationships as secure bases, places to which to return for reflection, caregiving, and compassion (Kahn, 2001). Personal support occurs in the context of various types of relationships, which include coaching and mentoring, peer, hierarchical, and group (cf. Hall & Kahn, 2002). Each type of relationship has the potential to provide meaningful personal support for individuals, which may be defined along a continuum ranging from concrete help with specific tasks to deeply engaged emotional support. Work relationships are the primary vehicle by which most support along this continuum is delivered.

Together, these five dimensions cover the spectrum of how relationships can be meaningful for people and help them feel connected, in different ways, to others at work. Work relationships serve other purposes for the organizations themselves, of course, such as coordination and control. However, I am interested here in developing the idea that work relationships are at the core of people's lived experiences of their work lives. The five dimensions described here are key to enabling people to be and to feel meaningfully connected to others in the context of work relationships that can meet people's various instrumental, expressive, cognitive, identity, growth, and relatedness needs.

RELATIONAL CONSTELLATIONS

The dimensions previously described may be understood as strands of positive relationships that have the potential to bind people to their work and their workplaces. To the extent that people have enough meaningful strands, or have strands that are thick and powerful and matter to them, they are more likely to feel personally engaged at work and attached to their workplace. I consider the sum total of such strands as the constellations of people's work relationships. A *relational constellation* is the entire set of relations that organization members draw on to meet their various needs. These constellations may assume different forms. They may be more or less effective in meeting people's needs. They may change as people move in and out of organizations or as people's needs change over time.

Relational constellations thus offer a particular avenue for exploring the positive nature of work relationships. Research and theory about job turnover, dissatisfaction, and lack of job commitment focus on workers' alienation. A focus on relational constellations and their impact on workers' personal engagement, on the other hand, is anchored in a concern for authenticity at work. It examines positive connections among individuals in organizational life as a fundamental source of people's attachments to work and their bringing forth their authentic selves in doing their work. They do this in the context of creating different relational constellations.

Antecedents

Relational constellations are created at the intersection of circumstance, opportunity, chance, and individual agency. There are, of course, situational constraints that shape people's relational constellations. Particular industries or organizations may attract certain types of people who prefer some relational dimensions, such as task accomplishment, to others, such as personal support, which shapes in powerful ways the types of constellations that might be created in those organizations. Certain circumstances— a company is a startup, undergoing significant downsizing, or mired in union–management strife—will likely shape the nature of available relational dimensions for organizational members. The type of work or job, such as blue-collar or low status, or type of organizational culture, imposes certain norms or barriers on what sort of relations people are tacitly encouraged or discouraged to pursue. Such situational factors—in combination with elements of chance and circumstance, which bring certain people into one another's orbits—impose certain constraints, and make possible certain possibilities, that shape people's relational constellations.

There are also the individual factors. A certain amount of individual agency is involved in the creation of relational constellations. People seek out, as best they can, certain types of meaningful connections with others. By reason of personal comfort and familiarity, style, predilections, and needs, individuals strive to create relationships that emphasize some relational dimensions over others. They might seek relationships that are heavily weighted toward task accomplishment or career development, or they might seek relationships focused on personal support or sense making. Still others will look for relationships that enable them to have a sense of meaning and purpose. Indeed, it is likely that people have different relational needs; that is, drives to create certain kinds of relationships in which certain of the relational dimensions described earlier are more likely to emerge. It is likely as well that people order these relational needs, consciously and unconsciously, into hierarchies that organize the relational dimensions in terms of importance. As people make more time and space for certain kinds of relations over others, they are implicitly prioritizing some dimensions as more and less important, relative to one another.

Such relational hierarchies are likely to be relatively enduring but amenable to change. The enduring quality reflects the ways in which people are emotionally and cognitively wired, through a combination of personality traits and personal histories, to move toward certain types of relationships and away from others. These prioritizations certainly are related to individual differences in need achievement, emotional intelligence, and other more or less enduring personality characteristics that shape people's wishes for and abilities to create certain relationships at work. The changing quality of relational hierarchies reflects the ways in which people's needs might alter, either urgently (according to sudden situational demands) or more slowly (according to people's own adult development sequences or career development and stages). Relational hierarchies are also likely to be related to gender, race, age, and other identity-group characteristics (cf. Ely & Thomas, 2001) that shape and constrain how people decide what dimensions are meaningful to them personally in the context of their workplaces.

It is thus at the intersection of individual and contextual factors that relational constellations are formed. The ensuing constellations look different for different people. They will take different forms, depending on the situational opportunities that present themselves to people and the conscious and unconscious choices that they make in regard to those opportunities. There is also the matter of ability. People vary in terms of their abilities to take advantage of opportunities to form certain types of relationships. They are constrained by their own skills at seeking out others and creating relationships along the dimensions I described earlier. Some people will be relatively skilled at creating or being receptive to such relationships, and others less so. This cannot help but influence the extent to which people are able to create positive relationships.

Types of Relational Constellations

It is possible to identify certain overarching types of relational constellations that people create at work by focusing on two dimensions: first, the extent to which individuals' sets of relations serve the complete set of func-

	COMPLETE	INCOMPLETE
DENSE	*Networked*	*Bounded*
SPARSE	*Concentrated*	*Scarce*

FIG. 10.1. Types of relational constellations.

tions that are necessary for people, in terms of meeting their needs; and second, the extent to which their sets of relations depend on many or few individuals; that is, to which those relations are dense or sparse. Four types of constellations take shape from these two dimensions, as pictured in Figure 10.1 and described next. These types reveal how the meeting (or not) of people's relational needs in certain ways creates or inhibits their experiences of positive relationships at work.

Concentrated Constellations.   A few key people serving individuals' relational needs define concentrated constellations. Individuals who create such constellations invest much in a few people and rely on them a great deal. Those few people more or less completely serve the individual's relational needs, along the dimensions that they seek and find important. The individual might turn to a senior figure in the organization to help with task accomplishment, career development, and sense making. He or she might turn to another colleague for provision of meaning and personal support. Or he or she might not seek out personal support because he or she does not experience a need for it or because he or she realizes that, for any number of contextual reasons, that need is unlikely to be met. In these constellations, however, the overall experience is positive, as the relational dimensions that are important to people are present, located in a few key people.

Networked Constellations.   Networked constellations offer the foundation for positive relationships as well. These constellations are marked by the presence of many people who may be relied on to offer the range of meaningful connections to a specific individual. By dint of situational and individual factors, the individual is able to look to an array of (rather than simply a few) others to meet his or her relational needs. He or she looks to some people for personal support, others for career development, and still others for task accomplishment or sense making or provision of meaning, to the extent that he or she values those dimensions. The ensuring network of relationships is strong, in the sense that it possesses the capability of providing for relational needs and positive relationships.

Bounded Constellations.   Bounded constellations are marked by a similarly large array of relationships, yet they prove less satisfying as sources of positive relationships. The individual's relational needs are incompletely met in spite of a relatively dense network on which to draw. The individual has many people on whom to depend for task accomplishment, for example—there are many colleagues who can help get a project going—but no one in the organization who can provide the type of personal support he or she desires. Or the individual has both formal and informal mentors who provide career development advice and support but no one who, because of his or her unique specialty, can provide help with task accomplishment. The network of relationships is large, but its ultimate effectiveness, relative to what the individual needs and desires, is limited. The intersection of opportunity and individual predilection and skills is overly bounded, and ultimately dissatisfying.

Scarce Constellations.   Scarce constellations are marked by few possible relationships that can only partly provide meaningful connections and meet an individual's relational needs. The individual relies on only a relatively few people to meet such needs and, as in bounded constellations, those needs remain largely unmet. For various reasons, the individual draws on a relatively circumscribed circle of others, much as in concentrated constellations—with the important difference that, in this case, those few others are inadequate. A worker focuses a great deal of energy into his or her relationship with a supervisor, who is ineffective at providing help with task accomplishment, career development, or personal support, all of which happen to be important to that worker. In such cases, the relational network is both small and ineffective.

These four types of relational constellations are the result partly of what sorts of relationships are available to people, and of the choices that those people make to reach out or be receptive to others at work in various ways and toward various ends. These choices may be conscious, as people think carefully about what they need from others at work. They may also be unconscious, as people instinctively move toward or away from certain types of relationships that make them feel comfortable or uncomfortable. The sum total of these choices leads people to create or shy away from sets of relations that have quite real consequences for both the ways in which they personally engage in (or disengage from) their work, and for the attachments that they form with others and with their organizations more generally.

The Nature of Organizational Attachment

I suggested earlier that relational constellations help shape the extent to which individuals personally engage in their work (Kahn, 1992). A set of positive relationships helps create the conditions under which individuals wish to move toward one another at work, and not incidentally, toward a more engaging way of being at work. I would like to press further on this idea by suggesting that when individuals are embedded in relational constellations that they experience as positive, they are more likely to attach themselves to others at work, and more generally, to their organizations as well.

The literature on organizational attachment focuses on the factors that shape when and why people leave their organizations or remain within them (see Mitchell, Holtom, Lee, Sablynski, & Erez, 2001). Researchers examine a variety of factors, including attitudes such as job satisfaction and commitment (Allen & Meyer, 1996), nonwork factors such as family and hobbies (Cohen, 1995), and job embeddedness (Mitchell et al., 2001). Work relationships occasionally show up in some of these studies as one factor among others that contribute to people's attitudes and, combined with job alternatives, shape turnover. The organizational attachment literature thus focuses on the literal meaning of attachment (i.e., whether someone works for an organization) rather than its psychological meaning (i.e., the extent to which someone feels personally connected to others).

I suggest here that the two meanings can be joined. Psychological attachments can influence literal attachments. People create psychological attachments in the context of relations with one another; their experiences of being supported, mentored, helped, developed, and invested in by others are what enable them to feel real attachments, or the lack thereof. Those feelings for a certain set of colleagues in an organization may then be generalized to the organization more generally, to the point that it affects the person's literal attachment. This formulation places relational constellation at the center of the person's lived experience of organizational life (see also Higgins, chap. 11, this volume; Kram, 1985). It suggests that those constellations help mediate people's movements toward or away not simply from one another, but toward or away from the organization itself. It is in the context of both—sets of relationships, and the organizations that contain them—that people attach, in one fashion or another, and strike various stances of engagement and disengagement.

Different types of constellations may thus help create the conditions for people's attachments to work. The building blocks for these categories are the dimensions, described earlier, of what I have called meaningful connections. These dimensions may be arrayed along a continuum stretching from those requiring less of people's deeper, emotional selves (e.g., task accomplishment) to those requiring more (e.g., personal support). People whose relational constellations consist largely of the former are likely to be less psychologically attached to others at work than those whose constellations consist largely of the latter. These differences are likely to show up as well in people's literal attachments to their organizations. When people invest their selves more heavily (in terms of depth and quantity) in relationships within, rather than outside, their organizations, they are more likely to remain attached to those organizations.

This notion assumes that people are placing bets, in one fashion or another, on where their attachments will meet with the most payoffs, in terms of crafting work lives that fit with their instrumental and expressive needs. It also assumes that people will seek to protect themselves from being hurt; that is, they will attach themselves more deeply to places (and relationships) in which they believe that they will flourish. One way to frame the issue of dispersion and concentration of people's relationships is to see where people are placing bets, as indicated by the types of constellations that they seek to create. People who concentrate the bulk of their relational needs on a few people, for example, might be signaling that they are more portable (i.e., less attached, more self-protective) than those who have more widely dispersed relationships across organizations; the latter have created "webs" spread out through an organization that help them "stick" to an organization, rather than those that are highly concentrated on just a few people. These are signals of a sort about the types of attachments that people want or are able to construct.

Such signals must, of course, be interpreted carefully. The work relationships in which people are embedded are shaped not simply by their wishes, desires, and skills, but also by the opportunities that are available to them. People are, at best, cocreators of their relationships with others. They seek out and are more receptive to some kinds of relationships than others, of course, and have different skills that enable them to be more successful in some efforts. Yet such success also has much to do with contextual factors, both macro (industry, organizational culture, nature of the job, types of workers hired) and micro (availability of suitable others, group composition and dynamics, others' willingness and abilities to cocreate useful relationships). The attachments that people work are due as much to these vagaries as they are to people's conscious and unconscious intentions.

IMPLICATIONS FOR POSITIVE RELATIONSHIPS AT WORK

I have used two relatively implicit definitions of positive work relationships throughout this chapter. One definition focuses on the particular ways in which people can meet others' relational needs. These are captured by the five dimensions of meaningful connections described earlier: People may be useful to one another in the service of task accomplishment, career development, sense making, provision of meaning, and personal support. These are positive dimensions. They enable people to feel competent and challenged. They enable people to understand more clearly what they are doing, and why. They enable people to feel supported and valued. The second definition focuses on how relationships influence the individual's ability to be authentic at work. I have suggested that positive relationships are those that enable people to personally engage in their work.

Different people will select differently from these definitions when framing for themselves the extent to which their work relationships are positive or not. They will select based on their own needs and predilections, the extent to which they quite naturally move toward instrumental or authentic work relationships. They will select on the basis of where they are in their own adult development and their careers. Hierarchy, role, and tenure will matter as well, in terms of the various presses they place on people to be instrumental or, conversely, the relative degrees of safety they offer for people to be more or less authentic. People will also frame their relations according to their identities; the more central work is to those identities, the more likely they will seek authenticity in the context of their work and work relationships. They will also select based on their own history of personal experiences, and the extent to which they have found it useful or rewarding to emphasize one or more relational needs, or authenticity more generally, in the context of creating positive work relationships.

From this perspective, positive relationships at work are a function of the choices that people are making, within the opportunities and contexts made available to them, to invest themselves in certain types of relations, toward certain ends that matter to them individually. We often frame positive relationships in terms of the characteristics and quality of interactions: They are marked by trust and integrity, for example, or intimacy and caring. This is certainly true for positive work relationships as well. Yet the work context also implies two dimensions that must be taken into account when conceptualizing the positive nature of relationships. First, there is always some element of instrumentality that is taken into account when people are making choices, conscious and otherwise, about the nature and quality of the relationships they construct at work. Organizations are not families, as much as their leaders might like to have themselves and others believe that they are, and work relationships are by definition conditional rather than unconditional. Second, positive relationships at work occur amidst constellations drawn from group and organizational settings. Individuals draw closer to some people, to serve some relational functions, and away from others, based on available populations.

These dimensions mean that positive work relationships are not simply a matter of people drifting toward one another as they sense possibilities for creating trusting, compassionate, and helping relationships. Although this process does occur, positive work relationships are more complicated. As noted earlier, people at work are placing bets, in terms of the relationships in which they invest and those in which they do not. They perform a certain calculus, based on various weightings: which dimensions do they care about or need to have served in the context of work relationships, weighted according to both personal preferences and contextual concerns and calculated in terms of probabilities shaped by what is available in their groups and organizations. Such calculations lead people toward and away from certain relationships and behaviors. These calculations are constantly performed, as relationships and conditions and people change, and individuals struggle to determine if they are getting "enough," however they define that threshold. Each set of calculations leads to another, and another, ad infinitum, propelling cycles of positive relationships (or not) and personal engagements (or not).

A Research Agenda

This formulation suggests a particular research agenda. First, we need to understand more precisely how, when, and why people create certain constellations of relationships at work, given the constraints and opportunities of their situational contexts. The five dimensions described earlier in this chapter offer a framework for this analysis. Using that framework, we can look closely at what types of constellations people create, both in terms of which relational needs people seek to meet and where they seek to do so. This research can also focus on the processes by which people move toward or away from certain relationships and functions—the process by which they invest in or divest from certain relationships, placing certain kinds of bets and hoping for certain kinds of payoffs. It can also focus on the various independent factors (e.g., gender, race, career stage, tenure, hierarchical role, organizational group, industry) that shape those processes.

Second, we need to trace the effects of the choices that people are making and the resulting relationships that they create. I have suggested in this chapter that the relationships and constellations that people construct have real implications for their engagements at work, and the attachments they experience to their organizations. At the specific level, people will have various relational needs met, or not, by the relationships they create: They will feel more or less supported, helped with tasks, and the like, with real implications for how much they personally engage at work. At the general level, they will feel more or less attached to their groups and organizations, held there by the constellations that they have created at work. This is an empirical question worth exploring. So, too, is the nature of the impact on, and from, the work groups and communities that give rise to certain types of relationships and constellations. The causality likely goes both ways, between the relations that people create and the nature of the contexts in which they do so, and research can indicate how those ways occur.

Third, we need to understand more clearly how people come to define their relationships at work as positive. Here, too, there are both specific and general levels to consider. At the specific level, there is the question of how people define certain relationships, which serve certain relational needs, as positive. Presumably, this has to do with the degree to which those needs are met. At the general level, there is the question of how people define the sum total of the relationships they have constructed—the constellations—as positive. I have suggested here that certain constellations (i.e., concentrated and networked) are positive, in the sense that they leave people feeling meaningfully connected to either many or a few others in ways that satisfy their more important relational needs. This is also an empirical question, worth testing. At both the specific and general levels, of course, there is much to learn empirically, such as whether there are certain tipping points that lead people toward or away from assessing relationships and constellations as positive.

Finally, there is the need for research related to the cycles that people inevitably fall into, for good or bad, in their work relationships. People create certain relationships by moving toward or away from others, and those relationships vary in terms of how positive they are. Over time, with repeated interactions, those relationships often become locked into certain patterns; they create a certain momentum, based on self-fulfilling prophecies, as people relate with one another that bring about predictable results. People thus create relationship cycles that can spin in positive or negative directions. For our purposes, there are two particularly interesting research questions: how can cycles of positive, functional relationships sustain their momentum, and conversely, how can cycles of negative, dysfunctional relationships be interrupted?

CONCLUSION

The overarching goal of the framework and research agenda presented in this chapter is to take seriously the centrality of work relationships in people's experiences of their work lives. These relationships—taken individually, and in terms of the constellations that people create—are key determinants of their attachments to their organizations. They are significant to their positive experiences of their work lives. In this context, people's relationships become the figure, not simply the background, of their work experiences and behaviors, and deserve to be examined as such.

REFERENCES

Albert, S., & Whetten, D. A. (1985). Organizational identity. In L. L. Cummings & B. M. Shaw (Eds.), *Research in organizational behavior* (Vol. 7, pp. 263–295).

Alderfer, C. P. (1972). *Existence, relatedness, and growth: Human needs in organizational settings.* New York: The Free Press.

Allen, N. J. & Meyer, J. P. (1996). Affective, continuance, and normative commitment to the organization: An examination of construct validity. *Journal of Vocational Behavior, 49,* 252–276.

Alper, S., Tjosvold, D., & Law, K. S. (1998). Interdependence and controversy in group decision making: Antecedents to effective self-managing teams. *Organizational Behavior and Human Decision Processes, 74,* 33–52.

Ancona, D., & Caldwell, D. (1992). Bridging the boundary: External activity in performance in organizational teams. *Administrative Science Quarterly, 37,* 634–665.

Baldwin, T. T., Bedell, M. D., & Johnson, J. L. (1997). The social fabric of a team-based MBA program: Network effects on student satisfaction and performance. *Academy of Management Journal, 6,* 1369–1397.

Bass, B. M. (1981). *Stodgill's handbook of leadership* (2nd ed.). New York: The Free Press.

Brass, D. J. (1984). Being in the right place: A structural analysis of individual influence in an organization. *Administrative Science Quarterly, 29,* 518–539.

Brass, D. J., & Burkhardt, M. E. (1992). Centrality and power in organizations. In N. Nohria & R. Eccles (Eds.), *Networks and organizations: Structure, form, and action* (pp. 191–215). Boston: Harvard Business School Press.

Brass, D. J., & Burkhardt, M. E. (1993). Potential power and power use: An investigation of structure and behavior. *Academy of Management Journal, 36*(3), 441–470.

Brass, D. J., Butterfield, K. D., & Skaggs, B. C. (1998). Relationships and unethical behavior: A social network perspective. *Academy of Management Review, 23,* 14–31.

Burkhardt, M. E. (1994). Social interaction effects following a technological change: A longitudinal investigation. *Academy of Management Journal, 37,* 869–898.

Burt, R.S. (1992). *Structural holes: The social structure of competition.* Cambridge, MA: Harvard University Press.

Cohen, A. (1995). An examination of the relationships between work commitment and nonwork domains. *Human Relations, 48,* 239–263.

Cohen, S., & Wills, T. A. (1985). Stress, social support, and the buffering hypothesis. *Psychological Bulletin, 98,* 310–357.

Cordes, C., & Doughtery, T. W. (1993). A review and an integration of research on job burnout. *Academy of Management Review, 18,* 621–657.

Ely, R. J., & Thomas, D. A. (2001). Cultural diversity at work: The moderating effects of work group perspectives on diversity. *Administrative Science Quarterly, 46,* 229–273.

Evered, R., & Selman, J. (1990). Coaching and the art of management. *Organizational Dynamics, 18*(2), 16–32.

Frost, P. (2002). *Toxic emotions at work.* Cambridge, MA: Harvard Business School Press.

Gersick, C., Bartunek, J., & Dutton, J. (2000). Learning from academe: The importance of relationships in professional life. *Academy of Management Journal, 43*(6), 1026–1045.

Granovetter, M. (1973). The strength of weak ties. *American Journal of Sociology, 78,* 1360–1380.

Hackman, J. R. (1987). The design of work teams. In J. Lorsch (Ed.), *Handbook of organizational behavior* (pp. 190–222). Englewood Cliffs, NJ: Prentice-Hall.

Hall, D. T. (1996). *The career is dead.* San Francisco: Jossey-Bass.

Hall, D. T., & Kahn, W. A. (2002) Developmental relationships at work: A learning perspective. In C. Cooper (Ed.), *The world of work* (pp. 49–74). Oxford, England: Blackwell.

Heaney, C. A., House, J. S., Israel, B. A., & Mero, R. P. (1995). The relationship of organizational and social coping resources to employee coping behavior: A longitudinal analysis. *Work and Stress, 9,* 416–431.

Hom, P. W., & Griffeth, R. W. (1995). *Employee turnover.* Cincinnati, OH: South/Western.

Ibarra, H. (1992). Homophily and differential returns: Sex differences in network structure and access in an advertising firm. *Administrative Science Quarterly, 37,* 422–447.

Ibarra, H. (1993). Personal networks of women and minorities in management: A conceptual framework. *Academy of Management Review, 18,* 56–87.

Josselson, R. (1996). *The space between us.* San Francisco: Jossey-Bass.

Kahn, W. A. (1992). To be fully there: Psychological presence at work. *Human Relations, 45,* 321–349.

Kahn, W. A. (1993). Caring for the caregivers: Patterns of organizational caregiving. *Administrative Science Quarterly, 38,* 539–563.

Kahn, W. A. (1998) Relational systems at work. *Research in Organizational Behavior, 20,* 39–76.

Kahn, W. A. (2001) Holding environments at work. *Journal of Applied Behavioral Science, 37,* 260–279.

Kahn, W. A. (2005). *Holding fast: The struggle to create resilient caregiving organizations.* London: Brunner-Routledge.

Kanov, J., Maitlis, S., Worline, M., Dutton, J., Frost, P., & Lilius, J. (2004). Compassion in organizational life. *American Behavioral Science, 47,* 808–827.

Kilduff, M., & Krackhardt, D. (1994). Bringing the individual back in: A structural analysis of the internal market for reputation in organizations. *Academy of Management Journal, 37,* 87–108.

Konovsky, M. A., & Pugh, S. D. (1994). Citizenship behavior and social exchange. *Academy of Management Journal, 37,* 656–669.

Krackhardt, D., & Porter, L. W. (1986). The snowball effect: Turnover embedded in communication networks. *Journal of Applied Psychology, 71,* 50–55.

Kram, K. E. (1985) *Mentoring at work.* Glenview, IL: Scott, Foresman.

Lawler, E. J., & Yoon, J. (1998) Network structure and emotion in exchange relationships. *American Sociological Review, 63,* 871–894.

Lincoln, J. R., & Miller, J. (1979). Work and friendship ties in organizations: A comparative analysis of relational networks. *Administrative Science Quarterly, 24,* 181–199.

Locke, E. A. (2000). Motivation, cognition and action: An analysis of studies of task goals and knowledge. *Applied Psychology, 49,* 408–430.

Louis, M. R. (1980). Surprise and sensemaking: What newcomers experience when entering unfamiliar organizational settings. *Administrative Science Quarterly, 25,* 226–251.

Miller, J. B. (1987). *Toward a new psychology of women.* Boston: Beacon.

Mitchell, T. R., Holtom, B. C., Lee, T. W., Sablynski, C. J., & Erez, M. (2001). Why people stay: Using job embeddedness to predict voluntary turnover. *Academy of Management Journal, 44,* 1102–1121.

Mitroff, I. (1993). *Crisis leadership.* New York: Wiley.

Podolny, J., & Barron, J. (1997). Relationships and resources: Social networks and mobility in the workplace. *American Sociological Review, 62,* 673–693.

Ragins, B. R. (1994). Gender differences in expected outcomes of mentoring relationships. *Academy of Management Journal, 37,* 957–971.

Rogers, C. R. (1958). The characteristics of a helping relationship. *Personnel and Guidance Journal, 37,* 6–16.

Smith, K. K., & Berg, D. N. (1987). *Paradoxes of group life.* San Francisco: Jossey-Bass.

Somers, M. R. (1994). The narrative constitution of identity: A relational and network approach. *Theory and Society, 23,* 605–949.

Sparrowe, R. T., & Liden, R. C. (1997). Process and structure in leader–member exchange. *Academy of Management Review, 22,* 522–552.

Stevenson, W. B., & Gilly, M. (1993). Problem-solving networks in organizations: Intentional design and emergent structure. *Social Networks, 22,* 92–113.

Stevenson, W. B., & Greenberg, D. (2000). Agency and social networks: Strategies of action in a social structure of position, opposition and opportunity. *Administrative Science Quarterly, 45,* 651–678.

Thomas, D. A. (1993). The dynamics of managing racial diversity in developmental relationships. *Administrative Science Quarterly, 38,* 169–194.

Tsai, W., & Ghoshal, S. (1998). Social capital and value creation: The role of intrafirm networks. *Academy of Management Journal, 41,* 464–476.

Van Maanen, J., & Schein, E. H. (1979). Toward a theory of organizational socialization. In B. Staw (Ed.), *Research in organizational behavior* (Vol. 1, pp. 209–264). Greenwich, CT: JAI.

Weick, K. (1995). *Sensemaking in organizations.* Thousand Oaks, CA: Sage.

Wenger, E. (1998). *Communities of practice: Learning, meaning and identity.* Cambridge, England: Cambridge University Press.

11

A Contingency Perspective on Developmental Networks

Monica Higgins

Recently, organizational scholars engaged in positive organizational research have suggested that high-quality connections (HQCs) at work are vital both to individuals and organizations (Dutton & Heaphy, 2003). Dutton and Heaphy suggested that high-quality connections are those that may be characterized as life-giving, as opposed to life-depleting, much as blood vessels connect vital organs within the human body. To the extent that connections are high quality, as opposed to low quality, they have the capacity to yield positive outcomes for individuals, such as resourcefulness (Quinn & Dutton, 2005) and health and well-being (e.g., Cohen, 2001), as well as positive outcomes for organizations, such as organizational learning and resilience (Weick, Sutcliffe, & Obstfeld, 1999). Still, as Dutton and Heaphy (2003) noted, HQCs may, either directly or indirectly, yield negative consequences.

Building on this research on HQCs, this chapter suggests that individuals engage in many different kinds of HQCs at work and focuses in particular on one important and well-researched kind of HQC, that of a developmental relationship. Similar to Dutton and Heaphy (2003), this chapter focuses on relationships that are life-giving, particularly from the perspective of the protégé. Further, and picking up on Dutton and Heaphy's final note on the potential negative effects of HQCs, this chapter does not assume that developmental relationships, although high quality, necessarily or always yield positive outcomes. Rather, the assumption is that developmental relationships may be more or less "positive," depending on the needs of the protégé; it therefore adopts a contingency perspective throughout.

In particular, this chapter considers the match between the needs of a protégé and the structure and quality of his or her network of developmental relationships. As Ragins and Verbos (chap. 5, this volume) suggest, a need-based approach is consistent with much of the research on mentoring and may advance our understanding of positive relationships at work more generally. By drawing on previous research on mentoring and integrating that work with recent positive organizational scholarship, this chapter aims to lend insight into the conditions under which networks of high-quality relationships do indeed yield positive outcomes for individuals.

At the same time, by proposing a contingency perspective on developmental networks, this chapter also advances recent research on mentoring (e.g., Higgins & Kram, 2001). This chapter considers the extent to which the set of dyadic mentoring relationships is positive and thus focuses explicitly on an individual's developmental network, as opposed to any one particular mentoring relationship, which has been the tradition in much of the mentoring research. Therefore, much as Dutton and Heaphy's (2003) recent work on HQCs has suggested that there are multiple dimensions along which one could consider the quality of one's connections and much as Kahn (chap. 10, this volume) considers the multiple functions that positive work relationships serve, this chapter explores multiple dimensions of developmental networks. Although within developmental networks, certain relationships may be viewed as high-quality or even "positive," the extent to which a protégé's entire network of such relationships is ultimately positive will depend, I propose, on the needs of the protégé. This therefore shifts the level of analysis up from two-person relationships, as research on HQCs (Dutton & Heaphy, 2003), relational mentoring (Ragins & Verbos, chap. 5, this volume), and positive relationships at work (Kahn, chap. 10, this volume) have considered, to a different level of analysis—to the level of the network.

As a final introductory note, although this chapter does pursue this contingency perspective on developmental networks from the perspective of the protégé, consistent with much of the mentoring research, I do want to acknowledge that this is an admittedly one-sided perspective. To truly consider the power of such HQCs, one would want to also consider the impact on the developer as a result of his or her connection with a protégé or network of protégés. Suggestions for such research are provided at the end of this chapter.

TOWARD AN INTEGRATION
OF MENTORING RESEARCH

Before introducing a contingency perspective on developmental networks, it is important to consider the foundations of research on mentoring, how this research has shifted toward a developmental network perspective

(Higgins & Kram, 2001; Thomas & Higgins, 1996), and how this work fits into recent research on HQCs and positive organizational scholarship. From there, we will be well positioned to consider the extent to which an individual's entire developmental network, as opposed to single dyadic HQCs, is indeed positive for a protégé.

About two decades ago, organizational research on mentoring began to proliferate. This work focused almost exclusively on the specific, special kind of developmental relationship known as mentorship. Kram's (1985) seminal book, *Mentoring at Work*, is the most comprehensive account of the dynamics of mentoring relationships. In that book, Kram acknowledged that mentoring may come from many sources, and she suggested that people likely have more than one developmental relationship at any given time. However, most of the organizational research that has followed has focused primarily on traditional forms of mentoring relationships—that is, a single relationship with an individual who is hierarchically superior to and in the same organization as the protégé. Similarly, practitioners have instituted formal mentoring programs in organizations that encourage the development and cultivation of a single mentoring relationship, generally with a superior from within the same organization.

More recently, however, and due in part to the demise of the lifelong employment relationship and to a greater awareness of the importance of social networks in today's career environment, researchers and practitioners have begun to return to Kram's original assertion that individuals are likely to have multiple developmental relationships at any given point in time. Therefore, although some individuals may still rely primarily on one strong relationship with a primary mentor, it is more frequently the case that individuals derive developmental assistance from many people at any given time. These "developers" may include peers, subordinates, or superiors, and these relationships may extend beyond the protégé's employing organization (Higgins & Thomas, 2001; see also Ragins & Dutton, chap. 1, this volume, for a review).

This shift toward a developmental network perspective also reflects recent career research that has incorporated a relational approach to careers (Hall, 1996) and so, considers the larger social context in which an individual learns and develops personally and professionally. Thus, much of the research on this particular kind of HQC has been viewed through a learning lens, as opposed to other possible frames, such as exchange theory, proposed recently by positive organizational scholarship (see Dutton & Heaphy, 2003, for alternative frames).

The relational view builds on assumptions that ground the majority of human resources practices and self-assessment courses—specifically, the notion that increasing an individual's understanding of himself or herself can improve one's ability to learn from experience. Increasingly, practitioners and scholars alike have come to recognize that much of this learning through experience also entails learning through others (see Ragins & Verbos, chap. 5, this volume, on relational learning). Such a relational model is based on the idea that connection in meaningful relationships is essential to professional learning and development. This view breaks from more traditional career and adult development theories that often conceptualize development as a series of stages in which the individual progresses from dependency on others toward an increasingly independent and autonomous self.

Building on this relational view, this chapter considers how, depending on the nature of the career context and thus, the needs of the protégé, some developmental networks may be more or less beneficial than others. Whereas prior research has suggested that some kinds of HQCs are more likely to lead to certain kinds of career outcomes, here, the perspective is that there is no one single best way or best developmental network structure. Rather, the perspective taken here is that individuals need to consider their own developmental needs and aspirations as well as the professional context in which they are working or aspire to work to determine the effectiveness of their developmental networks.

From this vantage point, although developmental networks may be comprised of distinct and uniquely positive relationships, the extent to which the overall structure and quality of that set of relationships turns out to be positive for the protégé may depend on a variety of conditions. This view departs from some social networks research that has proffered a particular position regarding desirable network structures. For example, research on social networks has often advocated network structures that are rich in structural holes and so, have connections to people who are otherwise disconnected from one another (see, e.g., Burt, 1992). Here, no one structural position or recommendation for developmental networks is advanced.

RESEARCH FOUNDATIONS OF MENTORING AND DEVELOPMENTAL NETWORKS

With decades of mentoring research now complete, there are some compelling reasons to believe that mentoring relationships are indeed one kind of HQC at work. That is, they are "life-giving" (Dutton & Heaphy, 2003) and have demonstrated the capacity for positive outcomes. Dyadic or two-person mentoring relationships have been associated with the following hard career benefits to protégés: greater career advancement (Kram, 1985; Phillips-Jones, 1982), greater career progress (Zey, 1984), and higher rates of promotion and total compensation (Whitely, Dougherty, & Dreher, 1991). In addition, there is substantial research that points to softer benefits of mentoring relationships, including the following: greater career satisfaction (Fagenson, 1989; Riley & Wrench, 1985; Roche, 1979) and clarity of professional identity and sense of competence (Kram, 1985).

In general, these findings come from research on intraorganizational mentoring and from studies of informal developmental relationships, as opposed to mentoring relationships that emerge through formal mentoring programs. Indeed, mentoring research has found that informal mentoring relationships are generally more effective than formal mentoring relationships (Chao, Walz & Gardner, 1992). In some contrast to this work, research on developmental networks has remained relatively agnostic as to how the relationships begin and so, may include relationships that are formal, informal or a mix of the two (Higgins & Kram, 2001; see also Ragins & Verbos, chap. 5, this volume).

One of the assumptions underlying much of the traditional research on mentoring is that the effectiveness of these positive relationships—that is, the extent to which the relationship that a protégé names is indeed "positive"—depends on the amount and kind of assistance provided. Beginning with Kram's (1985) original work, scholars have examined the amount and kinds of career support (e.g., exposure and visibility) and the kinds of psychosocial support (e.g., friendship and caring beyond the boundaries of work) that mentoring relationships provide. In contrast, the developmental network view offered here does not assume that more help is better (or that larger networks are better). Rather, the assumption here is that a collection of developmental relationships is likely differentially effective and depends on the specific career goals and challenges of the protégé. Thus, the true helpfulness or positive nature of the help that emerges from an entire network will depend, as we explore, on the needs of the protégé, including the nature of the career context in which the protégé works.

For example, in a knowledge-based economy in which information about customer needs and marketplace dynamics rests with front-line workers, more senior managers—those who are typically seen as the "mentors"—may be in need of developmental assistance as well. Further, changes in the career environment have led to an increase in the diversity in relationships that provide developmental support. For example, given the advancement of women and minorities in organizations, there is greater variance in the demographics of the composition of the workforce, which affects the breadth and diversity of resources available and also needed for support. Also, changes in the nature of work, including the need to work across divisions or geographical boundaries, has affected the sources of support to which people need to turn to solve complex career and work-related challenges (for a review of such changes, see Higgins & Kram, 2001).

Scholars also point out that changes in the current career environment have led to increased variation in the strength of ties that can provide such support, because people are moving across organizations more and more (Kram & Hall, 1996). Such trends reflect increasing globalization of businesses, for example, as well as the changing nature of the psychological employment contract (Rousseau, 1995). Whereas career paths were once relatively predictable and largely associated with a single organization, the "organization man" era has now passed. Individuals are not only more responsible for their own career development, they are also more likely to change organizations, making the sources of developmental assistance less relationally stable over time (Cummings & Higgins, 2006). The developmental network perspective incorporates this broader conceptualization of mentoring; it is a perspective that recognizes that traditional notions of mentoring may be insufficient in understanding the needs of the protégé operating in today's career environment.

In sum, past and present conceptualizations of mentoring can thus be contrasted in the following manner: From the traditional mentoring perspective, developmental relationships are viewed as hierarchical, single and dyadic (two-person) in nature, and intraorganizational. From the developmental network perspective, relationships that provide developmental support can occur at multiple levels in an organization, can be networked, and may extend beyond the boundaries of any one particular work organization (Higgins & Kram, 2001; see also de Janasz, Sullivan, & Whiting, 2003). This shift also reflects the growing recognition that multiple forms of positive relationships at work influence our careers and work lives and that exploring these groups, constellations, or networks of such connections can inform our understanding of how people think, feel, and behave at work (Kahn, chap. 10, this volume).

BOUNDARIES AND TERMINOLOGY

With this background on mentoring and developmental networks in mind, we can now turn to integrating this work into the emerging research on positive organizational scholarship. To do so, it is important to clarify several boundary conditions. First, at the most fundamental level, because developmental relationships do entail social interactions and so create mutual awareness and a "space between" (Berscheid & Lopes, 1997; Josselson, 1996), whether or not these are particularly intimate relationships (Dutton & Heaphy, 2003), they are indeed connections. Although developmental relationships are generally likely enduring as opposed to fleeting connections, the extent of communication may vary substantially from relationship to relationship, as discussed later.

Second, these are HQCs from the perspective of the protégé; they are people that the protégé names as having taken (sometime over the past year) an active interest and action to advance that individual's career by assisting with his or her personal and professional development (Higgins & Thomas, 2001; Thomas & Higgins, 1996). In this way, consistent with Dutton and Heaphy (2003), they are "life-giving" because their very existence, in the eye of the protégé, hinges on the transfer of some kind of developmental assistance. Developmental relationships also share the three core features of HQCs, as defined by Dutton and Heaphy (2003): (a) they have higher "emotional carrying capacity" than other kinds of passing or fleeting professional connections; (b) they have high "tensility" because they maintain strength, flexibility, and adaptability to accommodate a protégé; and (c) they have a "degree of connectivity" that is generative in kind—opening rather than closing options for a protégé.

Third, it is important to distinguish between the types of relationships that make up an individual's developmental network. In particular, the quality of developmental relationships may vary such that not all developers are best understood as true mentors. In line with this broader focus, researchers have begun to consider multiple sources of developmental assistance, however they are manifested in an individual's life, rather than focus exclusively on the special and intense kind of developmental relationship that is a "mentor." Employing one of the distinctions suggested by Dutton and Heaphy (2003), for example, only relationships that have the subjective experience of felt mutuality would mark this particular and true mentor kind of HQC. Therefore, within an individual's developmental network, he or she may have a host of different kinds of developmental relationships.

Here, I focus on the amount and kind of support provided as an indicator of developmental relationship type. This perspective builds directly on prior mentoring research and has been used to indicate the quality of different kinds of relationships (Higgins & Thomas, 2001; see also Dutton & Heaphy, 2003, for a review of conceptualizations of relationship quality).

Drawing on the foundational mentoring research of Kram (1985), developmental assistance has been found to take on one of two major forms: (a) the form of career assistance (advocacy, coaching, providing exposure and visibility, protection from potentially damaging political situations, and challenging professional opportunities), and (b) the form of psychosocial assistance (role modeling, counseling, acceptance and confirmation, and friendship; Kram, 1985; Thomas, 1993). If we consider different amounts of these two kinds of help, it is possible to differentiate between true mentors (those who provide high amounts of both career and psychosocial assistance), sponsors (those who provide high amounts of career but low amounts of psychosocial assistance), friends (those who provide high amounts of psychosocial but low amounts of career assistance), and allies (those who provide low amounts of each) as shown in Fig. 11.1. These are new terms in the mentoring literature and

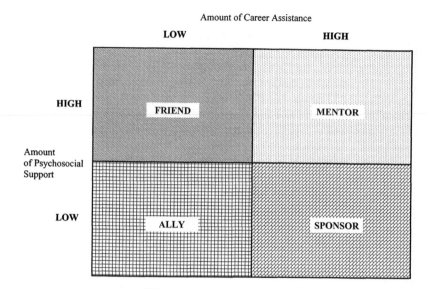

FIG. 11.1. Types of developers.

build on the distinction that Thomas and Kram (1988) made between a true mentor and a sponsor. These terms may be a useful way to classify different kinds of high-quality relationships and, specifically, different kinds of developers in one's developmental network.

It is important to note that by distinguishing between different amounts of support provided and hence, different kinds of developmental relationships, I am not suggesting that one kind of relationship is necessarily more "positive" than another—for example, that a mentor is necessarily better or more positive than a sponsor. Again, following a contingency model, such a determination could only come from understanding the particular needs of the protégé. To give a concrete example, if a protégé had a strong preference for bifurcating his or her discussions at work such that topics concerning home and his or her private life were truly preferred to remain off-limits, then receiving caring and sharing beyond the requirements of work and career from a developer might be quite off-putting to that protégé. As a result, efforts to try and turn that protégé's sponsor into a mentor would not necessarily be more positive for that individual. Put differently, more developmental assistance would not necessarily make that helping relationship more helpful. Similarly, an ally who provides low amounts of career and psychosocial support may be just the right kind of developer for an individual who occasionally needs some assistance but who, given his or her work demands, preferences, or life situation, may recoil from constant or high amounts of developmental support. In that particular case, turning an ally into a mentor would not be more positive for the protégé.

By extension, a network that is composed of all mentors, who provide high amounts of both career and psychosocial support, is not necessarily better or more positive than a network that has a variety of developers in it. As we consider, different protégé needs suggest different network structures—both in terms of the content and level of help provided as well as the social structure of these developmental networks.

First, however, let us consider what we mean by the term *developmental network* and how it differs from any set of HQCs at work. This raises a fourth set of boundary conditions—those that center around the entire network, as opposed to particular kinds of dyadic connections. Here, because we are interested in the protégé's view of who provides developmental assistance, this is a content-based network where the content consists of the developmental support that flows across the ties. These are not HQCs in general, but rather, those that provide a particular kind of support; other kinds of connections may be identified by other kinds of tie content or functions served, as Kahn (chap. 10, this volume) suggests. Further, unlike other more general kinds of social networks, a developmental network does not consist of anyone and everyone that a focal person communicates with. Because ego (the protégé) is the one naming the developmental relationships that constitute the developmental network (Higgins & Kram, 2001), in social network terms a developmental network would be considered an egocentric network.

Therefore, and consistent with research on HQCs (e.g., Heaphy & Dutton, 2003), what is important here is the subjective experience of the protégé—what the individual feels he or she is receiving in terms of developmental assistance rather than what a researcher or some other party may believe is "actually" being provided. This approach is also aligned with how mentoring scholars such as Kram (1985) have conceptualized mentoring relationships and with how informal mentoring relationships have been assessed in empirical research on mentoring and developmental networks (Ragins & Cotton, 1999).

The analogy of a personal board of directors may be useful here. You choose your own board of directors; you are the chairperson, of sorts. A proactive orientation provides individuals with the sense that they are active participants in the cultivation of developmental relationships and is consistent with current career theory and practice that has called for a more "protean" or self-authoring perspective to career development (Hall & Associates, 1996).

Regarding terminology, there are also many different ways to characterize a developmental network and the relationships that comprise it. The term *constellation* was Kram's (1985) original term and referred to the nexus of relationships that people rely on for support in their careers. In this chapter, the term *developmental network* rather than constellation or personal board of directors is used because the words *developmental* and *network* are useful to combine and consider. *Developmental* refers to the content of the support provided and reflects the learning lens adopted for studying these kinds of high-quality relationships (e.g., Fletcher, 1996). *Network* refers to the fact that this is not simply a cluster of individuals but rather a group of dyadic developmental relationships that may be tied to one another, like any other network.

Finally, in addition to the content of help that flows across the ties, it is important to consider the structure of the developmental network. Together, these two dimensions, network content and network structure may be useful in understanding when developmental networks yield positive outcomes for protégés.

One useful way to think about developmental network structure is to consider network diversity—that is, the extent to which the information provided by those in one's network is similar or redundant (Burt, 1992; Granovetter, 1973). One way to operationalize network diversity is in terms of the range or number of different social arenas from which these high-quality relationships come. Higher range developmental networks are ones that include diverse ties such as a combination of familial, community-based, and professional ties. As prior research shows, women tend to have more highly differentiated networks in general (Ibarra, 1992), and thus, may have higher ranging developmental networks.

A second way to operationalize network diversity is in terms of the density of a network—that is, how connected the developers are to one another. High-density developmental networks are comprised of people who tend to know one another and so provide similar kinds of information, whereas low-density developmental networks tend to be comprised of distinct dyadic (yet not highly networked or interconnected) ties; low-density developmental networks are more diverse. The underlying mechanisms are the same, irrespective of how one conceptualizes network diversity: Networks with greater diversity provide greater variety in the access to resources and information that could be valuable to you in your career (Brass, 1995). As prior research indicates, diverse networks may not only provide access to a variety of information, but they may also increase the cognitive flexibility of the protégé when it comes to contemplating career decisions, such as the decision to change careers (Higgins, 2001).

WHAT WE KNOW ABOUT DEVELOPMENTAL NETWORKS

Although relatively little empirical research has been conducted on developmental relationships utilizing this developmental network perspective, we do have some empirical findings that can inform our thinking about a contingency perspective. First, research on professionals shows that higher status developmental networks increase the likelihood of promotion and organizational commitment in hierarchical professions (e.g., law; Higgins & Thomas, 2001). Further, structurally diverse (i.e., high-range) developmental networks are associated with greater likelihood of changing careers (Higgins, 2001). Additionally, those with developmental networks that are characterized by strong ties and structural diversity are more likely to have greater clarity in their sense of professional identity, greater career-related self-efficacy, and greater sense of professional success (Higgins, 2002). Also, research on developmental networks that compares the amount and kind of developmental assistance provided shows that it takes just one tie, a good "friend" that provides high amounts of psychosocial assistance, to feel satisfied at work (Higgins, 2000).

In a nutshell, the research on mentoring and developmental networks suggests that it is not just what you know but who you know that matters. Taking personality tests may help an individual understand what his or her goals and values are, but to build a satisfying career, social and human capital matter. More specifically, positive relationships—that provide developmental assistance—matter. Further, as the recent work on developmental networks shows, these kinds of positive relationships affect not just our access to opportunities, which is how we typically think about the usefulness of networks, but they may affect how we think about our careers as well (Higgins, 2001).

INTRODUCING A CONTINGENCY PERSPECTIVE ON DEVELOPMENTAL NETWORKS

Although the research just described demonstrates that mentoring matters and that developmental networks matter, prior research has not examined when developmental networks, the focus of this chapter, matter. That is, can the same kind of developmental network be more or less useful depending on the circumstances? By examining this question, we can resist the temptation to assume that "more mentors is better" or that having a network of high-quality relationships must, necessarily, make the network yield positive results. Rather, we can now consider the conditions under which networks of positive relationships yield positive outcomes.

Of course, a contingency perspective could propose any number and variety of conditions as relevant to consider (Lawrence & Lorsch, 1967/1986). This chapter offers two dimensions, based on prior research, and then, in the final section, suggests additional dimensions as possible directions for future research. The two dimensions we consider here are the following: an individual's career goals and the professional context in which he or she is working. Prior research has, implicitly, considered each of these dimensions and so, provides a useful launching point for exploring a contingency perspective. For example, we know from prior research that some kinds of developmental networks are useful for career advancement and yet have no impact on work satisfaction, whereas other kinds of developmental networks are useful for work satisfaction and yet have no bearing on organizational commitment or promotion (see Higgins, 2000; Higgins & Thomas, 2001). These specific findings come from work that was done in the exact same professional context—the up or out context of white-shoe law firms. In that context, because partners vote on the promotions of their young attorneys, receiving career assistance such as exposure and visibility from such high-status colleagues is useful. An example of such a "positive" high-status developmental network is depicted in Figure 11.2.

However, consider this same developmental network depicted in Figure 11.2 and also the same professional context, but for a protégé with a very different career self-defined need or goal—one other than promotion. If the protégé is more interested in simply feeling satisfied at work than in getting ahead, then the developmental network in Figure 11.2 might not be that useful. Why? As depicted, such a developmental network would likely consist of many sponsors and perhaps an ally, but not necessarily any friends or mentors. The latter kinds of developmental relationships are the ones that provide psychosocial assistance, which, as prior research shows, is exactly

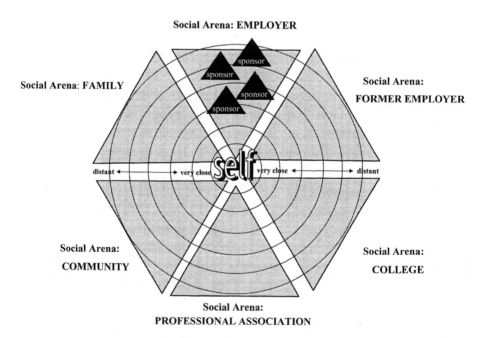

FIG. 11.2. Developmental Network 1.

the kind of developmental support that would be needed if one was seeking greater work satisfaction (Higgins, 2000).

Now, turning the prism once again, we can consider this same developmental network shown in Figure 11.2 and the same career goal but in a very different professional context. Suppose the protégé was working in a business development position in a large biotechnology firm. In such a context, there is no voting on promotion. Rather, one's professional reputation determines advancement and this depends on one's ability to do deals. Therefore, building developmental relationships that span organizational boundaries, with institutional investors and investment bankers or with those in major pharmaceutical companies, might be the most effective at satisfying goals for advancement. Such a positive developmental network might look like the network depicted in Figure 11.3, consisting of developmental relationships that provide career support from both inside and outside the firm.

Finally, returning to the Figure 11.2 developmental network, retaining the context of the biotech executive in business development, but shifting the career goal one last time, consider a new career goal: the desire to change careers. Here, a positive or useful developmental network might be comprised of strong ties, those that provide career as well as psychosocial support, but from multiple social arenas; this would offer the protégé the bene-

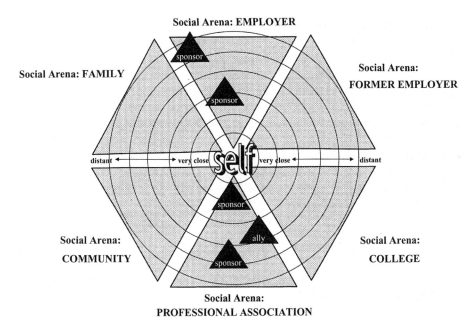

FIG. 11.3. Developmental Network 2.

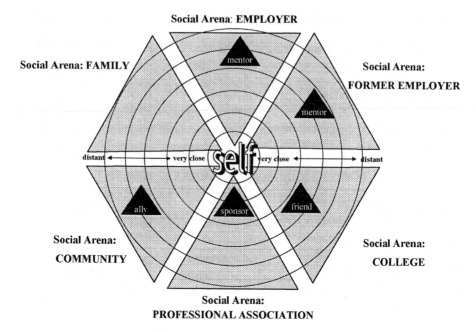

FIG. 11.4. Developmental Network 3.

fits of access to a variety of information as well as cognitive flexibility stemming from the support he or she receives from people who also care and share beyond the boundaries of work (Higgins, 2001). Such a developmental network might look like Figure 11.4.

As these figures and thought experiments suggest, there are likely to be important practical implications from conducting research that takes a contingency perspective on developmental networks. Additionally, just as the prior examples illustrate, by turning one dimension of the prism at a time— by changing career goals or professional context—future research might test specific propositions regarding this contingency view. Conducting comparative tests between individuals from similar professional contexts who have different career goals (or vice versa) would advance our understanding of the contingent nature of developmental networks.

SUGGESTIONS FOR FUTURE RESEARCH

The ideas presented here also raise some interesting questions for future research, questions that also speak to a contingency perspective on developmental networks as well as high-quality connections at work more generally. First, because this contingency perspective asks when developmental networks are more or less useful, it would be informative to examine the dynamics of developmental network structures. There is scant longitudinal research on mentoring or HQCs in general and even less on developmental networks (for an exception, see Dobrow & Higgins, 2005). Examining the dynamics of developmental networks would further our understanding of whether and how developmental networks change and then, whether those changes yield positive consequences with respect to certain career goals and, again, in certain career contexts.

For example, a longitudinal study of developmental networks could address whether the stability of network structures was critical to long-term outcomes such as psychological well-being, an outcome that has been of substantial interest to positive organizational scholarship. Recent research suggests that some kinds of ties, those that provide high levels of psychosocial support, tend to be more relationally stable over time (Cummings & Higgins, 2006). A next step would be to investigate whether the stability of that inner core affects longer term outcomes and if so, which outcomes, positive and negative, and under what circumstances. Drawing on prior research findings, it seems logical to expect that greater relational stability of an inner core of ties that provide high amounts of psychosocial assistance would yield greater satisfaction in one's career, but not necessarily greater career advancement, suggesting a trade-off between different kinds of positive career outcomes. Still, such a proposition remains to be tested.

A second possible avenue to explore is developmental network preferences. An examination of the preferences that a developer and protégé have for cultivating developmental networks could reveal that the matching of such preferences matters over the long run. Such an examination would advance the admittedly one-sided perspective adopted in this chapter and pick up on the dimension of felt mutuality that research on HQCs suggests may be critical to understanding the subjective experience of HQCs at work and the extent to which they yield positive benefits for the individuals involved.

For example, having a mentor as part of a diverse developmental network when that mentor prefers a monodyadic relationship with a protégé might clash with protégé preferences, impeding the pair's ability to have difficult conversations. Again, prior research shows that matching of preferences—for example, regarding the discussion of certain topics, such as race (Ely & Thomas, 2001)—enhances the quality of the work connections. Here, a corollary might be that the matching of preferences regarding developmental network structures could enhance the probability that the relationship will yield positive outcomes. More generally, matching interaction styles among members of HQCs may lead to more positive outcomes for both parties involved. Further, consistent with a contingency perspective, we could find that this kind of homophily based on structural or interaction style preferences matters for certain kinds of positive outcomes—such as career-related self-efficacy—but less so for others, such as career advancement. Such propositions remain to be tested.

Third, future research could consider the value of different developmental network structures during different stages of one's career and adult development. Although as mentioned at the beginning of this chapter, extant mentoring research has focused on early career mentoring, developmental assistance is important at any career stage, and perhaps even more so throughout one's career, given the changing nature of today's work environment. Therefore, examining when certain developmental networks are more or less positive for individuals—even for similar career goals but at different periods in their lives—would advance mentoring research as well as our understanding of windows of opportunity for HQCs to have a positive impact on individuals' careers and lives. It could be, for example, that later on in one's career, having a developmental network composed of subordinates could enhance one's sense of generativity (Bennis & Thomas, 2002) and so, contribute to work satisfaction, whereas early in one's career, peer-filled networks might be more useful with respect to this same kind of positive career outcome.

In addition to implications for research, the developmental network perspective and the contingency approach offered in this chapter open up areas of inquiry for practice. A contingency view offers individuals an opportunity to think about what is missing and what needs to change in the sources of support they rely on in their careers. Further, it helps us recognize that there is no one perfect kind of high-quality relationship, but that many people can and do provide helpful and growth-enhancing guidance in one's career. Moreover, and as this chapter suggests, the extent to which a particular set of high-quality relationships is indeed positive depends on much more than the sum of the help provided by each dyadic relationship; the structure of the whole, the collective, matters as well.

Finally, by taking the protégé's perspective, this work reinforces the notion that empathy is critical in cultivating effective relationships. Effective managers need to be keenly aware of their own interaction styles and preferences as well as those of others, rather than assume that one kind of advice, even if that advice seems "positive" or helpful, is necessarily helpful. As suggested here, even the same kinds of networks can be differentially positive. Therefore, understanding when high-quality relationships are truly positive may depend on aspects of the network in which the assistance was given, the processes related to the help-giving and receiving, as well as the specific needs of the individuals involved.

REFERENCES

Berscheid, E., & Lopes, J. (1997). A temporal model of relationship satisfaction and stability. In R. J. Sternberg & M. Hojjat (Eds.), *Satisfactions in close relationships* (pp. 129–159). New York: Guilford.

Brass, D. J. (1995). A social network perspective on human resources management. *Research in Personnel and Human Resources Management, 13,* 39–79.

Burt, R. S. (1992). *Structural holes: The social structure of competition.* Cambridge, MA: Harvard University Press.

Chao, G. T., Walz, P. M., & Gardner, P. D. (1992). Formal and informal mentorships: A comparison on mentoring functions and contrast with nonmentored counterparts. *Personnel Psychology, 45,* 619–636.

Cohen, S. (2001). Social relationships and the susceptibility to the common cold. In C. Ryff & B. Singer (Eds.), *Emotion, social relationships, and health* (pp. 221–232). Oxford, England: Oxford University Press.

Cummings, J., & Higgins, M. C. (2005). Relational instability at the core: Support dynamics in developmental networks. *Social Networks, 28*(1), 38–55.

de Janasz, S. C., Sullivan, S. E., & Whiting, V. R. (2003). Mentor networks and career success: Lessons for turbulent times. *Academy of Management Executive, 17*(4), 78–91.

Dobrow, S., & Higgins, M. C. (2005). Developmental networks and professional identity: A longitudinal study. *Special Issue on Mentoring, Career Development International, 10*(6–7), 567–583.

Dutton, J. E. & Heaphy, E. D. (2003). The power of high quality connections. In K. S. Cameron, J. E. Dutton, & R. E. Quinn (Eds.), *Positive organizational scholarship* (pp. 263–278). San Francisco: Berrett-Koehler.

Ely, R. J., & Thomas, D. A. (2001). Cultural diversity at work: The moderating effects of work group perspectives on diversity. *Administrative Science Quarterly, 46,* 229–273.

Fagenson, E. A. (1989). The mentor advantage: Perceived career/job experiences of protégés versus non-protégés. *Journal of Organizational Behavior, 10,* 309–320.

Fletcher, J. K. (1996). A relational approach to the protean worker. In D. T. Hall (Ed.), *The career is dead—Long live the career: A relational approach to careers* (pp. 101–131). San Francisco: Jossey-Bass.

Granovetter, M. S. (1973). The strength of weak ties. *American Journal of Sociology, 6,* 1360–1380.

Hall, D. T. (1996). Protean careers of the 21st century. *Academy of Management Executive, 10*(4), 8–16.

Hall, D. T., & Associates. (1996). *The career is dead—Long live the career: A relational approach to careers.* San Francisco: Jossey-Bass.

Higgins, M. C. (2000). The more, the merrier? Multiple developmental relationships and work satisfaction. *Journal of Management Development, 19,* 277–296.

Higgins, M. C. (2001). Changing careers: The effects of social context. *Journal of Organizational Behavior, 22,* 595–618.

Higgins, M. C. (2002, August). *Career consequences of developmental networks.* Paper presented at the Academy of Management annual meeting, Denver, CO.

Higgins, M. C., & Kram, K. E. (2001). Reconceptualizing mentoring at work: A developmental network perspective. *Academy of Management Review, 26*(2), 264–288.

Higgins, M. C., & Thomas, D. A. (2001). Constellations and careers: Toward understanding the effects of multiple developmental relationships. *Journal of Organizational Behavior, 22,* 223–247.

Ibarra, H. (1992). Homophily and differential returns: Sex differences in network structure and access in an advertising firm. *Administrative Science Quarterly, 37,* 422–447.

Josselson, R. (1996). *The space between us: Exploring human dimensions of human relationships.* Thousand Oaks, CA: Sage.

Kram, K. E. (1985). *Mentoring at work: Developmental relationships in organizational life.* Glenview, IL: Scott Foresman.

Kram, K. E., & Hall, D. T. (1996). Mentoring in a context of diversity and turbulence. In E. E. Kossek & S. A. Lobel (Eds.), *Managing diversity: Human resource strategies for transforming the workplace* (pp. 108–136). Cambridge, MA: Blackwell Business.

Lawrence, P. R., & Lorsch, J. W. (1986). *Organization and environment: Managing differentiation and integration.* Boston: Harvard Business School Press. (Original work published 1967)

Phillips-Jones, L. L. (1982). *Mentors and protégés.* New York: Arbor House.

Quinn, R., & Dutton, J. E. (2005). Coordination as energy-in-conversation: A process theory of organizing. *Academy of Management Review, 30*(1), 36–57.

Ragins, B. R., & Cotton, J. L. (1999). Mentor functions and outcomes: A comparison of men and women in formal and informal mentoring relationships. *Journal of Applied Psychology, 84,* 529–550.

Riley, S., & Wrench, D. (1985). Mentoring among female lawyers. *Journal of Applied Social Psychology, 15,* 374–386.

Roche, G. R. (1979). Much ado about mentors. *Harvard Business Review, 57,* 17–28.

Rousseau, D. M. (1995). *Psychological contracts in organizations: Understanding written and unwritten agreements.* Thousands Oaks, CA: Sage.

Thomas, D. A. (1993). Racial dynamics in cross-race developmental relationships. *Administrative Science Quarterly, 38,* 169–194.

Thomas, D. A., & Higgins, M. C. (1996). Mentoring and the boundaryless career: Lessons from the minority experience. In M. B. Arthur & D. M. Rousseau (Eds.), *The boundaryless career: A new employment principle for a new organizational era* (pp. 268–281). New York: Oxford University Press.

Thomas, D. A., & Kram, K. E. (1988). Promoting career-enhancing relationships in organizations: The role of the human resource professional. In M. London & E. Mone (Eds.), *The Human resource professional and employee career development* (pp. 49–66). New York: Greenwood.

Weick, K. E., Sutcliffe, K. M., & Obstfeld, D. (1999). Organizing for high reliability: Processes of collective mindfulness. *Research in Organizational Behavior, 21,* 81–123.

Whitely, W., Dougherty, T. W., & Dreher, G. F. (1991). Relationship of career mentoring and socio-economic origin to managers' and professionals' early career progress. *Academy of Management Journal, 34,* 331–351.

Zey, M. (1984). *The mentor connection.* Homewood, IL: Dow Jones-Irwin.

12

Structural Balance in Teams

Deborah Ancona
William Isaacs

What does it take to produce a healthy team? In this chapter we consider the literature on interpersonal relationships and their impact on team outcomes. Although it is difficult to generalize about such a broad and diverse literature, we observe that this literature is characterized by four attributes: (a) it tends to focus on dysfunction—not ongoing adaptation, health, and generativity; (b) it is fragmented; (c) it focuses primarily at the behavioral, not structural level of analysis; and (d) its basic paradigm derives from a mechanistic model. Teams are seen primarily as input–process–output devices (Gladstein, 1984; Hackman, 1990; McGrath, Kelly, & Machatka, 1984). Although some writers have advocated a "living system" approach, this is not the paradigm that dominates.

In this chapter we advocate taking a different point of view, one more in keeping with the positive organizations scholarship school with its emphasis on positive states, resilience, and virtuous cycles (Cameron, Dutton, & Quinn, 2003). We seek to look at the positive side of teams—what can we do to produce continued health and better team functioning over time? We want to shift the focus from dysfunction to repair and improvement. Also, although the dominant paradigm in the team literature highlights the outcomes of satisfaction, performance, and the ability of a team to remain together over time (Hackman, 1990), we would like to add the notion of generativity. That is, can team members work together to find new and innovative ways to deal with each other and with the environment that surrounds them? Can there be growth in functionality over time?

Second, we seek a more integrative model. Although it is in the nature of most team research to look at one dimension of teams (e.g., how members relate to one another or how team members make decisions), these different aspects of team activity often have an impact on one another. It is only in looking at multiple aspects of teams simultaneously that their interactions can be studied and the implications for outcomes assessed.

Third, the literature is dominated by a focus on team-member behavior. We can all identify the behaviors associated with groupthink (Janis, 1982) and convergent thinking (Nemeth, 1995). Here we seek to understand a level beneath behavior: structure. By structure we mean the underlying causal patterns of interaction that give rise to the visible manifestations of team behavior. We argue that behavior is the reflection of these underlying causal structures, and that lasting change needs to take place at the structural level. This line of thought opens the door to yet deeper levels of analysis, which relate to the causal determinants of structure, though this is not the focus here.

Finally, much of the functionalist school (Poole & Hollingshead, 2005) focuses on how to improve performance through attention to inputs and processes. Thus, to improve performance one presses one part of the input or process lever. The key to success involves putting just the right people onto the team, or creating the right incentive scheme or decision-making process to aid in performance. The interconnections are implied. The whole is assumed to be the sum of the parts. Instead of this piece-part mentality, we propose a systems paradigm whereby the system itself learns to reflect on its own functioning, identify where the process is not working, and shift to a better alignment among parts and the outside world.

In shifting the emphasis on relationships in teams to one that focuses on health and generativity, integration, structure, and systems thinking we build on the work of Kantor and Lehr (1975) in their articulation of the four-player model. This work stands in contrast to the existing literature and opens the way to a line of inquiry into the structural balance and conditions that make up a part of what we refer to as *dynamic wholeness*.

THE LITERATURE ON TEAMS: A FOCUS ON DYSFUNCTION

The extensive literature on teams reveals a pessimistic view of team-member relationships and a significant bias toward what can go wrong. Teams are seen as a pattern of relationships in which individuals feel the need to conform and so uniformity prevails (Sherif, 1966). There is a tendency toward groupthink (Janis, 1982) whereby individuals suppress doubts about what the group is doing, keep any conflicting evidence from reaching team members, and silence dissension—all in the name of maintaining agreement and positive feelings within the team. Teams are reported to have "disabilities" that lead them to fall to a low common denominator (Senge, 1990) or produce, in high-stakes environments, antilearning behavior that produces the appearance of functionality but seriously limits innovation and damages effectiveness (Edmondson, 1999).

The underlying assumption about team-member interactions in the literature is not charitable. Teams are presented as entities filled with shirkers, who avoid doing work when they can get away from it, and rate busters, who get punished by the team because they do too much work (Schachter, 1959; Shaw, 1976). Team members are described as people who are defensive, who hoard information, and who side with similar others (Marques & Paez, 1994). As a result, teams are not able to beat individuals on decision-making tasks, and are not usually able to pull the unique information that individuals have into the mix of team ideas (Gruenfeld, Mannix, Williams, & Neale, 1996).

Team collective behavior seems to reveal the worst, not the best of human experience. Teams fall into social inertia—they get stuck "knee deep in the big muddy" (Staw, 1976), where a decision once made is hard to unmake, even in the face of evidence suggesting that change is necessary. They are like myopic shoppers, making biased decisions based on limited data. Teams suffer from solution mindedness, in which the push to move quickly to a solution and alleviate the anxiety among members causes team members to lose their creative spirit and jump to support any solution that seems plausible.

This is something of a depressing survey. Despite claims of objectivity, there is a very strong normative slant driving this research. It carries a disease orientation—a focus on that part of the group process that is sick and needs to be cured. Despite the hype that teams are the key to corporate effectiveness; a mechanism to increase quality, commitment, and efficiency in organizations; and a way to ensure the satisfaction of members, most of the research points to the gap between this dream and reality. Teams are framed as dysfunctional and in need of help—in the form of consultation, structural change, or new leadership. However, these remedies do not necessarily get at the core of the problem and so we continue to search for the miracle cure.

SHIFTING THE PARADIGM

In this chapter we build on the positive organizational scholarship school by focusing on health, rather than disease, and on the requirements for generating positive sequences of interaction. This shift requires a move from a mechanistic input–output model to a systems approach.

In the organizational literature teams are seen as critical mechanisms for performance within an organizational context. They are studied by examining what goes into them, what goes on in them, and what comes out of them. This input–process–output mentality dominates (Gladstein, 1984; Hackman, 1990; McGrath et al.,1984). Teams are, in other words, seen as ingredients in a mechanistic sequence of activities designed to produce some measurable output.

The mechanistic frame draws its strength from the Industrial Age. Its orientation is on efficiency and optimization of the piece parts of any process or activity. In this view, producing the optimal effectiveness of each part leads to a more efficient whole. If a team in this light is inefficient, or underperforming, it must be fixed or upgraded. The trouble with this frame is that it fragments experience, and typically looks for what is not efficient or optimized. It is biased, in other words, toward a deficit mentality, on fixing parts, or removing them, if they no longer seem to fit. What is more, a machine is not expected to produce results beyond what it was programmed to do. It is unusual, given our current mechanistic frame, to see teams excel and expand beyond any preestablished limits. Generative outcomes—ones that produce unexpected levels of results—tend to be a mystery within the mechanistic frame.

Our work takes a different turn along two important dimensions. First, we make the assumption that teams are systems that can produce generative outcomes, and that these outcomes are created by underlying structural dynamics. In contrast with the mechanistic paradigm, we suggest that teams are living systems seeking a particular kind of homeostasis—a state of structural balance—that is healthy according to the norms of that particular team or context. In this frame, the team is not expected merely to fulfill its piece part, but to be a living entity, capable of creative action.

Teams that are healthy in this paradigm are able to produce divergent thinking, repair broken dynamics, and build new repertoires of behavior in response to changed environmental conditions. Structurally balanced teams are responsive to the precise context in which they function, and produce health according to that context, not just a standard arbitrarily imposed on it. They generate internal and external awareness and respond uniquely to circumstances; they also coordinate well across diverse actors.

Second, we highlight the concept of *structural balance,* which is the idea that teams are driven less by a collection of specific behaviors that are either dysfunctional or functional and more by a set of homeostatic-seeking underlying patterns and structures that create those behaviors (Alexander, 2004; Bateson, 1972; Capra, 2003). A positive or "balanced" team has in operation a set of structures that continuously monitor, correct, and produce healthy outcomes. Here we look beyond concrete instances of team member actions to examine the structural acts that those behaviors represent, how well those acts are performed, and the sequences of acts that are enacted. This sequence is the structure that determines whether or not healthy outcomes emerge.

FAMILY SYSTEMS THEORY APPLIED TO TEAMS

Our frame leads us to look for approaches that take seriously notions of systems, generativity, and structural dynamics in small groups. Surprisingly there is little in the organizations literature that shares these premises. We take our starting point instead from the world of family therapy and the path-breaking work of Kantor and Lehr's (1975) *structural dynamics.* Kantor and Lehr studied 19 families, nine of which had members who were emotionally dysfunctional. Through intense observation, interviews, continuous taping of family interactions, and analysis, they were able to identify a set of conditions associated with different types of healthy family systems.

Their notion is that family systems are self-regulating and work within particular norms. Healthy systems reach their targeted goals; unhealthy ones deviate from them. The essence of their approach is that social systems inherently seek health, as defined by them, and are thwarted from this only when the mechanisms available to them (in the form of emotional maturity of the individuals and the structure of the relationships among the individuals) do not work. We take here one aspect of their work as a starting point for our thinking.

In particular, we use Kantor and Lehr's (1975) model of the action patterns in human and family systems, which they call the *four-player model,* to introduce a frame for structural balance to the teams literature. The model suggests there are four core acts—move, follow, oppose, and bystand—that are the essential building blocks of both dysfunctional and healthy sequences of action in teams. They propose in effect a systems language for describing all group interactions, a language with four basic words, and a wide variety of sentences (sequences of words) that carry enormous nuance and subtlety. The four acts are key markers of critical forms of interaction in any group or team environment. They are each distinct, they each serve a different purpose in a team context, and they complement each other in particular dynamic circuits. Kantor and Lehr argue that healthy dynamics show balanced and enabled evidence of four acts in sequences that produce healthy and "successful" outcomes. The four provide, in different combinations, a basic pattern of health in a team context.

By healthy, we mean in this context, whole or complete. The Indo-European root of the word *whole* is *kailo* and means uninjured. This term is the same root as the words *health, whole,* and *holy,* and all point to a sense of completeness. A living system is whole and naturally seeks to remain so. In four player structural terms, a team achieves this by displaying these four acts in a balanced manner. To display health, teams need to move beyond simply enacting these roles to carrying each out effectively, in appropriate sequences and stages, and in sync with the context in which they exist and operate. Lack of health is the failure to reveal the full range of all four acts, in ways that enable the team to achieve its goals.

FOUR STRUCTURAL ACTS

We describe the four central acts or dimensions in this structural model—move, follow, oppose, and bystand—and then show how they together can create a system of balance and health. It is important to state that the way each of these acts appears is highly situationally dependent. This model is not an attempt to create a fixed personality typology, but a map for determining action and emergent structures among groups of people.

One of the main drivers in a team context is the initiation of action in a proposed direction. A person who acts in this way makes a "move." Someone must light the match. An example of a move might be, "Let's build Product X. Product X is the best idea out there and we would be crazy not to run with this idea before someone else gets their hands on it." What function does the act of a "move" serve? A move provides the team with direction and momentum. A move creates energy and a base that others can react to and engage. If there is no move, then there is no forward direction, and it becomes difficult or impossible for a team to make decisions, choose a path, and motivate members to produce results. A move sets social action in motion and establishes the social field.

Once someone in the team has made a move, several alternative acts are possible. One possibility is for someone else to *follow*. An example of a *follow* would be, "I agree. I have listened to all of your arguments and I think that product X is definitely the way to go. I support this idea and think that we should get to work immediately." The act of *following* is one of support and agreement.

The follow act serves the function of completion. A follower closes a circuit, backing the move, and thus gives it weight and momentum. If a mover opens the circle, the follower closes it. Without a follower, there is no one to complete the task that the mover has started. The follow act involves building something together and supporting members, thus setting the stage for team cohesion.

An alternative response to a move is the *oppose* act. Here the team member disagrees with or refutes the move that has been made. An example of an oppose act is, "No. I think that going with product X is a terrible idea. The data just don't support all of the claims that you are making. We would be in real trouble if we go down that road." Intriguingly, the oppose act brings not just a hindrance, but the potential for a correction to the social field by questioning the direction that a mover has initiated. The oppose act also introduces factors that the mover–follower agreement might have left out or discounted, in an effort to perfect, protect, or ensure the integrity of the idea.

Opposers are often underappreciated, because negative intentions are attributed to them, and their underlying intention and value-creating impact is missed. Opposers are typically seen as complainers or critics, or, in some cultures, as the "real" players—that is, the people who bring a dose of reality to ungrounded or uninformed discussion, but who are nevertheless difficult to control. Despite their reputation, however, opposers can open up the range of possibility so that team members can think about multiple options and perhaps even create new ones based on the opposing viewpoints that have now been introduced into the team. The oppose act perfects and actually often widens the field of consideration, by forcing everyone to include factors that they wanted to forget.

Finally, someone in a team can "bystand." The bystander act brings perspective and insight into the situation at hand. She introduces information into the scene, either from inside the group, or outside of it, that the team needs but does not yet have. In this sense the bystander has one foot inside and one foot outside of a team. The bystander might bring in data from another team, as in "The other group decided that the data that we are looking at might be biased in favor of Product G," or a more historic perspective, like "Last time we worked with this technology delivery was very late."

A bystander often provides information about the team process as well: "We have spent the last half-hour arguing back and forth over Product X or Product G, but it is not clear whether or not we have a way to resolve the disagreement." Or a bystander might say, "I have noticed that three components to the argument that were raised at the beginning have not come back in. Has anyone else noticed this?"

The bystand act provides perspective and invites the team to be more reflective. The bystander often remains a neutral player, not favoring one alternative over another. The bystand act helps others to step away from the action within the team and enables them to see what is going on through a different lens. As such the whole team may be able to shift dynamics and move the team forward. The bystand act is in some senses the most important act—particularly because in many team contexts it is the least active or enabled. Groups of people are notoriously unaware of the ways they suppress or limit individuals and produce unintended consequences in situations outside of themselves. It is important to note that bystanding is an active, direct move in a group. It is not the same as observing in the sense of being withdrawn and separated from the field of action. In that case the bystander might be termed "disabled."

These four acts have specific weight and impact in any group context, and they can, depending on the sequences in which they are deployed, contribute to health and positive outcomes or the lack of them. The four-player model is structural, not personal. The four are interactional roles or acts in any social context. In this sense, all four acts could be played out by two people, or conceivably intrapsychically, all four within one person.

These four acts, or structural elements, provide direction and energy; momentum and connection; correction and elaboration; and perspective taking, reflection, and openness to the external context. In the appropriate sequences, these acts enable team members to consider a wide range of alternatives, examine each alternative in some depth, refine and elaborate these alternatives with ideas from inside and outside the team, choose an alternative, and act. They are able to do this because team members alter and improve their interaction when these processes go off course.

INTENTION AND IMPACT

One key causal contributor to healthy or unhealthy sequences derives from the ability of the team to see and respond to the difference between the intentions of actors and the impact they may have on the situation. Often people react to the impact and ignore or bypass the intent. An ineffective or unhealthy act conveys unintended impacts or mixed messages, because the actor inserts "noise" into the situation—emotional reactions, excessive spin on their acts, heavy implications, or attributions. As a result, others tend to react to the noise, and sequences tend not to reach satisfactory resolutions. These intentions versus their unintended consequences can be summarized in Figure 12.1 This figure displays a key gap typically not grasped by teams. It is, for instance, difficult for an actor who is a mover to realize that his or her moves could come across as indecisive—but this is the case when he or she is always moving and always initiating, never allowing anyone else to follow or bystand what is happening.

A healthy team system is produced when there is a match between the intention and impact, or, when mismatches are noticed and corrected. A key determinant of effective acts is therefore that they be overt and enabled, not covert and disabled. A disabled actor is one who is thwarted by the rules of engagement or by his or her own limited repertoire. For instance, an opposer who is told that he or she is not a "team player" and should agree with others for the good of the team, and who buys into this line of thinking becomes disabled. Team members must be free to carry out the acts that seem appropriate to them at the moment that seems warranted. The team as a whole must also be free to make whatever act is required, whenever it is required.

	Actor Intends:	But sometimes comes across as:
Mover	Direction Discipline Commitment Perfection Clarity	Omnipotent Impatient Indecisive Scattered Dictatorial
Follower	Completion Compassion Loyalty Service Continuity	Placating Indecisive Pliant Wishy-Washy Over accommodating
Opposer	Correction Courage Protection Integrity Survival	Critical Competitive Blaming Attacking Contrary
Bystander	Perspective Patience Preservation Moderation Self-Reflection	Disengaged Judgmental Deserting Withdrawn Silent

© 1995 David Kantor

FIG. 12.1. Four player intention–impact gaps. Reprinted with permission of David Kantor.

TEAM BALANCE AND IMBALANCE

There are several ways the four-player model reveals and impacts positive or healthy outcomes. The first, as we have indicated, has to do with the way each act is carried out. Each act can, on its own, either enhance or destroy balance and health. Each act can either be inflated—too extreme—or deflated—disabled or too weak—to impact the social field, or to generate a balance with the other acts. Any of the acts can at one point in time dominate, creating imbalance and lack of health. Any of the four can be so weakly displayed, or actively suppressed, as to create a void in the team. Health arises when these acts are expressed distinctly, without overlays or distortion. Individuals can become stuck in any single act, unable to respond differently even though the situation calls for it, or may mix or compound acts—oppose when the need is for bystanding, or follow when the need is to move.

Second, there are collective dimensions to balance: The team can become stuck in a ritualized replaying of a particular sequence of moves, it can actively suppress one or more of the acts, or it can favor one sequence and punish others. In practice people combine acts, do one when they intend another, and get caught in patterns they would deem unproductive—indeed all the "negative" or deficit behaviors that the team literature outlines. However, the model also points to the way a more balanced way of functioning might be produced.

Balanced Acts

An effective or strong mover provides clear and unmixed direction. He or she inspires action or begins to make the case for a particular alternative. An effective mover—one that is in balance—initiates action that continues to let people be free to respond. He or she does not coerce or close things down. An ineffective or unbalanced mover is either stuck—moves too much, and suppresses alternatives—or is deflated and disabled—moving too little and inviting confusion. A team with a weak or disabled mover cannot find a direction or take a step. A team with a strong and balanced mover finds a direction and can reach resolution of its problems.

The follow act may also be done in a balanced or unbalanced manner. In balance, the follower engages because he or she authentically listens to or backs the direction of the mover, and reveals that qualitatively in his or her actions. His or her following has a strategic impact on the group, completing a circuit of thinking initiated by one or more movers, and brings the action toward unification and resolution. The follower might think that the leader, or the team, needs support for one of the ideas on the table rather than needing yet another idea that no one is focusing on. The effective follower is committed to helping to implement the idea; he or she is not just giving lip service to it.

In contrast, a weak follower either follows every move halfheartedly—never enabling anything to come to completion—or can only follow, following equally every initiative: "That's a great idea. And so is that." An unbalanced or stuck follower can get swayed by the most recent argument, or can attempt to minimize the impact of a dominating mover by following other weaker movers. A disabled follower cannot bring himself or herself to follow anyone, even though nothing can happen in the team without this.

The oppose act can also run in a constructive or destructive direction. A constructive opposer raises legitimate concerns about the situation—perhaps the move of another actor—and brings correction or change to the situation. Typically the opposer sees something missing in the interaction, or in the integrity of the information, and in the interest of survival and protection of the outcome, challenges what is happening. Opposers are typically branded as troublemakers, but that is not their intent. Although they themselves may not always be fully aware of it, we suggest they are seeking to bring into the situation some correction that has not yet been accepted or collectively understood. Children are, for example, genius opposers of their parents' requests to come to dinner or clean up their rooms—often the act of doing so is an attempt to establish some new level of listening in the family.

An ineffective or stuck opposer challenges everything. Typically these opposers argue that nothing else will work, that the overall situation requires opposing for any voice other than the dominant one to be heard—so they begin with this. However, this also becomes a habit, and others brand them as a result. An ineffective opposer can be internally weak—unable to produce an appropriately timed challenge when it is called for—or disabled—silenced or suppressed by themselves or by the team or system. A system that suppresses opposers is often one with a strong ideology, or an aversion to multiple takes on the truth. Equally a weak opposer is someone who has either been punished or put down for opposing, or who, rightly or wrongly, attributes that there is no room for his or her voice.

The bystand act can transform some of these limits. An effective bystander brings in information from both within and outside the team. A balanced bystander makes this information usable, raising the awareness of the team. He or she acts in these cases as something of a process consultant, providing observations of the team patterns and dynamics. An unbalanced bystand act can flood the system with information—adding too much perspective and confusing matters. Another sign of an unhealthy team dynamic is one where there is too little bystanding. This implies a lack in one of several directions: It is underdeveloped, meaning it is simply not adequately formed for new perspectives to be articulated; it is disabled, meaning the person in some way cannot find the courage or permission to bring out what he or she sees; or it is silenced, meaning there is an injunction on new views being brought in. This team embodies the equivalent of a lack of free press.

Collective Balance

However, it is not just the existence of all four acts, and the ability to carry out each act effectively, that makes a team a healthy system. The sequence and dynamics across acts determines what makes a team effective or not. Sequences of four-player acts are the structural revelation of the way the group works. When the sequences are ritualized and limited, the intelligence of the group is also limited. When there is flexibility and a capacity to respond to complex contexts, the group displays intelligence and adaptability. Each of these conditions can be traced to the presence or absence of a balanced set of four-player acts. Thus, whereas each individual act can be balanced or imbalanced, balance is also exhibited collectively at the team level.

There are several habitual patterns of interaction we have observed over time that reveal collective imbalance—situations where the team is stuck in an unproductive sequence of acts. For example, the sequence [move, move, move, move] we term a *serial monologue*—a situation where team members one after the other initiate a direction but without regard to any other move. The absence of all the other positions means it is predictable that no action will follow. Take a different sequence: [move, follow, follow, follow]. In this situation, a strong move is complemented by followers, but by nothing else. This could be a question-and-answer session, or a strong boss who proposes something that leads everyone else to agree. This sequence is the essence of politeness.

A third and common dynamic involves a repeating sequence: [move-oppose]. Here the team is locked in an infinite do-loop of conflict. This structure, like the others, is compelling, habitual, and seductive—it seems to draw you into it. Yet it ensures low collective intelligence and an unhealthy result for the team. Move-oppose dynamics arise whenever there is strong difference. It is quite possible to interrupt this sequence, but not by either moving or opposing—only through a combination of following and bystanding. Bystanding the dynamic itself often works: "Fred and Linda have pushed back on each other for the past hour, and I for one do not detect movement. Do others?"

Even when a team has created a balanced sequence of behavior, if this sequence is ritualized around a particular stance, such as always "fixing" things, as opposed to inquiry into what needs to be fixed, the team may suffer. For example, suppose a typical team meeting consists of a team member making a move: "Let's fix this problem using the standard procedure." Then another member follows, "Great idea, let's do it!" But a bystand act continues, "That didn't work very well the last time," and an oppose act adds, "We should recall that procedure is totally outdated and we should not use it." This leads to a follow and move combined: "I agree. Perhaps then we should try the procedure that we saw in that new video." After several other alternatives are discussed, the team moves into action and feels good about the process. However, this team's sequence always begins with a move that consists of a solution. If a team is locked in this pattern, when they face a situation in which no known solution exists, they may be unable to begin with the sensemaking needed to understand the problem before rushing to solution.

Collective balance, health, comes when the sequences that emerge in a group and that are managed by the group engage each of the four acts in a manner that produces resolution of the problem or issue at hand. This also however implies a continuous enlarging of vision and capacity to act—what we refer to as a "generative" capacity. The ability to produce healthy sequences represents a distinct collective capacity in a group of people, one that is immediately observable, and developable in them.

A NEW PARADIGM—MOVING TO STRUCTURE AND HEALTH

If we now return to the teams literature, we can see how the structural lens of the four-player model can illuminate many of the dynamics discussed there. However, we shift the analysis from describing behaviors (e.g., the team members all agreed with the president) to a structural analysis of move, oppose, follow, bystand dynamics. For instance one can describe groupthink (Janis, 1982) as a stuck sequence of moves and follows, with disabled or silenced opposers and suppressed bystanders. Team members follow the leader's move and block from awareness outside perspectives and dissension. A similar underlying sequence is evident in convergent thinking (Nemeth, 1995) and in escalation of commitment (Staw, 1976). In the former the initial move idea is supported by followers who move ahead quickly to elaborate the idea and squeeze out opposition. In the latter, once a move is supported by followers, the move becomes stronger and stronger, and opposition and bad news are discounted.

What is missing in each instance, again, is a balance of all four acts, performed in a manner that breaks the lock any one of them has on the situation. The structural rule of thumb is that absence of all four acts and limited structural sequences reduces collective intelligence.

Analyses like these yield interesting outcomes. For instance, these three types of team dysfunction are often viewed as distinct in the literature, but can actually be seen to be driven by very similar underlying structures. Second, the same limiting structure might be colored by a number of forces. For example, groupthink is created by team members not wanting to break the cohesion of the group, whereas convergent thinking is driven by anxiety and a desire to come up with an answer quickly. Escalation of commitment is driven by the momentum of the move after it has been supported by so many follows. One might conclude that escalation of commitment is simply a later stage of groupthink. In each case, though, the structural solution is the same: interruption of the repeating sequence by a strong set of opposing and bystanding acts. In each case, the analysis is done at the level of acts and sequences of acts, not behavior.

The Structure of Health

As we have argued, the four-player system's power is revealed in the way it describes and reveals sequences of interaction in social processes. Although any one act can have a defining influence on a situation, it is the composition of a set of acts, in a particular sequence, that determines the outcome of the events and the nature of the experience of the people concerned. Furthermore, it is the flexibility with which individuals can take on particular acts, and teams can vary their sequences of interaction, that accounts for health. Rigidity in roles and routines in the face of external change or error is a sign of dysfunction, because creativity and responsiveness are thwarted.

In adopting and applying this model to the field of positive relationships in teams and organizations, we aim to provide a way of seeing the mechanism by which health might emerge. In four-player terms, this means first making sure that all acts are enabled and balanced; second, reinforcing the bystand and oppose acts, the absence or imbalance of which often seems to be dominant in causing dysfunction; and third, working to maintain flexibility across acts and sequences of acts.

The presence of all four acts, in active and dynamic balance, creates a quality of interaction which serves as a new standard, a center point, from which all the other actions emerge. The emergence of this qualitative 'center' to a team's dynamic points to the potential for generative interaction, where the collective behavior of the team becomes more than the sum of the parts. The research on positive relationships in teams could be significantly advanced were there to be a theory describing the process by which this kind of deep innovation actually comes into existence.

When people know how to apply all four acts in healthy sequences, we posit that teams are able to engage in several critical kinds of behaviors that increase in generativity:

1. *Inclusiveness.* First, a team can accept increasing levels of information and complexity from its members and its environment. No one piece of information is fatally opposed by the team without a productive sequence, fitting for the team. No single point of view is allowed to dominate, and when it does, the team corrects, which points to a second facet of health.

2. *Repair.* A team that is in structural imbalance can correct—it can find its own center again, even when it deviates from it. Repair dynamics typically involve a recalcitrant opposer being offered something—usually by a follower, who says, in effect, "this oppose has some truth to it"; and where, at the same time, the opposer yields to a bystander's contention that there are other points of view besides his or her own. Repair dynamics involve a functioning and healthy bystander—one who can intervene despite the presence of a

powerful mover, and bring new angles that are listened to by the system, so that the system's goals can continue to be met.

3. *Adaptation.* A team must continue to find ways to respond to its environment. When all four positions are in effect, a team can respond to change without becoming rigid or defensive. When teams experiment with new sequences they generate new repertoires that may better match new external conditions. Without all four positions, this is very unlikely to happen.

4. *Differentiation.* Finally a healthy team lets each individual differentiate himself or herself more fully into his or her unique contribution, and does so without losing balance in the team. This is because the team can include and withstand greater levels of difference and continue, at increasingly high levels, to produce successful four-player sequences that do not allow any one person to dominate beyond the targeted goals of the group.

FUTURE RESEARCH

We have introduced the four-player model and have brought Kantor and Lehr's (1975) theory out of the realm of family systems and into team systems. However, we have also pointed to a new paradigm by which we might begin to understand generative relationships in teams, one based on a structural approach, that takes seriously the idea that there is a natural pattern of balance possible in any team context. However, many questions remain and much research is needed to move this theory to its next stage.

One direction might be to begin to link the existing body of literature to this new structural approach. Future research might involve a meta-analysis of the structural patterns underlying team dysfunctions. Although here we illustrated the similarity of structure across groupthink, convergent decision making, and overcommitment, there may be other bundles of similarity that highlight other underlying patterns of dysfunction. Once we know the key sequences and patterns of dysfunction it will be clearer whether the underlying problems of balanced acts, disabled bystanders and opposers, and lack of repair dynamics are the major inhibitors of health and generativity.

This linking to existing literature can also be done on the positive side. Future research can examine the structural patterns of teams that exhibit psychological safety (Edmondson, 1999), creativity (Amabile, Schatzel, Moneta, & Kramer, 2004), reflexivity (West, 1994), and other positive team outcomes. In this way, perhaps we can begin to further define the structural patterns that produce positive outcomes.

By applying the structural approach to organizational teams, future research will also begin to highlight some of the differences that might be found in the structural patterns in these types of teams as opposed to the families that Kantor and Lehr (1985) studied. For example, boundary spanning as a key component of an effective bystand act may be more important for organizational teams than it is for families. The former are more dependent on external information, coordination, and support. Such a research agenda could move this work from an emphasis on borrowed ideas to one with a firm footing in the organizational theory arena.

Although defining the structure that produces health and generativity will push the field to a deeper level of analysis, there are still yet deeper levels. What are the conditions under which these positive structural patterns emerge? Future research can begin to examine the role of skill, affect, and culture that help to create the initial conditions for positive structural patterns. A fair amount of literature is now pointing to the importance of safety in creating positive relationships in teams (Edmondson, 1999; Heifetz, 1994; Kahn, 2005). For a balanced team to emerge, individual team members need to feel supported in taking on the acts that they deem necessary for the team to move forward. Yet Kahn (2005) demonstrated that people are only capable of being self-reliant when they feel securely attached to others. There is a need for attention, validation, empathy, and support from others. Furthermore, he argued that team members may be disengaged by others who leave them isolated and alone. Kahn (2005), Heifetz (1994), Edmondson (1999), Isaacs (1999), and others use the notion of *holding environments* or *containers* whereby a supportive environment is created. More work is needed to determine whether such conditions are associated with balanced structural patterns of interaction, and how these conditions appear structurally.

Finally, this new structural approach to understanding the path toward healthy teams speaks to a more microfocus of data collection and analysis. Although the team literature refers to many of the behaviors illustrated in the move, oppose, follow, bystand framework, the timing and sequencing of these behaviors are somewhat different. For example, the literature includes reference to behaviors like reflection (West, 1994), devil's advocacy (Thompson, 2001), and brainstorming (Osborn, 1957). These might be understood as bystanding, opposing, and moving, for this is what these activities bring to the team. However, whereas these existing theories might predict the need for reflection at particular times in a team's history (e.g., the midpoint; Gersick, 1988; Hackman, 2004), our new structural theory points to the need for different acts and balance when they are needed for an effective sequence. A team needs a devil's advocate to oppose only when there is sincere disagreement with a move. Thus, our analysis may have to turn to a more microlevel (e.g., conversations within a meeting), rather than general behaviors over the course of the team's life.

In this chapter we have introduced a model of structural balance consisting of four acts—move, follow, oppose, and bystand—and the sequences of these acts. By shifting the focus to a structural level of analysis, and by attending to the systemic and collective sequences these generate, we can begin to see the possibility of more rigorously describing a route to achieving healthy and positive team dynamics. The structural language gives us a vehicle with which to see both health and dysfunction, in a framework that is observable, testable, and ultimately, actionable.

REFERENCES

Alexander, C. (2002). *The nature of order: Vol 1. The center for environmental structure*. Berkeley, CA:

Amabile, T. M., Schatzel, E. A., Moneta, G. B., & Kramer, S. J. (2004). Leader behaviors and the work environment of creativity: Perceived leader support. *The Leadership Quarterly, 15*, 5–32.

Bateson, G. (1972). *Steps to an ecology of mind: A revolutionary approach to man's understanding of himself*. New York: Ballantine.

Cameron, K., Dutton, J. E., & Quinn, R. E. (Eds.). (2003). *Positive organizational scholarship: Foundations of a new discipline*. San Francisco: Berrett-Koehler.

Capra, F. (2003). *The hidden connections*. London: Flamingo.

Edmondson, A. C. (1999). Psychological safety and learning behavior in work teams. *Administrative Science Quarterly, 44*, 350–383.

Gersick, C. J. G. (1988). Time and transition in work teams: Toward a new model of group development. *Academy of Management Journal, 31*, 9–41.

Gladstein, D. L. (1984). Work-groups; sales-personnel-psychology; performance-level. *Administrative Science Quarterly, 29*, 499–517.

Gruenfeld, D., Mannix, E., Williams, K., & Neale, M. (1996). Group composition and decision making: How member familiarity and information distribution affect process and performance. *Organizational Behavior and Human Decision Processes, 67*.

Hackman, J. R. (1987). The design of work teams. In J. Lorsch (Ed.), *Handbook of organizational behavior* (pp. 315–342). Englewood Cliffs, NJ: Prentice-Hall.

Hackman, J. R. (1990). *Groups that work (and those that don't): Creating conditions for effective teamwork*. San Francisco: Jossey-Bass.

Heifetz, R. A. (1994). *Leadership without easy answers*. Cambridge, MA: Belknap

Isaacs, W.(1999). *A pioneering approach to communicating in business and in life: Dialogue and the art of thinking together*. New York: Doubleday.

Janis, I. L. (1982). *Victims of Groupthink* (2nd ed.). Boston: Houghton-Mifflin.

Kahn, B. E. (2005). The power and limitations of social relational framing for understanding consumer decision processes. *Journal of Consumer Psychology, 15*, 28–34.

Kantor, D., & Lehr, W. (1975). *Inside the family*. San Francisco: Jossey-Bass.

Marques, J. M., & Paez, D. (1994). The black sheep effect: Social categorization, rejection of ingroup deviates and perception of group variability. In W. Stroebe & M. Hewstone (Eds.), *European Review of Social Psychology* (Vol. 5, pp. 37–68). New York: Wiley.

McGrath, J. E., Kelly, J. R., & Machatka, D. E. (1984). The social psychology of time: Entrainment of behavior in social and organizational settings. *Applied Social Psychology Annual, 5*, 21–44.

Nemeth, C. J. (1995). Dissent as driving cognition, attitudes, and judgments. *Social Cognition, 13*, 275–291.

Osborn, A. F. (1957). *Applied imagination*. New York: Scribner.

Poole, S. P., & Hollingshead, A. B. (2005). *Theories of small groups: Interdisciplinary perspectives*. Thousand Oaks, CA: Sage.

Schachter, S. (1959). *The psychology of affiliation*. Stanford, CA: Stanford University Press.

Senge, P. (1990). *The fifth discipline: The art and practice of the learning organization*. New York: Doubleday.

Shaw, M. E. (1976). *Group dynamics: The psychology of small group behavior*. New York: McGraw-Hill.

Sherif, M. (1966). *In common predicament: Social psychology of intergroup conflict and cooperation*. Boston: Addison-Wesley.

Staw, B. M. (1976). Knee deep in the big muddy: A study of escalating commitment to a chosen course of action. *Organization Behavior and Human Decision Processes, 16.*

Thompson, L. (2001). *Making the team: A guide for managers*. Upper Saddle River, NJ: Prentice-Hall.

West, M. A. (1994). *Effective team work*. Leicester, England: BPS Books.

13

Positive Relationships
and Cultivating Community

Ruth Blatt
Carl T. Camden

I can't work with people I don't like, and I don't know of any way to go into work every day with absolutely no emotional contact with anybody.
—Temporary test grader

It's better to feel the harmony and the unity than to feel division and separation.
—Temporary administrative assistant

Connecting with other people is an integral aspect of going to work. We work not only to perform a job but also to experience the feeling of "belonging together" that constitutes a sense of community. Organizational members are traditionally brought together into a community by history, continuity, repetition, stability, persistence, and predictability in the pattern of interactions (Kogut & Zander, 1996). This chapter explores the role of positive relationships in cultivating a sense of community at work when this kind of continuity is absent. In the work life of the new economy (Cappelli, 1999), in which organizations look more like markets than the traditional bureaucratic organizations of the Industrial Age, many employees are tied together neither by a shared past, common organizational membership, nor an anticipated future together. Yet we know little about how a sense of community can flourish under these circumstances. In fact, most of what we know about temporary employment points to the corrosion of community at work (Hulin & Glomb, 1999).

In this chapter, we ask where sense of community comes from in organizations typical of the new economy. We focus on what cultivates a sense of community when conditions for community development are unfavorable—when employment is temporary and individuals working together are relative strangers interacting in the short term. Our conclusions are based on a qualitative study of the experiences of community of veteran temporary employees. Our findings suggest that when we subtract continuity from organizations, positive connections in the present, which are experienced viscerally in the here and now, serve as a key mechanism for binding temporary employees to their coworkers, cultivating community, and facilitating the performance of work tasks. Whereas relationships at work involve continuity of interactions and build slowly over time (Gabarro, 1987), *connections* at work are bonds between people that are short and momentary and need not imply closeness or intimacy (Dutton & Heaphy, 2003). Connections are small units of relational microevents or micromoments (Collins, 1981). Connections are positive when they are subjectively experienced as such by the participants in them. Thus our use of positive refers to the experienced quality of the connection rather than its outcome (Dutton & Heaphy, 2003). We find that positive connections that help cultivate community are those that entail inclusion, a felt sense of being important to others, experienced mutual benefit, and shared emotions. Our findings suggest that positive connections improve individuals' experience of work and facilitate their task performance.

Our study contributes to the field of positive relationships at work by suggesting that sense of community under conditions of transience is cultivated by microrelational moves—small acts of positive connecting—enacted by individuals in the context of their ongoing doing of work, rather than by the macro-organizational practices that have traditionally sought to build community in work settings characterized by permanence and stable membership. These positive connections serve as substitutes to organizational practices for fostering community because for most temporary employees, organizational practices often exclude rather than include. Thus this chapter presents opportunities for relational research at the crossroads of the growing literatures on the relational foundation of work and the changing nature of work.

We begin by defining sense of community and presenting why it is important to understand its development in organizations. We then identify a gap in the organizational literature with respect to how community at work develops when workers are temporary, thereby lacking membership, a past, or a future in the organization. Under these conditions, organizational practices may in fact foster alienation and detachment rather than a subjective sense of belonging together for temporary employees. We then present an exploratory study of the experiences of community of a sample of veteran temporary employees. A thematic analysis of the data suggests that in the new world of work, acts of positive connecting between individuals that are part of the ongoing conducting of work help build a sense of perceived togetherness, thereby fostering a sense of community at work. Based on our findings, we discuss opportunities for future research.

SENSE OF COMMUNITY AT WORK

Defining Sense of Community at Work

Sense of community is a subjective sense of belonging together with others, a sense of solidarity with them (Weber, 1946). It is "a feeling that members have of belonging, a feeling that members matter to one another and to the group, and a shared faith that members' needs will be met through their commitment to be together" (McMillan & Chavis, 1986. p. 9). This use of the term *community* is relational rather than geographic (Gusfield, 1975). Sense of community is not circumscribed by time and space and it can develop even when people do not interact regularly, may rarely or never meet, or when their interactions are otherwise limited. When experiencing sense of community, individuals maintain their separateness and diversity simultaneously with their sense of togetherness and commonality. Sense of community reflects people's attraction to each other, but is partial in that members of the community may not share all aspects of their identities and may have a sense of belonging with other communities (Brodsky & Marx, 2001).

Several uses of the term *community* in the literature illustrate these properties. For example, occupational communities are defined according to perceived commonality in the nature of the work in which members engage, the kind of identity they draw from their work, and the values, norms, and perspectives they apply to their work (Van Maanen & Barley, 1984). Yet members of occupational communities may never meet. Moreover, they are also members of organizational communities, and their membership in both these communities is partial (Zabusky & Barley, 1997). Another example is provided by communities of practice (Orr, 1990), in which community refers to the experience of commonality around the meaning of work. Members of communities of practice engage in the same kind of work, but they are not necessarily members of the same organization, nor do they necessarily interact regularly. Their sense of community comes from interactions in which they construct a collective interpretation of their work, rather than from common organizational membership and long-term affiliation. A third example comes from Internet communities, in which people with common interests or life circumstances interact electronically, unrestrained by time and space (Rothaermel & Sugiyama, 2001). Internet communities provide people with information, social interaction, and emotional benefits through their contribution and connection with others (Sproull & Patterson, 2004). Yet members of Internet communities do not meet face to face, are not officially members of an organization (anyone may join or leave an Internet community), and their involvement in the community may be limited to a single time or may continue into the long term (Beenen et al., 2004).

In all three examples, community refers to a feeling of belonging together and commonality that can form between people even when they do not interact regularly, meet face to face, or share organizational memberships. Yet, in all three types of communities, members see the community as a reference group and often act in accordance with its norms (Van Maanen & Barley, 1984). They participate and contribute and in return enjoy informational, social, and emotional benefits. Communities "offer members positive ways to interact, important events to share and ways to resolve them positively, opportunities to honor members, opportunities to invest in the community, and opportunities to experience a spiritual bond among members" (McMillan & Chavis, 1986, p. 14).

Traditional Perspectives on Cultivating Sense of Community at Work

Organizational scholars, as well as seasoned managers, have long known that when employees experience a sense of community with the organization, they are likely to act on its behalf. People have a fundamental need to belong to a collective and form positive attachments to others, which, when met, leads them to transcend self-interest (Andersen & Chen, 2002; Baumeister & Leary, 1995). The feeling of belonging together that characterizes sense of community leads individuals to perceive a shared fate with the organization and thereby internalize its objectives and become committed to them. Accordingly, they are more likely to take actions that are aligned with organizational goals, values, and norms (McMillan & Chavis, 1986). Thus, sense of community at work benefits both individuals—by offering the experience of belonging rather than alienation at work—and organizations—which benefit from the increased contribution of their members.

Accordingly, a rich research tradition has explored how organizational practices can increase the sense of community of organizational members. Two mechanisms have been offered for how these practices exert their influence: organizational identification (Dutton, Dukerich, & Harquail, 1994; Tyler, 1999) and organizational culture (O'Reilly & Chatman, 1996). Organizational identification occurs when membership in an organization leads individuals to incorporate the organization into their self-concept (Pratt, 1998). Once an employee incorporates the organization in his or her social identity, then acts that benefit the organization are seen as benefiting the self (Dutton et al., 1994). Organizational practices that facilitate identification are those that increase the salience of common group membership and facilitate family-like cohesive dynamics between organizational members (Pratt & Ashforth, 2003).

Organizational culture is a system of shared values and norms promoting organizational interests that is internalized by organizational members. It brings organizational members together through their shared attitudes, norms, and interpretations of events (O'Reilly & Chatman, 1996). Organizational culture translates individuals' social attachment to the collective into behaviors that benefit the organization (O'Reilly & Chatman, 1996). Organizational practices that facilitate the internalization of organizational culture include rituals, displays of symbolic artifacts, use of unique language, telling stories, and norms that promote the values of the organization (Schein, 1992). The process of socialization into an organizational culture is lengthy; it takes time for newcomers to participate in, learn, and internalize the organization's unique norms (Van Maanen & Schein, 1979).

The Case of Temporary Employees

The processes of socializing into the organizational culture and developing identification are oriented to the long term. They are built over time with an implicit assumption of continuity in the organization. The changes in self-concept associated with organizational identification are relatively enduring (Rousseau, 1998) and socialization into the culture presumes a future in the organization. Moreover, both identification and socialization are more likely to occur when employees are also organizational members. Organizational identification requires the individual to be a member in the organization, because it is membership in the collective that triggers identification processes (Tajfel, 1978). Likewise, organizational membership is an important part of socialization into the culture, because the culmination of the socialization process is attaining the status of an "insider" (Van Maanen & Schein, 1979). In the absence of organizational membership, a shared history, or an expected future in the organization—as is the case for temporary employees—organizational practices that build a sense of community through identification and socialization into the culture are unlikely to be effective.

Moreover, the nature of temporary employment creates barriers to traditional community. Organizations are forced to actively differentiate temporary employees from permanent ones to avoid what is known as *coemployment,* when a company's relationship with the temporary employee takes on characteristics of traditional employment, rendering it legally liable for decisions regarding salaries, benefits, and termination that are made by the temporary agency (Barley & Kunda, 2004). This differentiation continuously reminds temporary employees of their outsider status and their inferior rights in the organization (Rogers, 1995).

In the absence of long-term membership to trigger identification and socialization into the culture, and against the backdrop of organizational practices that exclude rather than include temporary employees, perpetually reminding them of their outsider status, how does sense of community develop for temporary employees? The existing literature does not provide an answer to this question, which rises in importance as organizations increasingly employ temporary employees and contractors (Camden, 2003; Carre, Ferber, Golden, & Herzenberg, 2000). Does this imply that sense of community at work is impossible to achieve among temporary employees, that it is less important for them, or that if formed, community cannot be conducive to organizational goals? Some scholars have argued that temporary employees do not experience sense of community at work. Rather, they are alienated from others at work and consequently do not go beyond their narrow job descriptions to advance organizational goals. They maintain "arm's length" relations with the organization and its employees (Hulin & Glomb, 1999; Tsui, Pearce, Porter, & Hite, 1995; Wheeler & Buckley, 2000; Wiesenfeld, Raghuram, & Garud, 1999). Others, however, have observed that in fact, transience and short-term employment can go hand in hand with a sense of community at work and the associated commitment to organizational goals (Florida, 2002; Rousseau, 1998).

In this chapter, we side with and extend the latter view. We assumed that sense of community can and does occur under conditions of temporary employment and set out to empirically examine the factors that play a role in those instances in which temporary employees experience a sense of community at work. Our findings suggest that in the absence of organizational membership or long-term employment, connections with coworkers may play a more significant role in building community than the relationship with the organization at large. Our study sets the stage for exploring the role of relationships with coworkers in cultivating a sense of community, thereby increasing our understanding of how positive relationships can serve as a substitute to organizational practices. Moreover, we offer an alternative perspective to the current literature on temporary employees, which emphasizes their exclusion and alienation. By studying positive instances of sense of community, we pave the way toward building a vision of work in which individuals who are temporarily employed can feel a sense of belonging together with others, leading to positive individual and organizational outcomes.

METHODS

Given our goal to build theory about how sense of community is cultivated for temporary employees, for whom organizational practices that traditionally build community are less pertinent, we utilized an inductive, theory-building methodology (Eisenhardt, 1989). Our stance was that sense of community is context-specific and situated, which means that we cannot simply transfer the concept, which is well studied and specified in more stable contexts, to workplaces characterized by transience (Sonn, Bishop, & Drew, 1999). Thus, we set out to understand the experience of community from the perspective of the temporary employees themselves to identify constructs and images that realistically capture the new world of work (Barley & Kunda, 2001). To this end, our methods involved in-depth interviews with a sample of veteran temporary employees in various occupations.

Sampling

Our sampling was theory driven (Glaser & Strauss, 1967), whereby we sought to interview people who do different types of work, but in similar work arrangements (e.g., employees of a temporary employment agency who conduct their work on-site at a client firm). Our second criterion was to identify and interview people with significant experience as temporary employees. We assumed that veteran or "expert" temporary employees would have larger banks of experiences to draw from to identify and discuss experiences of sense of community at work. Third, we sought variance in the sample in the nature of their occupation, so that our conclusions about community would not be confounded with characteristics of the occupation. Thus, our sample was selected based on the following criteria: (a) the interviewee was working as a temporary employee for Kelly Services for at least 1 year; (b) he or she worked frequently (defined as within the top 30% of hours per year) for Kelly Services; and (c) he or she was in either the commercial division, which includes light industrial, administrative, and retail sales, or the professional division, which includes scientists, lawyers, and software developers. The last criterion was set to maximize variance in occupations and skill levels. We contacted 661 individuals who met these criteria and invited them to participate in the study. Of these, 92 employees expressed willingness to participate. Our final sample comprised 30 employees with whom we could conveniently schedule interviews. Interviewees were evenly split between the commercial and professional divisions and worked in the Washington, DC, Philadelphia, and Los Angeles areas. Their experience working as temporary employees ranged from 16 months to 15 years. Their ages ranged from 24 to 73 and their occupations spanned less skilled jobs such as retail sales or light industrial work to professional positions such as lawyers and scientists. Ten were men and 20 were women, reflecting the greater prevalence of women in the temporary workforce population (Bureau of Labor Statistics, 2005).

The interviews were all conducted by Blatt from June through September 2004 and lasted about 45 minutes each. Seventeen interviews were conducted in person and 13 were conducted over the phone. The interview protocol was developed to tap into people's situated knowledge about their life circumstances (Rubin & Rubin, 1995). The interviews began with background questions about the respondents—what they do, how they came to work as a temporary employee, and their day-to-day life in the current assignment. Next, they were asked to tell a story of a time from their tenure on a temporary assignment when they felt that they were part of a community. The meaning of the term *community* was not defined for them because we were interested in their understanding of the experience of community. During and following the telling of the story, probing questions such as "How did you know you were part of a community?", "What led up to or contributed to your experience of community?", and "How did this experience impact your work?" encouraged them to reflect on the meaning of this experience. Next, they were asked to tell a story of when they did not feel part of a community at work and were probed with similar follow-up questions. Finally, the interview concluded with a series of questions asking them to reflect on sense of community in general. Questions included, "Is feeling like a member of a community important to you? Why or why not? What do you think it means to be a part of a community? How does it feel when you are a part of a community? How do you think that sense of community at work built?" We did not specifically ask about the role of relationships with others but rather focused on how sense of community is experienced and built.

Analysis

The analysis proceeded in the following stages in accordance with the grounded theory approach (Glaser & Strauss, 1967). First, using qualitative data analysis software, we conducted "open coding" of the interviews (Strauss & Corbin, 1998), reading through the transcripts and attaching codes to units of text in a manner that was as open and inclusive as possible. In the next phase of the analysis, we read through the excerpts coded in each of the categories. For each category, we compared the various instances with one another in an attempt to elaborate the theoretical properties of the category: What are its dimensions? What are the conditions under which it is pronounced or minimized? What are its major consequences? What is its relationship to other categories? How does it relate to other properties? (Glaser & Strauss, 1967). In the final stage of theory building, we created tables in which we explored the theoretical properties of our constructs and assessed the extent to which we had empirical support for these properties.

FINDINGS

All respondents generated at least one story of a time when they felt a sense of community at work, lending credence to our conjecture that temporary employment and sense of community are not mutually exclusive. To our surprise, three of the respondents could not recall a time in which they did not feel a sense of community at work. Our analysis of the respondents' stories and their reflections on sense of community suggested several themes. Next we present our findings regarding what constitutes sense of community for temporary employees, how they perceive it to be created and cultivated, and how it impacts them.

What Is a Sense of Community for Temporary Employees

Given that community and temporariness do not traditionally go hand in hand in organizations, we first present our findings regarding what constitutes a sense of community among temporary employees. The stories revealed that sense of community for temporary employees is characterized by feelings of inclusion, felt sense of importance, experienced mutual benefit, and shared emotions with others. The first dimension is inclusion, which is similar to the notion of belonging that is a building block of sense of community in permanent settings (McMillan & Chavis, 1986) but without any implication of continuing to belong in the long term. Rather, inclusion is about belonging to the collective in the present moment. Many of the employees reported feeling a sense of community when they felt that they belonged to something. As a document reviewer said:

> A lot of times when you're a temp they don't include you in meetings because they feel it doesn't affect you, and when they started to include me in certain meetings, because they realized that if I'm a part of the project then it is obviously going to affect me. So community-wise, when they started inviting me to meetings or even out to lunches, it made me feel much more included . . . it made me feel like I could hear what everybody else was hearing. Obviously, I could take a part of the meeting and use it, they felt like I needed to take something from the meeting also.

The second dimension of sense of community was a feeling of importance to others. For example, a research assistant said that he felt a sense of community when coworkers

> acknowledge your work—your personal feelings. They take that into account when other stuff happens. For example, I was really, really busy with a school project, and I would usually tell them that during lunch or things like that and they would listen and they would remember it. So then if I'm really busy with the school project they will come to me with fewer requests. So I believe that they have listened to me and they have understood what I need. And they have been very considerate so I think that makes me feel like a part of a community.

For temporary employees, sense of community at work means being viewed not just as "a temp" but rather as a person whose unique situation other people care about.

The third dimension of sense of community is experienced mutual benefit, the feeling that one has made a contribution to others and that this contribution is reciprocated. As a chemist said, a sense of community means that "you contribute something towards others, you have really made camaraderie with other people, you are not afraid of talking to other people, you're not afraid to express your opinion." The sense of community hinges, however, on a perception that this contribution is reciprocated. Temporary employees are concerned about fairness, respectful treatment, and recognition. As an office manager said, a sense of community means "that you are thought of as a valuable person." There is a sense of mutual benefit. As a biologist said, sense of community means "providing strength in other people's weaknesses, providing help when it's needed, seeing things before you're asked to do them, being a cheerleader or at times being a leader, if that needs to be done, just overall supporting each other."

The final dimension that characterized sense of community is sharing emotions with others at work. An administrator gave an example:

> My son graduated from high school this year and my supervisor came to the graduation and he came to the graduation luncheon . . . I just felt like that he was like really involved and interested in my life and what I was doing as well even on a personal side so I thought that was good. The sense of community was that he wanted to share in my joy.

Our respondents' stories of experiencing a sense of community were full of celebrations, and moments of fun, joy, and laughter.

Sharing emotions also means that individuals feel understood by others; that others can empathize with their experience. As a paralegal told:

> I think there was a sense of community because we were all sort of the same age, not really sure what we wanted to do. There was a lot of camaraderie be-

cause we had similar backgrounds, we were similar ages and we had similar mindsets at that moment.

A unique feature of the shared emotions component of sense of community for temporary employees is that it is not based on a shared history, because there is relatively little history on which to build. Rather, shared emotions are based on shared felt experience, stance, and approach toward work life, regardless of whether the other person is a temporary employee.

In sum, our findings suggest that sense of community for temporary employees comprises four components: inclusion, felt sense of importance, mutual benefit, and shared emotions with others at work. We also found that the sense of community experienced by temporary employees did not develop over time, nor was it expected to last. It developed swiftly and lasted as long as the employees interacted, much like the "swift trust" that develops among temporary teams (Meyerson, Weick, & Kramer, 1996). In fact, some of the temporary employees talked about the importance of maintaining an optimal level of social distance lest they mistakenly feel that the sense of community has permanence that in reality, it does not. As a chemist said:

> I don't want to get—I don't want to get too ingrained in the—also because I've been, over the past 3 years, in four jobs. So I don't want to learn to love any place and feel too accepted there . . . It's nice to be able to eat with the people because you would take lunch together, and then to have something in common to talk about. It's good to be able to exchange jokes with them and it's good if you do have a common enemy and it's that sort of environment to all be on the same side, because then it's not just you against a world ... but you can take it too far because if you're looking at it from a temp angle, you don't know how long you're going to be there. So if you develop long-lasting or relationships that should be long-lasting with individuals there, then you deceptively feel now you're a part of the community because you have those relationships.

Although the particular friendships forged at work can last beyond a particular assignment, our respondents were well aware that the sense of community they felt was situated in the present. Their sense of community entailed momentary experiences of unity during which they appeared to remain aware of their separateness (Sandelands, 2003).

Where Does the Sense of Community Come From: The Role of Positive Connections

How does a sense of community develop? We found that positive connections were an important way that temporary employees explained the cultivation of a sense of community at work. Their stories suggested that it was in the space of interactions between coworkers that sense of community developed. Specifically, it was fostered through positive connections. Dutton and Heaphy (2003) defined positive, or high-quality, connections as the bond or "tissue" between people that occurs in social interaction. Positive connections need not imply a shared history or a future of interactions. Like sense of community, they occur in the present moment. Among the temporary employees we studied, positive connections occurred in conversations held as part of routine work, in rituals and celebrations, and in interactions beyond the content of work. In all of these contexts, they were experienced by our respondents as conduits of inclusion, importance, mutual benefit, and shared emotions that comprised for them the experience of sense of community and that, for the most part, were not formally granted or encouraged by the client organization.

The first component of where sense of community comes from is inclusion. Whereas permanent employees experience inclusion by virtue of their membership in the organization and the practices and policies that encourage identification and socialization, temporary employees are formally excluded from the purview of such practices by contract. Furthermore, informal organizational practices serve to remind them of their outsider status. A scientist gave a poignant example of organizational exclusion:

> One of the very first weeks I started, there were some permanents that had just been hired on, and we were in a safety meeting on a Friday morning, and they were introducing new people, and there were a few of us temporaries in there. And they were introducing some new employees so I got nervous thinking I was going to be put on the spot and what have you. But they really didn't even mention us, they only mentioned the new permanents. So yeah, it was somewhat of a slap in the face.

Being treated as a nonperson by the organization is the opposite of the experience of a sense of community. Rather than organizational practices fostering inclusion, our respondents credited momentary acts of inclusion enacted by their peers for cultivating their sense of community. To connect with others is to belong, to be no longer alone or on the periphery. An administrative assistant said:

> I appreciate that that they pull me into the fold. And like when they have special occasions, birthday parties, or someone does something good in their personal life, they give a little party or show appreciation, with food or a card or something and they extend that to me.

Acts such as this one, of extending an invitation to participate in social life, were talked about by our respondents as builders of a sense of community. In the moment of a connection, individuals are not alone; they become part of a social form that is greater than the sum of its parts (Sandelands, 2003). Moments of inclusion are particularly meaningful for temporary employees against the backdrop of their exclusion.

The second component of where sense of community comes from—felt sense of importance—means that others care about your unique situation and circumstances. Many permanent employees infer their importance by virtue of their role and membership in the organization. However, temporary employees' role in the organization as temporary undermines their feelings of importance. As a research assistant said, "I mean people would comment 'Oh, she's only a temp,' . . . because you're like a second citizen because of a lot of the privileges that aren't given to me as a temporary employee." Moreover, organizational policy often does not take the input of temporary employees into account in the work process, suggesting to them that their preferences are inconsequential. As a document reviewer recounted:

> The head of the document review process was leaving the company and she had a huge meeting with my boss, who was also her boss, and they talked about certain issues that needed to be done with the process. Well, because I was running it, I felt that I should've been in the meeting. Because then they turned around and gave me certain things to do with the process, but because they weren't running it, they gave me things that weren't reachable.

Against the backdrop of organizational practices that indicate to temporary employees that their role and input are not important, personal connections that signal that the other person is important can foster a sense of community. A test grader said:

> Part of the community is I guess when you walk in the door and people say, "Hello," to you and people greet you with your name. That there is some sort of recognition, identification, or seeing you as a person beyond just the number.

A different test grader told of how a coworker increased everyone's sense of community by recruiting people to participate in a talent show:

> One of the girls, who loves to make contact with like everybody, was going around extending personal invitations to people, "Will you be in the talent show and what's your talent?" kind of, pursuing that type of thing.

These personal invitations were moments of connecting in which the coworker signaled to others that they are important to others or that they have something unique to contribute, and they served to increase sense of community.

Positive connections also bolstered temporary employees' sense of mutual benefit. These served to counteract the common experience of lack of appreciation from the organization. For example, a microbiology technician recounted why she felt her contribution is not appreciated,

> I'm working here full time. I'd like to be counted as a full person, not a half of a person because I'm a temp. At corporate offices they said, "Oh, wow, microbiology lab. You guys handle so much with only a person and a half." And I was like, "Hello, wake up call! Person and a half?" That statement brought down to me and told to me that, you know, you're not counting me as a full person because I'm not fully employed by the company.

Being counted as a "half person" when in fact she is working full-time meant that there was no experience of mutual benefit with the organization, where she exchanged her effort for social and material rewards. The lack of mutual benefit undermines sense of community for temporary employees because they do not feel that their contribution is reciprocated with the appropriate appreciation and recognition.

However, when temporary employees experienced positive connections, they felt a sense of mutual benefit, as a result of which they made an effort to contribute something to others and receive something beneficial in return. The benefits they reported receiving were both instrumental to the work and also socioemotional, including emotional support. In the following quote, a chemist, herself an immigrant from Russia, who worked alongside coworkers from many nationalities, told how exchanges of help and support during moments of connecting at work help build a sense of community.

> Even if somebody doesn't ask, I just help and see what goes on and if something goes askew, they call me because they know that I help. So just, yes, it's a community. Because we are all good workers . . . [one of my coworkers is a] Buddhist and he is a very eloquent guy and kind; helpful. And I remember when I had problems with my grandson when he was a teenager, it was the Philippine woman said, "I will go to church; I will pray for him. I'll pray for him." I'm telling you, and this guy, Cambodian guy, and Chinese guy, how to say, they watch me. They want me to be effective. If something puts a cloud on my face, somebody is here. I appreciate it.

Similarly, a test grader told of how sense of community is built by exchanges of help:

> In fact, right now we just have a coworker that was in the hospital and we collected for a fruit basket and we sent her some cash to help her because she will not get paid because there are no sick days. There are no vacation days.

Dutton and Heaphy (2003) wrote about positive connections as vehicles for the exchange of resources and information, as a means of obtaining knowledge, and as means for personal growth. These features of positive connections increase the perception of mutual benefit between coworkers. In connections with others, our respondents helped others or were helped, taught others or were taught, and otherwise engaged in mutual support. Temporary employees appeared to largely rely on their coworkers, rather than organizational practices and policies, to gain a sense of a fair exchange at work that is an important building block of sense of community.

Finally, positive connections contributed to the shared emotions component of sense of community, because it was in moments of connecting that temporary employees shared positive and negative emotions. Within positive connections, temporary employees express themselves and thereby feel that they are understood. Not only are positive connections arenas for authentic interaction and self-expression, they are also opportunities for people to find points of similarity. This similarity increases liking and also creates opportunities for expressing empathy (Brickson, 2000). A test grader said that what increases a sense of community is that "we're all in the same position, have the same frustrations and all looking to do the best job that we can possibly do . . . if you have common interests you're more or less going to get together with that person."

Positive connections help build a sense of community by providing opportunities to share emotions even in the absence of a shared history or long-term relationship. Temporary employees do not usually stay long enough in a given workplace for their relationships with others to be founded on a shared history. As a chemist said, he did not feel a sense of community in a laboratory where friendships were based on shared history:

> They were sort of sorority girl types and they were very clique-y and I was coming in to do one kind of test, they were all doing another kind of test and they literally had one lab split into two halves. They all spent their day on that side of the room and if they wanted to go to lunch, they all went to lunch.

Rather than occurring in the context of long-standing friendships, emotions were shared between temporary employees and their coworkers during spontaneous moments of personal connection. As a document reviewer said:

> It's great because you can work and then you can joke around. When you're alone or by yourself, when no one's interacting with you, it makes the day go a lot slower and it makes you unhappy.

A biologist told of how a sense of community was built with two officemates through their connections with each other:

> It was an amazing thing because I found myself opening up more and these were two exceptional women, where we really melded together. We really encouraged each other, we were very open with each other, we built each other up. So it was really—it felt good and it was the first time I'd ever experienced that, and it was a really positive thing.

In sum, our analysis revealed that temporary employees credited positive connections with their coworkers as the building blocks of community, particularly against the backdrop of formal organizational policies that undermined their sense of community. These connections, albeit short-lived and spontaneous, were powerful vehicles for experiencing the inclusion, importance, mutual benefit, and shared emotions that help cultivate a sense of community at work. These connections helped enable the experience of belonging together at work even in the absence of a shared past, organizational membership, or an anticipated future.

What Are the Consequences of a Sense of Community Among Temporary Employees

Our findings suggest that sense of community among temporary employees both enhances their subjective experience of coming to work and helps enhance task performance. Our respondents felt that their experienced sense of community made the workplace a more fun place to be. It boosted their motivation to come to work every morning and increased the likelihood that they would stay despite alternative job offers. For example, an information technology worker said:

> I mean it definitely makes you want to come to work every day. It's kept me on. I've had several opportunities to leave and the community I think would be one of the things that I try to balance when I try to make those decisions. Like I don't want to leave these guys, you know, this is a good group of people and the fact that we're able to, every now and again, take a breather and just do something fun is a good thing.

Our respondents felt that when they felt a sense of community at work, going to work was a pleasant experience. This finding suggests that sense of community can serve to counteract the negative aspects of temporary work—such as alienation, depersonalization, and loneliness—that are often documented in the literature (Rogers, 1995).

Sense of community also appeared to enhance task performance by increasing their motivation to do a good job and by enabling them to communicate and collaborate with others. A biologist attested to his increased motivation, "[sense of community] makes you feel like you're more a part of the group and when that happens it kind of gives you more drive to do your job really well and go above and beyond." In contrast, a data entry worker told that lack of sense of community had the opposite effect: "It's impacted my work because I'm not as motivated now." This finding corroborates existing literature on the positive impact of sense of community at work on people's willingness to contribute to the goals of the collective (McMillan & Chavis, 1986). Moreover, sense of community helps task performance through its effect on communication and coordination. A research assistant said:

> I think [sense of community] has helped me because I can communicate with other people fairly easily. When I need to ask for something, I can just go straight to the person without any hesitation and just ask immediately and if I need to get some clarification, I will not feel embarrassed to ask them, because they're like good friends to me.

Conversely, our respondents reported that the absence of a sense of community hindered coordination and, consequently, task performance. As an office manager said, "It impacts me in the fact that I really have a hard time keeping up with what I need to do and what I'm assigned to do."

In sum, our findings suggest that sense of community at work for temporary employees enhances their personal subjective experience at work. Beyond the personal benefits they enjoy, they also reported increased motivation and effort to perform well, as well as an increased ability to do so through enhanced communication and coordination channels. Although our evidence speaks only to the experience of the temporary employees themselves, these findings suggest that coworkers, as well as the client organization at large, may benefit from these positive effects of sense of community for temporary employees.

DISCUSSION

Our study of the experience of community of temporary employees has identified positive connections as important building blocks of sense of community when employees lack membership, a past, or a future in the organization. There are several implications of these findings for research on positive relationships.

First, our findings suggest that positive connections may serve as substitutes for organizational practices as mechanisms for fostering a sense of community at work. The opportunity for relationships research lies in exploring microsituational mechanisms, whereby the agency of the actors, the contents of conversations, and the emotional energy of momentary interactions can account for observed social phenomena (Collins, 1981), rather than structural mechanisms, such as the norms, values, role expectations, and routine patterns of interaction (Scott, 1998), in contexts when transience and change weaken or counteract macroorganizational influence. In the new world of work, organizational practices of exclusion can undermine loyalty, identification, perceived justice, and prosocial behavior toward the organization (Ang & Slaughter, 2001; Chattopadhyay & George, 2001). As a substitute, microrelational moves enacted by people in the ongoing doing of work may have powerful effects toward furthering these ends. Paradoxically, lack of common and stable membership may strengthen the impact of positive connections on people's attitudes and behaviors. Future empirical research can assess whether temporariness moderates the relation between positive connections and outcome variables that are known to be impacted by organizational practices, such as identity (Whetten & Godfrey, 1998), meaning (Brief & Nord, 1990), and prosocial behavior (Brief & Motowidlo, 1986). This implication echoes Golden-Biddle, GermAnn, Reary, and Procyshen's (chap. 16, this volume) finding that under conditions of organizational turmoil, positive relationships have powerful effects on people's ability to adapt to organizational change.

A second implication of our findings is that positive connections that give people a sense of commonality and belonging together may be an important means of organizing to accomplish work. Current research distinguishes between work-related and "private" interactions at work (Tschan, Semmer, & Inversin, 2004). Yet, to the extent that nontask interactions help cultivate a sense of community that contributes to the accomplishment of work, a more fruitful avenue of research may be to examine which aspects of interactions facilitate the accomplishment of work and why. For example, McGinn (chap. 14, this volume) highlights the important role of shared language for maintaining community in the face of transience and external threat. Other research has shown that interactions that build trust (Adler, 2001), enable people to take the perspective of another (Heath & Staudenmayer, 2000), and establish mutual respect (Gittell, 2003) can facilitate coordination, particularly when organizational coordinating mechanisms such as standards, structures, and routines are ineffective. Further research is needed to understand these relatively understudied mechanisms for organizing.

Another fruitful avenue for relational research suggested by our findings is to explore the relational competencies that facilitate adaptation to the new world of work. At the individual level, our findings suggest that certain skills, such as the ability to form connections easily and the ability to detach oneself from the organization without negative emotions, may play an important role in adapting to a transient work life. The fact that three of our respondents could not think of a time they did not experience a sense of community at work suggests that for our respondents, positive connections with others were salient. One interpretation of this finding is that those temporary employees who develop the competence to quickly and positively connect with others are more likely to persist in temporary work than individuals for whom negative experiences of disconnections are salient. Moreover, our findings suggest that fostering positive connections is in itself valuable work. As such, future research can explore the possible costs of engaging in this work, such as depletion of emotional resources or lack of recognition from the organization for performing it (Fletcher, 1998).

At the organizational level, adapting to the new world of work may necessitate developing a different paradigm for how employees attach to organizations. Organizations may seek a model of attachment that is strong but that enables employees to detach easily and without damage either to the individual or to the organization. Under traditional models, attachment is strong and long-lasting, but separation can cause damage to both sides. Practices for building community under these models have included strengthening markers of identity and culture, but these tactics may backfire with temporary, virtual, or part-time employees. One mechanism based on a new relational stance toward employees would be for organizations to acknowledge tenure of association with the organization, rather than continuity of employment, as a marker of status. Even if employees work for the organization intermittently, the tenure of that relationship would be recognized and their contribution appreciated. Employees who leave would maintain contact with the organization as part of an "alumni network." Another mechanism would be to acknowledge contribution based on an employee's relative added value to the product or service, rather than the terms of employment. Under this criterion, bonuses would be given to those who contributed most to accomplishing organizational goals, regardless of their formal membership status. A new model of the employee–organization relationship would enable blended workforces of permanent and temporary workers to organize more integrated communities and enjoy the benefits of such. Staffing firms, which employ individuals to work on-site at other organizations, would also need to develop a relational competence to ensure continuity of contact with employees, even when they are on extended assignment elsewhere.

More broadly, we found that removing an apparently essential elements of organizations—continuity—yields paradoxical consequences, namely that organizational practices that foster community among permanent employees can have the opposite effect on temporary employees. We raise the possibility that fostering community in the absence of continuity involves interventions not at the organization level but at the level of interactions among members; interactions that raise the salience of the present and enhance the positive experience of the here and now. As work life increasingly becomes infused with flux, discontinuity, and multiplicity, people's need for a sense of belongingness, commonality, and unity remains. This chapter suggests that positive relationships can make a difference.

ACKNOWLEDGMENTS

We are grateful to Jane Dutton and Emily Heaphy for their helpful comments on earlier versions of this chapter.

REFERENCES

Adler, P. S. (2001). Market, hierarchy, and trust: The knowledge economy and the future of capitalism. *Organization Science, 12,* 215–234.

Andersen, S. M., & Chen, S. (2002). The relational self: An interpersonal social-cognitive theory. *Psychological Review, 109,* 619–645.

Ang, S., & Slaughter, S. A. (2001). Work outcomes and job design for contract versus permanent information systems professionals on software development teams. *MIS Quarterly, 25,* 321.

Barley, S. R., & Kunda, G. (2001). Bringing work back in. *Organization Science, 12,* 76–95.

Barley, S. R., & Kunda, G. (2004). *Gurus, hired guns, and warm bodies: Itinerant experts in a knowledge economy.* Princeton, NJ: Princeton University Press.

Baumeister, R. F., & Leary, M. R. (1995). The need to belong: Desire for interpersonal attachments as a fundamental human motivation. *Psychological Bulletin, 117,* 497–529.

Beenen, G., Ling, K., Wang, X., Chang, K., Frankowski, D., Resnick, P., et al. (2004, November). *Using social psychology to motivate contributions to online communities.* Paper presented at the ACM CSCW04 Conference on Computer Supported Cooperative Work, Chicago.

Brickson, S. (2000). The impact of identity orientation on individual and organizational outcomes in demographically diverse settings. *Academy of Management Review, 25,* 82–101.

Brief, A. P., & Motowidlo, S. J. (1986). Prosocial organizational behaviors. *Academy of Management Review, 11,* 710–725.

Brief, A. P., & Nord, W. R. (Eds.). (1990). *The meaning of occupational work.* Lexington, MA: Lexington Books.

Brodsky, A. E., & Marx, C. M. (2001). Layers of identity: Multiple psychological sense of community within a community setting. *Journal of Community Psychology, 29,* 161–178.

Bureau of Labor Statistics. (2005). *Contingent and alternative employment arrangements.* Washington, DC: U.S. Department of Labor, Bureau of Labor Statistics.

Camden, C. T. (2003). Benefits for the free agent workforce. In O. S. Mitchell, D. S. Blitzstein, M. Gordon, & J. Mazo (Eds.), *Benefits for the workforce of the future* (pp. 241–248). Philadelphia: University of Philadelphia Press.

Cappelli, P. (1999). *The new deal at work.* Boston: Harvard Business School Press.

Carre, F., Ferber, M. A., Golden, L., & Herzenberg, S. A. (Eds.). (2000). *Nonstandard work: The nature and challenges of changing employment arrangements.* Champaign, IL: Industrial Relations Research Association.

Chattopadhyay, P., & George, E. (2001). Examining the effects of work externalization through the lens of social identity theory. *Journal of Applied Psychology, 86,* 781–788.

Collins, R. (1981). On the microfoundations of macrosociology. *American Journal of Sociology, 86,* 984–1014.

Dutton, J. E., Dukerich, J. M., & Harquail, C. V. (1994). Organizational images and member identification. *Administrative Science Quarterly, 39,* 239–263.

Dutton, J. E., & Heaphy, E. D. (2003). The power of high-quality connections at work. In K. S. Cameron, J. E. Dutton, & R. E. Quinn (Eds.), *Positive organizational scholarship* (pp. 264–278). San Francisco: Berrett-Koehler.

Eisenhardt, K. M. (1989). Building theories from case study research. *Academy of Management Review, 14,* 532.

Fletcher, J. K. (1998). Relational practice: A feminist reconstruction of work. *Journal of Management Inquiry, 7,* 163–186.

Florida, R. (2002). *The rise of the creative class.* New York: Basic Books.

Gabarro, J. J. (1987). The development of working relationships. In J. W. Lorsch (Ed.), *Handbook of organizational behavior* (pp. 172–189). Englewood Cliffs, NJ: Prentice-Hall.

Gittell, J. H. (2003). A relational theory of coordination. In K. S. Cameron, J. E. Dutton, & R. E. Quinn (Eds.), *Positive organizational scholarship: Foundations of a new discipline* (pp. 279–295). San Francisco: Berrett-Koehler.

Glaser, B. G., & Strauss, A. L. (1967). *The discovery of grounded theory: Strategies for qualitative research.* New York: Aldine de Gruyter.

Gusfield, J. R. (1975). *Community: A critical response.* New York: Harper & Row.

Heath, C., & Staudenmayer, N. (2000). Coordination neglect: How lay theories of organizing complicate coordination in organizations. In B. M. Staw & R. Sutton (Eds.), *Research in organizational behavior* (Vol. 22, pp. 153–191). Greenwich, CT: JAI.

Hulin, C. L., & Glomb, T. M. (1999). Contingent employees: Individual and organizational considerations. In D. R. Ilgen & E. D. Pulakos (Eds.), *The changing nature of performance: Implications for staffing, motivation, and development* (pp. 87–118). San Francisco: Jossey-Bass.

Kogut, B., & Zander, U. (1996). What firms do? Coordination, identity, and learning. *Organization Science, 7,* 502–518.

McMillan, D. W., & Chavis, D. M. (1986). Sense of community: A definition and theory. *American Journal of Community Psychology, 14,* 6–23.

Meyerson, D., Weick, K. E., & Kramer, R. M. (1996). Swift trust and temporary groups. In R. M. Kramer & T. R. Tyler (Eds.), *Trust in organizations: Frontiers of theory and research* (pp. 166–195). Thousand Oaks, CA: Sage.

O'Reilly, C. A., & Chatman, J. A. (1996). Culture as social control: Corporations, cults, and commitment. In B. M. Staw & L. L. Cummings (Eds.), *Research in organizational behavior* (Vol. 18, pp. 157–200). Greenwich, CT: JAI.

Orr, J. E. (1990). Sharing knowledge, celebrating identity: Community memory in a service culture. In D. Middleton & D. Edwards (Eds.), *Collective remembering* (pp. 169–189). London: Sage.

Pratt, M. G. (1998). To be or not to be? Central questions in organizational identification. In D. A. Whetten & P. C. Godfrey (Eds.), *Identity in organizations: Building theory through conversations* (pp. 171–207). Thousand Oaks, CA: Sage.

Pratt, M. G., & Ashforth, B. E. (2003). Fostering meaningfulness in working and at work. In K. Cameron, J. E. Dutton, & R. E. Quinn (Eds.), *Positive organizational scholarship* (pp. 309–327). San Francisco: Berrett-Koehler.

Rogers, J. K. (1995). Just a temp: Experience and structure of alienation in temporary clerical employment. *Work and Occupations, 22,* 137–166.

Rothaermel, F. T., & Sugiyama, S. (2001). Virtual Internet communities and commercial success: Individual and community-level theory grounded in the atypical case of TimeZone.com. *Journal of Management, 27,* 297–312.

Rousseau, D. M. (1998). Why workers still identify with organizations. *Journal of Organizational Behavior, 19,* 217–233.

Rubin, H. J., & Rubin, I. S. (1995). *Qualitative interviewing: The art of hearing data.* Thousand Oaks, CA: Sage.

Sandelands, L. E. (2003). *Thinking about social life.* Lanham, MD: University Press of America.

Schein, E. H. (1992). *Organizational culture and leadership.* San Francisco: Jossey-Bass.

Scott, W. R. (1998). *Organizations: Rational, natural, and open systems* (4th ed.). Upper Saddle River, NJ: Prentice-Hall.

Sonn, C. C., Bishop, B. J., & Drew, N. M. (1999). Sense of community: Issues and considerations from a cross-cultural perspective. *Community, Work, and Family, 2,* 205–218.

Sproull, L., & Patterson, J. F. (2004). Making information cities livable. *Communications of the ACM, 47,* 33.

Strauss, A. L., & Corbin, J. (1998). *Basics of qualitative research: Grounded theory procedures and techniques* (2nd ed.). Thousand Oaks, CA: Sage.

Tajfel, H. (1978). Social categorization, social identity, and social comparison. In H. Tajfel (Ed.), *Differentiation between social groups: Studies in the social psychology of intergroup relations* (pp. 61–76). London: Academic.

Tschan, F., Semmer, N. K., & Inversin, L. (2004). Work related and "private" social interactions at work. *Social Indicators Research, 67,* 145–182.

Tsui, A. S., Pearce, J. L., Porter, L. W., & Hite, J. P. (1995). Choice of employee–organization relationship: Influence of external and internal organizational factors. *Research in Personnel and Human Resource Management, 13,* 117–151.

Tyler, T. R. (1999). Why people cooperate with organizations: An identity-based perspective. In B. M. Staw & L. L. Cummings (Eds.), *Research in organizational behavior* (Vol. 21, pp. 201–246). Greenwich, CT: JAI.

Van Maanen, J., & Barley, S. R. (1984). Occupational communities: Culture and control in organizations. In B. M. Staw & L. L. Cummings (Eds.), *Research in organizational behavior* (Vol. 6, pp. 287–365). Greenwich, CT: JAI.

Van Maanen, J., & Schein, E. H. (1979). Toward a theory of organizational socialization. In B. M. Staw & L. L. Cummings (Eds.), *Research in Organizational Behavior* (Vol. 1, pp. 209–264). Greenwich, CT: JAI.

Weber, M. (1946). *From Max Weber* (H. H. Gerth & C. W. Mills, Trans.). New York: Galaxy.

Wheeler, A. R., & Buckley, R. M. (2000). Examining the motivation process of temporary employees: A holistic model and research framework. *Journal of Managerial Psychology, 16,* 339–354.

Whetten, D. A., & Godfrey, P. C. (Eds.). (1998). *Identity in organizations: Building theory through conversations.* Thousand Oaks, CA: Sage.

Wiesenfeld, B. W., Raghuram, S., & Garud, R. (1999). Communication patterns as determinants of organizational identification in a virtual organization. *Organization Science, 10,* 777–790.

Zabusky, S. E., & Barley, S. R. (1997). "You can't be a stone if you're cement": Reevaluating the emic identities of scientists in organizations. In B. M. Staw & R. Sutton (Eds.), *Research in organizational behavior* (Vol. 19, pp. 361–404). Greenwich, CT: JAI.

14

History, Structure, and Practices: San Pedro Longshoremen in the Face of Change

Kathleen L. McGinn

White collar workers increasingly rely on group interaction rather than individual expertise to generate knowledge and create innovative responses to new questions (Bechky, 2003). Blue collar workers, in contrast, increasingly work outside the archetypal work gang and operate machinery or computers in isolation from others. As manual labor evolves to require more interaction with machines and less coordination and communication with other workers, highly valued relational aspects of blue-collar work are dwindling. How can positive communities among workers be enhanced while work becomes progressively more asocial?

Many groups of people who share location, interests, or activities are considered communities. An urban neighborhood can be a community; an online forum of deco art enthusiasts can be a community; a group of bikers that ride together on weekends can be a community. Regardless of whether the basis for a community is geographical, conceptual, or behavioral, a community is a *positive* one when its members actively participate in a network of supportive relationships. This definition assumes that it is the quality of the connection among community members that connotes a positive community. Membership in a positive community enhances the "quality of character of human relationship" (Gusfield, 1975, p. xvi). Attending to the "quality . . . of relationship" entails a pervasive, intentional, and constructive focus on mutual support and on members as individuals. Positive communities endow the group and its individual members with a primary source of identity, a basis for interpretation, and a channel of influence outside the community (McMillan & Chavis, 1986).

If the positive aspects of community remain and even strengthen during "unsettled" (Swidler, 1986) times, membership in the community has the potential to shape new ways in which members think about themselves and one another, their work, their workplaces, and their role in society. Through the community, the changing nature of work can be interpreted, support can be made available, and voice can be solidified and given weight. In this chapter, I focus on the sources of adaptation and flexibility that allow a community to heighten its dominant and positive role in workers' lives as the world around them changes. I explore a dynamic, positive community during a time of dramatic transformation. This exploration reveals three factors that underlie the strengthening of a positive community when it is confronted with external change: shared history, a densely connected structure of interaction, and regular communication across members.

The theory presented in this chapter is based on my study of the longshoremen[1] in San Pedro, California. This community, located on a peninsula incorporated within the city of Los Angeles but 27 miles south of downtown, is home to the largest group of longshoremen residing in one location in the United States. Longshoremen and their families have made up the majority of San Pedro's population for over half a century. The community among the longshoremen in San Pedro blends the occupational communities discussed by Van Maanen and Barley (1984), the neighborhood communities considered in social capital research (Putnam, 1993) and community psychology (McMillan & Chavis, 1986), and the social worlds described by Strauss (1993). On the job, longshoremen carry out all of the physical and logistical tasks associated with loading and unloading ships. All longshoremen in San Pedro and across the West Coast of the United States are members of the International Longshoremen's and Warehousemen's Union (ILWU). They are employed by more than 70 companies, mostly foreign-owned, connected through the Pacific Maritime Association (PMA). Throughout the second half of the 20th century, the single voice of the ILWU dictated the terms of employment with the loosely tied, diverse set of maritime employers.

In 2002, when I began my interviews and observations, the maritime employers in San Pedro were moving toward broad-scale implementation of information technology on the ports. The longshoremen were facing a fundamental economic and technological transformation of their work after more than 30 years of incremental change (Rosenkopf & Tushman, 1998). Beginning in 1971, longshore work gradually incorporated the many features of

---

[1]Fourteen percent of ILWU members are women. San Pedro is home to three ILWU locals: Local 13, the longshoremen local; Local 63, the clerk local; and Local 94, the foreman local. Foremen, because of their supervisory responsibilities and necessary ties with management, tend to have weak ties with members of the longshoreman community. I use the term *longshoremen* when referring to registered longshoremen and clerks in San Pedro, regardless of gender.

containerization.[2] Interpersonal and collective relationships among long-shoremen and the day-to-day interactions between employers and workers slowly altered to accommodate these changes. In the late 1990s, employers initiated small forays into new information technologies for tracking cargo containers as they were moved from ship to port to truck or train. The onset of these changes shook the community awake. San Pedro's longshore-men braced themselves for "the second revolution of the intermodal trans-portation industry" (Venieris, 2000). Many felt the imperative to rekindle the community spirit that had been dwindling during the years of incremen-tal change. They believed that renewed unity would help them cope with the new technologies. Using data from observation, interviews, and archival research, I worked iteratively over a 30-month period to develop a grounded understanding of the evolution of community among the workers as they faced the changing environment.

The study of San Pedro's longshoremen revealed how shared history, shared structure, and shared communication practices allow a commu-nity to adapt and increase its focus on mutual support during "unsettled times" (Swidler, 1986). Shared history is perhaps the most prominent fea-ture of the longshoreman community. For more than 150 years, San Pedro has been home to the majority of the men and women who work on the docks of Los Angeles and Long Beach. Every longshoreman in San Pedro knows the stories of those who have come before him. Shared history pro-vides the base, the core that members turn to for identity as individuals and as a group. History recalls the collective actions taken in other unset-tled times, and thereby provides a narrative conveying the belief that the community can be powerful and effective in the face of today's change. Shared structure—the set of relationships among the workers, their em-ployers, the local community, and society—is the flexible backbone of a strong community. Through the myriad links in this network, members hold themselves together in the workplace and in their daily lives outside work (Sewell, 1992). Supported by a foundation of shared history and structure, communities accommodate high uncertainty during periods of upheaval through shared communication practices. Communication prac-tices, the "strategies of action" (Swidler, 1986) that keep the community alive and fluid, offer a daily dose of identity and connection to the work-ers. Through regular communication across its reach, the positive com-

---

[2]Until the 1960s, maritime cargo was loaded, transported, and unloaded crate by crate. Once on the docks, crates were moved onto pallets. Forklifts moved the pallets into trucks and ware-houses. A standardized, sealed shipping container was invented in the 1950s. In the second half of the 20th century, new shipping systems designed around these large (20, 40, or 45 feet long by 8 feet wide 8.5 feet high), interchangeable containers drastically increased transport efficiency, allowing the seamless movement of cargo between ships, trucks, and trains. By 2000, approxi-mately 90% of all maritime cargo was shipped in containers.

munity is continually responding to and shaping its own history, its network structure, and its external environment.

HISTORY: THE BASIS FOR BELIEF
IN THE COMMUNITY

The longshoremen of San Pedro are a throwback to simpler times, days of physical labor and families living and working together. Paradoxically, they are also an exemplar for modern employees, independent workers in a contingent relationship with employers, enjoying generous benefits and job security. Their status rests on an amalgamation of the globalization of trade, the constraints of physical space (you cannot outsource a port), government intervention, competition across employers, and the history of labor in the United States. Stories told in conversation and in writing reinforce the longshoremen's belief in their status, their place in society. The tales include the bloody labor battles of 1934 in which two San Pedro longshoremen were shot and killed during a protest march, the 99-day strike of 1937 that established the union-controlled hiring halls still in operation today, the Modernization and Mechanization agreement of 1960, and the strike of 1971 that opened the door for the technological transformation of the ports. Retelling these stories reminds the longshoremen that their work is important and valued, that their efforts add up to more than a paycheck. It communicates their shared history as well as their shared future.

Bourdieu (1977) offered the concept of *habitas,* the idea that history produces more history through an integration of past experiences into present "perceptions, appreciations, and actions" (p. 82). Events that embody the pervasive, intentional and constructive focus on mutual support within a community are enlarged and reified over years of retelling. The assimilation of workers into the San Pedro community and the socialization into shared values is accomplished through stories of fellow workers of the past, their struggles, and the resolution of those struggles through joint action. Through recounting their shared history, the longshoremen not only define and exert control over their work (Van Maanen & Barley, 1984), they define themselves.

Stories of workers long gone meld multiple affiliations (McMillan & Chavis, 1986). They integrate ties based on territory, work, and shared ideals into a single affiliation with the community of workers. These stories give the workers a reason to coalesce during times of change, by highlighting the ways in which community played a critical role when those who preceded them were faced with similar threats and challenges. Storytelling conveys a place in the larger society even as that place is threatened and altered. Each struggle their predecessors endured is a reason for the longshoremen's unity in the face of current threats; each success their predecessors secured is a source of collective pride today.

Shared history lays the foundation for a positive community when it illuminates the benefits that accumulate from unity. Although history inevitably canonizes its individual heroes, to foster community it needs to also laud the multitude of players, named and unnamed, who contributed to the accomplishments of the whole. A shared history communicates that the group, rather than any one person, has earned the respect of the outside world. To belong to the community is to command that respect, that place in society.

STRUCTURE: A FOUNDATION OF RELATIONSHIPS

The San Pedro community exhibits cohesion and structural equivalence (Burt, 1987). Each element of the social structure played a role in reinforcing the positive community as new technologies came into the ports. In San Pedro, social cohesion is to some extent a product of proximity. Longshoremen are relatives of and neighbors to other longshoremen. They interact daily in coffee shops, grocery stores, gyms and restaurants. Proximity and face-to-face interaction, though not necessary for strong communities (Van Maanen & Barley, 1984), reliably lead to community building (Homans, 1961; McMillan & Chavis, 1986; Vaughn, 2002). But cohesion is in San Pedro is due to shared preferences for mutual interaction as well as shared location. Many of the longshoremen I met had compelling interests outside work. They were in school, running small businesses, traveling, raising children and engaged in side careers. In spite of these other avenues for interaction, their close friends, the people they chose to be with outside work, were often other longshoremen.

Unlike most employees who work for one employer in one workplace, most longshoremen work for a different employer on a different ship each day.[3] This feature of their work has the potential to strain any cohesion among community members. Having experienced the costs of this dispersion early in their history, West Coast longshoremen secured the union-controlled hiring hall. Each person wanting to work on a given day comes to the hiring hall to get his port assignment. The hiring hall decreases the conflict between the administrative control of work (hierarchy, rules and procedures, etc.) and "communal principles of control" (Van Maanen & Barley, 1984, p. 290). For longshoremen, the daily interaction with one another

---

[3]The Mechanization and Modernization Agreement instituted the use of "steadies," who report to the same pier and employer every day. This has strained the community, but is somewhat mitigated by steadies reporting to the hiring hall for extra work whenever there is insufficient work for them in their steady position.

in the hiring hall, outside the purview of management, affords the community significant influence over the identities and activities of its individual members. The constant rotation of workers at an employer's pier or ship constrains management's influence over the longshoremen's interpretations of new stimuli in the environment. During times of tumult, technological and economic changes are discussed and interpreted in the hiring hall rather than under the roof of the employer.

In addition to strong cohesion, San Pedro's longshoremen exhibit a notable level of structural equivalence. Because of the hiring hall process for assigning work, every longshoreman is a potential coworker of every other longshoreman. Longshoremen are also structurally equivalent in their relationships with their employers and their work. There are multiple job classifications, ranging from lashers who secure the containers on the ships, to crane operators who operate the huge cranes that move the containers from ship to land and vice versa. After those registered at a certain job classification have taken the jobs they want for the day, other longshoremen can take any job for which they have the required training. This reduces differences in experiences as well as differences in income. Longshoremen are also structurally equivalent relative to local, state and federal government and the public. Viewed from the outside as powerful, unified, and willing to exercise their muscle, one longshoreman is the same as another and they are all separate and different from the mainstream. Accepting employment as a longshoreman means taking on the larger role in society as well.

Shared structure forms the relational foundation for a community of workers. Physical proximity, preferences for within-community interaction, and structural equivalence provide consistent reinforcement of meaning through complementary messages across relationships and activities (Small & Supple, 2001). Increasing interpersonal cohesion boosts trust (Jehn & Shah, 1997; McGinn & Keros, 2003) and enhances attraction among group members (Zaccaro & Lowe, 1988). Cohesion and structural equivalence lead to a convergence in emotions (Anderson, Keltner, & John, 2003) and a common way of making sense of the issues faced by the community (Fletcher & Fitness, 1996; Wegner, Erber, & Raymond, 1991). These shared emotions and cognitions further enhance the sense of connection and belonging among members. As with shared history, shared structure encourages a collective response to environmental change.

COMMUNICATION PRACTICES:
KEEPING THE COMMUNITY FLUID

Among San Pedro's longshoremen, face-to-face communication in the hiring hall allows the development of a common language supporting the goals and ideals of the community of workers (Bechky, 2003). As the language is spoken, work takes on a meaning beyond the task. Longshoremen have developed a language of safety (Van Maanen & Barley, 1984), economics and unity that identifies and solidifies their community. The language of safety, economics, and unity is spoken in the hiring halls and on the docks, as well as during casual social interactions among longshoremen. Talk of safety and economics ties the community together, exposes members of the community as members, and helps the longshoremen interpret changing circumstances. Talk of unity emphasizes that the collective is valued, active, real, and that the power of the collective serves its members even in the face of change or challenge. This language shapes the members' responses to and understandings of the changes surrounding them.

Safety has been essential to the culture of longshoremen since they first started loading and unloading ships. Their jobs are objectively dangerous, with a fatality rate of 16.6 per 100,000 in 2003, putting longshoremen into the second most dangerous occupational group and industry in the United States.[4] Although the tasks carried out by a longshoreman fundamentally changed with the introduction of containerization, fatality and injury levels remained high. The number of recent deaths and the details of the latest injuries are a common topic in hiring hall conversations. But talk of safety conveys more than high injury rates; it expresses the physical, masculine identity of individual longshoremen and of the community of longshoremen. Longshoremen pride themselves on masculinity, but most of their jobs no longer involve strenuous physical labor. The ideals of masculinity and physicality are kept in the collective conscience through a constant discussion of safety and an ongoing litany of the dangers of longshore work. When the employers proposed new technological changes, the longshoremen translated the proposition into a question of safety. It was that translation that was offered to the public, thus shaping the negotiations with employers.

Talk of economics is heard throughout the hiring hall and on the docks. Longshoremen incessantly discuss how much they make per hour, how much more one job pays over another, and how much they earned last week, last month, and last year. There are repeated references to their role in the larger economy, the value of the goods passing through the ports each month, and the critical place they hold in international commerce. Longshoremen are among the best paid laborers in America (Kanter, 1999). A Class A longshoreman working 40 hours per week, 50 weeks per year, earns more than $100,000. Clerks, crane operators, and those who choose to work overtime can earn significantly more. Longshoremen communicate in-

---

[4]In terms of dangerous occupational groups, longshoremen are second only to agricultural workers, which include fishermen, farmers, and loggers. In terms of industry fatalities, the construction industry ranks number one.

ternally and externally that their key position in international trade justifies their high pay. Employers, seeking to impose technological changes, waged a campaign to raise public and governmental awareness of the millions of dollars in daily costs incurred during work slowdowns on the ports. The employers' efforts only served to increase the longshoremen's security about their critical role in the economy. While any one longshoreman spends his days performing the tedious tasks required for loading and unloading ships, talk of economics says that longshoremen together keep the national and international economy moving.

Unity among longshoremen is summed up in ILWU's motto, "An injury to one is an injury to all." This message is conveyed through banners in the hiring hall, on the locals' newspapers' letterhead, on the locals' Web sites, and in speeches made by local and international officers. Members are "brothers and sisters." Whether waiting in the hiring hall for work (the best jobs each day go to the longshoremen who have worked the fewest hours that month), discussing employer treatment (favoritism is strongly frowned upon even if it benefits a member), or making contributions to other unions (San Pedro families "adopt" and support families in other worker communities during work stoppages), the mantra of unity and solidarity is reinforced. As conversations around the new technologies take place in the hiring hall and on the docks, the longshoremen's responses are voiced in the language of unity—we will accept the changes only if the work is kept within the community and all are trained in the new systems.

The language of safety, economics, and unity underlies external as well as internal communication practices. During a time of upheaval, a positive community shapes its external message in a way that draws public attention to the impact of the change on the community. This is accomplished by translating the conditions facing the community into the community's language, rather than allowing external players to drive public understanding of those conditions (Checkoway, 1995). When new technologies first emerged on the docks, the longshoremen's first response was outright rejection. Some employers continued with implementation, creating the impetus for the longshoreman community to develop a shared understanding and response. Their shared history and structure shaped the contours of this response. History showed the futility of fighting implementation over the long run; cohesion ensured that the community would not be willing to trade clerk jobs (which would gradually be eliminated through the use of new information technologies) for more longshoreman work (which would increase as volume and turnover increased in response to more efficient information technologies); and structural equivalence dictated that any new technology would have to be understood and accepted by all if it were to be effectively used on the ports. The longshoremen's response was communicated to the employers and the public through the shared language of safety, economics, and unity. The changes would be welcomed by the long-shoremen as long as they did not further threaten the safety of the workers, the additional profits from the new efficiencies were shared with the workers, and those in jobs most affected by the new technologies would continue to be able to earn the same wages as others in the community.

Social worlds are built and linked to the larger society through communication practices (Strauss, 1993). The influence a positive community has on members during a time of discontinuous change comes not only through shared history and structure, but also through the interactions taking place in the community during the upheaval. Communication practices include day-to-day interactions among community members. They also include the messages exchanged with parties external to the community, either explicitly through the media or other outlets, or implicitly through the outsiders' observations of community members. Communication, whether internal or external, informal or formal, establishes the tone and the details of the community's response to new technologies (Bechky, 2003). When confronted with change, communities respond in ways that are congruent with their history and structure (Kelley & Steed, 2004). Communication, improvised in the moment, acts as the avenue for rapid adaptation (Turner, 1991). This fluidity enabled by communication and steeped in history and structure gives positive communities the potential for shaping both the change itself and the community's response to that change.

Like structure, which provides a snapshot of a community at a specific point in time but is continuously evolving, communication practices mirror the realities of the present while adapting to environmental shifts. Like history, which embodies the meaning behind membership, communication practices encourage visible and visceral statements of the values of membership. Communication practices offer constant reminders of what the community stands for, who its members are, and what members are expected to do and believe in the face of change.

CONCLUSION

A positive community enhances the "quality of character of human relationship" (Gusfield, 1975, p. xvi) across its members. This enhancement is revealed in a pervasive, intentional and constructive focus on mutual support and on members as individuals as well as contributing parts of the group. As the chapters across this volume illustrate, a positive community of workers is a tangible, vital, influential force in the workplace. When confronted with changes largely out of their control, community may become more central to the identity, interpretation, and influence of traditional workers. A critical question is how positive communities can grow and thrive in changing work environments, when workers are especially in need of mutual support and understanding. This chapter has attempted to begin to address that question.

Blatt and Camden (chap. 13, this volume) suggest that in "settled" times, mutual support may be self-reinforcing, fed by the daily interactions among community members. Maintaining a positive community in settled times may not require much beyond simple, mutually beneficial communication. During "unsettled" times, however, these actions may be insufficient. The example of San Pedro's longshoremen suggests that three features interact to strengthen a positive community among workers during times of radical change: shared history, shared structure, and shared communication practices. A shared history offers a belief system carved out of the realities of the past—it illuminates the continuities that govern mutual support within the community. Shared structure, which reproduces quality connections among community members during stable times, binds the community together when external changes are pulling its members in different ways. Shared communication practices foster a mutually developed basis for translation and interpretation of the new circumstances confronting the community.

Through shared history, shared structure, and shared communication practices, positive communities of workers endow the group and its individual members with identity, a lens for interpretation, and a channel of external influence in a changing world. History cannot be changed, but interpretation of history can. Structure and communication are constantly in a state of flux. Future research can help us understand the dynamic processes within positive communities that allow historical interpretations, social structure, and communication practices to evolve while ensuring continued mutual support to members during times of change.

REFERENCES

Anderson, C., Keltner, D., & John, O. P. (2003). Emotional convergence between people over time. *Journal of Personality and Social Psychology, 84,* 1054–1068.

Bechky, B. A. (2003). Sharing meaning across occupational communities: The transformation of understanding on a production floor. *Organization Science, 14,* 312–330.

Bourdieu, P. (1977). *Outline of a theory of Practice.* Cambridge, England: Cambridge University Press.

Burt, R. S. (1987). Social Contagion and Innovation: Cohesion versus Structural Equivalence. *American Journal of Sociology, 92,* 1287–1335.

Checkoway, B. (1995). Six strategies of community change. *Community Development Journal, 30,* 2–20.

Fletcher, G. J. O., & Fitness, J. (Eds.). (1996). *Knowledge structures in close relationships: A social psychological approach.* Mahwah, NJ: Lawrence Erlbaum Associates.

Gusfield, J. (1975). *Community: A critical response.* Oxford, England: Blackwell.

Homans, G. C. (1961). *Social behavior: Its elementary forms.* New York: Harcourt, Brace & World.

Jehn, K., & Shah, P. (1997). Interpersonal Relationships and Task Performance: An examination of mediating processes in friendship and acquaintance groups. *Journal of Personality and Social Psychology, 72,* 775–790.

Kanter, L. (1999, February 22). On the waterfront: Possible strike by longshoremen threatens L.A.'s economy. *Los Angeles Business Journal.*

Kelley, G. J., & Steed, L. G. (2004). Communities coping with change: A conceptual model. *Journal of Community Psychology, 32,* 201–216.

McGinn, K. L., & Keros, A. T. (2003). Improvisation and the logic of exchange in embedded negotiations. *Administrative Science Quarterly, 47,* 442–473.

McMillan, D. W., & Chavis, D. M. (1986). Sense of community: A definition and theory. *Journal of Community Psychology, 14,* 6–23.

Putnam, R. D. (1993, Spring). The prosperous community: Social capital and public life. *American Prospect, 4,* 13.

Rosenkopf, L., & Tushman, M. (1998). The coevolution of community networks and technology: Lessons from the flight simulation industry. *Industrial and Corporate Change, 7,* 311–346.

Sewell, W. H. (1992). A theory of structural duality, agency, and transformation. *American Journal of Sociology, 98,* 1–29.

Small, S. A., & Supple, A. (2001). Communities as systems: Are communities more than the sum of their parts? In A. Booth & A. Crouter (Eds.), *Does it take a village? Community effects on children, adolescents and families* (pp. 161–174). Mahwah, NJ: Lawrence Erlbaum, Associates.

Strauss, A. L. (1993). *Continual permutations of action.* New York: Aldine de Gruyter.

Swidler, A. (1986). Culture in action: Symbols and strategies. *American Sociological Review, 51,* 273–286.

Turner, J. H. (1991). *The structure of sociological theory* (5th ed.). Belmont, CA: Wadsworth.

Van Maanen, J., & Barley, S. R. (1984). Occupational communities: Culture and control in organizations. *Research in Organizational Behavior, 6,* 287–365.

Vaughn, D. (2002). Signals and interpretive work: The role of culture in a theory of practical action. In K. A. Cerulo (Ed.), *Culture in mind: Toward a sociology of culture and cognition* (pp. 28–54). New York: Routledge.

Venieris, M. (2000, February). Modernization and mechanization: A tradition of partnerships. Second Annual ILWU State of the Trade and Transportation Industry Town Hall Meeting. (Press Release). Retrieved February 15, 2005 from *www.uces.csulb.edu/Files/PressReleases/ilwupressrel.html*

Wegner, D. M., Erber, R., & Raymond, P. (1991). Transactive memory in close relationships. *Journal of Personality and Social Psychology, 61,* 923–929.

Zaccaro, S. J., & Lowe, C. A. (1988). Cohesiveness and performance on an additive task: Evidence for multidimensionality. *Journal of Social Psychology, 128,* 547–558.

15

Commentary: Positive Relationships in Groups and Communities

William A. Kahn

The chapters in this part of the book illustrate the meaning and the momentum of positive relationships in work groups and communities. These relationships are created when people perform certain acts that are meant as, and received as, positive in the context of social situations and structures that enable and sustain such acts. This is a straightforward formulation: People simply act in positive ways toward one another, and are enabled to do so by communal structures, cultures, and processes. These actions create relationships among people that enable them to feel valued and valuable, seen and witnessed, cared for and appreciated, productive and engaged. People are contained within rather than left outside the shelter and movement of their groups and communities. Members are reasonably authentic, saying what they think and feel and acting in ways that feel real to them. They do good work together.

The simplicity of this formulation belies the difficulty of actually creating, and then sustaining, positive relationships in groups and communities. Indeed, such relationships are relatively rare, at least in their pure form, as people struggle just to make their social systems function. Work groups and communities are filled with people trying their best to accomplish various tasks in circumstances that vary from ideal to miserable, with a lot of room in between. They feel somewhere between a lot and a little sense of connection, commitment, and belonging, as they manage the ambivalence between wanting to run into and run away from groups with which they may feel more, or less, identified. They carry the histories of their previous experiences of group and communal life into their present circumstances, for better or for worse. They also operate within larger contexts—organizations, institutions, and political realities—that shape and constrain their experiences and behaviors.

Given these factors, it is no surprise that life in groups and communities involves some struggle, as people try to make sense of their tasks and environments, join with one another across gulfs of intent and desire, and get work done. When people rise above those struggles, and create something remarkable—havens of and for positive relationships—it is a marvelous, fragile thing. The chapters in this section suggest that certain conditions help create positive relationships in groups and communities, and that those conditions are in turn supported by various structures. In this chapter I describe those conditions, and the implications of positive relationships in groups and communities, before turning to thoughts about ongoing research.

CREATING CONDITIONS

The chapters in this part point to four underlying conditions that, taken together, help create and sustain positive relationships in groups and communities. These conditions—abundance, safety, boundaries, and positive spirals—are necessary if positive relationships are to become characteristic of groups and communities and not simply a function of the particular individuals who happen to be members of those systems.

Condition 1: Abundance

Sartre (Laing & Cooper, 1964) argued that felt scarcity—of attention, honor, humor, love, or whatever is wanted—is the fundamental disturbance of group life. If scarcity is the disturbance, then it stands to reason that abundance is the repair. By abundance, I mean many acts: of gratitude, compassion, selflessness, love, and concern. When group and community members reach out to one another, unbidden, they add to the underlying stores or reserves of the collective; they create a surplus from which all can draw. They replenish themselves and combat felt scarcity. They create the foundation for positive relationships.

The chapters in this part illustrate the various ways in which members of groups and communities can perform acts that create an abundance of positive connections with one another. Blatt and Camden (chap. 13) describe how positive connections, embedded within work interactions, create attachments among temporary organization members and enable them to positively engage one another and their work. McGinn (chap. 14, this volume) illustrates how the ongoing language of unity, and the communication practices more generally, among of a group of longshoremen bespoke a current of positive energy that coursed throughout the community. Ancona and Isaacs (chap. 12, this volume) write about how the use of certain acts among group members, selectively performed, create real movement in the group and enable members to create positive work relationships. Higgins (chap. 11, this volume), in her discussions of developmental networks, and Kahn (chap. 10, this volume), in his discussions of relational constellations, both suggest various ways in which people may invest in one another by performing acts that provide mentoring, career assistance, and other forms of support.

In each of these chapters, a steady stream of acts that people construe as positive creates the foundation for positive relationships. Members move toward one another in positive ways, over and again, with their language, their support, their assistance, and their warmth. They create an abundance of connection with one another, stockpiling goodwill and positive energy that they draw on in the course of their work with one another.

Condition 2: Safety

When people feel safe, they act as if their contributions—no matter how awkward or profound—will be regarded with some sort of appreciation. Members sense acceptance rather than rejection of who they are. Safety evolves from a series of repeated acceptances by group and community members of one another. Those acceptances sustain the abundance noted earlier; people are reinforced for moving toward one another in positive ways by how they are received. They feel safe in continuing to move toward one another. Safety—necessary for trust, intimacy, and authenticity—thus helps sustain the momentum of positive relationships in groups and communities (Smith & Berg, 1987).

Safety appears in different guises within the chapters in this part. McGinn (chap. 14) describes how the longshoreman community is marked by a certain cohesion—a set of bonds among members—that allows for an almost unconditional acceptance and the safety it entails. Higgins (chap. 11) notes that various levels of intimacy and investment mark relationships between developers and protégés, with implications for how safe the latter feels in accepting the support of the former. Kahn (chap. 10) echoes this, in his descriptions of the different types of relationships that make up the constellations that people create for themselves. Ancona and Isaacs (chap. 12) describe how group members who experience a sense of safety allow themselves, and one another, to perform particular moves, according to what the group needs, without needing to retreat to habitual acts that leave them and their groups mired in unproductive patterns. Blatt and Camden (chap.

13) note that when temporary workers experience the sense of being under-stood, of being taken in by and joined with one another, they feel safe enough to create a community with one another that compensates for their lack of ties to the organization itself.

In each of these chapters, safety operates as a lever of sorts, which, once triggered, enables people to move more closely toward one another in posi-tive ways. Over time, amidst the abundance of positive acts, safety be-comes a property of the collective; groups and communities become known as safe places in which members can make themselves vulnerable, in their words and acts (Schein, 1999).

Condition 3: Boundaries

Positive relationships occur within the context of boundaries that enable people to feel safe. Boundaries define our groups and communities. They show who is clearly inside. They enable people to feel contained within a social system. They therefore recognize themselves and are recognized by others as members, their contributions are accepted, their distress is ab-sorbed, and their support is given and received. In positive groups and communities, members are not abandoned; they are not dropped or iso-lated. Nor are members intruded on. Their autonomy remains intact, allow-ing them to move toward others without fear that they will lose something of themselves in the process of doing so. Positive relationships require such gatekeeping (Kahn, 2005). It is only when we are clearly within some sort of bounded space that we are able to express ourselves authentically and draw closer to others, certain in the knowledge it is reasonably safe to do so (Smith & Berg, 1987).

Boundaries are invoked in various ways in this section. Higgins (chap. 11) suggests that developmental relationships are marked by useful bound-aries that implicitly guide the shape and depth of what occurs between de-veloper and protégé. Such boundaries enable those relationships to flour-ish. Ancona and Isaacs implicitly invoke boundaries when they describe how team members remain within rather than exit or disengage from one another in the course of their performance of various effective moves. McGinn (chap. 14) offers a more literal, physical sense of boundaries in de-scribing the centers, such as the hiring hall, around which the community forms. These centers exist within the larger context of a community that shares a distinct occupation, a geographical place, and a language, all of which help create bonds among its members. Blatt and Camden (chap. 13) and Kahn (chap. 10) each describe how the nature of interactions creates networks, or constellations, that bind members to one another and help create attachments that exist in lieu of more formal, structural identifica-tions. In positive groups and communities, such attachments are sturdy enough to create boundaries that contain members who might otherwise drift away.

Implicit in these conceptions of boundaries is an optimal permeability (Alderfer, 1980). The boundaries that separate groups and communities from their environments are permeable enough to allow members to absorb useful information and feedback, yet impermeable enough to enable members to remain protected from noxious influences. Within that optimal zone people are able to engage in positive ways in the course of their work together.

Condition 4: Positive Spirals

Positive relationships in groups and communities are created through ongoing, self-perpetuating, mutually reinforcing acts that both offer and generate positive energy among their members. The resulting conditions, necessary for creating these ongoing relationships, are positive spirals: endlessly looping positive acts that, like energy, transform and reverberate and alter form but never simply come to a halt. Positive spirals are marked by begetting: A positive movement from one group or community member to another begets another, and another, and another, ad infinitum, until the acts take on a life of their own, or more precisely, until they become woven into the life of the group or community so deeply that they become cultural and outlast the turnover of any particular member (Schein, 1999). These positive spirals are crucial; they create and maintain momentum for positive acts that members contain to perform in the context of situations in which those acts might otherwise be difficult to conjure.

The chapters in this part invoke positive spirals in distinct ways. Ancona and Isaacs (chap. 12) describe positive teams as self-regulating; team members create useful patterns of moves, filling in acts as needed, which enable them to repair their teams in the course of their work together. Higgins (chap. 11) notes that positive relationships between developers and protégés are mutually reinforcing; positive moves toward one another are reciprocated, leading to further connection among those embedded in developmental relationships. Similarly, Blatt and Camden (chap. 13) and Kahn (chap. 10) describe how positive acts breed more positive acts, binding people more closely in the context of their organizational communities and relational constellations. McGinn (chap. 14) notes how the longshoreman community is sustained by the stories of its members; the resulting oral history, tapped into and created anew by each generation, weaves a fabric that surrounds and binds members to their community.

Each of these is an example of a positive spiral. Positive acts are met with positive acts. Investments yield dividends: Group and community members find that the positive energy that they emit toward one another is returned, and added to, prompting them to invest again. These spirals become self-regulating. Enough goodwill is created that positive energy becomes stored, like caches, to be drawn on during the inevitable moments when being positive—optimistic, caring, warm, inquiring, helpful—is difficult to come by. Positive spirals survive such hiccups, with only momentary pauses.

THE TIES THAT BIND

The positive relationships described in this part create, within the formal structures of groups and communities, relational structures defined by ties among members. These relational structures stem from positive acts that blossom into positive relationships, which, over time, become embedded within work groups and communities. Blatt and Camden (chap. 13) write about the emergent structure that appears among temporary workers; through the course of their interactions with one another, they create a community of peers that supplants a relatively minimal organizational structure. Similarly, Kahn (chap. 10) notes that the relational constellations that people form provide for them a specific way to attach to their organizations that has more power and meaning than the more abstract attachment of "organizational identification." Ancona and Isaacs (chap. 12) describe how the moves that members of positive teams make create centers that hold them in place as they go about their work. Each of these is a shadow structure, of sorts, that binds members in positive, healthy ways in the context of more formal group and organizational systems.

The ties that bind members together in positive groups and communities serve them well, in various ways. McGinn (chap. 14) describes how the ties among the longshoremen enable them to join together and create collective responses in the face of significant changes and turbulence in their industry, political contexts, and institutions. Blatt and Camden note that, in the lives of temporary workers who lack organizational membership or long-term employment, the sense of community that workers create with one another through daily interactions anchors them to their work. In both cases, community members are held fast in potentially difficult environments by the attachments that they create with one another through ongoing positive acts. These attachments sustain communities, to the point that they remain positive and healthy even as particular members come and go. As Ancona and Isaacs (chap. 12) suggest in regard to teams, positive relationships not only sustain groups but also render possible ongoing learning, health, and deep innovation.

The ties of positive relationships also have quite specific implications for individuals' experiences within their groups and communities. Higgins (chap. 11), in emphasizing the protégé as the center of the developmental network, articulates the desirable outcomes—career support, learning, and personal development—that emerge from positive developmental relationships, as modified by career goals and professional context. Blatt and Camden (chap. 13) and Kahn (chap. 10) both describe how individuals embedded in positive relational contexts are more likely to personally engage in their work, buoyed by a sense of meaning, safety, and connectedness with others. It is the particular nature of positive groups and communities to create what Ancona and Isaacs refer to as centers—which are created by and exist amongst the relationships among their members rather than in any particular spatial or temporal context—that anchor those members to one another and to the work that they do alone and with others.

NEXT STEPS

Each chapter in this part suggests some future directions for research into specific areas related to positive groups and communities. My aim here is to point to research that would be useful in developing increased knowledge about how the four conditions already articulated—abundance, safety, boundaries, and positive spirals—are created in groups and communities, to the point that they help trigger and maintain positive relationships. We know some things about these conditions, at least in a general way, but there is more specific knowledge that we need to create. Toward that end I offer three general categories of future research.

Research Focus 1: Structure

How groups and communities are organized—in terms of systems of coordination, authority, communication, control, design of tasks, and the like—unquestionably facilitates and undermines how members engage with one another. The overarching question here is what particular structural dimensions enable people to move toward one another in positive ways and help create mutually reinforcing positive relationships. It seems likely that one type of answer to this question involves forums of one sort or another. Forums—like work groups, mentoring relationships, community meetings, retreats and conferences, departmental gatherings, and even lunchrooms—bring people together and, structured appropriately, enable them to interact in positive ways. The research questions here include the following: What forums can different types of groups and communities best use to create the conditions for positive relationships among their members? How should these forums operate? How do they connect with other structural dimensions?

Research Focus 2: Courage

Smith and Berg (1987) noted the inherent paradox of safety: It does not exist in a group or community unless members act as if it already does. People must do or say something that they feel safe doing even though it may not, in fact, be safe to do so. Positive relationships, often enough, are a product of people taking the risk of moving closer to others—providing support or help without being asked to do so, acting in a warm or caring fashion, or reacting honestly—even though the group or community does not yet have a history of such acts. This requires courage. So too does the act of confronting others who act in ways that negate positive relationships, through their cynicism, hurtful actions, and withdrawals. Confronting this effectively requires people to make themselves vulnerable, in the face of possible rejection. The research questions here include the following: How do groups and communities promote such courage in their members? What structures, processes, and norms enable rather than disable such courage?

Research Focus 3: Leadership

Acts of leadership, from formal and informal leaders both, are necessary to interrupt the negative spirals that may mark groups and communities: the self-perpetuating cycles of battling, cynicism, despair, and other arenas of disconnection. We know a great deal about leadership, of course, in its various guises and situations, and about the characteristics of effective leaders. In the special case of positive groups and communities, however, we need to identify the leader's role. The leader needs to look carefully at a particular group or community, first to see where positive relationships do and do not occur, and then to see if those relationships flourish at the expense of negative relationships elsewhere in the system. The leader needs to interrupt negative spirals, by personally starting or contributing to positive spirals, with acts small and large. The leader also needs to be positive, maintaining a positive outlook while remaining authentic. The research questions here include the following: What enables leaders to perform such acts? What is it about them personally, their roles, their authorizations by others, their contexts? What enables them to remain resilient in the face of negativity?

GOOD HARBOR

The chapters in this part offer different versions of the ways in which groups and communities can offer their members good harbor: places that provide shelter from the inevitable storms of organizational life; that enable people to move toward one another in bounded, safe ways; and that give shape and meaning to people's work and their work experiences. Positive relationships sustain, and are sustained by, such work groups and communities. These relationships are difficult to create and sustain; they are fragile, and once disrupted, often difficult to re-create. Nor are they marked by unalloyed joy; they are not simply the linking of arms and singing "We are the world," although that gives off a nice feeling. They involve the acknowledgment of both the shadow and light of who people are when they are in sustained relation with one another. Groups and communities contain the best and worst of who we are. In this context, positive is about staying the course, about struggling well, and about hope and resilience. Ultimately, our agenda—research and otherwise—is about figuring out how to do that.

REFERENCES

Alderfer, C. P. (1980). Consulting to underbounded systems. In C. P. Alderfer & C. L. Cooper (Eds.), *Advances in experiential social processes* (Vol. 2, pp. 267–295). New York: Wiley.

Kahn, W. A. (2005). *Holding fast: The struggle to create resilient caregiving organizations.* London: Brunner-Routledge.

Laing, R. D., & Cooper, D. (1964). *Reason and violence: A decade of Sartre's philosophy, 1950–1960.* London: Tavistock.

Schein, E. H. (1999). *Organizational culture and leadership* (2nd ed.). San Francisco: Jossey-Bass.

Smith, K. K., & Berg, D. N. (1987). *Paradoxes of group life.* San Francisco: Jossey-Bass.

POSITIVE RELATIONSHIPS: ORGANIZATIONS AND ORGANIZING

16

Creating and Sustaining Positive Organizational Relationships: A Cultural Perspective

Karen Golden-Biddle
Kathy GermAnn
Trish Reay
Gladys Procyshen

Positive relationships at work, especially high-quality connections, have been shown to enhance individual and organizational well-being and effectiveness (Dutton 2003ba). In particular, they foster communication and the coordination of highly interdependent work (Fletcher, 1998; Hofer-Gittell, 2001, 2002), and they lead to the development of vibrant work environments that facilitate individual and organizational well-being (Worline et al., 2005). As such, they are a vital part of individuals' lives in accomplishing work in organizations (Dutton, 2003ba; Dutton & Heaphy, 2003; Worline et al., 2005). Yet, in spite of their benefits, such relationships are not typical in organizations. For example, Fletcher's (1998) study of an engineering firm shows how relational practices and their benefits "get disappeared" into the system through a process that constructs them as nonwork and dismisses them as inconsequential. Thus, although we are beginning to understand how positive relationships shape outcomes, we still have little understanding of the dynamics involved in creating and sustaining them in organizations (Baker, Cross, & Wooten, 2003; Bradbury & Lichtenstein, 2000; Dutton, 2003a, 2003b; Fletcher, 1998).

We gained insight into these dynamics when we encountered the case of Wetoka Health Unit (WHU) in Alberta, Canada, which has been recognized nationally and provincially for its innovation and excellent performance in public health. For years, leaders and staff of WHU generated positive relationships in delivering public health and community services that focus on preventing disease, and protecting and promoting individual and collective health and well-being. Serving the community in the health unit, as well as in homes, schools, and workplaces, the programs of WHU were established to protect and enhance population health and well-being. The members of WHU believed in serving clients and their communities the best way they could, and in supporting each other and the community as they accomplished this work. As a result, the positive relationships created in WHU transcended organizational boundaries to include clients and community partners.

This world was disrupted in the early 1990s when members of Wetoka Health Unit faced mandated disestablishment of their organization. Part of a provincial initiative to restructure the health delivery system by merging more than 200 hospital districts and 27 health units into 17 health regions, in 1995, the WHU was divided into two sections, each merging with a different region. For the first time, members of WHU would work in organizations that consisted not only of public health, but also acute and long-term care facilities. In one of the regions that would absorb a section of WHU, for example, public health would account for only 12% of the staff and 6% of the budget. As well, they would encounter challenges associated with merging different organizational cultures and service philosophies into a new entity. Facing the end of their organization, members of WHU intentionally sought to bolster the cultural forms and positive relationships that had come to represent their organization.

In this chapter, we draw on this empirical case to shed light on the dynamics of creating and sustaining positive organizational relationships in two respects. First, the case shows how the persistent and focused long-term work of leaders in WHU fostered the creation of cultural symbolic forms that not only shaped, but also were shaped by the enactment of positive relationships. Second, the case shows how this interdependent dynamic between culture and positive relationships resourced the ability of WHU leaders to navigate a situation of change that required that they dissolve their own organization but carry on their work. Our analyses point to how organizational members' capacities to create and sustain positive relationships can be fostered through the creation of central cultural forms. More generally, they point to the importance of culture for understanding how positive relationships in organizations are generated and institutionalized. We begin by providing the conceptualizations of positive relationships and culture that inform our analytic work. Then, we portray the dynamics of creating and sustaining positive relationships in the case of WHU. We end the chapter with a discussion of future research possibilities.

POSITIVE RELATIONSHIPS AND CULTURE

In this chapter, we use the term *positive organizational relationships* to mean those patterns of interacting that are characterized by a recurring but not necessarily intimate bond in which groups of people develop a sense of mutuality, positive regard, and respect for one another. People in these relationships feel enriched and perhaps even energized by them, rather than feeling reduced or threatened (Surrey, 1991). Moreover, people care about and actively strive to maintain these relationships, even during difficult times.

Positive organizational relationships are both similar to and different from high-quality connections (Dutton & Heaphy, 2003). They are similar in their features of regard, mutuality, and respect, but different in that they are more than temporary connections. As we use the term in this chapter, positive relationships are longer lasting high-quality connections among groups of people that imply at a minimum a recurring bond in the doing of work. They have a history (a past), a present, and an anticipated future that together influence the nature of the relationship. The energy generated in positive relationships therefore ebbs and flows over time and in concert with changes in the circumstances in which they are embedded.

There are various definitions of organizational culture (for comprehensive discussions, see Martin, 2002; Martin, Frost, & O'Neill, 2006). A predominant one is causal: Culture determines action through values that define desired ends (Martin, 2002; Swidler, 1986). In this view, the leader's role is one of managing symbols, such as value statements, to control organizational processes and influence behavior toward these desired ends (Martin, 2002; Smircich, 1983). Such symbols are conceived as vessels that carry meanings and provide models of reality (Feldman, 1986; Smircich, 1983). However, this conceptualization not only has encountered difficulties attempting to explain this causal relation (Martin et al., 2006; Swidler, 1986), but also lowlights the dynamics of culture.

Consequently, here we use a different conceptualization that regards culture as consisting of symbolic forms, or representations such as language, goals, beliefs, or mission, through which people in organizations experience and express meaning (Feldman, 1986; Golden, 1992; Martin, 2002; Rosen, 1985; Smircich, 1983; Swidler, 1986). Symbolic forms are publicly accessible, having been created and materialized. Organizational members draw on particular symbolic forms to interpret and take action. Thus, culture, as constituted in symbolic forms, shapes organizational members' capacities to create and sustain patterns of interaction such as positive relationships.

The connection between positive organizational relationships and culture is rendered visible when one considers symbolic forms as more than

inert vessels that simply carry meaning. Rather, symbolic forms have a creative force as people draw on and reshape them in enacting new ways of relating, such as positive relationships, and in sustaining these meaningful
patterns of interaction. As Swidler (1986) noted, when certain symbols "become more central in a given life, and become more fully invested with
meaning, they anchor the strategies of action people have developed" (p.
281). Applied to the present case of WHU, we are especially interested in understanding how particular symbols shape people's capacities to cultivate
positive relationships in organizations, and how these relationships can be
sustained over time in part by anchoring them in central symbolic forms.
As well, our analyses extend prior work by showing how positive relationships also shape culture, and how together, positive relationships and culture create a dynamic that resources leadership ability to navigate difficult
situations of change.

CREATING AND SUSTAINING POSITIVE
RELATIONSHIPS IN WETOKA HEALTH UNIT

The WHU was established in 1956 as one of 27 health units in the province
of Alberta, Canada. Through the years, WHU came to be recognized for its
innovation and excellence in public health. As a former CEO commented,
"We did strategic planning, continuous quality improvement. We did a lot of
firsts in the province. We were the first health unit to have an Employee Assistance Program. We were the first for many provincial pilots and new programs." In early 1995, just before it was split into two sections, WHU had 120
employees throughout four offices serving a population of 40,000 in a geographical area of 3,100 square miles.

As in organizations more generally, the people of WHU created a variety
of symbolic forms as they conducted their work, including business plans,
goals, reports, and local language terms. From these various symbolic
forms, we sought to discern which particular ones were central and meaningful for life in Wetoka, and specifically for shaping members' capacities to
generate and sustain positive relationships. Our analyses identified three
central symbolic forms: (a) WHU mission, (b) Wetoka Web, and (c) Wetoka
tailored public health principles. In describing these symbolic forms, we
draw special attention to their interdependence with positive relationships;
that is, how these symbolic forms shape people's recurring connections at
work, and how people's positive interactions keep these forms alive by continually reinfusing them with local significance. We also highlight the persistent and hard work undertaken by Wetoka leaders over the years in fostering this mutually reinforcing dynamic between symbolic forms and positive
relationships.

Symbolic Forms in Wetoka Health Unit

> The Wetoka Health Unit works in partnership with individuals, families, and communities throughout all stages of life to achieve and maintain the best possible level of health and well-being.

The first symbolic form, the WHU mission statement, was initially developed in 1982 and continued to evolve, being "revised several times to reflect the changing needs of our community and our changing times" (internal document). Staff of the time noted, "Our purpose is expressed clearly in our mission statement. . . . As employees, we've had a part in drawing up these documents; because we've shared in their creation, they are more functional and credible to us."

As a symbolic form in WHU, the mission represented partnership as central in delivering public health and community based services that fostered health and well-being. It combined the work of WHU in health services with "the belief in being responsive to the community and respecting their involvement" (internal document). The mission was continuously kept alive, as one leader told us, through "evangelization" of it on a day-to-day basis, first by leaders and then by other members who enacted it in their work, discussed it in conversations, and embellished it in strategic planning processes. Seeing service delivery as a partnership with the community—being responsive to the community and respecting community involvement—helped members weave together the principles of public health with the strategic direction and work of WHU within the community and health system. As a result, the mission as symbolic form shaped positive relationships by infusing them with the significance of work and its accomplishment through partnership. In turn, the enactment of these relationships kept the mission alive, rendering it central in the doing of work, and thus preventing it from becoming a meaningless statement.

The second symbolic form critical to the establishment of positive relationships was the Wetoka Web. For employees, being part of WHU was like being part of a caring family. One person depicted WHU as a "leader-full" organization that cared deeply about every member and about doing important work—serving the community with excellence. Staff suggested that this attention to participatory management and inclusion of all was illustrated in the Wetoka Web, an organizational chart adapted from the work of Hegelsen (1990), which is depicted in Figure 16.1. These staff explained that the web showed "the interconnectedness and interdependence of all our programs . . . the need to pull together and be supportive when a sag or weakness develops" (internal document).

For leaders, the Wetoka Web represented an inclusive and caring relational stance that was developed from much work over many years with

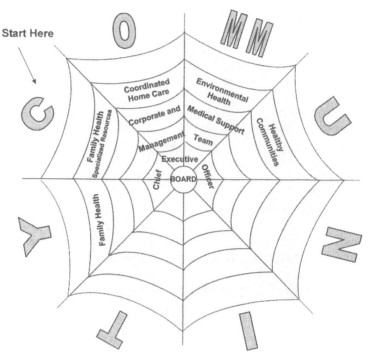

FIG. 16.1. Wetoka Web.

staff and board members to get to the point where people felt valued. As one leader commented, "that was how people were expected to be treated ... it was back to, if you look after the team and treat the people right, that's how they will treat others and the rest looks after itself." Another leader commented,

> I used to draw the organizational chart as a web and we'd talk about when any one program is hurting or weak, you've got a sag in the web, and if we don't reinforce that collectively, it brings us all down. Staff was able to quickly move to where the sags were and support each other. So when there was a crisis, people would just step up to the plate.

Thus, the Wetoka Web as symbolic form represented the "interconnectedness and commitment of all WHU staff to provide the best service [they could], not only to ... customers and clients, but also to ... community partners and to each other at the health unit" (internal document). In particular, it highlights the value and respect of people and renders prominent the everyday leader work essential in supporting such a positive relational stance. As one leader commented, "We were always mindful of reinforcing the tendrils of the web—not just in crisis but in everyday interactions." As a result, when members drew on the Wetoka Web in enacting positive relationships, it infused them with the importance of being inclusive and caring with people in accomplishing work. In turn, enacting these relationships put the web into concrete practice, keeping it visible for all to see and use in interpreting and expressing meaning associated with working in WHU.

The third symbolic form consisted of Wetoka-specific principles of public health. Since its inception, staff and board leadership of WHU held general and long-standing public health principles such as "Apply the greatest good for the greatest number at least cost and risk," or "Understand that improvements in health status occur by influencing the determinants of health, many of which are outside the purview of health." Over time, WHU members tailored these generic principles into a set of Wetoka-specific public health principles, creating a sense of personal ownership of and commitment to the principles. Representative statements from the WHU-specific public health principles include:

- We promote healthy public policies and fair access to all resources for health.
- We explore innovative approaches to global health issues and apply what we learn to local circumstances.
- We encourage creativity in delivering programs and services, minimizing duplication and maximizing efficiency and effectiveness.
- We encourage personal growth and development for staff to meet emerging challenges.

In time, these principles were printed on a laminated sheet and given to all new staff in orientation packages. The printing of this sheet and its wide circulation throughout WHU rendered this symbolic form publicly accessible, creating the opportunity for the principles to become infused with more meaning and to occupy a more central place in WHU members' lives. Underscoring the work of WHU, members used these tailored principles to guide their everyday work and relating with communities and each other as they created a "community of caring" in accomplishing their mission. As symbolic form, the principles infused relating in WHU with a larger purpose—that of helping to make a healthier community. In connecting significance of work and caring relational stance, this form helped cultivate members' capacities to enact positive relationships. In turn, extending the enactment of positive relationships beyond the organizational borders of WHU invested the principles with a significance and vibrancy that rendered this symbolic form especially central and meaningful in the lives of staff and community members associated with WHU.

Over the years, then, leaders actively worked to continuously energize and persistently renew the significance of these symbolic forms. As a result, members drew on them in enacting positive relationships with staff, clients, board, and community partners as they conducted their work. In turn, these positive relationships enlivened the symbolic forms, infusing them with a greater significance and depth of meaning in the lives of people associated with WHU. Enacting positive relationships came to mean that members sought to deliver services to clients that promoted health and well-being, in the best way they could, being mindful of supporting each other, clients, and community members in partnership.

Notably, the leadership work in WHU was dedicated both to continually renewing the significance of these three symbolic forms and to enacting positive relationships in the doing of work. This work not only supported the creation of vibrant symbolic forms and positive relationships, but also over time led to their interdependence. As these particular symbols became more central to life in WHU, they anchored the enactment of positive relationships. Similarly, as positive relationships became more significant and meaningful to life in WHU, they infused the symbolic forms with relevance to everyday life. As a result, a dynamic was generated that sustained each in their interdependence with the other. Members of WHU developed a community of caring constituted by a variety of partners and filled with rich symbols that sustained supportive interactions in accomplishing the meaningful work of delivering quality (and continuously improving) public health and community services.

RESOURCING THE NAVIGATION OF MANDATED DISSOLUTION OF WETOKA HEALTH UNIT

In the late 1980s and early 1990s discussions and commissioned reports in the province about the need to restructure health services led to the dismantling of more than 200 organizations (including Wetoka) and their reassembly into 17 Regional Health Authorities. This began a series of changes experienced as tumultuous in the province's health system that continues to the present day. In this section, we depict how leaders in WHU navigated this mandated dissolution of their organization. In particular, our analyses show how the mutually reinforcing system of culture and positive relationships created in WHU resourced leadership's ability to engage others in the work of sustaining positive relationships and meaningful work in spite of, and while experiencing a tremendously difficult situation.

Members of WHU speculated what dissolution would mean for their organization, themselves, and their partners because they knew that health units would cease to exist. One leader shared, "I had never been in an experience where what we have built was going to be destroyed ... like how do you prepare for something like that with so many unknowns?" The CEO of WHU at the time explained that one of the provincial commissioned reports, known as the Rainbow Report, offered an opportunity to dialogue with staff and managers about what this change would mean:

> I went out to all offices, and said, "These are the themes. This is what it says. This is what I think it means, what do you think it means? How do we prepare for this? How do we move forward?" We realized the organization we had so mindfully built together and tended was about to be torn apart and reassembled into a larger organization that would now include acute care and long term care services. We needed to firm up what it was we were there for, what business we were in, what our mission was, what our ... principles were.
>
> So, where do we put our energies? Well we would put our energies into ... being able to carry that critical mass forward ... I think it all comes right back down to what are your principles ... what do you want to see moving forward? What have we learned on this journey that we will take forward? That transition year, once we knew how the organizations would be merged—that was a time of really coming to ... what really is holding us now as we move forward.

As just conveyed vividly, in preparing to dismantle WHU as an organizational entity and join two newly created health regions, leaders intentionally and immediately sought to dialogue with all members in an effort to identify what it was from WHU they wanted to "firm up" and where they would devote their energies. When push came to shove, and their world was crumbling, instead of worrying about events over which they had no control, they sought to bolster the positive relationships and central symbolic forms that had come to signify the purpose of their organization.

Going forward, leaders tapped into the dynamic of positive relationships and symbolic forms to resource their efforts. In particular, they engaged all members of WHU in dialogue to reaffirm the foundational principles that formed the significance of work as accomplished in partnership. Seeking to reinforce these principles, WHU and community members collaborated in creating a new symbolic form, represented as the Wetoka Wheel, which is depicted in Figure 16.2.

The CEO at the time explained,

> In our dialogues with staff, partners, and the public, we affirmed Wetoka's strong, respectful culture and a deeply held set of principles that guided our everyday work with communities and with each other in our own community of caring. Interestingly, we'd never written these down anywhere. They couldn't be found framed and hanging on a wall—instead, they lived in our hearts and souls. So I met with all the staff in focus groups and we talked about, in their words, what was it that they saw and felt and experienced by working at

FIG. 16.2. Wetoka Wheel.

Wetoka. Out of that we were able to articulate those values and spin them into this wheel that was very pictorial. Even though Wetoka was to be dismantled as a formal organization, that anchor would not change for us. . . . We decided to put our energies into keeping our principles intact wherever we went, because that is what had guided and would continue to guide our interactions and our work. Engaging in these dialogues allowed the development of a common playing field for all of us to work from as we moved forward in the change.

And, one staff member of the time portrayed:

I vividly remember an office meeting where we developed our list of what we value and the principles we work by, and the managers saying that if you're committed to those principles, it doesn't matter to whom you report. What happens is you will still have the same ethics, the same outlook on the work we do and why it matters. We all see the broad picture. We see how we fit. We see how our managers believe in public health and how they stick up for it and that's set the stage for us.

Significantly, the cocreation of this wheel materialized the foundational principles for the first time, which up to this point had lived in their hearts but had not been recorded. Although the Wetoka-specific public health principles were related, these foundational principles underlay all that WHU stood for. In creating the wheel, WHU members expressed these fundamental and central principles in written form for the first time, and in so doing, vitalized the organizational legacy of positive relationships in the accomplishment of work directed to enhancing population health and community well-being. They also bolstered the other symbolic forms of mission, Wetoka Web, and specific public health principles. Consequently members were able to draw on these vibrant symbolic forms to move forward into the new organizations in a manner that sustained the significance of their work and the positive relationships used in accomplishing this work.

Leaders also realized that their leader work of actively maintaining the symbolic forms and positive relationships became even more significant, and certainly more labor intensive and time consuming now that they faced mandated disestablishment of their organization. Consequently, they developed and provided training on change and transition that not only assisted people in dealing with change, but also helped them recognize and honor that people dealt differently with change. A leader commented:

> Once I realized the "people part" of change was crucial to successful change implementation, then I was able to really move forward. People are ripe for learning in times of change, so we focused a lot on helping people develop new skills, or hone existing ones, helping them realize what strengths and gifts they had to offer the new organization. We worked a lot on learning about how people respond differently to change. We capitalized on the safe, trusting, and caring relationships we had with each other and our staff, ensuring we were accessible for people "just to talk." We talked with staff about what we could control and influence (our zone of influence) and what we simply had to accept. And we focused on ensuring staff were continually updated on any news relating to the change, whether it was good, bad, or ambiguous.

A staff member shared:

> Our managers kept us right up to date with what was happening in the change. And we trusted they were telling us the truth because they've proven over and over again they're trustworthy. And they kept their doors open so we could come and ask questions, or cry, or vent. It was so helpful just to be listened to and really heard. And we helped each other, too. The training sessions on dealing with change helped us understand and accept that different people deal with change differently—for me it is quite invigorating, but for others it is frightening.

Thus, leadership moved forward with a mindfulness of sustaining positive relationships by fostering opportunities for people to continue growing, learning, and contributing to the significant work of the organization.

First and foremost in their efforts to navigate change was the leaders' investment of their own energy and attention in people. This took time and was hard work, but as one of the leaders shared with us, even though culture building takes an inordinate amount of energy, it takes much less energy to build a life-sustaining culture than it takes to work within a toxic culture.

Sadness, fear, frustration, and anxiety were recognized and acknowledged, but this was accompanied by continual redirection toward the positive and energizing each other by celebrating successes and putting fun into work. The leaders sought to transform negative spirals into positive bubbles and further into positive spirals. Attending to people by hearing the negative and allowing people space to cry, vent, and express disappointment, they also nudged them to move on to what they could control and influence. Even though their organization was being dismantled, they were dedicated to preserving their legacy through continuing positive relationships and bolstering symbolic forms that supported a caring relational stance and the incorporation of foundational principles.

In moving into one of the newly formed health regions, former Wetoka members recalled how they explicitly sought to integrate the symbolic forms and positive relationships into this new context. For example, they took a lead role in creating a health service Teams in Transition, bringing staff and managers from all parts of the new organization together—frontline workers, managers—with the agenda of getting to know each other and helping all realize they had an equally important role to play in the new organization's work. As one of the leaders shared:

> Focusing on respect for the different roles got us over the "turf" hurdle. People came to realize how important a sense of community is in the workplace and what skills could be used to create that. As we worked together, we got energized. We were exhausted yet we could see the results that were happening for the greater good . . . these positive bubbles of activity—and that just fueled us to work harder and longer and better.

Leaders of WHU had worked over many years to develop and sustain positive relationships that were shaped by the symbolic forms of mission, representing significance of work and partnering in its conduct; Wetoka-specific public health principles shared with all staff; and the Wetoka web, representing inclusion and support. Moreover, in cocreating with the community a materialized form of their foundational principles—the Wetoka wheel—they bolstered these forms and crystallized what the WHU stood for as it had developed over the years. Importantly, leaders did not initiate these efforts only when facing disruptive change, nor did they rest on their past efforts. Instead, they redoubled their attention and efforts in the face of this change by extending the creation of symbolic forms and positive relationships to new staff in the newly forming organizations. Some leaders of the time indicated that it would have been easy to let go, especially because there was so much else to do in dealing with the disestablishment of WHU. However, they were able to keep going because they believed in the importance of these efforts in creating a better health system and because they provided much support to each other in their efforts. Drawing on the sustained and interdependent dynamics between the WHU symbolic forms and the established pattern of positive relationships to resource their efforts, leadership and other members not only looked after relationships in the midst of implementing a difficult situation, but also purposefully sought to re-create this dynamic in the new organizations.

We have presented here only a snippet of our findings to date; space limitations preclude further elaboration. Gladys Procyshen experienced Wetoka as it developed and was dismantled. The other coauthors studied the organization known as Crossroads, 10 years after Wetoka's dismantlement. What they found were pockets of life and energy where the spirit and principles of Wetoka were alive and well and leaders at various levels who continued reaching outward to the rest of the organization. In these pockets, staff and managers alike described an open atmosphere of friendliness and positive interaction, a place where people felt valued, respected, and heard. At a time when staff morale was at an all-time low in most other health organizations, people here seemed to be thriving as they drew on the heritage of WHU in anchoring their actions in the new organization of Crossroads.

CONCLUSION

Although much research has focused on the linkages between positive relationships and organizational outcomes, our interest in this chapter has been in explicating the dynamics by which positive relationships in organizations are generated and become institutionalized. Our case study of WHU contributes to the growing work on positive relationships in organizations in two specific ways. First, it showed how symbolic forms shaped and were shaped by the enactment of positive relationships. Just as symbolic forms nurture and sustain positive relationships in organizations, enacting positive relationships keeps the symbolic forms alive, continually reinfusing them with significance and meaning. Second, it depicted how organizational leaders drew on the dynamic between organizational culture and positive relationships to resource their efforts during times of turmoil (e.g., difficult organizational change). We have developed a model (Figure 16.3) that depicts the general framework discerned in these two sets of analytical relationships. We discuss each of these points next.

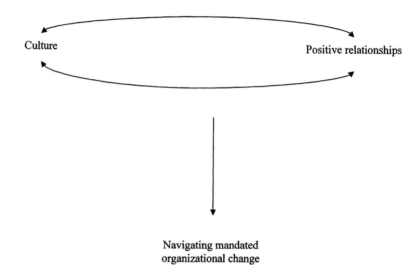

FIG. 16.3. Creating and sustaining positive relationships.

Adopting a cultural lens, we have shown how organizational leaders and other members draw on symbolic forms to foster the creation of meaningful positive relationships in the conduct of work, and to nurture and support their ongoing enactment. In turn, enacting these relationships revitalizes the symbolic forms, helping them stay meaningful and full of life rather than becoming lifeless and meaningless documents never to be used. We have shed particular light on how leader work can foster this dynamic and in so doing, cultivate a cultural capacity that facilitates the sustained enactment of a pattern of positive relationships. In the case of WHU, we identified three symbolic forms that shaped the generation and endurance of positive relationships: mission, web and wheel. Two forms—the Wetoka mission and Web—were developed long ago and were continually renewed through the years. One form—the Wetoka Wheel—materialized through staff and community dialogue during a very difficult time of change. All of these forms were created through a combination of leader work and meaningful staff participation. As such, these particular symbolic forms celebrated the spirit and shaped members' capacities to enact positive relationships. Moreover, because all three had become central and significant in the lives of people associated with WHU, they not only helped to create, but also to sustain the enactment of positive relationships beyond the dismantlement of a particular organization.

In highlighting the dynamics of culture, and the interdependent relation between culture and positive organizational relationships, our study also highlights that the use of central and meaning-rich symbolic forms in shaping positive relationships (or being shaped by them) is far from a linear or straightforward endeavor. Clearly, symbols do not become central, significant, and meaning infused on their own. Rather, "using" symbolic forms involves their complicated enactment and reconstitution in everyday work. We saw in WHU the dedicated and unceasing attention by leaders and staff to continually explicate the meaning of these symbols in everyday organizational life.

We can also discern at least two subprocesses associated with the use of symbolic forms. First, use involves the materialization of symbols so that they are rendered publicly accessible. Yet, although important and necessary, cultivating their "thing-ness" is not a sufficient condition to ensure their meaningfulness and endurance in shaping positive relationships. If it was, any group or organization could introduce them without translation efforts and without ongoing attention. Second, use involves rendering symbolic forms significant during the ongoing enactment of everyday organizational life. Consequently, use means the everyday materialization and signifying of symbols as people go about their work, pursue new initiatives, and engage across hierarchical levels in strategic conversations (Westley, 1990). Such persistence and daily attention to use is hard work—but necessary and essential work in ensuring that positive relationships do not "disappear" (Fletcher 1998) into a cultural system that renders them meaningless or "fluff," or into a political system that dismisses them as inconsequential.

Future research in this area should examine the development and use of symbolic forms that enhance cultural capacity for cultivating positive relationships in organizations. There is much to learn, for example, about which symbolic forms in which specific contexts become central and meaningful in developing positive relationships. As well, we know very little about how particular symbolic forms become central in sustaining positive relationships. Finally, future research needs to continue to problematize the use of symbolic forms to disclose subprocesses that constitute use, and to render visible the microlevel conversations and ongoing interactions that are so important to nourishing the significance and centrality of positive relationships in organizations.

Our case further suggests that leaders can tap into the dynamic between positive relationships and culture to resource (Feldman, 2004) the navigation of difficult change. When this happens, positive relationships, in combination with symbolic forms rendering them meaningful, become life-enriching and energy-producing resources that broaden people's repertoires for dealing with difficult change. Suggesting that positive relationships and symbolic forms can become resources in dealing with difficult change may sound naive at first glance. However, on closer inspection we see how they can foster the reframing of a difficult situation from an experience of hopelessness and lacking all control over events, to an experience of hope and being able to enact purposeful action. In particular, this case shows how connecting positive relationships and symbolic forms resources the generation of confidence in dealing with a disruptive change by calling on belief in a time of tremendous ambiguity and doubt (Weick, 2001).

Most generally, this chapter contributes to prior work by highlighting the cultural dynamics in generating and sustaining positive relationships in organizations. Although positive relationships are patterns of interaction, and are essential social networks, they are also, and significantly, cultural products. Attention to the symbolic meaning of positive relationships, and to the symbolic forms that vitalize and are revitalized by them, thus helps us see how people create and sustain meaningful relationships in which they can experience and express respect, positive regard, and purposeful work, even during times of turmoil.

REFERENCES

Baker, W., Cross, R., & Wooten, M. (2003). Positive organizational network analysis and energizing relationships. In K. Cameron, J. Dutton, & R. Quinn (Eds.) *Positive organizational scholarship. Foundations in a new discipline* (pp. 328–342). San Francisco: Berrett-Koehler.

Bradbury, H., & Lichtenstein, B. (2000). Relationality in organizational research: Exploring the space between. *Organization Science, 11,* 551–564.

Dutton, J. (2003a). Breathing life into organizational studies. *Journal of Management Inquiry, 12,* 5–19.

Dutton, J. (2003b). *Energize your workplace: How to create and sustain high-quality connections at work.* San Francisco: Jossey-Bass.

Dutton, J., & Heaphy, E. (2003). Coming to life: the power of high quality connections at work. In K. Cameron, J. Dutton, & R. Quinn (Eds.), *Positive organizational scholarship* (pp. 263–278). San Francisco: Berrett-Koehler.

Feldman, M. (2004). Resources in emerging structures and processes of change. *Organization Science, 15,* 295–309.

Feldman, S. P. (1986). Management in context: An essay on the relevance of culture to the understanding of organizational change. *Journal of Management Studies, 23,* 587–607.

Fletcher, J. (1998). Relational practice: A feminist reconstruction of work. *Journal of Management Inquiry, 7,* 163–186.

Golden, K. (1992). The individual and organizational culture: Strategies for action in highly-ordered contexts. *Journal of Management Studies, 29,* 1–21.

Hegelsen, S. (1990). *The female advantage—Women's ways of leadership.* New York: Doubleday/Currency.

Hofer-Gittell, J. (2001). Supervisory span, relational coordination and flight departure performance: A reassessment of post-bureaucracy theory. *Organization Science, 12,* 467–482.

Hofer-Gittell, J. (2002). Coordinating mechanisms in care provider groups: Relational coordination as a mediator and input uncertainty as a moderator of performance effects. *Management Science, 48,* 1408–1426.

Martin, J. (2002). *Organizational culture: Mapping the terrain.* Thousand Oaks, CA: Sage.

Martin, J., Frost, P. J., & O'Neill, O. A. (2006). Organizational culture: Beyond struggle for intellectual dominance. In S. Clegg, C. Hardy, W. Nord, & T. Lawrence (Eds.), *Handbook of organization studies* (2nd ed.). London: Sage.

Rosen, M. (1985). Breakfast at Spiro's: Dramaturgy and dominance. *Journal of Management, 11,* 31–48.

Smircich, L. (1983). Concepts of culture and organizational analysis. *Administrative Science Quarterly, 28,* 339–358.

Surrey, J. (1991). The self-in-relation: A theory of women's development. In J. Jordan, A. Kaplan, J. Baker Miller, I. Stiver, & J. Surrey (Eds.), *Women's growth in connection* (pp. 51–66). New York: Guilford.

Swidler, A. (1986). Culture in action: Symbols and strategies. *American Sociological Review, 51,* 273–286.

Weick, K. (2001). *Making sense of the organization.* Oxford, England: Blackwell.

Westley, F. (1990). Middle managers and strategy: Microdynamics of inclusion. *Strategic Management Journal, 11,* 337–351.

Worline, M., Dutton, J., Frost, P., Kanov, J., Lilius, J., & Maitlis, S. (Invited revision). *Fertile soil: The organizing dynamics of resilience in work organizations.*

17

My Family, My Firm: How Familial Relationships Function as Endogenous Organizational Resources

Mary Ann Glynn
Krysia Wrobel

For better or for worse, family relationships are arguably the most enduring of all relationships. The comedian George Burns captured the emotional equivocality of familial ties when he said, "Happiness is having a large, loving, caring, close-knit family in another city." Yet, it is precisely the high emotionality and enduring nature accompanying familial relationships that make them such potent social ties.

In organization studies, the notion of family has been an oft-used metaphor. Figuratively it is a term often applied to organizations, their cultures, and the relationships among organization members. For instance, Cameron and Quinn (1999) described the "clan" culture of organizations as one of extended family. Casey (1999) described how many organizations invoke the sense of family to attract potential employees:

> Many companies, from manufacturing operations and supermarket chains, to hospitals and airline companies, promote themselves in the marketplace and to employees as caring, familial communities, inviting both employees and customers to "Come, join our family" through their involvement with the company....
>   Both family and team, are, in normative conditions, positive and generative social practices. Therefore, their deliberate installation as part of the new organizational culture fundamentally assumes their reasonable incontestability and universal attractiveness. (p. 155)

In this chapter, we extend the use of family literally and focus on familial relationships as positive resources endogenous to organizations. By *posi-*

tive, we refer to those relationships that serve as "connections between individuals at work that are experienced as rewarding, desirable, and enriching" (Dutton & Ragins, chap. 21, this volume). By *endogenous,* we mean that familial relationships are a resource that comes from within the organization, primarily through its people and cultural values. Thus, as part of the human and social assets or inputs to production, that are both tangible (in terms of the work people do) as well as intangible (in terms of the reputational capital or positive regard that people convey), familial relationships are endogenous resources that organizations control, mobilize, or access on a semipermanent basis; it is in this way that we believe that familial relationships function as an endogenous "resource" (Helfat, 2003).

In this chapter, we examine how multigenerational family relationships may be created in, and displayed by, organizations to create "positive" identity; that is, an identity that is attractive, legitimate, or desirable that serves as a touchstone for customer, employee, or public identification and that legitimates its products and services. We propose that familial relationships can confer an organization identity, when the family of the founder, CEO, or other iconic firm figure is displayed as part of the identity of the organization. Perhaps this is most transparent in family businesses or when firms carry the family name, such as Dell, Martha Stewart Living Omnimedia, or Hewlett-Packard, or in firm names that evoke family ties, like Grandma's Fudge Factory. In cases such as these, namesake firms signal how personal identity and organizational identity become intertwined. As such, we address a critical gap in the identity literature by examining how organizational identities may be grounded in personal identities that spring from family relationships. Moreover, we seek to contribute to this volume on positive relationships in a number of ways: (a) by showing how family can be a source of positive relationships in organizations that are endogenous and embedded in the human capital of the firm; (b) by showing how family relationships can function as a touchstone for individuals' identification with, and organizational construals of, the firm's identity; and (c) by showing how familial relationships can legitimate, sustain, and solidify the values, beliefs, and ideology of the organization, by serving as important institutionalization mechanisms in firms.

We relate positive family relationships in organizations to the mechanisms of institutionalization in firms. Borrowing from institutional theorists such as Scott (1995), we define an institution as a set of values and beliefs that guide behavior. We propose that family is an institutional mechanism that, when associated with a focal organization, helps to engender trust in its products and services. We can see this in namesake products, such as Dell Computer, Smucker's jellies, the *Oprah* television show or *Martha Stewart Living* magazine, as well as in brands like MOTHERS car polishes, waxes, and cleaners; Family Dollar Stores; or My Sister's Store. We position the joining of familial relationships to organizational products and services as a process whereby one key institution (family) is grafted to another (business) so that family becomes a part of the ideology of the firm and changes over time in response to the firm's needs. By suggesting change over time, we reinforce the call from institutionalists for a more life-cycle view of the process of institutionalization (Haveman & Rao, 1997).

Last, although the concept of family has entered the business literature to a greater degree in recent years, we extend the conversation from a conflict-based perspective that has focused on problems of succession and the work–family interface (e.g., Perlow, 1998) to a more positive view of the way in which family functions in service of business goals. In our conceptualization, family and business converge in a productive way that both preserves the family and advances the goals of the business. By further breaking down the myth of separate spheres of work and family, we recognize the important function family relationships fill at the organizational level.

In our focus on familial relationships, we examine an understudied form of relationships at work. Our central assumption is that family ties are positive relationships that constitute a form of social capital for the firm; in turn, family relationships function as an endogenous resource to identify and legitimize the corporate firm. Specifically, we theorize that the display of family relationships by an organization is used to characterize, enliven, and legitimate a firm and its offerings to public audiences. Unpacking these three verbs—*characterize, enliven,* and *legitimate*—reveals how family relationships function as positive relationships. First, family relationships characterize firms by serving as a source of identify for the firm, either literally, by invoking the name, face, and personal attributes of founders, such as Bill Gates, Walt Disney, or Oprah Winfrey; or figuratively, in terms of the resemblance of the firm's culture or orientation to one's family. The traits of the family founders and members map onto the attributes that constitute the organizational identity. Second, family relationships enliven an organization, as well as its products and services, by literally and figuratively "breathing life" into the organization. Having living, breathing, family members, such as Martha Stewart (and even her mother and daughter) display the organization makes it real, with all the ups and downs that implies. Finally, family relationships legitimate organizations by making them more comprehensible and understandable (Suchman, 1995). Although it may be more difficult to discern (and thus identify with) the workings of a tool-and-die maker or a power company, it is easier to relate to institutions that we know (i.e., family). We leverage our understanding of family relationships, or what it means to be a parent, a sister, an aunt, or a relative, to understand what it means to be a member of an organization or to understanding its particular offerings (e.g., Mother's jellies). Thus, by grafting the institution of family to that of the firm, organizational legitimacy can be enhanced.

We organize the chapter as follows. First, we review the relevant literatures on work relationships, family relationships, and organization; we
close this section by advancing two primary research questions that drive
the formation of our theoretical framework. Next, we offer a conceptual
framework for theorizing family as a positive and endogenous resource for
organizations. Finally, we conclude with suggestions for future research.

TOWARD A DYNAMIC VIEW OF POSITIVE
RELATIONSHIPS AT WORK

We seem to know a lot about relationships at work. Organizational scholars
have studied relationships in the employment context from a variety of perspectives. Social and organizational psychologists have explored the dynamics of coworkers and the group processes that underlie relationships
among them (e.g., Dutton, 2003; Robinson & O'Leary-Kelly, 1998); organizational researchers have identified antecedents and consequences of positive and negative relationships among colleagues, supervisors, and subordinates (e.g., Pearson, Andersson, & Porath, 2000; Rook, 1984; Tepper, 2000);
social network theorists have examined the structural characteristics of
patterns of relating at work that lead to high energy (Baker, Cross, &
Wooten, 2003; Cross, Baker, & Parker, 2003); and strategists have even discovered the outcomes of relationships between members of various stake-
holder groups, such as the CEO and the chairman of the board of directors
(e.g., Mizruchi, 1983). In spite of this scholarship on relationships at work,
the examination of "family" relationships at work has been far more limited,
discussed primarily by scholars interested in either succession planning in
the family business literature or on the conflict between employees' work
and family roles and responsibilities.

We attempt to reverse this trend by examining the positive aspects of
family relationships at work; in so doing, we believe that understanding
family relationships can be particularly generative for understanding positive relationships at work, for several reasons. First, family relationships
tend to be enduring, and thus can complement those positive relationships
at work that tend to be more fleeting or temporary. In the same way that
family relationships can endure over time and space, as when geographic
relocations occur or family circumstances change (through marriage or divorce, the births of children, or the deaths of older generations), it may provide a framing of how positive relationships that are seeded at work can
grow and change even as the contexts for those relationships change
(through organizational shifts or personnel movements). Second, as much
as family ties can be a source of positive relationships they can also be a
source of negative energy or toxic emotions; understanding how relation-

ships endure, in spite of changing feelings about those relationships (both positive and negative), can illuminate how seemingly positive relationships at work may also include elements of friction, tension, and even negativity. Finally, an understanding of family can locate positive relationships within a broader social network of relationships. At work, as in families, interpersonal relationships tend to tie into other sets of relationships, such as those with different coworkers, bosses, department members, and even international colleagues, that begin to resemble the sometimes far-flung web of familial relationships. We can understand better, for instance, the positive relationships between pairs of people (mother–son or supervisor–employee) when we also understand those relationships in the context of other relationships, for example, how a mother relates to her other children, her husband, or her sister, or how a supervisor relates to her other employees, her peers, or her bosses. By so doing, we can understand positive relationships at work in terms of their embeddedness in hierarchies, cultural systems, and traditions of engagement that may be transparent at family events (e.g., weddings, christenings, deaths) or holidays. Thus, by adding an understanding of endurance and stability over time, positive aspects that may also include negativity, and a socially embedded perspective on interpersonal relationships, examining familial ties permits a more expansive perspective on positive relationships.

In conceptualizing familial ties as a form of positive relationships, we borrow from definitions offered by our colleagues in this text: "By positive relationships we mean connections between individuals at work that are experienced as rewarding, desirable, and enriching" (Dutton & Ragins, chap. 21, this volume). More specifically, we conceptualize *positive relationships* as both a noun and a verb. As a noun, we are concerned with positive familial relationships. As a verb, we focus on the way in which familial relationships serve as a way to relate positively to others, thereby forming new relationships.

This dynamic view of relationships, as both an outcome and a process, is not new. The notion of social capital captures this idea well. At the societal level, Putnam (2000) defined social capital in his influential treatise, *Bowling Alone:*

> Whereas physical capital refers to physical objects and human capital refers to the properties of individuals, social capital refers to connections among individuals—social networks and the norms of reciprocity and trustworthiness that arise from them. In that sense social capital is closely related to what some have called "civic virtue." The difference is that "social capital" calls attention to the fact that civic virtue is most powerful when embedded in a sense network of reciprocal social relations. (p. 19)

In the social capital literature, relationships with others have been identified as important sources of currency that can be activated to gain other, more difficult-to-achieve resources. Conceptualized as a noun, *social capital* is defined as a resource residing in networks of relationships (Baker, 2000). Used as a verb, it is a "resource for action" enacted for substantive profit (Coleman, 1988, p. 95). As a resource that can be enacted to gain additional resources, social capital is a productive resource. As Coleman (1988) described it, "The function ... of 'social capital' is the value of these aspects of social structure to actors as resources they can use to achieve their interests" (p. 101). In the case of new ventures, for example, social capital can be used as a type of entrepreneurial resource capital (Lounsbury & Glynn, 2001).

Familial relationships, like all social relations among persons, are a form of social capital (Baker, 2000). Children, because of their social relationships to parents, siblings, and extended family members, are able to profit from the human capital embodied in their family members. Although seemingly intangible, the social capital of the family has been measured. Coleman (1988) assessed the strength of familial social capital using variables such as the physical presence of two adults, the amount of attention given to the child by the adults, number of siblings, nuclear structure, mother's expectations of child attending college, and the frequency with which the child talks with the parents about personal experiences. Through these measures, the social capital of the family can be used as a resource for children's education, just as is financial and human capital (Coleman, 1988).

However, without actively enacting the relationships, family members do not gain from social capital within the family. "If the human capital possessed by parents is not complemented by social capital embodied in family relations, it is irrelevant to the child's educational growth that the parent has a great deal, or a small amount of human capital" (Coleman, 1988, p. 110). It is only through the process of relating—and, clearly, positive relating, or that which is "rewarding, desirable, and enriching" (Dutton & Ragins, chap. 21, this volume)—that social capital in the family can be realized. Therefore, to realize the potential of social capital in the family, familial relationships must be identified, preserved, and institutionalized. In an organizational setting, familial relationships are identified when they are made explicit (e.g., in executive speeches), preserved when they are used respectfully (e.g., not defaming one's own or others' families), and institutionalized when they become fixtures of the organization (e.g., in the naming of products).

However, family as a source of positive relationships at work has been largely neglected. Research on work relationships to date has tended to focus almost exclusively at the interpersonal or intergroup level of analysis. As informative as this work has been, the emphasis on this particular level of analysis has led to a neglect of examining other kinds of relationships that may hinge the organization to broader aspects of social relationships. Thus, a paternal founder of an organization prompts identity attributes associated with one's father or permits us to locate our relationship to the organization as analogically like the one we have with our father. We believe that family relationships constitute a potentially important aspect of the social context that embeds organizations. Because the processes underlying the relationship between family and firm are inherently social, we propose that these processes involve both identity and institutional mechanisms. Mechanisms offer plausible explanations or understandings (Hedstrom & Swedberg, 1998) of "the cogs and wheels" behind observed events or relationships (Davis & Marquis, 2005). In particular, we propose that identity and institutional mechanisms offer explanations of how familial relationships function as endogenous resources for firms.

We argue that family relationships work as endogenous resources for firms through two fundamental theoretical mechanisms—institutionalization and identification—that can elucidate how positive relationships become embedded in the organization and how they function as endogenous resources to define the firm. More generally, we view the display of family in the business context as a form of social capital in service of firm goals. We also postulate that these relationships can be used in a dynamic way: to develop other relationships of interest to the business, such as between the firm and its customers, or between the firm and its employees. In this way, family relationships serve as a touchstone for institutionally based trust (Zucker, 1986) that supersedes interpersonal relationships and benefits the firm.

Identity mechanisms claim familial relationships as core attributes of the firm, layering them in affect, as a display of the character of the firm; in this case, personal and organizational identities become intertwined in a dynamic process (Glynn & Lacey, 2004). The richness of relationships, grounded in both family and organizational roles, invites individuals to form a deeper connection to the firm and perhaps a more emotionally laden identification. For instance, an organizational name like "Jones & Sons" signals a family-run (and potentially family-owned) business, in which organizational relationships (among coworkers or between boss and subordinates) are overlaid with, and reinforced by, family relationships. Thus, trust can operate at multiple levels, at the contractual or business level, where consumers purchase services, and at a familial level, where, ideologically, we would believe that sons would not betray their father by doing substandard work. Further, we can think about these relationships on multiple levels; the firm moniker invites us to think about the business partners (Jones & Sons) as if they were our sons, our brothers, or our cousins, just as the business model invites economic considerations of producers and consumers.

Researchers in the entrepreneurship literature have identified the myriad ways that entrepreneurs' personal resources become firm resources (see Lounsbury & Glynn, 2001). The tie between the individual and the organization is perhaps most evident in symbolic aspects of organizations, particularly through the naming of the firm or its offerings. For instance, Donald Trump has attached his family name to a number of his prominent organizational offerings (e.g., Trump Tower, Trump Place, and Trump's Taj Mahal Casino). Moreover, his family members, including his ex-wife and children, have been featured organizational members, lending their style and managerial talents to all things Trump. The Trump identity was perhaps cemented in his rise as a celebrity and entertainer, featured in the television show, *The Apprentice,* with his new wife by his side in several shows, even while she was still his fiancée. Thus, the family is displayed as being part of the business, part of the show (if you will), in a way that amplifies and identifies the persona of the founder and CEO, Donald Trump. (As an aside, it is interesting to note that his ex-wife, Ivana Trump, retains his name in her own business holdings, seemingly to signal the enduring familial relationship, in spite of the legal severance of the marriage.)

On a smaller scale, with less media glare, there seem to be countless numbers of plumbing, contracting, construction, or auto service firms who append family relationships to their name (e.g., "Smith and Sons" or more recently, ". . . and Daughters"). More visibly, several larger firms have done the same (e.g., piano manufacturer Steinway & Sons; financial services giant AG Edwards & Sons, Inc.; and fine tea purveyors Harney and Sons). In scarcer supply were firms identified by their daughters. However, one urban fine foods specialty store, Russ and Daughters, which advertises itself as a "New York institution since 1914," explicitly calls on family relationships as firm resources. The history of the firm recounts the history of the family, complete with scrapbook photos and this cite from *The New York Times Magazine:* "A fourth-generation business, Russ & Daughters is a reminder of the people that, historically, make this city what it is. You know them, you trust them, and they promise to do right by you" (from the company's Web site, www.russanddaughters.com). Thus family relationships serve both to identify the firm and to map a set of attributes that engender credibility (e.g., trustworthiness) that advantage the business.

As well, family relationships are not simply symbolic but strategic as well, rallying, as families often do, in times of trouble to help one another. For instance, the Levi Strauss and Company (LS&CO) was founded on family relationships: "LS&CO traced its roots to the 1850s, when a Bavarian-born immigrant, Levi Strauss, came to San Francisco from New York and joined his brother-in-law's dry goods business" (Paine & Katz, 2002, p. 433). The company prospered over its first 100 years, remaining a private company with family members owning nearly all the stock. The company went public in 1971, needed funds for an expanding business, but fell on hard times in the early 1980s, with the jean market declining. Family rallied to help save the firm:

> In 1984, Robert D. Haas, the great-great-grand-nephew of founder Levi Strauss, became president and chief executive officer, following in the footsteps of both his uncle, Peter Haas, and his father, Walter Haas, Jr. . . . In 1985, under Robert Haas's leadership, certain descendants of Levi Strauss's family repurchased publicly held shares for $50 a share—a 42 percent premium over the market price . . . at that time the biggest leveraged buyout in history. In 1993, 95 percent of the company's stock was held by descendants of Levi Strauss. (Paine & Katz, 2002, p. 433)

Thus, familial relationships can serve as a productive resource for firms, both strategically and symbolically, shoring up the vitality of the firm and legitimating its enterprises. Vitality emerges not only from positive relationships, which are enriching (Dutton & Ragins, chap. 21, this volume) and enlivening, but from identities that are connected to living, breathing family members (or the memory of living, breathing family members). Institutional mechanisms are also at work in attaching one trustworthy social institution (family) to an unfamiliar one (the new firm). In addition to defining the firm, through identity mechanisms, institutional mechanisms legitimize its offerings, making the company's products credible and trustworthy.

Grafting family relationships onto the firm is evident in the communications of several firms. For instance, Volvo cars, with its tag line of "Volvo for life" claims "We treat you like one in the family," in addressing both employees and customers (www.volvocars.com). Similarly, Santa Rosa Medical Center says, "We treat you like family," as an encouragement to use its services. Other companies describe themselves as a family, even though it may be far-flung in terms of interests and geography. For instance, on its Web site (www.nike.com), Nike claims to be a family, using the institution of family to explain its smallness while growing big:

> As small as we feel, the Nike family is a fairly vast enterprise. We operate on six continents. Our suppliers, shippers, retailers and service providers employ close to 1 million people. The diversity inherent in such size is helping Nike evolve its role as a global company. We see a bigger picture today than when we started, one that includes building sustainable business with sound labor practices. We retain the zeal of youth yet act on our responsibilities as a global corporate citizen.

As well, CEOs of companies sometimes act like family, sending traditional family greetings. For instance, Anita Roddick, founder and CEO of The Body

Shop, posted this public message on the Internet (http://www.anitaroddick
.com/topicdetails.php?topicid=24:)

An Immense Holiday

Posted By Anita Roddick on 2004-12-15 12:30:01
Topic: <u>Friends & Family</u>

My husband Gordon sent out this message to his colleagues,
friends, and family this week. I thought I'd share it with you.

This is to wish you an immense Christmas and festive season and a big thank
you to all those with whom I have shared a glass over the past year. I feel a revolution coming on.

From these examples, it becomes evident that a primary mechanism for
institutionalization of familial relationships, in society and in organizations,
is the narrative (Bartunek & Lacey, 1998). Families generally have defining
narratives that guide behavior that can be considered institutionalized stories. Storytelling is essential to family groups because it provides a shared
meaning of events experienced by members. All families narrate their identity through stories, and it is through this storytelling that the sense of family endures over generations. When families "remember the time that . . ."
they engage in forming and re-forming a collective memory, and this shared
experience strengthens the familial relationships. It is also through narrative that family members connect with more distant relatives. For example,
the narrative thread running through the stories of a family of holocaust
victims may be one of survival. This family will certainly use the theme of
survival to portray ancestors' experiences during World War II, and they
may also use it to express their identity as a family in everyday trials and
tribulations. By serving as a point of pride, the family's narrative connects
members in a positive way and continually communicates a sense of who
they are (survivors).

Often less dramatically but no less significantly, families preserve their
history through not only oral but written narratives, such as those embedded in birthday and holiday missives, letters from school, postcards from
travels, home videos, and written memoirs. By weaving together the history
of the family, stories make the social capital of the family accessible. Companies such as Levi Strauss, Russ and Daughters, and others do this with
the public through their published Web sites and brochures. Without the
deliberate acts of remembering and sharing memories, the human capital
resources of the family would be isolated within individual members, but
by both remembering and storytelling the resources are shared through social capital. The family must endure for it to serve its members as social
capital, and the act of remembering family is what enables family to endure.

In this important way, storytelling is the critical means by which familial relationships provide social capital to members.

Although the social capital of the family has been established in the literature as a means by which individuals gain other resources (Baker, 2000; Coleman, 1988), we are interested in how familial relationships also provide social capital for the firm. Further, by theorizing shifts in the depiction of familial relationships (and the degrees to which those relationships are positive or negative) with organizational changes in structure, strategy, governance, or culture, we can begin to develop a theoretical understanding of the use of family as an endogenous resource over the life cycle of the firm, through significant phases of organizational life such as new venture formation, establishment, and growth, that sometimes map onto the trajectory of individual lives. Martha Stewart Omnimedia, for instance, seems to have ridden a roller coaster of highs and lows, mapping the business cycle of returns to its founders' ups and downs. And so, we ask:

Research Question #1: How Might Familial Relationships Be Used as Social Capital at the Level of the Firm?

We also seek to explain how familial relationships are used in the service of firm goals. We know from the strategic management literature that resources matter and are deployed strategically (e.g., Barney, 1991), in response to changes precipitated by either internal organizational shifts (as, for instance, in governance structures) or external perceptions (e.g., changed corporate reputations). In the case of Levi Strauss and Martha Stewart more recently, where her daughter Alexis became primary shareholder (purchasing 58.74% of the stock of her firm, Martha Stewart Living Omnimedia) during her mother's incarceration, we can see how family relationships infuse firms with needed financial and social capital. By purchasing stock when the company is under threat, family members signify their confidence, trust, and investment in the enterprise. As a result, we expect that a firm's social capital, like other firm resources, will be deployed to meet changing organizational needs. Because familial relationships as social capital have not been studied as a source of resources available to the firm, we investigate how they might be used strategically. We also ask:

Research Question # 2: How Does a Firm's Strategic Use of Familial Relationships Change in Response to Organizational Needs and Environmental Demands?

To address these questions, we offer a conceptual framework that examines how positive familial relationships function as endogenous organizational resources, changing in response to organizational needs over the corporate life cycle. Our objective is simply to initiate the start of theorizing how familial relationships function as social capital, using the theoretical lens of identity and institutional mechanisms. Admittedly, our approach is not exhaustive; we only hope to stimulate ideas for future research on family relationships in the firm.

THEORIZING POSITIVE FAMILIAL RELATIONSHIPS AND SOCIAL CAPITAL IN ORGANIZATIONS

To address our two primary research questions, we offer a conceptual framework for considering how positive family relationships function as endogenous resources for the firm. In focusing on the first research question, how familial relationships are used as social capital, we suggest that positive familial relationships might be used as a form of social capital to signal the firm's abundance; to highlight the founder's ample social and human capital; to emphasize positive organizing dynamics; and to enhance the expertise, legitimacy, and trustworthiness of the firm's products and services. In these myriad ways, family relationships may function as a productive resource for the firm. Some examples serve to illustrate.

A health plan provider, Cimarron, summarizes how it crafts a bridge from its organizational family to client families with this slogan: Cimarron is committed to taking care of your family. That's why we say "Let our Family Take Care of Yours." OshKosh B'Gosh, a maker of children's clothes and accessories, claims to be "America's Family Brand since 1895." And, perhaps more explicitly, Martha Stewart, founder, former CEO, and cultural icon, expressed it best when she said: "I take the simple things of life and teach others how to do them, everyday things ... [my goal] is to teach, to inform, and to inspire all of you in the preservation and extension of traditional family values and activities" (1997, p. 12).

Our approach to how positive family dynamics function as a form of social capital for organizations is summarized in Table 17.1. In the table, we organize and elaborate our key arguments, which we summarize here as follows. We propose that the display of positive family relationships works as a mechanism for social capital in a number of ways, notably, signaling the abundance of social capital (that is available to the firm through family ties that are multigenerational and multicontextual, which amplify the business resources); making the firm "real" and trustworthy (by literally displaying family members or by analogy to the institution of family); maximizing social capital for the iconic leader, founder, or CEO by making him or her the focal point of interest, both in the family and the firm; linking to the core businesses both symbolically (e.g., through the name) or strategically (by differentiating the firm competitively); highlighting other forms of capi-

TABLE 17.1
Positive Familial Relationships as Social Capital for the Organization

How Positive Family Relationships Are Displayed	Effects of Displaying Positive Family Relationships
Abundance of social capital, suggested by abundance of family ties that are multigenerational and in multicontexts, from home to vacations, everyday to special occasions, and so on.	Contextualizes the firm in a web of relations, making it more "real," accessible (and thus something with which you can identify), and trustworthy (like your own family members).
Social capital maximized for firm principals.	Leader, founder, or CEO tends to be silhouetted against the family as a featured member without peer; minimal use of siblings means that more social capital accrues to the individual executive (see Coleman, 1988)
Family relationships are directly *linked to the core businesses* so as to leverage this social capital.	Concretizes the firm's offerings by associating it with trusted experts, thus increasing legitimacy and trustworthiness of business. Social capital leverages business interests.
Social capital highlights and *enhances managers' human capital.* Family stories used to communicate valuable leadership traits, which are easily convertible into profitable business characteristics.	Founder's role in the family is used to present a personal identity that is beneficial and easily transferable to the firm. This is how familial relationships further the process of founder imprinting. Founder uses family to provide a storied context for their own accomplishments and personality. Through effective branding, this is transferred to the firm.
Positive portrayal of familial relationships as social capital (not social debts).	Use of family in the memoir style is possibly the most positive way to portray family—especially because they are invoked in service of greater (firm) goals.
Positive family roles convey *an expertise that is not authoritarian*—it is more friendly and charismatic, bridging interests from theirs to yours.	The display of familial relationships enlivens the firm by making it seem more accessible and "real" to consumers and to employees.

tal (especially human capital) through storytelling; portraying social capital as a form of wealth (not indebtedness or obligation); and, finally as a conveyance of expertise that is not authoritarian, but rather friendly, accessible, and familiar. Table 17.1 elaborates each of these points, noting how familial relationships function as a source of social capital that can benefit business.

To address our second research question, how the strategic use of familial relationships shifts to meet organizational needs, we suggest that a fruitful approach might be to focus on two key organizational changes: changes in governance structure and changes in the image of the firm. We focus on these two changes because they are concerned with two central aspects of organizations: structure, as assessed by ownership and governance, and symbol, as displayed in image and identity. Both seem to be at play recently at Martha Stewart Living Omnimedia, confronting the scandalized image of its iconic founder and leader, Martha Stewart, and the economic burdens of declining revenues and reduced advertising interest. It was at this point that her daughter purchased the necessary shares, often at a disadvantaged price, to not only keep family control of the business but to signal the family commitment to keeping the firm viable and competitive.

Depending on the business's needs, family relationships may be used to infuse capital where it might do the most good, for example, at the founding of the firm or during downturns, precipitated by market declines or image threats. We can speculate that the use of family as social capital would not deployed willy-nilly, with firms protecting the family (like other forms of capital) against the taint of scandal or economic distress. Thus, the portrayal of relationships seems highly attuned to organizational needs and to using social capital to purchase benefits for the firm.

As well, family relationships would seem to bolster the trustworthiness of the firm, such that the basis of trust shifts from a personal basis in the founder, CEO, or leader to become more institutionally based (Zucker, 1986) in the firm. Dependency on the personal identity of the founder can be risky, as we have seen in the case of Martha Stewart, a convicted felon, and the recent trials of other CEOs associated with scandals at Enron, Worldcom, Tyco, and other firms. Thus, less personal relationships may be useful to maintain and strengthen legitimacy, in the face of a scandalized corporate leader.

More generally, we believe that portraying positive relationships through familial relationships is a mechanism that engenders trust, a critical task to get customers to purchase the company's products or services. With a name like Mothers, car waxes and polishes have to be good! The branding using family—and especially the iconic symbol of mother—is used as a device to say, "I'm like your mother, grandmother, or aunt who knows how to clean and make things look the way you want them to." There is an institutional mechanism at work in the marriage of one social institution (the family or motherhood) to another (the firm or the workplace). By transferring a highly trusted institution (family) to a new, unknown entity such as an entrepreneurial enterprise or a small business, corporations can signal trustworthiness and credibility in the firm and its offerings (Zucker, 1986). The firm is legitimated through strategies of appropriation from one social institution (family) to another (business; see Suchman, 1995), with the result that positive relationships become endemic to the business and its success.

DISCUSSION AND FUTURE DIRECTIONS

We have explored the use of family as social capital in service of firm goals and demonstrated the manner in which familial relationships were displayed as a source of social capital for the firm. As any competitively advantageous resource, social capital (in our case, residing in positive familial relationships) can be deployed strategically for maximum benefit to the firm. Our discussion in this chapter suggests that this form of social capital can be deployed differently to meet changing firm needs. We offer potential reasons for the use of familial relationships as social capital and call for future research to extend and test these ideas.

First, we propose that the display of familial relationships as social capital benefits the firm by defining its identity. By embedding its founder in a web of family relationships, the social capital of the family enlivens the firm and its key personality. Especially for a new firm, this creation of identity (by transferring identity from family to CEO) offers an effective means for securing a socially desirable firm identity for its internal constituents (employees) as well as a desirable and appropriate image that appeals to its external constituents (investors, customers). We might speculate that the use of familial relationships, as a way to craft an organizational identity and establish a firm, might be used early in a firm's history, as was the case for Levi Strauss and Company. Later, as the company expands it business, and with a public offering, the prominent role of family might decrease or may change the form of attributes or values with which it endows the identity. We speculate that, as the governance structure of the firm shifts toward public ownership, concerns about the strong reliance on a leader's personal or familial identity make it more vulnerable to the impact of factors outside the firm that are not under its control. Both to signal trust and authority, we believe that firms would downplay the display of familial relationships with growth, change, investors, and stakeholders who bring more visible and more public scrutiny. Yet, in times of stress, organizations may well recover through the use of family relationships, as for instance, when family members invest in the firm through stock purchases or assuming organizational roles or formal positions that signal confidence in the firm, as we saw for both Levi Strauss and Martha Stewart Living Omnimedia.

Second, we suggest that the invocation of family relationships in the business context operates as a mechanism of legitimation. By marrying one known social institution (family) to another ambiguous one (the new corporate firm), trust is produced for the new entity. By characterizing the new firm as a familiar, familial organization (through the identity mechanisms described earlier), the firm and its offerings are thus legitimated, and this production of trust follows the institutional-based paradigm described by Zucker (1986).

We call for future research further explicating these processes and identifying the conditions under which they occur. We have found that familial relationships serve as social capital for the firm, so understanding the specific parameters of the successful deployment of this resource would have both important theoretical and managerial implications.

We have explored a particular type of social relationship, that of the family, as an endogenous resource benefiting organization needs. By taking an institutional perspective, we have suggested that a central aspect of life (family), previously cast as either separate from, or in competition with, work is actually a potential resource for organization goals. At the individual level, scholars have discovered the synergy between family roles and work roles (Rothbard, 2001). We contribute by bringing the discourse to an institutional level by suggesting that there can be positive synergy between the institution of family and the institution of the firm.

This view of positive relationships at work has both theoretical and managerial implications. Theoretically, the display of familial relationships as a mechanism for identity creation advances our understanding of the way in which the personal identity of the entrepreneur is intertwined with the identity of the new firm (Lounsbury & Glynn, 2001). In addition, following the changes in the organization's use of family relationships as a means for the production of trust and legitimacy in the firm's offerings reveals a more life-cycle view of the process of institutionalization. For managers, the discovery that the family entity, perhaps misunderstood as competitive with firm goals, is potentially an endogenous organizational resource may lead to a more refined strategy and the ability to more effectively capitalize on the advantages available in the notion of family. Overall, this chapter contributes by further making known the complex ways in which positive relationships at work function at the organization level.

REFERENCES

Baker, W. (2000). *Achieving success through social capital: Tapping the hidden resources in your personal and business networks.* San Francisco: Jossey-Bass.

Baker, W., Cross, R., & Wooten, M. (2003). Positive organizational network analysis and energizing relationships. In K. Cameron, J. Dutton, & R. E. Quinn (Eds.), *Positive organizational scholarship* (pp. 328–342). San Francisco: Berrett-Koehler.

Barney, J. B. (1991). Firm resources and sustained competitive advantage. *Journal of Management, 17,* 99–120.

Bartunek, J., & Lacey, C. (1998). The roles of narrative in understanding work group dynamics associated with a dramatic event: Confronting alcoholism. In J. Wagner (Ed.), *Advances in qualitative organizational research* (Vol. 1, pp. 33–66). Greenwich, CT: JAI.

Cameron, K., & Quinn, R. E. (1999). *Diagnosing and changing organizational cultures.* New York: Addison-Wesley.

Casey, C. (1999). "Come join our family": Discipline and integration in corporate organizational culture. *Human Relations, 52,* 155–180.

Coleman, J. S. (1988). Social capital in the creation of human capital. *American Journal of Sociology, 94*(Suppl.), 95–120.

Cross, R., Baker, W., & Parker, A. (2003). What creates energy in organizations?. *Sloan Management Review, 44,* 51–56.

Davis, G. F., & Marquis, C. (2005). Prospects for theory about organizations in the early 21st century: Exemplars from new institutional theory. *Organization Science, 16,* 332–343.

Dutton, J. E. (2003). *Energize your workplace.* San Francisco: Jossey-Bass.

Glynn, M. A., & Lacey, R. (2004, August). Celebrity CEO and personalization of the organization identity: Illustrations from Martha Stewart. Paper presented at the 2004 Academy of Management meeting, New Orleans, LA.

Haveman, H. A., & Rao, H. (1997). Structuring a theory of moral sentiments: Institutional and organizational coevolution in the early thrift industry. *American Journal of Sociology, 102,* 1606–1651.

Hedstrom, P., & Swedberg, R. (1998). *Social mechanisms: An analytical approach to social theory.* Cambridge, England: Cambridge University Press.

Helfat, C. E. (2003). Stylized facts regarding the evolution of organizational resources and capabilities. In C. Helfat (Ed.), *The Blackwell/Strategic Management Society handbook of organizational capabilities: Emergence, development, and change* (pp. 1–14). Malden, MA: Blackwell.

Lounsbury, M., & Glynn, M. A. (2001). Cultural entrepreneurship: Stories, legitimacy and the acquisition of resources. *Strategic Management Journal, 22,* 545–564.

Mizruchi, M. S. (1983). Who controls whom? An examination of the relationship between management and boards of directors of large American corporations. *Academy of Management Review, 8,* 426–435.

Paine, L. S., & Katz, J. P. (2002). Case study: Levi Strauss & Co: Global sourcing (A). In T. Donaldson, P. H. Werhane, & M. Cording (Eds.), *Ethical issues in business* (7th ed., pp 432–471). Upper Saddle River, NJ: Prentice-Hall.

Pearson, C. M., Andersson, L. M., & Porath, C. L. (2000, Fall). Assessing and attacking workplace incivility. *Organizational Dynamics, 29,* 123–137.

Perlow, L. A. (1998). Boundary control: The social ordering of work and family time in a high-tech corporation. *Administrative Science Quarterly, 43,* 328–359.

Putnam, R. (2000). *Bowling alone: The collapse and revival of American community.* New York: Simon & Schuster.

Robinson, S. L., & O'Leary-Kelly, A. M. (1998). Monkey see, monkey do: The influence of work groups on antisocial behavior of employees. *Academy of Management Journal, 41,* 658–672.

Rook, K. S. (1984). Negative social interactions: Impact on psychological well-being. *Journal of Personality and Social Psychology, 46,* 1097–1108.

Rothbard, N. P. (2001). Enriching or depleting? The dynamics of engagement in work and family roles. *Administrative Science Quarterly, 46,* 655–684.

Scott, W. R. (1995). *Institutions and organizations.* Thousand Oaks, CA: Sage.

Stewart, M. (1997). Letter from Martha, *Martha Steward Living* magazine, April, p. 12.

Suchman, M. C. (1995). Managing legitimacy: Strategic and institutional approaches. *Academy of Management Review, 20,* 571–610.

Tepper, B. J. (2000). Consequences of abusive supervision. *Academy of Management Journal, 43,* 178–190.

Zucker, L. G. (1986). Production of trust: Institutional sources of economic structure, 1840–1920. *Research in Organizational Behavior, 8,* 53–111.

18

Enabling Positive Social
Capital in Organizations

Wayne Baker
Jane E. Dutton

This chapter identifies and elaborates organizational practices and social mechanisms that create and sustain positive social capital in work organizations. It adds to the understanding of positive relationships at work by considering the resource-producing capabilities of high-quality connections (HQCs) and reciprocity. By being in this form of connection and practicing this type of interaction, dyads, teams, and organizations create valuable assets, such as trust, confidence, affirmation, energy, and joy. These are durable resources that have impact beyond the initial connecting point between two or more individuals (Fredrickson, 1998). This chapter shows how two forms of positive social capital (HQCs and reciprocity) expand the capacities of both individuals and groups. Further, it identifies key enablers of each form of positive social capital. Finally, it articulates the underlying mechanisms (motivation and opportunity structures) linking enablers and outcomes.

Social capital refers to the resources that inhere in and flow through networks of relationships (Adler & Kwon, 2002; Coleman, 1988). These resources include knowledge, information, ideas, advice, help, opportunities, contacts, material goods, services, financial capital, emotional support, and goodwill (Adler & Kwon, 2002). Social capital can be positive or negative. For example, a group inside a company can band together and use their collective power for their own gain, as engineers in a tobacco plant did (Crozier, 1964).[1] Or, investment managers may favor their friends and family in

---

[1] In this case, the plant had recently automated. The engineers threw out the operation manuals and made modifications to the machinery. This way, they could not be replaced, and management was forced to rely on the engineers and acquiesce to their demands.

the allocation of profits to investors, using money stolen from other investors (Baker & Faulkner, 2004). To be positive, we must consider the means by which social capital is created, and the ends to which social capital is used. Social capital is positive if the means by which social capital is created expands the generative capacity of people and groups. *Capacity* refers to the abilities of people and groups to achieve their personal and professional goals. Capacity is generative when it is able to reproduce and renew itself, expand abilities, and enable the combination and recombination of resources in new and novel ways. Social capital is positive if it helps people grow, thrive, and flourish in organizations and thereby achieve their goals in new and better ways. For example, acts of kindness and generosity between two people expand each person's emotional resources (e.g., joy or gratefulness) and openness to new ideas and influences (Dutton & Heaphy, 2003). If a pair uses this openness to innovate, create better solutions to problems, or work more efficiently or effectively, then this dyadic interaction has created positive social capital that was used for positive purposes. Even if these ends are achieved only in part, social capital is still positive if the purpose is positive.

Our chapter is organized around two fundamental forms of positive social capital in organizations: HQCs and reciprocity. In Table 18.1 we summarize both forms of social capital, the capacities that they expand, and the outcomes they produce. In brief, an HQC refers to a particular form of positive connection between two people. Like any HQC, a work relationship can be high quality even if the interaction is short. Basic or two-party reciprocity involves the mutual exchange of aid and benefit between two people; generalized reciprocity is a system of mutual exchange, aid, and benefit among members of a network. There are, of course, other forms of positive social capital. We focus on these forms for two reasons. First, each describes a pervasive form of social capital. For example, all treatments of social capital, regardless of discipline, identify reciprocity as an essential element. Second, although rarely explicitly defined, all of the forms of human ties that compose social capital vary in quality. Together, both forms link micro (the dyad) and macro (the system), revealing the essential complementary of the two. HQCs and reciprocity are mutually reinforcing: HQCs foster the practice of reciprocity; reciprocity builds new connections and improves the quality of connections. They both represent forms of positive deviance in organizations. Positive deviance is a term used in positive organizational scholarship to refer to extraordinary positive outcomes and the means that produce them (Cameron, Dutton, & Quinn, 2003). Applied to social capital, positive deviance means that social capital is used to achieve extraordinary results, and that it does so by building and broadening the generative capacity of individuals and groups. After defining each form of positive social capital, we identify several key practices that enable it by in-

TABLE 18.1
Two Forms of Positive Social Capital, Capacities, and Outcomes

Form of Positive Social Capital	What Capacities Are Expanded?	What Outcomes?
High-Quality Connections	Emotional carrying capacity Tensility Connectivity	Physiological functioning Learning Engagement at work Attachment and commitment Cooperation and coordination Individual and project performance
Generalized reciprocity	Ability to exchange more resources, more quickly Connectivity of the network (thus access to more resources) Ability to combine and recombine resources Ability to match resources and needs Elevates trust (hence willingness to make riskier requests, and to have confidence of repayment for help given)	Better resource utilization Discovery of new resources More problems solved, faster Reduces duplication of effort Cost reduction Time savings

creasing the motivation to engage in HQCs and reciprocity, and by creating opportunity structures for both forms of social capital.

TWO FORMS OF POSITIVE SOCIAL CAPITAL AND THEIR OUTCOMES

High-Quality Connections

HQCs are connections made between two people that are marked by vitality, mutuality and positive regard (Dutton & Heaphy, 2003). We intentionally use the word *connection* instead of *relationship* to assert that these interactions can be momentary and short term, rather than being enduring and lasting. In an HQC, both participants feel more alive and experience a heightened sense of energy. HQCs are marked by a particular subjective experience for both people in them, and connection is distinguished by several capacities (Dutton & Heaphy, 2003). First, HQCs have higher emotional carrying capacity, which is indicated by both the expression of more emotion by people in this kind of a tie, and more variety in the emotions expressed when compared to people in a lower quality tie. Second, an HQC has greater levels of tensility, which is the capacity to bend and withstand stress in the face of setback or challenges. Finally, an HQCs between two people is marked by a higher capacity for connectivity. Connectivity is a term used by Losada (1999) and Losada and Heaphy (2004) to capture a connection's generativity and openness to new ideas and influences, and its capacity to deflect actions or behaviors that would stifle or hinder these generative processes.

As implied by their defining features, HQCs have lasting impact on people and organizations (Dutton, 2003) as they enhance physiological functioning (Heaphy & Dutton, 2005; Reiss, Sheldon, Gable, Roscoe, & Ryan, 2000), enable heightened engagement in work (Kahn, 1990), facilitate coordination of interdependent people or units (Gittell, 2003), promote learning through heightened positive emotions (Fredrickson, 1998), strengthen organizational attachment and commitment (Labianca, Umphress, & Kaufmann, 2000), foster individual resilience and growth (Carmeli, 2005) and facilitate individual and project performance (Baker, Cross, & Parker, 2003; Cross, Baker, & Parker, 2002; Losada & Heaphy, 2004).

Reciprocity

The reciprocity principle operates when a person does something of value for you "without expecting anything immediately in return and perhaps without even knowing you, confident that down the road you or someone else will return the favor" (Putnam, 2000, p.134). Reciprocity is a form of cooperation that involves the exchange of resources between two or more people. Reciprocity does not involve legal contracts or formal agreements; often, the expectation of repayment is vague, undefined, or tacit. Because future repayment is not formally specified, reciprocity is sometimes defined as a combination of short-term altruism and long-term self-interest (Taylor, 1982). However, it is not necessary to invoke altruism to define reciprocity. Systems of reciprocity can arise and thrive even when all participants are only self-interested (e.g., Axelrod, 1984; Seabright, 2004).

Reciprocity can be present in varying degrees, and it can involve varying numbers of people. Basic reciprocity involves the exchange of resources between two people. This is also called two-party reciprocity because the exchange and expectation of repayment are limited to two people. Generalized reciprocity occurs in larger systems and involves more people. Generalized reciprocity is sometimes called third-party reciprocity because the exchange of help and assistance takes place among three or more people in a chain of reciprocity. For example, when John Clendenin managed the logistics group at Xerox, he instituted a practice called "huddles" (Podolny, 1992). If a person needed help, he or she could round up the people needed and request a 15-minute huddle. Those asked to help dropped what they were doing and participated, knowing that when they needed help in the future, they too could call huddles. Generalized reciprocity exists in degrees. At the pinnacle, people willingly help anyone who needs it—even if it has not been requested yet. For example, at IDEO, people routinely offer their expertise and insight to others, even if they are not officially assigned to these projects (Gada, Glover, & Tsai, 2004). Generalized reciprocity is a hallmark of communities of practice. "Members of a healthy community of practice have a sense that making the community more valuable is to the benefit of everyone," noted Wenger, McDermott, & Snyder 2002, p. 37). "They know that their contributions will come back to them. This is not a direct exchange mechanism of a market type where commodities are traded. Rather, it is a pool of goodwill—of 'social capital' to use the technical term—that allows people to contribute to the community while trusting that at some point, in some form, they too will benefit." Simply put, people help others knowing that others will help them when they need it.

The practice of generalized reciprocity expands capacity by increasing the volume, velocity, and efficiency of exchanges. It expands capacity by increasing the flow of resources through networks, by enabling the combination and recombination of resources, and by increasing the probability that the right resource will get to the appropriate need. Finally, it increases capacity by elevating trust and improving the connectivity and cohesion of a group. A wealth of research demonstrates the vital role of generalized reciprocity for the health of communities and organizations, as well as for individual health and well-being (e.g., Brown, Nesse, Vinokur, & Smith, 2003). Generalized reciprocity is essential for the strength of democracy and the economic development of nations (e.g., Putnam, 2000). Similarly, it is essential for healthy corporate cultures and business performance, and leadership plays a key role in creating it (Adler & Kwon, 2002; Baker, 2000; Cohen & Prusak, 2001; Flynn, 2003; Kouzes & Posner, 2002). For example, reciprocity improves productivity, promotes learning, and builds a climate and culture of trust (Flynn, 2003). By implementing some of the enablers we discuss next, such as collaborative practices and technologies, we have observed that generalized reciprocity improves the efficiency and effectiveness of resource exchange. It enables groups to discover new resources, solve more problems faster, and save time and money.

ENABLERS OF POSITIVE SOCIAL CAPITAL

In general, an *enabler* is any practice or condition that makes a process or state more likely to occur. Enablers differ from causes in that they suggest a probabilistic but not deterministic connection between one condition and another. We propose that enablers of positive social capital work through two major means: motivation and opportunity structures. More specifically, the enablers impact positive social capital by either increasing employees' motivation to engage in HQCs or in reciprocity, or by providing opportunities for employees to engage in HQC or generalized reciprocity.

We focus on clusters of organizational practices that promote positive social capital. By practices we mean the recurrent, materially bounded, situated activities of a particular unit or organization (e.g., Orlikowski, 2002). Practices refer to routine "ways of doing" in an organization that create and are created by structures (Giddens, 1984). More recently, there is recognition that everyday practices in organizations cultivate resources and resourcefulness in organizations (Feldman, 2004; Spreitzer, Sutcliffe, Dutton, Sonenshein, & Grant, 2004; Worline, Dutton, Frost, Lilius, & Kanov, 2004). Consistent with these perspectives, the practices we consider are patterns of everyday doing that produce positive social capital in organizations by motivation for or opportunity to engage in HQCs or reciprocity.

We argue that various organizational practices activate and affirm employees' motivation to participate in connections and a system of relationships that are generative. For example, organizational practices that foster employee recognition motivate HQC and generalized reciprocity by affecting people's perceptions of each other, attracting them to each other, and instilling expectations of mutual regard. In addition, we assume that the motivation to relate or connect in a certain way is more likely to create positive social capital if employees have the means and chance to connect that is captured by the idea of opportunities to engage. The motivation and opportunity to engage in HQCs increase when a practice facilitates respectful engagement (interacting in a way that communicates a sense of worth and value), evokes higher trusting (interacting in a way that communicates a belief in the integrity and reliability of another's actions), or strengthens task enabling (interacting in a way that facilitates the other person's capacity to perform their task more effectively). All three of these forms of interacting make higher quality connections more likely (Dutton, 2003) and thereby explain why some organizational practices build this form of positive social capital.

Reciprocity is natural: People are "hard-wired" for it; it is rooted in evolution, because it improves survival, and many argue that is what made society possible (e.g., Cialdini, 1993; Gouldner, 1960; Seabright, 2004). Yet many obstacles get in the way, such as incentive systems that measure and reward only individual efforts, separation in time and space, negative cultures, and so forth. These obstacles reduce the motivation to engage in generalized reciprocity and decrease the opportunities to do so. However, the natural tendency to engage in reciprocity can overcome obstacles to it. For example, business unit managers at British Petroleum (BP) have developed an informal system of reciprocity, evident in their informal "peer assists" and "personnel transfers" (Pfeffer & Sutton, 2000, pp. 216–217). Unit heads will loan their talented people to other units. BP, however, does not provide formal incentives for these practices and does not measure the results. Furthermore, the lender loses the contributions of the people on loan. By making loans, unit leaders know they can make requests for people when they need them. Although people can overcome obstacles and still engage in reciprocity, enablers increase the frequency and extent of these forms of interaction.

Enablers exert their positive effects when they increase motivation, opportunities, or both. A specific enabler may affect only one—motivation or opportunities. For example, the establishment of a formal system to measure and reward collaboration will increase the motivation to engage in reciprocity, but (without other changes) opportunity structures would remain the same as before. Participatory selection practices increase opportunities for reciprocity (because these practices expand social networks and awareness of others' needs) but they do not by themselves increase the motivation to engage in reciprocity. Of course, the most potent enablers increase motivation and opportunities (see examples that follow).

Table 18.2 summarizes the arguments for the main effects of six clusters of social capital enablers. (A blank cell in the matrix indicates the absence of a main effect, although there may be a minor effect.) These social capital enablers are illustrative and not exhaustive. They bring to light the intriguing possibility that everyday ways of doing in an organization cultivate the quality of social capital, which in turn, is associated with many desirable individual and collective outcomes.

Some Enablers of Positive Social Capital

Organizations are distinctive in the practices that create or destroy positive social capital. From the moment that employees begin to engage with an organization, until the day an employee exits, practices cultivate or eliminate certain conditions for interaction (Baker, 2000) that are the foundation of positive social capital. We identify, describe, and illustrate six clusters of practices here, using them as a vehicle for unpacking the theoretical mechanisms underlying the creation of positive social capital. Some of the practices are what organizational scholars might call human resource practices (selection, socialization, evaluation, rewards), whereas others are more fo-

TABLE 18.2

Links Between Enablers, Motivation to Engage, and Opportunity Structure for Two Forms of Positive Social Capital

	Motivation		Opportunity Structure	
Enabler	To Engage in HQC	To Engage in Generalized Reciprocity	To Engage in HQC	To Engage in Generalized Reciprocity
Selecting on relational skills	More experience and desire to build connections that call on these strengths	More likely to understand and be willing to engage in exchange with others	Endows individuals with competence to build HQC	—
Participatory selection practices	Participation in selection builds investment in new recruit, making trusting and task enabling more likely	—	More occasions to meet new members	Creates social networks, which are necessary for exchange; increases interpersonal knowledge; greater and earlier exposure to others' needs and potential contributions
Relational socialization practices	Cultivates conditions of trusting and respectful engagement	Decreases the motivation to misuse the reciprocity principles to trigger unwanted exchanges or create unfair debts	Creates more connections earlier and creates more opportunities for task enabling, trusting, and respectful engagement	Expands social networks, which are necessary for exchange; increases interpersonal knowledge; greater and earlier exposure to others' needs and potential contributions

Rewarding for relational skills	Strengthens skills for respectful engagement, trusting, and task enabling	Increases willingness to continue practicing reciprocity, and to seek new opportunities to do so		—
Using group incentives	Group incentives reward task enabling	Group incentives link and align self-interest (individual rationality) to collective interest (collective rationality)	—	
Relational meeting practices	Cultivate trusting and respectful engagement		Increase frequency of authentic connecting opportunities making respectful engagement and trusting more likely	Provides new and more venues and occasions for exchange
Using collaborative technologies		Increases willingness to practice reciprocity if technologies make it faster or more efficient	Creates occasions in which individuals interact in ways that increase respect and trust, and facilitate task enabling	Provides means (tools) for practicing reciprocity; may increase the efficiency of exchange

Note. HQC = high-quality connection.

cused on everyday work practices (conduct of meetings, collaborative technologies, practices of interpersonal helping) that undergird the conduct of work. There are other classes of enablers that we might consider (e.g., formal structure, mentoring programs, leadership behaviors, and physical architecture; Baker, 2000; Cross & Parker, 2004; Dutton, 2003; Ragins & Verbos, chap. 5, this volume), but due to space limits we do not consider them here.

In practice, multiple enablers often appear together, creating an organizational system that fosters positive social capital. In organizations with high positive social capital, these enablers are practices that are institutionalized along with a set of norms and values. Moreover, there may be congruency across practices, so that it is unlikely that one would be established without others. Although we discuss each enabler separately, note that just changing one may not improve positive social capital. For those who wish to put these enablers into practice, we advise a systems perspective in which these six (and others that we have not enumerated) are considered together.

1. Relational Selection. Beginnings matter. How an organization recruits and selects its employees shapes the terms on which people in an organizational initially connect. Selection practices leave their imprint on employees' expectations and images of their work organization. From the point of first contact, selection processes are powerful shapers of employees' future behavior patterns. Selection practices also are potent carriers of symbolic messages about what are desired employee attributes and what are valued ways of interrelating.

Two features of an organization's selection practices are particularly conducive to building positive social capital. First, selection practices that put a premium on hiring people for interpersonal skills and strengths shape the probability that people build HQCs. For example, some organizations explicitly select an individual's team-building competences, communication skills, or conflict management capabilities. Other organizations select individuals for how they have demonstrated collaborative behavior. For example, Cross and Parker (2004) described an organization that uses group problem-solving tasks during selection to favor individuals who excel in this form of collaborative skill. Researchers who have studied and articulated the idea of relational practice (e.g., Fletcher, 1999) have identified a host of relational skills that if used as a basis for employee selection, are likely to increase the motivation for and opportunity to engage in both the building of HQCs and generalized reciprocity. For example, Fletcher (chap. 19, this volume) identifies empathic competence (ability to understand others' experiences and perspectives), emotional competence (ability to understand and interpret emotional data), authenticity (ability to access and express one's own thoughts and feelings), and fluid expertise (ability to move easily from expert to nonexpert role) as skills that foster what she called a relational stance, which facilitates growth-enhancing (high-quality) connections between people. If people are routinely selected for membership in an organization using these kinds of criteria, they are likely to be more motivated to and capable of engaging in respectful engagement, task enabling, or trusting, which are three forms of interacting that build HQCs. In addition, selection practices that favor relational skills further motivate employees to form HQCs because the practices cultivate a model of desirable interacting that others copy and imitate. Thus, selection practices that favor people with relational skills directly and indirectly motivate HQCs by affecting the supply of people who are skilled in interacting this way and by activating a modeling or imitation dynamic that further spreads high-quality connecting behaviors.

A second selection practice that enables the building of positive social capital involves participatory selection practices, which as the name denotes means that multiple people are involved in selecting an individual to join the organization. This type of participatory practice means that people acquire a stake in helping someone succeed if they have had input in their selection. This motivation is more likely to increase people's investment in the new recruit, and increasing trusting and task enabling, making the situation ripe for building HQCs. At the same time, joint participation in the selection of a new recruit means more people have opportunities to connect with the employee, jump-starting the possibility of building higher quality connections.

Selecting on relational skills influences the practice of generalized reciprocity primarily through motivation: People who have good relational skills from the start are more likely to understand the importance of generalized reciprocity and be willing to engage in it, compared with those with poor relational skills. Participatory selection practices are a hallmark of companies with rich social capital, such as UPS, Capital Partners (pseudonym of a commercial real estate development firm), Russell Reynolds (executive recruiters), and many others (Baker, 2000; Cohen & Prusak, 2001; Prusak & Cohen, 2001).

Participatory selection practices lay the initial groundwork for generalized reciprocity, and exert their influence primarily through the creation of opportunities to engage in it. Reciprocity involves exchange, exchange requires knowledge of needs and resources, and this knowledge is transferred via social networks. Participatory selection practices create early opportunities for social contact, which increases interpersonal knowledge about needs and contributions. These practices expand a person's network of contacts, enabling one to spot and act on more opportunities to engage in generalized reciprocity.

2. Relational Socialization. Socialization describes the formal and informal processes that are used to bring new organizational members on board in an organization. An organization's practices are more relational when they provide multiple connecting opportunities for a new member to meet "old" members, the connecting opportunities are substantive (allowing for authentic communication), when others are specifically rewarded from bringing someone on board, and new employees are well equipped with the information and contacts that they need to do their job well (Dutton, 2003; Fernandez, Castilla, & Moore, 2000).

Socialization processes that rotate people though multiple departments when they first enter an organization actively jump-start new entrants' opportunities to build HQCs (Cross & Parker, 2004). In addition, if the organization's practices introduce the new recruit in ways that authentically and meaningfully allow others to value a new person, these practices cultivate high-quality connecting by creating a foundation for trusting and respectful engagement. Formal mentoring programs are good examples; not only do they build HQCs between mentors and mentees, but such programs facilitate "intergenerational" reciprocity as former mentees become mentors (see Ragins & Verbos, chap. 5, this volume). Some organizations provide specific occasions for people to meet a new recruit, and also equip organizational members with extensive useful information about a newcomer's background experiences or talents. The organizations facilitate new members' telling of their story about who they are, which are powerful means for connecting. "By revealing vulnerabilities and creating empathy 'I stories' build trust" (Putnam & Feldstein, 2003, p. 181). The use of these kinds of practices also provides more opportunities for connecting under conditions in which the connections are likely to be of higher quality. These kinds of socialization practices stand in sharp contrast to organizations where new recruits, or people on temporary assignments, are left on their own to navigate a new organizational context and to introduce themselves to others on an "as needed" basis (Dutton, 2003).

Relational socialization practices increase the motivation to engage in the proper uses of generalized reciprocity by decreasing the motivation to engage in the misuses and abuses of reciprocity. The social rule of reciprocity is so overpowering that it can be misused to create unwanted debts and trigger unfair exchanges (Baker, 2000; Cialdini, 1993). Cialdini (1993) described several unethical techniques and practices that "compliance professionals" use to unfairly invoke the principle of reciprocity. Relational socialization practices communicate the norm of proper generalized reciprocity as they communicate the prohibitions against its misuses and abuses. Further, relational socialization practices model appropriate reciprocity behaviors, such as observing acts of contribution and helping. For example, a global pharmaceutical firm incorporated generalized reciprocity in its high-performance teams program. Among other goals, this program helped to socialize newcomers (and reinforce for old-timers) about the proper uses of generalized reciprocity.

Relational socialization practices create opportunities to engage in generalized reciprocity by expanding knowledge of needs, resources, and possibilities of exchange in the organization. These socialization practices expand networks of HQCs, creating new opportunities to practice generalized reciprocity. The example of the pharmaceutical firm noted earlier had this effect as well: Participants made an expanding number of new HQCs, and discovered many new opportunities to help one another through the practice of generalized reciprocity. According to evaluations of the program, participants attributed hundreds of thousands of dollars of value and thousands of hours saved to the practice of generalized reciprocity.

3. Rewarding Relational Skills. In organizations designed for the creation of positive social capital, people are not only selected on relational skills, but they are also meaningfully rewarded for their development and strengthening. The rewarding of relational skills may be informal (e.g., praise or on-the-spot recognition) or formal (requiring more elaborated and explicit monitoring and measurement systems). Having practices that reward relational skills also means having a capacity to monitor and assess their development and having some way of assessing improvements. For example, organizations that include 360° feedback on whether a person provides effective support for others or whether a person displays empathetic or emotional competence (two of Fletcher's relational skills) would have a basis for monitoring, assessing, and rewarding relational skills. One could imagine real variance across organizations in the way that this feedback is done, and in the degree to which it motivates individuals to display and improve relational skills.

Where individuals receive meaningful rewards for displays or improvements of these skills, one would expect to see people more motivated to create HQCs (as the skills necessary to build them are clearly valued). At the same time, because the system is designed to detect effective relational skill development, one would expect more formal and informal opportunities to emerge for building these forms of connections.

Practices involving rewarding for relational skills do not have to be a formal, grand system to make a difference in building positive social capital (Dutton, 2003). In many organizations, informal, smaller rewards such as public spot awards, can be effective in creating the conditions for creating positive social capital. A well-known example is Southwest Airlines, which supports "agent of the month awards" that are fully determined by fellow employees, and given to employees who make outstanding efforts to enable the success of others, and the airline as a whole (Gittell, 2003).

Practicing generalized reciprocity is itself a relational skill. Rewarding the development and strengthening of relational skills increases the motivation to engage in generalized reciprocity. Even for those who are favorably disposed to engage in it, many do not know how to engage this way. It is often necessary to demonstrate the practice of generalized reciprocity, and to provide opportunities to experiment with it. The global pharmaceutical company mentioned earlier provided experiential training to develop and strengthen relational skills specifically aimed at promoting generalized reciprocity.

4. Use of Group Incentives.   One of the single biggest obstacles to positive social capital is the incentive system (e.g., Baker, 2000). Many leaders hope for positive social capital but reward only individual performance. As Cross and Parker (2004) noted, the most important question to ask is, "Do you reward collaborative behaviors or focus heavily on individual accomplishment?" (p. 125). Typical incentive systems focus on individual accomplishment and not collaboration and thus fail to promote high levels of positive social capital.

The use of group incentives in addition to individual incentives shapes the context for positive social capital. By group incentives we mean the linking of rewards to group-level rather than individual-level outcomes. For example, companies like Nucor, which have a significant proportion of employees' variable pay tied to team-level outcomes, create and maintain conditions conducive to the generation of positive social capital (Collins, 2001). When team-level pay is operational, individuals are more likely to be attuned to treating each other in ways that generate HQCs. For example, with this type of pay scheme there are incentives to enable the successful performance of other teammates because it directly contributes to one's own rewards. Thus, task enabling is more likely to take place when group incentives exist, and group members are more attentive to, and over time, more skilled at facilitating each other's performance.

Generalized reciprocity aligns individual and collective, and at times, can even blur the distinction (Baker, 2000). As noted earlier, it is possible for systems of generalized reciprocity to arise even when participants are only self-interested (e.g., Axelrod, 1984; Seabright, 2004), but it is much more likely if group incentives are added to individual incentives. Doing so increases the motivation to engage in generalized reciprocity. When people know their contributions to the welfare of others will be monitored and rewarded, they are more likely to practice generalized reciprocity and to look for opportunities to do so.

5. Relational Meeting Practices.   Meetings are a dominant social arena for the conduct of work in organizations. They are major sites for interaction—both virtual and face to face. They are social forums in which people in organizations spend a significant amount of time. They often bring people together physically and socially, which are conditions ripe for a heightened sense of connection (Homans, 1961) as well as rapport-building. They are the places where people share narratives, personal and collective, that social theorists have argued are so important to the building of social capital (Putnam & Feldstein, 2003).

Organizations vary considerably in both the qualities of the space allocated to conduct meetings and in the relational practices that typify how the meetings are conducted. For example, some organizations make extra efforts to allow for face-to-face meetings, such as UPS and Hewlett-Packard (Cohen & Prusak, 2001), because there is an explicit valuing of "good conversational spaces." Other organizations go to great lengths to do the background preparatory work to enable each person to enter a meeting better equipped to add value. They do this by letting people know what the meeting will cover, inviting people to meaningfully contribute, and giving people adequate time to prepare.

Relational practices in meetings that facilitate HQCs include encouraging listening, equipping individuals with information and opportunities to contribute, and providing opportunities for people to interact that are playful and fun (Dutton, 2003). Meetings in which people are encouraged to meaningfully contribute, where there are norms for respectful treatment of each other's inputs, and where people have chances to problem solve in ways that enhance the performance of the collective (e.g., a unit or the organization as a whole) are conditions that are more likely to create and affirm HQCs.

Relational meeting practices foster the practice of generalized reciprocity by providing new and more venues and occasions for exchange. The quarterly management meetings at Nucor Corporation are good examples, as Cross and Parker (2004) described: "People read material beforehand and use their precious time together for collaborative problem solving. For example, employees form teams from various functions or physical locations, and these groups not only solve problems but also help to form relationships across boundaries" (p. 127). These new relationships become conduits for the continuing practice of generalized reciprocity.

6. Using Collaborative Technologies. Building and using social capital requires time and face-to-face interaction; generally speaking, technology is not a good substitute (Cohen & Prusak, 2001). However, we believe that technology has its place. Similarly, Cross and Parker (2004) argued that technology can enhance work processes, but warn that managers first have to understand how work really gets done—the tasks, the people, the informal networks—and then explore how technology could assist. They document positive examples of various communication and collaboration technologies: instant messaging, skill-profiling systems (the equivalent of searchable online résumés), and group support systems, such as Web conferencing, Microsoft NetMeeting, chat rooms, and team rooms (e.g., eRooms). For example, BP's Virtual Teamwork Program enables engineers from around the globe to collaborate in real time and diagnose and solve technical problems quickly (Pfeffer & Sutton, 2000). Collaborative technologies ease the difficulties of making contact with other people when physical distance or structural impediments are barriers. Although these technologies cannot guarantee high-quality connecting, they increase the possibility of interacting by some means, making trusting, task-enabling, and respectful engagement at least a possibility.

If used properly, collaboration technologies increase the motivation to engage in generalized reciprocity and provide the opportunities to do so. Technology can make exchange faster and more efficient, and expand the reach of reciprocity well beyond what is possible in a face-to-face group. We know of only one collaboration technology that actually creates generalized reciprocity, the Virtual Reciprocity Ring™ (www.reciprocityring.com). This tool is explicitly designed to implement the principle and practice of generalized reciprocity. It is built around a structured process that enables participants to make requests, to make contributions to requests, and to follow up with one another. Data show that most exchanges are not between two parties (e.g., A helps B, B helps A) but third-party exchanges (e.g., A helps B, B helps C, C helps D, and D helps A). Third-party exchanges are the hallmark of generalized reciprocity. Participants report that they spend most of their time making contributions to others, and they trust that their requests will be met along the way. Consistent with observations of reciprocity in the workplace (Flynn, 2003), using this tool improves productivity, promotes learning, and builds a climate and culture of trust. Of course, other practices, such as transparent decision making, building a shared vision, employee ownership, and job security further contribute to a climate of trust (e.g., Abrams, Cross, Lesser, & Levin, 2003; Leana & Van Buren, 1999).

RESEARCH IMPLICATIONS

This chapter has outlined the contours of a framework for explaining and studying how organizational units or organizations as a whole are more or less likely to cultivate positive social capital. By adding the modifier "positive" to the widely used concept of social capital, we wish to assert that the means and the outcomes of social capital can vary. A focus on positive social capital highlights the particular value of connections between people that are generative or resource and capacity creating. We suggest that

HQCs and generalized reciprocity are two distinct but complementary and mutually reinforcing forms of positive social capital. Both forms highlight that positive relationships are not static entities, but are active mechanisms in the creation and sustenance of capacities and resources that create value to people who are in connection, and also to the unit or organization of which they are a part.

There are several research opportunities opened up by this perspective on positive relationships at work. First, the assumption that HQCs and generalized reciprocity build capacity for a social entity (like an organizational unit or organization as a whole) deserves further empirical validation. We have discussed (and summarized in Table 18.1) a variety of ways that these forms of positive social capital build and expand capacity, and implied that these help to account for the range of desirable outcomes also documented in Table 18.1. Our ongoing research supports the argument that these HQCs and generalized reciprocity build capacity and generate resources, but more research is needed.

Testing the first argument—that these forms of positive social capital are capacity generating—suggests important theoretical assumptions that must be tested as well. Implicit in our framework is an assumption that positive relationships at work (represented by HQCs and reciprocity) are resource producing. Thus, just by being in one these forms of connection, people create valuable assets like trust, confidence, affirmation, energy, and joy, which are durable resources that have impact beyond the initial connecting point between two or more individuals. In this way, our theory is consistent with Glynn and Wrobel's (chap. 17, this volume) claim that positive relationships can be an engine of resource production that adds to a social unit's capacity to act, to think, or to adapt. The idea that resources can be unleashed or unlocked from within a connection between people is an example of a broader idea of endogenous resourcefulness—that is, that there are resources that are released in the process of interacting, in doing, and in organizing that add value to human and organizational functioning (Dutton, Worline, Frost, & Lilius, 2005; Feldman & Dutton, 2005). This assertion, in turn, builds on Feldman's (2004) ideas that resources are built and changed in practice. In our case, we place at center stage the relational practices that undergird positive social capital, arguing that these practices are generative (i.e., resource producing).

Third, our perspective invites empirical investigation into how everyday practices of selecting, socializing, rewarding, meeting, and collaborating create or destroy positive social capital. At a very concrete level, our analysis suggests that, in the units or organizations with the enablers in place that we identify as conducive to positive social capital, we should observe frequent and pervasive high-quality connections and generalized reciprocity. Even within a single organization, we would expect to observe meaningful variance across units in positive social capital, explained in part by the presence, extent, and combinations and permutations of enablers that shape both the motivation and opportunity for these forms of interrelating.

Fourth, we need to examine the extent to which there is congruency among the practices. It might be unlikely that one enabler could appear without others; perhaps only a constellation of enablers could be used in practice. For example, it might be unlikely that an organization would reward for relational skills but fail to hire on the basis of these skills. Additional research would tell us if it is possible to have situations with high levels of some enablers, but just moderate (or even low) levels of others.

CONCLUSION

This chapter introduces the concept of positive social capital in work organizations. Positive social capital takes into account both the means by which social capital is created, and the ends to which it is used. Social capital is positive if the means by which it is created expands the generative capacity of people and groups. Social capital is positive if it helps people grow, thrive, and flourish in organizations and thereby achieve their goals in better ways.

We focus on two forms of positive social capital—HQCs and reciprocity. These forms create and sustain positive social capital by expanding the resource-producing capabilities of positive relationships at work. HQC captures a particular configuration of positive characteristics of a relationship between two people (mutuality, positive regard, and felt energy). Basic reciprocity refers to mutual exchange, aid, and benefit between two people; generalized reciprocity refers to a system of mutual exchange, aid, and benefit among members or a group or organization. HQCs and reciprocity are complementary forms of social capital where one reinforces the other. We argue that positive social capital ensues when members of a group or organization are motivated to engage in HQCs and generalized reciprocity, and have opportunities to do so. We identify six types of enablers of positive social capital that operate through the mechanisms of motivation and opportunities: selecting on relational skills, participatory selection practices, relational socialization practices, rewarding for relational skills, using group incentives, relational meeting practices, and using collaborative technologies. These enablers can be present or absent in organization, and they exist along a continuum. Different combinations and permutations of these are possible, although we expect that certain combinations would appear together in practice

We presented a sample of enablers, so one area of future work is to identify and validate other enablers of positive social capital. For example, what aspects of an organization's or unit's culture are most conducive to HQCs and generalized reciprocity? Are there particular patterns of shared values and beliefs that encourage patterns of interrelating that represent positive social capital? For example could justice, and in particular, interactional justice (e.g., Bies, 2001) be a shared organizational value or belief that is conducive to the production of positive social capital (see Greenberg, chap. 8, this volume)? Alternatively, are there particular strategic goals or ways of competing that are conducive to creating positive social capital? One might expect that for certain strategies (ones that rely heavily on collaboration and cooperation within and across organizational boundaries, e.g., alliance strategies; Bamford, Gomes-Casseres, & Robinson, 2003), enablers of positive social capital would be critical to sustained economic success. In these organizations, strategic goals and strategic priorities should be enablers of positive social capital. Finally, our set of enablers of positive social capital touch on some of the human resource practices that Vogus (2004) argued affect respectful interaction at work. His empirical study of nursing units suggests that bundles of human resource practices (including extensive training, developmental performance appraisal, selective staffing, performance-based rewards, employee empowerment, and job security) together contribute to patterns of respectful interaction that are conducive to HQCs and to generalized reciprocity. Future research should consider how these practices alone, and in combination with other practices, enable the creation and sustenance of positive social capital.

More research is needed to understand and validate precisely how these forms of positive social capital increase the generative capacity of individuals and groups, how they combine, and how they can be an engine of resource production. Such research would contribute to a fuller understanding of positive relationships at work—their dynamics, enablers, underlying mechanisms, and outcomes.

REFERENCES

Abrams, L. C., Cross, R., Lesser, E., & Levin, D. Z. (2003). Nurturing interpersonal trust in knowledge-sharing networks. *Academy of Science Executive, 17,* 64–77.

Adler, P. S., & Kwon, S. (2002). Social capital: Prospects for a new concept. *Academy of Management Review, 27,* 17–40.

Axelrod, R. (1984). *The evolution of cooperation.* New York: Basic Books.

Baker, W. (2000). *Achieving success through social capital.* San Francisco: Jossey-Bass.

Baker, W. E., Cross, R., & Parker, A. (2003, Summer). What creates energy in organizations? *Sloan Management Review, 44,* 51–56.

Baker, W. E., & Faulkner, R. R. (2004). Social networks and loss of capital. *Social Networks, 26,* 91–111.

Bamford, J. D., Gomes-Casseres, B. J., & Robinson, M. S. (2003). *Mastering alliance strategy.* San Francisco: Jossey-Bass.

Bies, R. J. (2001). Interactional (in)justice: The sacred and the profane. In J. Greenberg & R. Cropanzano (Eds.), *Advances in organizational justice* (pp. 85–108), Stanford, CA: Stanford University Press.

Brown, S. L., Nesse, R. M., Vinokur, A. D., & Smith, D. M. (2003). Providing social support may be more beneficial than receiving it: Results from a prospective study of mortality. *Psychological Science, 14,* 320–327.

Cameron, K. S., Dutton, J. E., & Quinn, R. E. (Eds.). (2003). *Positive organizational scholarship.* San Francisco: Berrett-Koehler.

Carmeli, A. (2005). *Fostering vitality, growth, resilience and learning processes in organizational members: The role of high-quality connections* (Working paper). Ramat Gan, Israel: Bar-Ilan University.

Cialdini, R. B. (1993). *Influence: The psychology of persuasion.* New York: Quill/William Morrow.

Cohen, D., & Prusak, L. (2001). *In Good company: How social capital makes organizations work.* Boston: Harvard Business School Press.

Coleman, J. S. (1988). Social capital in the creation of human capital. *American Journal of Sociology, 94,* S95–S120.

Cross, R., Baker, W. E., & Parker, A. (2002). *Charged up: The creation and depletion of energy in social networks* (Working paper). Cambridge, MA: IBM Institute for Knowledge-Based Organizations.

Cross, R., & Parker, A. (2004). *The hidden power of networks.* Boston: Howard Business School Press.

Crozier, M. (1964). *The bureaucratic phenomenon.* Chicago: University of Chicago Press.

Collins, J. (2001). *Good to great.* New York: HarperBusiness.

Dutton, J. (2003). *Energize your workplace.* San Francisco: Jossey-Bass.

Dutton, J., & Heaphy, E. (2003). The power of high quality connections. In K. Cameron, J. Dutton, & R. Quinn (Eds.). *Positive organizational scholarship* (pp. 263–278). San Francisco: Berrett-Koehler.

Dutton, J. E., Worline, M., Frost, R., & Lilius, J. (2005). *Explaining compassion organizing competence* (Working paper). Ann Arbor: University of Michigan, Center for Positive Organizational Scholarship, Stephen M. Ross School of Business.

Feldman, M. S. (2004). Resources in emerging structures and processes of change. *Organization Science, 15,* 295–309.

Feldman, M., & Dutton, J. (2005, August). *Creating capacity from within: Understanding endogenous resourcefulness in organizations.* Paper presented at the National Academy of Management meetings, Honolulu, HI.

Fernandez, R., Castilla, E., & Moore, P. (2000). Social capital at work: Networks and employment at a phone center. *American Journal of Sociology, 105,* 1288–1356.

Fletcher, J. (1999). *Disappearing acts.* Boston: MIT Press.

Flynn, F. J. (2003). How much should I give and how often? The effects of generosity and frequency on favor exchange on social status and productivity. *Academy of Management Journal, 46,* 539–553.

Fredrickson, B.L. (1998). What good are positive emotions? *Review of General Psychology, 2,* 300–319.

Gada, H., Glover, M., & Tsai, T. (2004). IDEO: The enabling of positive social capital for innovation. Team project, Social Capital for Managerial Effectiveness (MO624), Fall.

Giddens, A. (1984). *The constitution of society.* Cambridge, England: Polity Press.

Gittell, J. F. (2003). *The Southwest Airlines way: Using the power of relationships to achieve high performance.* New York: McGraw-Hill.

Gouldner, A. W. (1960). The norm of reciprocity. *American Journal of Sociology, 25,* 161–178.

Homans, G. (1961). *Social behavior: Its elementary forms.* New York: Harcourt, Brace & World.

Kahn, W. A. (1990). Psychological conditions of personal engagement and disengagement at work. *Academy of Management Journal, 33,* 692–724.

Kouzes, J., & Posner, B. (2002). *The leadership challenge* (3rd ed.). San Francisco: Jossey-Bass.

Labianca, G., Umphress, E., & Kaufmann, J. (2000). *A preliminary test of the negative asymmetry hypothesis in workplace social networks.* Paper presented at the National Academy of Management meetings, Toronto.

Losada, M. (1999). The complex dynamics of high performance teams. *Mathematical and Computer Modeling, 30,* 179–192.

Losada, M., & Heaphy, E. (2004). The role of positivity and connectivity in the performance of business teams: A nonlinear dynamics model. *American Behavioral Scientist, 47,* 740–765.

Orlikowski, W. (2002). Knowing in practice: Enacting a collective capability in distributed organizing. *Organization Science, 13,* 249–273.

Podolny, J. (1992). *Interview with John Clendenin* [video]. Stanford, CA: Stanford Business School.

Pfeffer, J., & Sutton, R. I. (2000). *The knowing-doing gap.* Boston: Harvard Business School Press.

Prusak, L., & Cohen, D. (2001, January). How to invest in social capital. *Harvard Business Review, 79,* 86–93.

Putnam, R. D. (2000). *Bowling alone: The collapse and revival of American community.* New York: Simon & Schuster.

Putnam, R., & Feldstein, L. M. (2003). *Better together: Restoring the American community.* New York: Simon & Schuster.

Reiss, H. T., Sheldon, K. M., Gable, S., Roscoe, J., & Ryan, M. (2000). Daily well-being: The role of autonomy, competence and relatedness. *Personality and Social Psychology Bulletin, 25,* 419–435.

Seabright, P. (2004). *The company of strangers: A natural history of economic life.* Princeton, NJ: Princeton University Press.

Spreitzer, G., Sutcliffe, K., Dutton, J., Sonenshein, S., & Grant, A. (2004). A socially embedded model of thriving at work. *Organization Science, 16,* 537–549.

Taylor, M. (1982). *Community, anarchy, and liberty.* New York: Cambridge University Press.

Vogus, T. (2004). *In search of mechanisms: How do HR practices affect organizational performance?* Unpublished doctoral dissertation, University of Michigan, Ann Arbor.

Wenger, E., McDermott, R., & Snyder, W. N. (2002). *Cultivating communities of practice.* Boston: Harvard Business School Press.

Worline, M., Dutton, J., Frost, P., Lilius, J., & Kanov, J. (2004). *Fertile soil: The organizing dynamics of resilience in work organizations* (Working paper). Ann Arbor: University of Michigan.

Leadership, Power,
and Positive Relationships

Joyce K. Fletcher

We survive only as we learn how to participate in a web of relationships.
—Margaret Wheatley (2001, p. 20)

The goal of this chapter is to explore the construct of leadership as a particular kind of positive relationship at work (Dutton, 2003; Dutton & Heaphy, 2003). First, I discuss the notion of leadership itself and the characteristics of emerging models of leadership that highlight its relationality. Second I identify opportunities for learning about relational leading as revealed by certain gaps and limitations of these models. Finally, I offer a particular perspective on positive relational interactions informed by Stone Center relational cultural theory (RCT) and use it to unpack a number of relational leadership constructs and identify key opportunities for future research.

LEADERSHIP AND POSITIVE RELATIONSHIPS
AT WORK

In many ways, the construct of leadership is and always has been inherently relational. Although there are many different theoretical perspectives on what constitutes good leadership (cf. Bryman, 1996; Yukl, 1998), all perspectives implicitly acknowledge the fundamental relationship between leader and follower. And the relationality of leadership has become more explicit and increasingly central to models of leadership effectiveness in recent years as the nature of work has changed. For example, the complexity of knowledge work means that it is unlikely that any one person will have all the necessary capability and competence to achieve effective outcomes. Instead, it is recognized that positional leaders must be learners, open to influence from multiple sources, able to empower and inspire others (Bryman, 1996; Manz & Sims, 2001) as well as foster organizational learning, adaptability, and innovation (Heifitz & Laurie, 1999; Senge, 1990b). Theorists have many different labels to describe this new leadership prototype, such as authentic leadership (Luthans & Avolio, 2003), quiet leadership (Badarraco, 2002) humble leadership (Collins, 2001), transformational leadership (Bass, 1998), and connective leadership (Lipman Blumen, 1996). Although there are important distinctions among these subprototypes, what they have in common is a recognition of the importance of being able to work effectively in the "spaces between" (Bradbury & Lichtenstein, 2000); that is, to work in and through relationships and to foster relational health in their organizations. Indeed, popular (e.g., Kouzes & Posner, 2003; Wheatley, 2001) as well as scholarly approaches (e.g., Graen & Scandura, 1987; Graen & Uhl-Bien, 1995; Pearce & Conger, 2003b) increasingly define leadership itself as a relationship and leadership practices as occurring in the context of relational interactions.

RELATIONAL CHARACTERISTICS OF NEW MODELS OF LEADERSHIP

There are three characteristics that distinguish new, more explicitly relational models of leadership from more traditional conceptualizations: leadership skills, leadership processes, and leadership outcomes.

Leadership Skills

As the requirements of good leadership practice have shifted, so too has the discourse around what skills, competencies, and attributes are needed to enact this practice. Relational and emotional intelligence are considered key to effective leadership and the skills required include things such as empathy, vulnerability, self-awareness, self-regulation, humility, resilience, and resolve (Badarraco, 2002; Collins, 2001; Cox, Pearce, & Sims, 2003; Goleman, 1998; Goleman, Boyatzis, & McKee, 2002; Luthans & Avolio, 2003; Sutcliffe & Vogus, 2003; Vera & Rodriguez-Lopez, 2004).

Leadership Processes

New models of leadership emphasize the role of social interactions in the process of enacting leadership. The practice of leadership is portrayed as a dynamic, multidirection activity that, like all human action and cognitive sense making, is embedded in the social context in which it occurs (Lave & Wenger, 1991; Suchman, 1987). The microprocesses of leadership are conceptualized as occurring in and through the relational interactions that make up these relationships and networks of influence (Fletcher & Kaeufer, 2003; Gardner, 1990; Hosking, Dachler, & Gergen, 1995; Kahane, 2004; Mayo, Meindl, & Pastor, 2003; McNamee & Gergen, 1999). In particular, the relational interactions that typify good leadership are characterized as egalitarian, mutual, collaborative, and two-directional, with followers playing an integral, agentic role in the leadership process (Aaltio-Marjosola, 2001; Harrington, 2000; Pearce, 2004).

Leadership Outcomes

New models of leadership recognize that effectiveness in a knowledge-intensive workplace depends less on the individual, heroic efforts of a few, and more on the degree to which an organization has constellations of positive collaborative working relationships throughout (Badarraco, 2002; Bass, 1998; Beer, 1999; Conger, Spreitzer, & Lawler, 1999; Hargadon, 2003; Heifitz & Laurie, 1999; Pearce & Sims, 2000; Senge & Kaeufer, 2001; Yukl, 1998). Thus, the practice of leadership is increasingly conceptualized as the ability to create conditions under which relational outcomes such as coordinated action, collective achievement, and shared accountability can be achieved (Conger, 1989; Gittell, 2003; Hosking et al., 1995; Kanter, 2001; Lipnack & Stamps, 2000; Seely Brown & Duguid, 2000; Thompson, 2004; Wheatley, 2001; Yukl, 1998). Multilevel learning is the key organizational outcome of good leadership: dyadic learning when the relationship is between individuals, group learning in teams and communities of practice, and ultimately organizational learning that results in positive action (Agashae & Bratton, 2001; Heifitz & Laurie, 1999; Kim, 1993; Senge, 1990a). Thus, the conventional distinction that managers "do things right" and leaders "do the right thing" (Zaleznik, 1992) is increasingly blurred as the knowledge of the right thing is conceptualized as something that is cocreated and emergent from positive, learning relationships distributed throughout an organization (Day, Gronn, & Salas, 2004; Hill, 2004; Kayes, 2004; Kim, 1993; Vera & Crossan, 2004; Watkins & Cervero, 2000) and the leadership task is conceptualized as creating organizational conditions in which all relational interactions at work are

high-quality connections (Dutton, 2003) that enhance organizational learning, innovation, and adaptation.

OPPORTUNITIES TO EXPLICATE LEADERSHIP
AS A RELATIONAL CONSTRUCT

Despite the increasing acceptance of the relationality of leadership, there
are a number of gaps in the development of the construct that limit the ability to research, identify, and evaluate leadership as a relational entity
(Fletcher & Kaeufer, 2003). These limitations present new opportunities to
explicate the construct of leadership and connect it to the emerging literature on high-quality connections and positive relationships in the workplace (Dutton, 2003; Dutton & Heaphy, 2003; Losada & Heaphy, 2004). In this
section I identify two of these gaps and the resulting opportunities. In the
following section I offer a perspective on positive relational interactions informed by a particular theory of relational interaction (RCT) and identify
several constructs within this perspective that could help theorists and
practitioners begin to address the gaps and enhance the construct of relational leadership.

Opportunity 1: A Need to Explicate the Characteristics
and Microprocesses of Positive Relational Interactions
in a Leadership Context

Conceptualizing leadership as an example of a positive relationship at work
highlights the need to explicate the microprocesses within leader–follower
interactions at the level of one leadership interaction or what Dutton (2003)
calls one high-quality connection. For example, new models of leadership
implicitly acknowledge that the process of enacting leadership is more egalitarian, two-directional, and collaborative than traditional top-down leadership perspectives. However, these new models are largely silent on the
specific microprocesses between leaders and followers that would operationalize two-directional concepts such as egalitarianism or mutuality in a
leadership context. Nor do these leadership models explicate or give a theoretical frame for understanding the process by which outcomes achieved
at the dyadic level link to broad leadership outcomes such as organizational learning and adaptability. Moreover, although the skills necessary to
enact relational leadership are aligned with tenets of emotional and relational intelligence (Goleman et al., 2002) there is little discussion about the
motivating set of beliefs or "logic of effectiveness" (Fletcher, 1999, 2004) that
would prompt someone to use these skills to enact mutuality and two-
directionality in a context that traditionally has been neither. Thus, there is

an opportunity to connect the literature on leadership with the emerging field of positive relationships at work to explore the characteristics of positive relational interactions between leaders and followers and the process by which those dyadic interactions can achieve organizational-level outcomes.

Opportunity 2: A Need to Embed the Construct of Relational Leadership Within the Larger Social Context in Which It Occurs

The second opportunity is the need to address what Jacques calls the abstraction of relational principles (Fletcher & Jacques, 2000) in the leadership literature. New models of leadership offer a more relational paradigm of leadership practice as well as a new, more relational prototype (Lord & Maher, 1993) of the skills, characteristics, and attributes of an ideal leader. Too often, however, both paradigm and prototype are abstracted or lifted from the larger organizational and societal context and presented as context-neutral concepts. For example, although the emotional and relational skills needed to enact a more relational model of leadership are identified, the literature is largely silent on how individual-level social identity characteristics such as race, class, or gender might influence one's ability to enact these more relational skills and still be perceived as a strong leader. Thus, there is an opportunity to embed relational leadership within the larger organizational and societal context to better understand the external forces that influence the ability and motivation to adopt relational leadership practice.

In the next section I overview a particular perspective on positive relational interactions I believe has relevance to the construct of relational leadership and identify how this perspective can help theorists begin to address these two gaps. The perspective I offer has been informed by RCT (Jordan, Kaplan, Miller, Stiver, & Surrey, 1991; Miller, 1976; Miller & Stiver, 1997), a type of relational psychology that highlights the gender and power implications of relationality, and draws on the emerging field of relational practice (Fletcher, 1999, 2004; Fletcher & Jacques, 2000; Fletcher & Kaeufer, 2003; Gittell, 2003; Jacques, 1993; Jordan, 1999; Walker, 2002) a body of work that applies relational concepts to the workplace with their gender and power dynamics intact.

STONE CENTER RELATIONAL CULTURAL THEORY

Relational cultural theory is a model of human growth developed by feminist psychologists and psychiatrists at the Stone Center for Developmental Services and Studies at Wellesley College. Its tenets detail a process of human development the authors call growth-in-connection (Jordan 1986, 1991; Jordan et al., 1991; Miller, 1976, 1984; Miller & Stiver, 1997; Surrey, 1985). The theory's hallmark is that it privileges connection as the primary site of human growth and carefully delineates the relational microprocesses that account for this growth.

The origins of this relational theory of growth reside in the early 1970s, when psychiatrist Jean Baker Miller began to question prevailing models and images of mental health that she believed were inadequate in capturing the full range of human experience. In particular, Miller (1976) noted that mainstream theories of human growth that had been developed by studying the experience of men, did not fit women very well. Listening to and learning from women's experience, she proposed a new, more inclusive theory of human growth and development that she called growth-in-connection. The central difference between this theory and what at the time were more mainstream theories of human development is the image of growth it offers. Rather than conceptualizing human growth as a process of separating and individuating oneself from others, RCT posits growth and development as a process of increasing proficiency in connecting to others. This is not a trivial difference. What sets RCT apart from other relational ideologies is what Miller (1976) called a new way of seeing. That is, rather than adding relationality to existing models of human development, RCT offers new principles, guidelines, and definitions of what it means to grow, develop, and achieve. Working with colleagues at the Stone Center, Miller identified the critical relational skills and attributes that were needed to engage growth-in-connection, the microprocesses that characterized it, and the orientation toward others that motivated its enactment (Jordan et al., 1991; Miller, 1976; Miller & Stiver, 1997).

Although the general literature on positive relationships at work has drawn on a wide range of theoretical perspectives, many of which include RCT as one thread (e.g., Baker, 2000; Dutton, 2003; Gittell, 2003; Kram, 1996; Ragins, 2005), there are three reasons that specific tenets of RCT are worth revisiting to further the construct of relational leadership. First, RCT is a theory with a very specific definition of what constitutes a "positive" relational interaction at the microlevel of what the positive relationship literature calls one high-quality connection (Dutton, 2003). This definition, which integrates personal growth with achievement, action, and learning is particularly appropriate for the study of leadership where achievement and action are integral to the desired outcomes of a positive relationship. Second, the RCT definition of positive is based not only on a set of relational constructs but also on a theory or logic of effectiveness about how growth and achievement occur. Third, its tenets focus not only on the microprocesses within one relational interaction that lead to these positive outcomes for both members of the interaction, but also offer a framework for thinking about the process by which individual-level outcomes can spiral outward to affect the larger community. Finally, the theory has a feminist orientation and deals directly with the issue of power differences in relational interactions. That is, its tenets have not been abstracted from the cultural context but instead have been explicitly located within a social context of patriarchy and other power dynamics. This makes the theory uniquely suited to studying the construct of relational leadership as a positive relationship that, by definition, occurs in a context of power differences.

In the following section I define some of the key tenets of RCT and relate them to the construct of relational leadership as an example of a positive relationship at work. First, I describe the outcomes of positive relational interactions identified in RCT and suggest a process by which these outcomes are achieved. Next I define some key characteristics of the growth-in-connection process and describe how outcomes at the dyadic level can spiral outward. Last, I introduce the RCT perspective on gender and power and discuss its implications for the study of relational leadership.

Key Tenets of Stone Center Relational Cultural Theory

Outcomes. RCT defines a positive relational interaction as one in which mutual growth-in-connection has occurred and offers specific evaluative criteria to assess whether this condition has been achieved. Specifically, Miller and Stiver (1997) state that when mutual learning and growth have occurred, both members in the interaction achieve *five good things*. These five things, which are congruent with more recent lists of outcomes of positive relationships (e.g., Cross, Baker, & Parker, 2003; Dutton, 2003) are defined as:

- *Zest.* Connection with the other that gives both members a sense of increased energy and vitality.
- *Empowered action.* Motivation and ability to put into practice some of what was learned or experienced in the relational interaction.
- *Increased sense of worth.* Increased feelings of worth that come from the experience of having used one's relational skills to achieve mutual growth-in-connection.
- *New knowledge.* Learning that comes from the experience of having cocreated new knowledge in the interaction through a fluid process in which members fully contribute their own thoughts and perspective while being influenced by the thoughts, experiences, and perspective of the other.
- *Desire for more connection.* A desire to continue this particular connection or establish other growth-fostering connections, leading to a spiral of growth that extends outward, beyond the initial participants.

There are several aspects of the definition of positive embedded in these outcomes that have significance for the construct of relational leadership. First, the definition of positive has to do with two-directional, mutually achieved growth that has affective, cognitive, and behavioral dimensions. That is, all five of these outcomes must be mutually achieved in an interaction for that interaction to be classified as positive. This means it is not enough for only one member of the relationship to experience the five good things. If the outcomes are not mutual, the ideal has not been met. In the same vein, all dimensions of the outcomes must be achieved. So, for example, if cognitive outcomes are achieved but do not have positive affective and behavioral dimensions, the ideal has not been met. Applied to leadership, this would mean that if, for example, a follower is not moved to empowered action as a result of a relational interaction with a leader but instead remains in the mode of directed action, or if a leader has not gained new knowledge or a desire for more connection, mutual growth-in-connection has not been achieved. Moreover, if some but not all of the outcomes have been achieved (e.g., teaching between leader and follower has occurred but the process has not resulted in zest and increases in sense of worth for both members), the ideal has not been met.

This high standard for mutual growth-in-connection has a lot to offer the construct of relational leadership. Traditionally, models of leadership have focused on one-directional impact (cf. Pearce & Conger, 2003a) and the degree to which a leader's behavior influences others to follow. Newer, more relational models of leadership acknowledge the need for mutuality but focus on it as a general, descriptive characteristic of a relationship between leaders and followers that evolves over time. The issue of specific growth, development, and learning benefits to leaders and followers at the level of a single high-quality connection has received little attention. In addition, the outcomes of positive interactions in general and leadership interactions specifically, have tended to address thoughts, feelings, and actions as separate entities. RCT, on the other hand, offers a model of growth that integrates its cognitive, behavioral, and affective dimensions and posits that all dimensions be mutually achieved for the interaction to qualify as growth-in-connection. That is, for growth-in-connection to have been achieved, both members must achieve

- *Cognitive outcomes*. The acquisition of new knowledge that has been cocreated in the interaction.
- *Affective outcomes*. Zest, increased sense of worth, a desire for more connection.
- *Behavioral outcomes*. The ability and motivation to take empowered action, putting into practice what was learned in the interaction.

The high standard that all outcomes be mutually achieved in a single interaction is especially appropriate for assessing leadership as a particular type of positive relationship at work. Unlike other positive relationships at work that might serve the function of providing personal closeness, friendship, or emotional support, the construct of relational leadership is implicitly tied to organizational-level outcomes such as organizational learning, innovation, and adaptability. Thus, it is reasonable to expect that a higher, more integrative standard be applied to dyadic interactions that can be labeled relational leadership and distinguished from other positive relationships at work.

In sum, RCT's perspective on growth and the implicit definition of positive embedded within it offer an evaluative, integrative framework that could be used to assess the degree to which relational leadership has been achieved at the level of one interaction. Moreover, as discussed in more detail in the next section, RCT suggests a process by which the integration of the cognitive, behavioral, and affective dimensions of growth are achieved.

Proposition 1: Relational interactions between leaders and followers at the dyadic level can be classified as positive when both members experience zest, increased feelings of worth, and a desire for more connection; acquire new knowledge, and are motivated to take empowered action.

Process.   Another contribution RCT makes to the construct of relational leadership is the process it suggests for how mutual growth-in-connection outcomes are achieved. As noted, RCT growth outcomes are multidimensional, achieved not separately but in concert. Feminist relational psychology, an area of inquiry that uses the tenets of RCT to explore workplace phenomena, suggests that mutual growth-in-connection begins through a process of cocreation that results in new knowledge (Fletcher, 1999; Fletcher & Jacques, 2000). More specifically, findings from a study of relational practice in the workplace suggest that it is the presence of "fluid expertise" (Fletcher, 1999) in the process of cocreating new knowledge that leads to the acquisition of the affective and behavioral outcomes associated with mutual growth-in-connection. Fluid expertise has been defined as a process in which

power and/or expertise shifts from one party to the other, not only over time but in the course of one interaction. This requires two skills. One is a skill in empowering others: an ability to share—in some instances even customizing— one's own reality, skill, knowledge, etc. in ways that made it accessible to others. The other is skill in *being* empowered: an ability and willingness to step away from the expert role in order to learn from or be influenced by the other. Expecting mutuality in this type of interaction implies an expectation

that others will have both sets of skills and will be motivated to use them, regardless of the individual status of the parties involved. (Fletcher, 1999, p. 64)

Fluid expertise, then, is a process of cocreation that depends on relational skills that enable each member of the relational interaction to move
easily from expert to nonexpert role, with a genuine openness to being influenced by and learning from the other member. It requires not only a belief that others are a source of learning, but also a willingness to engage
with others in a way that will encourage them to share what it is they have
to offer. In contrast to social exchange theories that emphasize the reciprocal exchange of commodities as the basis of relational benefits (Graen &
Uhl-Bien, 1995), fluid expertise highlights the process of cocreation and the
relational stance toward others that is required to achieve it.

Although the notion of relational stance has not been fully developed, it
is an important concept to explore in understanding the relevance of RCT
to relational leadership. As noted previously, RCT includes not only the relational skills and competencies that growth-in-connection requires, but
also the underlying beliefs about human growth. It is this set of beliefs or
what Miller (1976) called a way of seeing, that gives rise to a relational, wel-
coming stance toward others. Interactions in which both members have
this stance would be characterized by mutuality (Jordan, 1986) in which
both members of the interaction recognize the need for others, each feels a
responsibility to contribute to the growth of others (Fletcher, 1999), and
each approaches relational interactions expecting to grow from them.
Thus, the notion of relational stance reconceptualizes the notion of other
embedded in relational interactions. Whereas the interactional other is often characterized as a source of growth for the self (e.g., Levinson, 1978) or
the receiver of one's self-representation (Brewer & Gardner, 1996) or one's
impression management activities (Goffman, 1959), the concept of relational stance suggests a multidirectional, interactional process of influence
similar to what Follett (1924) called circular response.

The notion of relational stance is especially important for a discussion of
relational leadership because it suggests that the motivation to engage in
relational leadership and develop the skills necessary to enact it effectively
will be influenced by the degree to which one accepts the role of mutual
growth-in-connection in one's own achievement and development as well as
the development and achievement of others. Thus, it is reasonable to assume that operating from a relational logic of effectiveness in which mutual
growth-in-connection is central, is likely to motivate the enactment of relational leadership.

The centrality of the cocreation process in the enactment of positive relational interactions is supported by several frameworks of positivity of-

fered in the emerging field of positive relationships at work. For example, many of the microprocesses and behaviors identified in the positive relationships literature as leading to moments of high-quality connection entail the enactment of regard. This is operationalized by behaviors that communicate social respect, such as recognizing and valuing the contribution and worth of others (Dutton, Debebe, & Wrzesniewski, 1998), being present and genuine in your everyday interactions with others (Dutton, 2003), and communicating an eagerness to learn from others (Vera & Rodriguez-Lopez, 2004). These examples all suggest that positivity begins with an invitation to engage with another person that communicates a belief in the inherent value and potential contribution of that person. Implicit in this invitation is a willingness to influence and be influenced by the other regardless of that member's relative status or position. The notion of fluid expertise further explicates this process and suggests that growth-in-connection requires not only that such an invitation be mutually extended, but also that it be mutually accepted and acted on such that something new is cocreated in the interaction.

Explicating cocreation as a process in which fluid expertise is mutually enacted has special relevance for the construct of relational leadership. As discussed earlier, theories of relational leadership do not specify how characteristics such as egalitarianism can be operationalized, measured, or evaluated. RCT and studies of relational practice offer the concept of fluid expertise as one microprocess through which egalitarianism is operationalized. Moreover, this perspective suggests that when the process of cocreation is actively engaged and new knowledge is mutually achieved, its effects will be experienced affectively as zest, increased sense of positive worth, and a desire for more connection, and behaviorally as empowered action.

Again, the study of positive relationships at work offers some support this for model. Specific behaviors identified as energizers that create zest and vitality in workplace interactions include things related to the cocreation process such as cognitively engaging with others, using one's expertise appropriately, engaging in inclusive processes that foster empowerment, and being flexible in considering others' ideas (Cross, Baker, & Parker, 2003; Feldman & Khademian, 2003). Other studies of high-quality connections at work such as Gittell's (2003) work on relational coordination, Feldman and Khademian's (2003) work on empowerment, and Fredrickson's (2003) work on the role of positive emotions in expanding cognitive and behavioral repertoires support the process link to organizationally positive action that is internally rather than externally motivated.

In sum, the tenets of RCT, when applied to relational leadership, suggest the following propositions.

Proposition 2a: Growth-in-connection in leader–follower interactions begins with a process of cocreation in which both members have the skills and relational stance necessary to enact fluid expertise.

Proposition 2b: The mutual enactment of fluid expertise is the vehicle through which egalitarianism is operationalized in leader–follower interactions.

Proposition 2c: When fluid expertise is enacted in leader–follower interactions such that new knowledge is cocreated and mutually achieved, its effects will be experienced affectively as zest, an increased sense of positive worth and a desire for more connection.

Proposition 2d: When fluid expertise is enacted in leader–follower interactions such that new knowledge is cocreated and mutually achieved, its effects will be experienced behaviorally, as empowered (as opposed to directed) action.

Growth-in-Connection Spirals. A third contribution RCT makes to the construct of relational leadership is that it includes the vehicle by which individual-level outcomes extend beyond the dyad to impact the broader community. RCT suggests that an interaction cannot be classified as positive unless both members leave the interaction hungry for more connection. Significantly, the desire for more connection is conceptualized both as a desire to continue growth-in-connection with that specific partner as well as a more generalized desire for high-quality connection with others. This high standard of evaluation is especially important to the construct of leadership because it highlights—and offers for further study—the specific process by which dyadic interactions between leader and followers can lead to broader organizational outcomes such as organizational learning, innovation, and adaptability. Specifically, RCT suggests that the affective desire for more connection will result in behavioral attempts to engage the mutual growth-in-connection process with others in one's relational network. In a work setting this could include coworkers, bosses, clients, suppliers, and customers. To the extent these attempts are successful, the outcomes of growth-in-connection, including the cocreation of new knowledge and the desire for more connection, will spiral outward from the initial dyadic interaction.

Again, there is support for this image of spiraling growth in the positive relationships at work literature, where positive emotions such as joy or gratitude have been hypothesized as fueling upward spirals of optimal organizational functioning because these emotions expand people's modes of thinking and acting (Fredickson, 2003). RCT, however, suggests that it is not only through positive emotions that such spirals are engaged, but through a cocreation process in which fluid expertise has been mutually exercised.

It should be noted, however, that fluid expertise must be enacted by both members of the relational interaction for growth-in-connection to occur. Thus it is reasonable to assume that the spiraling effects of relational leadership will be dependent on the extent to which others in the organization have the relational skills and stance required to recognize and respond to an invitation to engage in mutual growth-in-connection. It is also reasonable to assume that even the smallest experience of enacting fluid expertise successfully will enhance the relational skills and stance of each member of the interaction such that the chances of further engaging the spiral are increased.

In sum, RCT brings specificity to the notion that leaders affect the relational climate of an organization by modeling relational behavior. That is, RCT suggests that the practice of relational leadership affects others not only because they observe leaders acting in more relational, egalitarian ways and therefore feel free to act that way themselves. Rather, RCT suggests that growth-in-connection leadership interactions have an organizational effect because they create a hunger for more growth-in-connection, thereby increasing the chances that the five good things will be achieved repeatedly at multiple levels in the organization. Thus, RCT offers one specific mechanism by which organizational-level leadership outcomes such as innovation, organizational learning and empowered action can be achieved. This leads to the following propositions.

Proposition 3a: Relational leadership is likely to spiral outward through a process in which a mutual desire for more connection leads to behavioral attempts to engage the mutual growth-in-connection process with others in one's network, thereby increasing the chances that the five good things will be achieved repeatedly at multiple levels within the organization.

Proposition 3b: Relational leadership has the potential to influence the relational climate of an organization because episodes of mutual growth-in-connection provide opportunities to practice relational skills and develop a relational stance toward others, which in turn increase the chances that the number of episodes of mutual growth-in-connection will increase throughout the organization.

Power

Unlike many relational ideologies, RCT does not abstract relationality from its broader cultural context. Rather, its tenets are explicitly located within the social context of patriarchy and other power dynamics in which they occur. Explicating the theory in this broader context makes visible two important questions: Why, if connection is the basic site of growth and human development, have conventional models of development so emphasized separation, independence, and individuation? And why, if relational skills and attributes are key to the growth-fostering process for all humans, have they been historically associated with femininity and the private sphere of life and so devalued in the public realm? Miller (1976) offered a gender and power analysis to explain these contradictions. She noted that in Western society men are socialized to devalue and deny in themselves the relational skills needed to survive psychologically. Instead, they tend to rely on women to provide these attributes. Women, on the other hand are socialized to provide these skills, usually invisibly and without acknowledgment that the provision of these attributes is needed or that something valuable has in fact been done. In this way, women become the "carriers" of relational strengths in Western society, responsible for creating relational connections for others and meeting basic relational needs without calling attention to the needs themselves. Rather than strengths, these relational attributes are surrounded by what Miller (1976) called a language of deficiency (e.g., emotionally needy, codependent, or overly dependent on relationships, low ego strength, etc.) and in the psychological domain often characterized as the source of psychological problems rather than psychological strength. Miller (1976) observed that the invisibility and devaluing of relational activity allows society to perpetuate a myth of self-reliance and independence, even though most people have a network of people supporting their "individual" achievement.

Miller asserted that the belief that independence is a state that can be achieved belies the essentially interdependent nature of the human condition. Moreover, she asserted that the myth of individual achievement is actually a discursive exercise of power whereby some in society are expected to provide the collaborative subtext of life invisibly so others can enact the myth of individual achievement without acknowledging that this collaborative subtext of support is needed and important. Growth-in-connection depends on a belief that interdependence (not independence) is the natural human state. However, the myth of individual achievement that permeates Western society precludes that belief and makes growth-in-connection difficult to achieve. The theory points out that both a gender power dynamic associated with patriarchy and a more general power dynamic are involved in sustaining these so-called myths of independence and individual achievement.

Gender.   RCT places the construct of relationality within the discourse on the social construction of gender (West & Zimmerman, 1991), highlighting the fact that relationality is not a gender-neutral concept. Gender socialization, especially in Western society, assigns to women the task of creating the relational conditions under which human growth-in-connection can occur (Chodorow, 1978; Fairbairn, 1952; Miller, 1976; Miller & Stiver, 1997; Winnicott 1958), especially as it relates to the private sphere of family and motherhood. The result is that enacting relational skills and adopting a relational stance is one way in which women "do gender" (West & Zimmerman, 1991) in Western society. The fact that at a societal level women are the carriers of relationality and expected to provide conditions of growth invisibly may inappropriately associate the stance and the relational skills it takes to engage it with femininity.

Power. In addition to this gender power dynamic there is a more general power dynamic influencing relationality. In systems of unequal power (e.g., inequities based on race, class, organizational level, or sex) it behooves those with less power to be ultrasensitive and attuned to the needs, desires, and implicit requests of the more powerful (Jost, 1997; Miller, 1976). In other words, in systems of unequal power, what marks you as more powerful is the entitlement of having others anticipate your needs and respond to them without being asked; what marks you as less powerful is being required to do the anticipating and accommodating without any expectation of reciprocity. The fact that those with less power need to develop a distorted, nonmutual relational stance toward others to survive may inappropriately associate the stance, and the relational skills it takes to engage it, with powerlessness and vulnerability (Bartolome & Laurent, 1988; Miller, 1976).

The RCT analysis of gender and power dynamics has important relevance for the study of relational leadership. Specifically, it suggests that the inappropriate association of relationality with femininity and powerlessness is an important factor to consider in understanding the experience and consequences of enacting relational leadership. First, let us consider femininity. Those who emphasize the social construction of identity (e.g., Goffman, 1959) note that whenever we interact with others we enact our self-image and social identity, a good part of which is our gender identity (Foldy, 2002). Thus, all social interactions, including those at work, become occasions to "do gender" (West & Zimmerman, 1991), whereby we convey our gender identity in the way we respond and react to others or in how we choose to do our work. An example of this dynamic is found in the work of Martin and Collinson (Martin, 1996; Martin & Collinson, 1998), who noted that work is often used as an occasion to display stereotypically masculine attributes such as toughness and physicality, even when those attributes are not required of the work itself. Further, they suggested that because men have dominated the work world for so long, doing masculinity and doing work has gotten conflated, such that everyone (men and women) experiences subtle pressure to "do masculinity" at work to be perceived as competent.

The concept of doing gender at work adds another layer of complexity to the context in which leadership is practiced. As noted, the skills and attributes needed to practice relational leadership are aligned with stereotypical images of femininity. Thus, in the same way competence at work has traditionally required that both men and women engage in displays of masculinity, the new leadership can be thought of as requiring both men and women to engage in displays of femininity (Fletcher, 2004). This suggests that the experience of enacting relational leadership is likely to be different for women and men and that the sex of the participants in the leader–follower interaction is an important contextual factor to consider in studying and understanding these leadership interactions (Fletcher, 2004; Fletcher & Kaeufer, 2003; Sinclair, 1998).

Descriptions of the behavior, skills, and organizational principles associated with new leadership, however, are typically presented as gender neutral in practice, that is, as if the sex of the actor is irrelevant to how the behavior is understood, perceived, and experienced by leader and followers. In contrast, the RCT perspective, which is congruent with work in the social cognition domain (cf. Fiske & Taylor, 1991) highlights the way interpretations and perceptions are always contextual and filtered through cognitive schemas that are influenced by many factors, including the social identity characteristics (sex, race, class, organizational title, etc.) of the actor as well as that of the observer. Gender schemas (Valian, 1998) are particularly powerful cognitive schemas through which we observe and interpret behavior. The result is that the experience of putting relational leadership into practice is likely to be different for women and men (Babcock & Laschever, 2003; Rudman & Glick, 2001; Wade, 2001). For example, because behavior is filtered through gender schemas and the different expectations we have of male and female behavior, it is likely that men who enact behavior that is unconsciously associated with femininity, although they might be in danger of being called soft, may have an easier time being seen as doing something new. Women, on the other hand, may have a harder time distinguishing what they do as something new, because it looks like they are just doing what women do (Fletcher, 1999). Indeed, studies using RCT to study workplace phenomena suggest that women who enact relational practice have their competence "disappeared" because of this association with femininity (Fletcher, 1999). When applied to leadership the association of relationality with femininity may have an even more pernicious effect on women. For example, the expectation that women will provide the conditions for relational growth invisibly, without calling attention to the need for these conditions or the expectation that these conditions will be provided for them in return, makes it difficult for women to embed an invitation to mutuality and reciprocity in their practice of new leadership (Fletcher, 2004). Thus it appears that although the association of relationality with femininity may complicate the practice of relational leadership for both men and women, the effects are likely to create special dilemmas for women.

Proposition 4a: The sex of the participants is an important contextual factor to consider in studying the experience and consequences of enacting relational leadership.

Proposition 4b: The conflation of displays of relationality with displays of femininity is likely to create special dilemmas for women who enact relational leadership.

The second dynamic the RCT perspective on gender and power highlights is the way in which displays of relationality may be conflated with and misinterpreted as displays of powerlessness. This is particularly relevant to a discussion of leadership because leadership is, by definition, linked to the exercise of power. There are two specific contributions an awareness of this potential conflation can make to the study of relational leadership as an example of a positive relationship at work. The first is that it highlights a key dynamic undercutting the practice of relational leadership in the workplace. As discussed previously, enacting relational leadership requires that both leaders and followers have the willingness and ability to enact fluid expertise and operationalize egalitarianism to engage the cocreation process. Whereas traditional notions of leadership often incorporate the need to empower others, new leadership requires an openness to *being* empowered and visibly acknowledging it. This means that leaders who traditionally are expected to have all the answers and to be help-givers rather than help-seekers will need to engage in nontraditional behavior themselves as well an invite nontraditional behavior from their followers. This new requirement entails risk. Indeed, it has been noted that workers avoid help-seeking behavior because it is negatively associated with positional power through its association with dependence (Lee, Caza, Edmondson, & Thomke, 2003) and lack of competence. Thus it appears that the risk for leaders of having their relational behavior conflated in others' eyes (as well as in their own) with a display of powerlessness and incompetence may well act as a deterrent, undermining the practice of relational leadership in the workplace.

The second contribution to relational leadership made by an awareness of the potential conflation of relationality with powerlessness is that it highlights the need to unpack the concept of power. Specifically, RCT calls us to expand the concept of power beyond positional authority to include systemic dynamics associated with other aspects of social identity. As noted, there is a gender dynamic inherent in practicing relational leadership such that the experience is likely to be different for men and women because of the different expectations we have of ourselves and others. However, gender is not the only social identity characteristic implicated in the RCT perspective on gender and power. Rather, the RCT perspective suggests that any social identity characteristic that signals membership in a group with a history of societal-level power differences (i.e., the legacy of patriarchy, the legacy of slavery, the history of homophobia, etc.) is going to influence the relational process. Thus, RCT highlights the fact that enacting egalitarianism through, for example, engaging fluid expertise and the process of cocreation is going to be influenced not only by the power of one's organizational level but also by the social identity characteristics of the actors and the history of power relations between them. For example, because of racial stereotypes related to competence and advancement, men of color may be at greater risk of suffering from the unconscious association of relationality with powerlessness than White men and experience greater constraints in enacting relational leadership. In a similar vein, although all women may have a difficult time embedding an invitation to mutuality and reciprocity in their relational leadership, the situation may be exacerbated for women of color for whom the legacy of racism and slavery may have created additional expectations that they defer to others or engage in self-less giving and service. Although the manifestations of different permutations of leader and follower social identity characteristics are too numerous to enumerate or predict, what RCT helps us see is that the intersection or what Holvino (2001) calls the simultaneity of social identity characteristics within as well as between leader and follower will affect the practice of relational leadership. This leads to the following proposition.

Proposition 5: The social identity of the participants in leader–follower relational interactions and the history of power relations between their identity groups is an important contextual factor to consider in studying the experience and consequences of enacting relational leadership.

Although this discussion has focused on the role of gender and power in leadership interactions, it should be noted that current work on positive relationships at work could also benefit from the RCT perspective on these issues. For the most part, the emerging field of positive relationships at work treats relational interactions as gender and power neutral, as if, for example, the sex, race or organizational level of the actors has little bearing on the relational process or the generation of positive outcomes. The RCT perspective suggests that this is unlikely to be true. Rather, it is likely that the ability to adopt the practices associated with creating high-quality connections at work will be influenced by these subtle and not so subtle power dynamics such that they should be taken into account as important contextual factors in any study of the phenomena.

In sum, the RCT perspective on gender and power dynamics inherent in relational interactions indicates that both the study of relational leadership and the more general study of positive relationships at work would benefit from including these dynamics as objects of study. Specifically, it suggests that although articulating the value of positive relational interactions at work is an important first step, there are powerful contextual factors influencing the relational process that must be taken into account before we can understand the implications and implementation issues inherent in enacting positive relational behaviors at work.

CONCLUSION AND DIRECTIONS
FOR FUTURE RESEARCH

The perspective presented here suggests a number of important opportunities for future research and theory development for the construct of relational leadership as an example of a positive relationship at work. Currently, leadership is most often integrated into the positive relationships at work literature as an external influence (for an exception see Luthans & Avolio, 2003). That is, the role of leadership in the study of positive connections at work is presented as a factor in, for example, the creation of safe spaces for positive connection (Kahn, 1998; chap. 10, this volume) or as a forum for modeling the practices that foster positive connections at work (Dutton, 2003) or the vehicle for the design of organizational structures that would support and enhance the flourishing of positive connections at work (Baker & Dutton, chap. 18, this volume; Dutton, 2003; Ragins & Verbos, chap. 5, this volume). Using the principles of RCT to explore the construct of relational leadership suggests an additional, more direct influence of leadership on the flourishing of positive connections at work. More specifically, this discussion of relational leadership has suggested that one way positive leader–follower interactions lead to organizational outcomes is through the fifth of the five good things, namely the desire for more connection. One avenue for future research would be to further delineate this movement and map the specific microprocesses by which desire for more connection spirals outward from the individual-level relational interaction between a leader and follower to effect organizational-level outcomes such as learning, adaptation, and innovation.

A related avenue for exploration would be to be to reconceptualize current leadership concepts such as power, from an RCT perspective and connect them to RCT concepts such as fluid expertise or the RCT location of relationality within a larger social context. For example, applying RCT principles to the workplace suggests that a willingness to operate in a context of fluid expertise requires three things: a view of other as a potential source of learning regardless of where that other resides in the organizational hierarchy; a relational view of self such that engaging in mutually growth-fostering interactions with another will be experienced positively regardless of where that other resides in the organizational hierarchy; and a desire to contribute to the learning, well-being, and development of another, regardless of where that other resides in the organizational hierarchy. As noted, this suggests that notions of positional power and the status markers associated with it are important influences in achieving the desired outcomes of new leadership. More specifically, it suggests that the notion of power embedded in fluid expertise is also fluid, evoking a more symmetrical pattern of influence perhaps captured better by the phrase "power with" (Follett, 1924; Miller & Stiver, 1997) than the more common conceptualization of power as an asymmetrical pattern of influence. Developing, exploring, and testing such a concept could greatly enhance the understanding of new leadership. As noted previously, descriptions of shared leadership and empowering practice refer to the importance of a participatory style and more egalitarian power relations. However, there is no single construct to describe this more fluid notion of power relations. Developing the construct of "power with" could fill this void and further the understanding of fluid expertise and the relational stance needed to engage it.

Another fruitful area for research would be to delineate the concept of relational followership as an integral part of relational leadership. This chapter has focused on the construct of relational leadership and the relational skills, stance, and behaviors of a leader. However, meeting the growth-in-connection definition of positive requires mutuality and the mutual achievement of all five of the five good things. This raises the question of the relational skills, stance, and behaviors of followers in the leader–follower interaction. Are they the same? Are they different? In what ways is movement from cognitive to affective to behavioral outcomes for followers similar to or different from that of leaders? What is the followership experience of achieving each of the five good things? Is, for example, the affective experience and behavioral manifestation of a desire for more connection different for followers? Future research on relational leadership could provide an in-depth analysis of the differences and similarities in leader and follower roles, functions, and behaviors in relational interactions and rather than treat followers as a separate entity (Aaltio-Marjosola, 2001; Agashae & Bratton, 2001; Berg, 1998) embed the notion of follower in all aspects of positional leadership.

The association of relational leadership with displays of femininity and powerlessness has received little serious attention in the leadership literature. Although the alignment of feminine attributes with the changing requirements of work has long been recognized (Calvert & Ramsey, 1992; Fletcher, 1994, 1996; Fondas, 1997; Helegson, 1990) and continues to be a topic of discussion (Peters, 2003) an exploration of the specific gender dynamics inherent in practicing relational leadership is in its infancy (Fletcher, 2004; Fletcher & Kaeufer, 2003). One glaring gap, for example, is that whereas those who have used RCT to study workplace phenomena have found that women who enact relational practice often have their efforts "disappeared" as competent action (Fletcher, 1999), little is known about the effects of relational gender dynamics on men. Studies of relational leadership that explore the different experiences of men and women and delineate the role of the body in relational leadership interactions could make a significant contribution to the understanding of how gender dynamics play out in these interactions. In the same vein, both the relational leadership and the positive relationships at work literatures have largely ignored the role of social identity in the relational process. The RCT perspective on gender and power as systemic variables offers an opportunity to unpack the multiple dimensions of social identity characteristics and their effect on leader–follower interactions. One avenue for exploration would be to use the concept of simultaneity (Holvino, 2001) to explore the intersection of social identity characteristics such as race and class or sexual orientation and race within each member of the interaction as well as between members. Research such as this could make an important contribution to both relational leadership and the more general domain of positive relationships at work by furthering our understanding of the individual and systemic constraints, risks and opportunities in enacting positive relationality at work.

In conclusion, RCT provides a perspective on relational leadership that can further the understanding of this important construct. In addition it has the potential to further the understanding of some of the paradoxes associated with relational leadership (Fletcher & Kaeufer, 2003) and identify the constraints to its practice that would help explain why we are not seeing the transformation effects of this kind of leadership to the degree we might expect (Beer, 1999; Heifitz & Laurie, 1999; Khurana, 2003).

REFERENCES

Aaltio-Marjosola, I. (2001, September). *Charismatic leadership, manipulation and the complexity of organizational life*. Paper presented at the MIT Sloan School of Management Organizational Studies Seminar Series, Cambridge, MA.

Agashae, Z., & Bratton, J. (2001). Leader–follower dynamics: Developing a learning environment. *Journal of Workplace Learning, 13*(3–4), 89–103.

Babcock, L., & Laschever, S. (2003). *Women don't ask*. Princeton, NJ: Princeton University Press.

Badaracco, J. (2002). *Leading quietly*. Cambridge, MA: Harvard Business School Press.

Baker, W. (2000). *Achieving success through social capital*. San Francisco: Jossey-Bass.

Bartolome, F., & Laurent, A. (1988). Managers: Torn between two roles. *Personnel Journal, 67,* 72–83.

Bass, B. M. (1998). *Transformational leadership.* Mahwah, NJ: Lawrence Erlbaum Associates.

Beer, M. (1999). Leading learning and learning to lead. In J. Conger, G. Spreitzer, & E. Lawler (Eds.), *The leader's change handbook* (pp. 127–161). San Francisco: Jossey-Bass.

Berg, D. (1998). Resurrecting the muse: Followership in organizations. In E. B Klein, F. Gaibelnick, & P. Herr (Eds.), *The psychodynamics of leadership* (pp. 27–52). Madison, CT: Psychosocial Press.

Bradbury, H., & Lichtenstein, B. (2000). Relationality in organizational research: Exploring the space between. *Organization Science, 11,* 551–566.

Brewer, M., & Gardner, W. (1996). Who is this "we"? Levels of collective identity and self representations. *Journal of Personality and Social Psychology, 71,* 83–88.

Bryman, A. (1996). Leadership in organizations. In S. Clegg, C. Hardy, & W. Nord (Eds.), *Handbook of organization studies* (pp. 276–292). London: Sage.

Calvert, L., & Ramsey, V. J. (1992). Bringing women's voice to research on women in management: A feminist perspective. *Journal of Management Inquiry , 1,* 79–88.

Chodorow, N. (1978). *The reproduction of mothering.* Berkeley: University of California Press.

Collins, J. (2001). *Good to great.* New York: Harper Business.

Conger, J. (1989). Leadership: The art of empowering others. *Academy of Management Executive, 3,* 17–24.

Conger, J., Spreitzer, G., & Lawler, E. (Eds.). (1999). *The leader's change handbook.* San Francisco: Jossey-Bass.

Cox, J., Pearce, C., & Sims, H. P. (2003). Toward a broader leadership development agenda: Extending the traditional transactional-transformation duality by developing directive, empowering and shared leadership skills. In S. Murphy & R. Riggio (Eds.), *The future of leadership development* (pp. 161–180). Mahwah, NJ: Lawrence Erlbaum Associates.

Cross, R., Baker, W., & Parker, A. (2003). What creates energy in organizations. *MIT Sloan Management Review, 44*(4), 51–56.

Day, D., Gronn, P., & Salas, E. (2004). Leadership capacity in teams. *The Leadership Quarterly, 15*(6), 857–868.

Dutton, J. (2003). *Energize your workplace: How to create and sustain high quality connections at work.* San Francisco: Jossey-Bass.

Dutton, J., Debebe, G., & Wrzesniewski, A. (1998, January). *Being valued and devalued at work.* Paper presented at ICOS Seminar, University of Michigan, Ann Arbor, MI.

Dutton, J., & Heaphy, E. (2003). The power of high-quality connections. In K. Cameron, J. Dutton, & R. Quinn (Eds.), *Positive organizational scholarship* (pp 263–278). San Francisco: Berrett-Koehler.

Fairbairn, W. D. R. (1952). *An object relations theory of personality.* New York: Basic Books.

Feldman, M., & Khademian, A. (2003). Empowerment and cascading vitality. In K. Cameron, J. Dutton, & R. Quinn (Eds.), *Positive organizational scholarship* (pp. 343–358). San Francisco: Berrett-Koehler.

Fiske, S., & Taylor, S. (1991). *Social cognition.* New York: McGraw-Hill.

Fletcher, J. K. (1994). Castrating the female advantage. *Journal of Management Inquiry, 3,* 74–82.

Fletcher, J. K. (1996). A relational approach to developing the protean worker. In D. T. Hall & Associates (Eds.), *The career is dead—Long live the career.* San Francisco: Jossey-Bass.

Fletcher, J. K. (1999). *Disappearing acts: Gender, power and relational practice at work.* Cambridge, MA: MIT Press.

Fletcher, J. K. (2004). The paradox of post heroic leadership: An essay on gender, power and transformational change. *The Leadership Quarterly, 15,* 647–661.

Fletcher, J. K., & Jacques, R. (2000). *Relational practice: An emerging stream of theorizing and its significance for organizational studies* (CGO Working Paper). Boston: Simmons School of Management, Center for Gender in Organizations.

Fletcher, J. K., & Kaeufer, K. (2003). Shared leadership: Paradox and possibility. In C. Pearce & J. Conger (Eds.), *Shared leadership: Reframing the hows and whys of leadership* (pp. 21–47). London: Sage.

Foldy, E. (2002). *Be all that you can be.* Unpublished doctoral thesis, Boston College, Boston.

Follett, M. P. (1924). *Creative experience.* New York: Longmans Green.

Fondas, N. (1997). Feminization unveiled: Management qualities in contemporary writings. *Academy of Management Review, 22,* 257–282.

Fredrickson, B. (2003). Positive emotions and upward spirals in organizations. In K. Cameron, J. Dutton, & R. Quinn (Eds.), *Positive organizational scholarship* (pp. 163–175). San Francisco: Berrett-Koehler.

Gardner, H. (1990). *On leadership.* New York: The Free Press.

Gittell, J. (2003). A theory of relational coordination. In K. Cameron, J. Dutton, & R. Quinn (Eds.), *Positive organizational scholarship* (pp. 279–295). San Francisco: Berrett-Koehler.

Goffman, E. (1959). *The presentation of self in everyday life.* New York: Doubleday.

Goleman, D. (1998). *Working with emotional intelligence.* New York: Bantam.

Goleman, D., Boyatzis R., & McKee, A. (2002). *Primal leadership.* Cambridge, MA: Harvard Business School Press.

Graen, G. B., & Scandura, T. A. (1987). Toward a psychology of dyadic organizing. In L. L. Cummings & B. M. Staw (Eds.), *Research in organizational behavior* (pp. 175–208). Greenwich, CT: JAI.

Graen, G. B., & Uhl-Bien, M. (1995). Relationship-based approach to leadership: Development of leader-member exchange (LMX) theory over 25 years: Applying a multi-level multi-domain perspective. *Leadership Quarterly, 6,* 219–247.

Hargadon, A. (2003). *How breakthroughs happen.* Cambridge, MA: Harvard Business School Press.

Harrington, M. (2000). *Care and equality.* New York: Routledge.

Heifitz, R., & Laurie, D. (1999). Mobilizing adaptive work: Beyond visionary leadership. In J. Conger, G. Spreitzer, & E. Lawler (Eds.), *The leader's change handbook* (pp. 55–86). San Francisco: Jossey-Bass.

Helgeson, S. (1990). *The female advantage.* New York: Doubleday.

Hill, L. (2004). New manager development for the 21st century. *The Academy of Management Executive, 18*(3), 121

Hirschorn, L. (1990). Leaders and followers in a postindustrial age: A psychodynamic view. *Journal of Applied Behavioral Science, 26*(4), 529–542.

Holvino, E. (2001). *Complicating gender: The simultaneity of race, gender and class in organizing change(ing)* (CGO Working Paper No. 13). Boston: Simmons School of Management, Center for Gender in Organizations.

Hosking, D., Dachler, H. P., & Gergen, K. J. (Eds.). (1995). *Management and organization: Relational alternative to individualism.* Aldershot, England: Ashgate.

Howell, J., & Shamir, B. (2005). The role of followers in the charismatic leadership process: Relationships and their consequences. *Academy of Management Review, 30,* 96–112.

Isaacs, W. (1999). *Dialogue and the art of thinking together.* New York: Doubleday Currency.

Jacques, R. (1993). Untheorized dimensions of caring work: Caring as a structural practice and caring as a way of seeing. *Nursing Administration Quarterly, 17*(2), 1–10.

Jordan, J. (1986). *The meaning of mutuality* (Working Paper No. 23). Wellesley, MA: Centers for Women.

Jordan, J. V. (1991). *The movement of mutuality and power* (Working Paper No. 53). Wellesley, MA: Wellesley College Centers for Women.

Jordan, J. (1999). *Toward connection and competence* (Working Paper No. 83). Wellesley, MA: Centers for Women.

Jordan, J., Kaplan, A., Miller, J. B., Stiver, I., & Surrey, J. (Eds.). (1991). *Women's growth in connection.* New York: Guilford.

Jost, J. (1997). An experimental replication of the depressed entitlement effect among women. *Psychology of Women Quarterly, 21,* 387–393.

Kahane, A. (2004). *Solving tough problems.* Berkeley, CA: Berrett-Koehler.

Kahn, W. (1998). Relational systems at work. In B. M Staw & L. L. Cummings (Eds.), *Research in organizational behavior* (Vol. 20, pp. 39–76). Greenwich, CT: JAI.

Kanter, R. M. (2001). *E-volve!* Cambridge, MA: Harvard Business School Press.

Kayes, D. C. (2004). The 1996 Mount Everest climbing disaster: The breakdown of learning in teams. *Human Relations, 57,* 1263–1285.

Khuruna, R. (2003). *Searching for a corporate savior: The irrational quest for charismatic CEOs.* Princeton, NJ: Princeton University Press.

Kim, D. H. (1993), The link between individual and organizational learning. *Sloan Management Review, 34,* 37–50.

Kouzes, J., & Posner, B. (2003). *The leadership challenge* (3rd ed.). San Francisco: Jossey-Bass.

Kram, K. (1996). A relational approach to career development. In D. T. Hall (Ed.), *The career is dead—Long live the career: A relational approach to careers* (pp. 132–157). San Francisco: Jossey-Bass.

Lave, J., & Wenger, E. (1991). *Situated learning: Legitimate peripheral participation.* New York: Cambridge University Press.

Lee, F., Caza, A., Edmondson, A., & Thomke, S. (2003). NCW knowledge creation in organizations. In K. Cameron, J. Dutton, & R. Quinn (Eds.), *Positive organizational scholarship* (pp. 194–206). San Francisco: Berrett-Koehler.

Levinson, D. J. (1978). *Seasons of a man's life.* New York: Knopf.

Lipman Blumen, J. (1996). *The connective edge.* San Francisco: Jossey-Bass.

Lipnack, J., & Stamps, J. (2000). *Virtual teams.* New York: Wiley.

Lord, R. G., & Maher, K. J. (1993). *Leadership and information processing: Linking perceptions and performance.* Boston: Routledge.

Losada, M., & Heaphy, E. (2004). The role of positivity and connectivity in the performance of business teams. *American Behavioral Scientist, 47*(6), 740–765.

Luthans, F., & Avolio, B. (2003). Authentic leadership development. In K. Cameron, J. Dutton, & R. Quinn (Eds.), *Positive organizational scholarship* (pp. 241–258). San Francisco: Berrett-Koehler.

Manz, C. C., & Sims, H. P., Jr. (2001). *The new superleadership: Leading others to lead themselves.* San Francisco: Berrett-Koehler.

Marsick, V., & Watkins, P. (1999). *Facilitating learning organizations: Making learning count.* Aldershot, England: Gower.

Martin, P. Y. (1996). Gendering and evaluating dynamics: Men, masculinities and managements. In D. Collinson & J. Hearn (Eds.), *Men as mangers, mangers as men* (pp. 186–209). London: Sage.

Martin, P. Y., & Collinson, D. L. (1998). Gender and sexuality in organizations. In M. M. Ferree, J. Lorder, & B. Hess (Eds.), *Revisioning gender* (pp. 285–310). London: Sage.

Mayo, M., Meindl, J. R., & Pastor, J. (2003). Shared leadership in work teams: A social network approach. In C. Pearce & J. Conger (Eds.), *Shared leadership: Reframing the hows and whys of leadership* (pp. 21–47). London: Sage.

McNamee, S., & Gergen, K. J. (1999*). Relational responsibility: Resources for sustainable dialogue.* Thousand Oaks, CA: Sage.

Miller, J. B. (1976). *Toward a new psychology of women.* Boston: Beacon.

Miller, J. B. (1984). *The development of women's sense of self* (Working Paper No. 12). Wellesley, MA: Wellesley College Centers for Women.

Miller, J. B., & Stiver, I. (1997). *The healing connection.* Boston: Beacon.

Pearce, C. (2004). The future of leadership: Combining vertical and shared leadership to transform knowledge work. *The Academy of Management Executive, 18*(1), 47–57.

Pearce, C., & Conger, J. (2003a). All those years ago: The historical underpinnings of shared leadership. In C. Pearce & J. Conger (Eds.), *Shared leadership: Reframing the hows and whys of leadership* (pp. 3–13). London: Sage.

Pearce, C., & Conger, J. (2003b). A landscape of opportunities: Future research on shared leadership. In C. Pearce & J. Conger (Eds.), *Shared leadership: Reframing the hows and whys of leadership* (pp. 285–304). London: Sage

Pearce, C., & Sims, H. (2000). Shared leadership: Toward a multi-level theory of leadership. In M. Beyerlein, D. Johnson, & S. Beyerlein (Eds.), *Advances in the interdisciplinary studies of work teams* (Vol. 7, pp. 115–139). New York: JAI.

Peters, T. (2003). *Re-imagine!* New York: DK Publishing.

Ragins, B. R. (2005). *Towards a theory of relational mentoring.* Unpublished manuscript.

Rudman, L., & Glick, P. (2001). Gender effects on social influence and hireability: Prescriptive gender stereotypes and backlash toward agentic women. *Journal of Social Issues, 57*(4), 743–762.

Seely Brown, J., & Duguid, P. (2000). *The social life of information.* Cambridge, MA: Harvard Business School Press.

Senge, P. (1990a). *The fifth discipline.* New York: Doubleday.

Senge, P. (1990b). The leader's new work: Building learning organizations. *Sloan Management Review, 32*(1), 7–23.

Senge, P., & Kaeufer, K. (2001). Communities of leaders or no leadership at all. In S. Chowdhury (Ed.), *Management 21C* (pp. 186–204). New York: Prentice-Hall.

Sinclair, A. (1998). *Doing leadership differently.* Carlton, Victoria, Australia: Melbourne University Press.

Suchman, L. (1987). *Plans and situated actions: The problem of human–machine communication.* New York: Cambridge University Press.

Surrey, J. (1985). *The self in relation* (Working paper No. 13). Wellesley, MA: Wellesley College, Centers for Women.

Sutcliffe, K., & Vogus, T. (2003). Organizing for resilience. In K. Cameron, J. Dutton, & R. Quinn (Eds.), *Positive organizational scholarship* (pp. 94–110). San Francisco: Berrett-Koehler.

Thompson, L. (2004). *Making the team* (2nd ed.). Upper Saddle River, NJ: Prentice-Hall.

Valian, V. (1998). *Why so slow?* Cambridge, MA: MIT Press.

Vera, D., & Crossan, M. (2004). Strategic leadership and organizational learning. *Academy of Management Review, 29,* 222–240.

Vera, D., & Rodriquez-Lopez, A. (2004). Strategic virtues: Humility as a source of competitive advantage. *Organizational Dynamics, 3,* 393–408.

Wade, M. E. (2001). Women and salary negotiations: The cost of self-advocacy. *Psychology of Women Quarterly, 25,* 65–76.

Walker, M. (2002). *Power and effectiveness: Envisioning an alternative paradigm* (Working Paper No. 94). Wellesley, MA: Wellesley College, Centers for Women.

Watkins, K.E., & Cervero, R. M. (2000). Organizations as contexts for learning: A case study in certified accountancy. *Journal of Workplace Learning, 12*(5–6), 187–194.

West, C., & Zimmerman, D. (1991). Doing gender. In J. Lorber & S. Farrell (Eds.), *The social construction of gender* (pp. 13–37). Newbury Park, CA: Sage.

Wheatley, M. (2001). *Leadership and the new science: Discovering order in a chaotic world.* London: Sage.

Winnicott, D. (1958). *The maturational process and the facilitating environment.* New York: International Universities Press.

Yukl, G. P. (1998). *Leadership in organizations* (4th ed.). Englewood Cliffs, NJ: Prentice-Hall.

Zaleznik, A. (1992). Managers and leaders: Are they different? *Harvard Business Review, 70,* 126–136.

20

Commentary: Following the Resources in Positive Organizational Relationships

Denise M. Rousseau
Kimberly Ling

During the 1972 American presidential campaign, the informant Deep Throat told the investigators of the Watergate break-in that to really understand what was going on they needed to "follow the money." The essential point Deep Throat implied is that complicated or mysterious human activity might be most readily understood by looking into the resources the activity involves. This commentary reflects on the critical role resources play in positive organizational relationships (PORs) in terms of the distinctive contributions relational partners offer each other.

Evident in the four organizationally focused chapters on which we comment is that PORs is an enhanced form of resource exchange. PORs efficiently deploy available resources by more effectively timing and targeting the resources partners exchange. Critically, PORs entail the production of new resources of a particularly scarce and valued nature via interactions that give exchanges special significance. From the intimate support that derives from sharing personal and professional risks (as in complex organizational change, described by Golden-Biddle, GermAnn, Reay & Procyshen, chap. 16, this volume) to the development and application of fluid, often tacit expertise (Fletcher, chap. 19, this volume), PORs provide an affirming and heady mix of supports and supplies. By virtue of their enhanced resources, PORs substantially multiply the potentialities of people and organizations.

This commentary highlights the attributes of PORs-related resources. It places the centrality of resources for POR in the context of the broader history of workplace psychodynamics, in particular the focus on constructive organizational relationships as championed by Levinson and others nearly 50 years ago (cf. Meckler, Drake, & Levinson, 2003) and the positive psychology zeitgeist. Last, it develops implications for future research exploring the dynamics of PORs and its resource exchanges as well as its limiting, boundary conditions.

ATTRIBUTES OF POR's RESOURCES

Resources are forms of wealth; that is, supplies (e.g., money or goods) or supports (e.g., information, status, services, affiliation, or love) having economic, social, or emotional value. Certain resources are themselves relationship-creating, as when the employer's promise of future opportunities for personal and career development leads an employee to develop a psychological contract in employment of a relational character—and to behave accordingly (Rousseau, 2005). PORs invite deeper connections (Fletcher, chap. 19, this volume; Glynn & Wrobel, chap. 17, this volume) over time, making their participants resource-rich. Several mechanisms account for this abundance.

1. *PORs create efficiencies in use of resources.* Time and money are saved when coordination is easier and problems are solved faster (Baker & Dutton, chap. 18, this volume). By PORs' broader distribution of resources, requests for cooperation among people and organizational units are more readily fulfilled, targeting supplies and supports to where they may be most needed. Golden-Biddle and colleagues (chap. 16, this volume) point out that by encouraging creativity in the delivery of services, PORs can further enhance efficiency. By promoting ease of action the zest Fletcher (chap. 19, this volume) speaks of energizes member efforts on behalf of the organization, its clients, and its customers. When fewer resources are consumed in the exchange, there is more conservation and less waste. The emotional carrying capacity associated with PORs (Baker & Dutton, chap. 18, this volume) can mean that participants experience fewer strains in challenging work settings, conserving their energies for more productive activity. In effect, PORs are the opposite of Williamson's (1985) transaction costs.

2. *PORs create resources* and importantly via their resource production capabilities expands the array of available resources ("the pie"). In Baker and Dutton's (chap. 18) words, PORs are a "resource that can be enacted to gain additional resources." The essence of PORs is generative through their creation and support of resource-rich interactions among members and the broader organization. Generative means having the power to originate and propagate something that would not exist otherwise. Martha Stewart's ser-

vice mission demonstrates generativity through teaching people things that inspire family preservation where "family ties generate social capital" (Glynn & Wrobel, chap. 17, this volume). Her readers receive emotional gratification via multigenerational connections including skills that connect them to their own grandmother (if she cooked!), and future grandchildren, generating future family traditions via newly acquired capabilities and associated symbols (e.g., abundance at the table and in the garden).

Exchange, or perhaps a better term here, *giving*, is central to PORs. By making people more able and willing to give to one another, PORs become in Baker and Dutton's (chap. 18) terms generalized reciprocity. They are a catalyst, a veritable chemical reaction, making resource exchange generative as well as efficient. PORs expand the pie, turning 2 + 2 into 5 (or more). This expanded pie derives not only from efficient use of existing resources but also by additional resources that are only produced by high-quality connections. These additional resources are particularistic, deriving their meaning from the party who offers them, the party who receives them, and the relationship between them (Foa & Foa, 1974). Particularistic resources are the most sought after, impossible to demand, and given freely or not at all, as in the case of love, friendship, mentoring, and deep trust.

PORs create resources through multiple mechanisms: positive feedback via reciprocity, repeated cycles of exchange over time, and new meanings that PORs introduce into the resource exchange, including willingness to support new members as well as the organization and member future interests.

a. PORs inherently involve positive feedback cycles, generating greater levels of activity, information exchange, and mutual activity (Baker & Dutton, 2005). Indeed certain exchanges motivate recipients to give more to others consistent with Fletcher's notion of a constellation of spirals. For example, fundamental to the relational self is the notion of paying forward, anticipating the needs of others and responding without being asked. With no obligation to match resource for resource, the relational self is able to fulfill the other's higher level needs for adaptation and development, flexibly responding to the needs of others, without tit-for-tat exchange. PORs are gifts that keep on giving. Drilling down into the mechanisms underlying Fletcher's spirals, we infer that over time, participation in positive exchanges predisposes people to anticipate and experience benefits, especially of a particularistic and personal nature (e.g., status, care) in their subsequent interactions. Similarly, prior negative exchanges (e.g., loss of status, withholding of rewards) project negativity into subsequent encounters. From the perspective of high-quality connections as described by Baker and Dutton, even deviance can become a positive where it creates extraordinary results, broadening the generative capacity of groups and individuals. In the sense that positive feedback cycles are expansive (as opposed to negative feedback, which seeks consistency and equilibrium), growth and change are inherent in PORs.

b. *PORs expand the time horizons of the exchanges involved.* PORs-based resource flows exist not only in the present. They can reach into the past and forward to the future. The past is activated by memories of prior enjoyable exchanges, which form the basis for present and future behavior. Recollections of salient contributions earlier members have made can create greater willingness to pass on benefits to future generations. Research on intergenerational justice demonstrates that people tend to behave toward future generations the way one's own generation was treated (Wade-Benzoni, 1996). As such, generosity or opportunism in the present is shaped by how the past is viewed and interpreted. In consequence, PORs can generate a multigenerational view of the organization that lends itself toward appreciation of predecessors, restraint and responsibility in the present and investment in the future. In a similar vein, Martha Stewart's family imagery primes readers to recall (or imagine) childhood holidays and pleasures, energizing efforts to create memories for future generations (Glynn & Wrobel, chap. 17). PORs' orientation toward the future is conducive to delayed gratification, commonly involving exchanges that give the parties reason to stay together over time (Leana & Rousseau, 2001; Rousseau, 2005). Participants demonstrate greater willingness to give today in hope of future return. They invest in resources that grow in value over time, often giving them access to resources that simply cannot be obtained in the short term (e.g., development of self and others). This future orientation permits amortization and expansion over time of the available resources. In doing so, it can aid the organization and its members in coping with disruptive change as we observe in the PORs change process Golden-Biddle and colleagues (chap. 16) describe, making people more mindful about the future (and less focused on the end of the old organization). The result is that people move forward, enriched rather than debilitated by past difficulties.

c. *PORs give rise to new meanings that in themselves create or free up resources.* When several resources are exchanged in combination, they constitute a bundle that can take on richer meanings beyond that of its parts. Bundles characterize relationship-based exchanges generally, in contrast with narrower economic transactions. Although all relationships need not involve multiple resources, PORs do. In their capacity to mix and match resources, PORs develop distinctive symbolism and meanings. Training a worker (a service, not unlike giving someone direction via a help line) can be transformed into personal and career development via mentoring and feedback provided patiently over time; the shift from training to development is the expansion from providing a mere service to coupling it with hard-to-obtain information, status, and care. Combining resources can give rise to a multiplex of meanings that no single resource can signal on its own.

Meanings in and of themselves can create resources (adding to their volume and variety), as we have seen in the context of Martha Stewart's use of family imagery. Ascribing the notion of family to an organization in a credible fashion permits certain kinds of investments that individuals might otherwise shy away from making to a conventional business. In Glynn and Wrobel's (chap. 17) portrayal of family-like relationships, the resources created include trusting ties, multigenerational relationships senior and older members have with their junior and younger counterparts, and robustness in the face of adversity. The frame of family can powerfully alter the meaning of day-to-day activities, much in the same way that Nelson Mandela and his fellow political prisoners used the concept of "university" to shift Robben Island from a place of imprisonment to a center for political education and personal growth (e.g., Buntman, 2003; Cascio & Kellerman, 2005). In the context of PORs, there is power in combinations. Just as new meanings can result from providing resources in combination (e.g., coupling training with care), shared meanings can permit the flow of resources not otherwise available. Mandela and his compatriots acted together to reframe their incarceration as a time of personal development, community education, and political expression. This shared frame led to investment of efforts to learn and share, creating a political culture that deepened mutual respect among political prisoners and capacity for rapprochement with their captors.

Personal betterment is rarely an outgrowth of a prison experience, let alone the capacity to forgive and affirm the dignity of others. Similarly, organizational restructuring often creates more costs for its participants than benefits. However, by energizing rather than enervating their participants, PORs can transform adversity into growth.

3. *POR makes difficult-to-access resources available.* Some resources to which access is restricted become available by virtue of the high-quality connections underlying PORs. Certain resources can only be produced and offered in trusting relationships as in the case of services such as mentoring or emotional support, which, like psychotherapy, can only be provided by someone trusted (Foa & Foa, 1974). As Glynn and Wrobel (chap. 17) point out, when circumstances affirm individual identity, certain exchanges become more possible. Attempts to mentor or support fall flat absent the necessary relationship between the parties.

Even where tangible resources are concerned, a broader array is available in the context of PORs when coworkers are not overly sensitive to differential treatment or issues of equity (Rousseau, 2005). The generalized reciprocity Baker and Dutton describe serves to increase the support PORs participants offer fellow members who seek special help or accommodation. In many workplaces, coworkers frequently react adversely to special accommodations made to peers, such as reduced work hours or limited duties (Collela, 2001). When the overall organizational climate is supportive, as in the context of generalized reciprocity, members are more likely to endorse as legitimate those scarce resources allocated to certain workers and not others. PORs's embedded ties ease the targeting of resources otherwise likely to be withheld in lower quality exchanges whose parties monitor each interaction for inequity.

4. *PORs make resource exchanges less subject to disruption.* The Wetoka Health Unit's culture, as Golden-Biddle and colleagues (chap. 16) describe, is a bundle of resources in symbolic form imbuing even a disruptive change with opportunities for individual and collective action. Wetoka ultimately perpetuates the "good things" its member relationships embody by sustaining its culture despite the original organization's traumatic restructuring. Its core values themselves involve resources—from members' trust in each other to an affirming attachment to client service—making it possible for Wetoka and its members to perpetuate their relationships as the erstwhile formal organization passes away.

PORs create a behavioral plasticity, broadening the organization and its members' repertoires of behavior, thereby allowing learning and adaptation (Golden-Biddle et al., chap. 16). Plasticity means greater variety in member behavior and organizational practices during times of change, enhancing adaptability. PORs also heighten emotional carrying capacity (Baker & Dutton, chap. 18), protecting employees from some of the more disruptive aspects of job demands, workplace stressors, and environmental turbulence.

PORs, Ancient History in Organizational Scholarship, and Positive Psychology

PORs resurrect and revitalize one page of organizational scholarship's ancient history and unite it with the movement toward positive psychology. Humanistic and socioemotional matters such as personal development and growth, affiliation, and mutuality were a major theme in organizational research in the 1950s and 1960s (e.g., Argyris, 1962; Levinson, 1962). Levinson's early notion of the psychological contract, as a mutual arrangement between employer and worker meeting deep-seated human needs, centered on promoting a psychologically healthy organization. The shift of organizational research from social science and human service departments to business schools led to the downplaying of research with this humanistic and developmental focus.

The positive organizational scholarship movement, of which this volume is a part, provides an impetus for organizational research to revisit these socioemotional concerns. Positive psychology is the study of positive emotions, character traits, and enabling institutions (Seligman, Steen, Park, & Peterson, 2005). A central psychological process throughout positive psychology is hope. Hope entails beliefs about one's ability to set and achieve goals and control the self and one's environment consistent with those goals. Not a fixed trait, hope can be enhanced by training and development, and very likely the conditions of an individual's workplace. Hope is related to optimism, another core concept in positive psychology, reflecting a positive outlook on life and the future promoting perseverance, happiness, health, and accomplishment (Peterson, 2000). Both are linked to self-efficacy, an individual's confidence in his or her abilities to engage in a course of action to execute a particular task (Stajkovic & Luthans, 1998). Last, positive psychology focuses attention on resilience and thriving, the capacity to respond to change or high demands with strength, energy, and enhanced self-confidence (Cascio & Kellerman, 2005). In combination, these features produce a willingness to delay gratification in pursuit of meaningful, challenging goals, even in the face of adversity, confident skills that one is willing to share with others without feeling threatened by making them capable, too. The reader will probably not be surprised that hope, opportunity, and possibility are three common synonyms for resources (see Merriam-Webster, 2005). An organizational perspective to positive psychology is intrinsically tied to the resource flows that underlie it.

There are three reasons that resources are critical to implementing a positive psychology approach to organizations. First, PORs-based resources are the source of hope, opportunity, and possibility in organizations because they provide a means for building a future even from a stressful and turbulent present. A compelling future, individual growth, and support are hallmarks of a positive workplace. Similarly, the preceding example of Nelson Mandela and his compatriots on Robben Island (Cascio & Kellerman, 2005) is an exemplar of positivity demonstrating how hope, opportunity, and possibility can be maintained despite adverse conditions. Second, as this volume argues, a distinct feature of PORs is that they are resource rich for both direct exchange partners and their constituents. PORs are sustained because over time they provide self-perpetuating flows of resources that make hope, opportunity, and possibility realistic. Third, and very important in the contemporary climate of high-demand workplaces with superficial promises of engagement and employability, the depth and nature of the resources that organizations make available to their members are the acid test of the quality of the employment relationship. Corporate mission statements frequently purport that "people are our most important asset," but poor employee treatment says otherwise. Actual corporate values and exhortations printed in mission statements are two different things. Real lived values are manifest in the way key decisions are made, in particular how an organization allocates limited resources such as money, people, and time. It is easy for a CEO to claim he or she values people, safety, or some other laudable humanistic goal. Such claims in themselves can be mere cheap talk, easy to make, requiring little more than a catchy slogan. In contrast, actual resource exchanges are tough to fake. Any CEO seeking to merely look supportive without actually being so may talk a good line but stop short of actually expending valued resources on behalf of that support. Faking values by actually expending resources would be an expensive proposition! Therefore, the way organizations allocate their staffing, money, and leadership time and effort (e.g., in support of development and well-being) are credible signs regarding true corporate values, discernible even to outsiders and new recruits. So, too, are the resources that flow to employees from the firm. When long-standing members enjoy thriving careers, whether they remain with the firm or go elsewhere, we observe a valuable resource exchange that can be verified. Organizations can readily claim that they are enlightened and supportive, but let them demonstrate the actual investments they have made in people and the resulting socioemotional responses this promotes. The resources inherent to PORs are the crucial evidence that PORs do, in fact, exist. Evidence that firms vary widely in the degree to which employees are energized or exhausted by their work experience (e.g., Welbourne, 2005) indicates that PORs are not the norm.

FUTURE RESEARCH

Viewing resource flows as central to PORs generates a host of interesting theoretical and empirical questions. We divide these questions into several domains.

Distribution and Allocation of PORs-Related Resources

The ways in which resources are distributed among members and units in PORs is an important theoretical and empirical issue. It is unclear from scholarly treatment of PORs to date whether equality, equity, need, or some combination thereof provides the appropriate basis for resource allocation among members. This is particularly important to PORs where organizational rewards such as compensation and advancement are concerned.

Organizations send very different signals based on whether rewards are distributed contingent on performance (the employee's or the organizations'), allocated to all in a similar manner, based on position or hierarchical level, systematically or in an ad hoc manner (Rousseau & Ho, 2000). One possibility is that PORs are linked to broadly available rewards given to all to energize cooperation. Allocations among highly interdependent people tend to be based on equality, or at least follow distribution rules that promote more similarity than difference in the outcomes members obtain. Nonetheless, different reward allocations may function equally well with appropriate supports. For example, a merit system can undermine collaboration when compared to an equality-based system, except where merit is measured in a credible fashion and the basis for allocations is transparent. Equality-based systems may be poor motivators of high performance unless workers are highly interdependent and hold a commitment to the organization's mission that transcends their own personal interests.

A comprehensive theory of PORs must ultimately address resource allocation rules and distribution processes. The sensitivity of PORs to differential allocation rules is an important question in real-world settings that seek both individual contributions and cooperation. Because individuals do differ, we need to understand how much difference in individual treatment, contribution, and compensation is possible while maintaining positive organizational relationships.

The Self in POR

The essential role of the self in PORs is, as Fletcher argues, self in relations. As such, the interplay between PORs and such inherently individual constructs as career orientation, self-management, autonomy, and personal idiosyncrasy is unclear. PORs may necessitate individual accommodations to broader collective forces in much the same way that organizational cultures assert demands on the type of people recruited, the kinds of behaviors they must acquire to fit in, and the conditions that cause "misfits" to exit (Schneider, 1987). To learn about the functioning of PORs it is useful to know its limits, in particular its sensitivity to differences among people. How can high-quality relationships overcome the challenges of highly dissimilar members, geographic distance, or status or cultural differences? Further, certain work contexts, such as military units, can downplay individual differences where demands for teamwork necessitate sacrificing one's individuality to the group. Are PORs possible in such settings? Are there limits on the types of people or work settings conducive to PORs?

Control Systems and Negative Feedback in PORs

Positive feedback cycles are replete in the four chapters in the organizational part of this book. As such, growth and change are inherent in PORs because positive feedback cycles are expansive (as opposed to negative feedback, which promotes consistency and equilibrium). Yet no system can sustain continuous expansion, a surfeit of resources, and growth without attention to equilibrium and self-regulation. Regulation is necessary to sustain effective action, coordinate efforts, and suppress dysfunctional behavior. One issue not addressed yet in organizational treatments of PORs is the role of negative feedback and ways of achieving consistency and stability.

How organizations characterized by PORs regulate themselves and member behavior is unclear. Issues include how much control is achieved by self and group-level regulation as opposed to top-down controls.

Contexts for PORs Present and Future

Although PORs may be likely to flourish in some settings more than others, we might reflect on the potential PORs have for creative design of future workplaces. The instances of PORs described in this volume characterize settings where highly interdependent workers collaborate face to face. Yet, a good deal of future work may be geographically distributed among people who communicate through technology. People do show evidence of learning how to create quality relationships among distributed workers and workers from different cultural backgrounds (e.g., Baba, Gluesing, Ratner, & Wagner, 2004). Although PORs today might flourish in certain environments, it need not mean that organizations and their members cannot learn to make PORs thrive elsewhere. It is important to investigate the necessary as well as sufficient conditions that make possible the particular resource exchanges characteristic of PORs.

To what extent are PORs generalizable to other kinds of work and societies? Fletcher described self in relation as a readily recognizable feature of knowledge work where it is unlikely that a single person can possess sufficient knowledge without ties to what others know. Are PORs generalizable to other forms of work, or is a knowledge-component critical to the allow PORs-based resource exchanges between workers and the organization? Are PORs generalizable to other societies? We note that value-driven interventions such as total quality management have been successfully implemented in third-world-based organizations via local adaptation (D'Iribarne, 2002), incorporating Islam in Morocco and community service in Mexico. There may be numerous possible local instantiations of PORs giving us insight into the drivers of PORs.

Developing Valid and Representative Indicators of POR-Related Resources

Although organizations often use employee willingness to work long hours or make sacrifices on the company's behalf as evidence of engagement and involvement, we are skeptical that these are appropriate indicators of PORs. There is a difference between finding zest in one's work and being addicted to it. Throughout this volume the resources exchanged generate positive feedback; that is, escalating resource quantity and quality. A realistic appraisal of the resources exchanged must also consider how limited resources such as personal time and physical energy are affected or consumed in the employment relationship. PORs may alter how members and organizations consume scarce, limited, or otherwise fixed resources while making other resources more available. If so, the array of resources workers enjoy provide a critical indicator of both whether PORs exist as well as the employment relationship's true quality.

CONCLUSION

This volume's organizational chapters highlight the essential connection between PORs and the resources organizations and their members exchange. Through PORs's web of interactions both tangible and intangible resources flow, multiplying over repeated cycles of exchange. Resources flow among networks of individuals, top down from the organization and its leadership to individual workers, and bottom up as energized, competent, and trustworthy members shape their organization. Abundant resources are not the initial cause of PORs. Yet the existence of PORs is confirmed by the distinctive attributes of the resources they involve. Through the criticality of resource exchange and creation for PORs, the PORs perspective positions us to raise important and challenging questions regarding the nature of connections organizations achieve with their members.

REFERENCES

Argyris, C. (1962). *Interpersonal competence and organizational effectiveness*. Homewood, IL: Dorsey.

Baba, M., Gluesing, J., Ratner, H., & Wagner, K. H (2004). The contexts of knowing: natural history of a globally distributed team. *Journal of Organizational Behavior, 25*, 547–587.

Buntman, F. L. (2003). *Robben Island and prisoner resistance to apartheid*. Cambridge, England: Cambridge University Press.

Cascio, W. F., & Kellerman, R. (2005). *Leadership lessons from Robben Island: A manifesto for the moral high ground*. Unpublished manuscript.

Collela, A. (2001). Coworker distributive fairness judgments of the workplace accommodation of employees with disabilities. *Academy of Management Review, 26*, 100–116.

D'Iribarne, P. (2002). Motivating workers in emerging countries: Universal tools and local adaptations. *Journal of Organizational Behavior, 23*, 243–256.

Foa, U. G., & Foa, E. B. (1974). *Societal structures of the mind*. Springfield, IL: Thomas.

Leana, C., & Rousseau, D. M. (2001). *Relational wealth: The advantages of stability in a changing economy*. New York: Oxford University Press.

Meckler, M., Drake, B. H., Levinson, H. (2003). Putting psychology back into psychological contracts. *Journal of Management Inquiry, 12*, 217–228.

Merriam-Webster. (2005). *On-line Thesaurus*. Retrieved September 27, 2005, from http://www.m-w.com/cgi-bin/thesaurus?book=Thesaurus

Peterson, C. (2000). The future of optimism. *American Psychologist, 55*, 45–67.

Rousseau, D. M. (2005). *I-deals: Idiosyncratic deals workers bargain for themselves*. New York: Sharpe.

Rousseau, D. M., & Ho, V. (2000). Psychological contract issues in compensation. In S. Rynes & B. Gephart (Eds.), *Compensation* (pp. 273–310). San Francisco: Jossey-Bass.

Schneider, B. (1987). The people make the place. *Personnel Psychology, 40,* 437–453.

Seligman, M. E. P., Steen, T. A., Park, N., & Peterson, C. (2005). Positive psychology progress: Empirical validation of interventions. *American Psychologist, 60,* 410–421.

Stajkovic, A., & Luthans, F. (1998). Social cognitive theory and self-efficacy: Going beyond traditional motivational and behavioral approaches. *Organizational Dynamics, 26,* 66–77.

Wade-Benzoni, K. (1996). *Intergenerational justice: Discounting, reciprocity, and fairness as factors that influence how resources are allocated.* Unpublished paper. Evanston, IL: Northwestern University, Kellogg School.

Welbourne, T. (2005). *The energy-engagement cycle: Is it broken in your organization?* Retrieved August, 14, 2005, from www.umich.edu

Williamson, O. (1985). *The economics institutions of capitalism: Firms, markets, relational contracting.* London: Collier Macmillan.

CONCLUSION

21

Moving Forward: Positive Relationships at Work as a Research Frontier

Jane E. Dutton
Belle Rose Ragins

We began this volume with a belief that crossing theoretical boundaries and crossing levels of analysis with a focus on positive relationships at work (PRW) would yield new insights and open new frontiers for inquiry in organizational studies. By unpacking the construct of PRW we recognize that a focus on *relationships* is a corrective to the more atomistic accounts of behavior in and of organizations (Bradbury & Lichtenstein, 2000; Kahn, 1998; Leana & Rousseau, 2000). A focus on *positive* directs attention to connections that are mutually beneficial in some way. The focus on *work* situates understanding of these relationships in a context of social structures in which people live and are employed for temporary or more extended periods of time. The chapters in this volume are full of insights and directives for future inquiry. Although no concluding chapter can do full justice to 16 original chapters and 3 integrative discussion chapters, we look across these contributions and see two major ways that a PRW lens adds value to organizational studies: through explanation and through extension. We use these two major clusters of contributions to articulate how a focus on PRW is a high-prospect research frontier.

A PRW LENS EXPLAINS

Through focusing on PRW the chapters in this book offer three types of explanatory contributions: (a) a better understanding of the theoretical mechanisms that explain work relationships; (b) a more situationally embedded account of the nature and effects of work relationships; and (c) a deepened investigation of generative dynamics involving PRW.

PRW and Theoretical Mechanisms

It is exciting to consider the chapters' insights about the kinds of theoretical mechanisms that explain how PRW are created, sustained, challenged, and repaired, as well as insights on how PRW influence organizational, unit, and individual-level outcomes. A focus on PRW opens up the investigation of theoretical mechanisms underlying work relationships. By mechanisms we mean "the theoretical cogs and wheels that explain why one thing leads to another" (Anderson et al., 2006, p. 1). Mechanisms describe how one variable or construct influences another. By opening up we mean that the focus both introduces new theoretical mechanisms and expands the consideration of old mechanisms to understand relational dynamics or relational impacts.

The chapters offer numerous new theoretical mechanisms that are worthy of study. Many of these came from importing ideas from other disciplines that are not typically connected to organizational studies. These new mechanisms augment current theoretical models in use, and invite new types of theoretical inquiries about relational theories and phenomena in organizations. For example, Heaphy's (chap. 3, this volume) focus on the human body (—its physiological systems, its subjective experience, and its cultural interpretations—) offers three novel and different ways to understand how positive relationships shape behavior, through how they affect the body. One illustration of the mechanisms in her account involves explaining how PRW prompt physiological reactions (e.g., reducing blood pressure, strengthening immune system functioning, and activating neuroendocrine responses) that increase health. Ancona and Isaacs (chap. 12, this volume) apply ideas from family systems theory to propose the mechanisms through which teams create healthy outcomes. They elaborate a mechanism of structured interaction patterns that explains whether and how a team achieves sustainable effective performance. Their model proposes how structured patterns of interactions, composed of a particular set of acts that capture how team members interact with one another, allow a team to monitor, and correct itself over time, producing a set of healthy outcomes. Fletcher (chap. 19, this volume) brings in ideas from the Stone Center relational theory as a model of human development to reconstrue leadership as relational activity, highlighting the importance of considering issues of power and gender as central constructs. All three chapters illustrate the possibilities for using related areas of inquiry to open new domains of theoretical exploration for the study of PRW.

Other authors articulate mechanisms through which PRW work by creatively grafting and blending theoretical accounts that already have some currency in organizational studies. For example, Roberts (chap. 2, this volume) describes three paths through which positive relationships with others at work foster the creation of a more fulfilling identity for an individual. Her identity-enhancement mechanisms include self-learning, inspiration creation, and social support provision. Ragins and Verbos (chap. 5, this volume) use ideas from relational cognition theory to unpack the way that individuals see and act in connection to each other, and they apply these insights to explain the development of high-quality relational mentoring. Davidson and James (chap. 7, this volume) link relationship conflict with ideas from learning theory to posit under what conditions people can constructively build PRW across the divide of social and individual differences. Blatt and Camden (chap. 13, this volume) have a more interaction-based account of how PRW affect a sense of community. They suggest that in PRW, those people who interact in ways that create emotional sharing with others, experienced inclusion, felt importance, and generation of mutual benefits, which together create felt community even for individuals who have a temporary association with an organization. Kahn (chap. 10, this volume) describes a full set of mechanisms that underlie the power of PRW to attach people to their work and to their workplaces. These mechanisms include task accomplishment, career development, sense making, provision of meaning, and personal support. Glynn and Wrobel (chap. 17, this volume) marry positive relationships to forces of institutionalization, opening up consideration of how PRW are symbols that convey meaning and thus participate in the process of organizational and individual legitimation and status. To the best of our knowledge their chapter is the first in organizational studies to use the mechanism of institutionalization to explore and explain how positive relationships shape legitimacy and identity at the organizational level.

A different form of theoretical blending is illustrated by chapters that consider how PRW develop or change. For example McGinn (chap. 14, this volume) theorizes and illustrates how a shared history, a densely connected structure of interaction, and regular communication within a community of longshoremen strengthens positive community during a time of duress. Baker and Dutton (chap. 18, this volume) combine a variety of literatures to develop propositions about how clusters of organizational practices affect the creation of positive social capital, which is how they define and elaborate PRW. They examine how these practices create the motivation to interact and opportunity to interact in particular ways.

A fourth category of mechanism-based contributions comes from the authors who seek to unpack or reinvent core relationship-related constructs. For example, Pratt and Dirks (chap. 6, this volume) offer an account of trust and trust repair, based on a commitment rather than social-exchange-based view of trust. Greenberg (chap. 8, this volume) challenges how we think about ideas of justice (and interactional justice in particular) by redirecting attention away from how injustice is prevented and toward how positive organizational justice is enabled.

A critical contribution of a PRW lens is to complicate and enrich the set of theoretical mechanisms used to explain relational dynamics and relational outcomes. A natural next step is to put these new insights to the empirical test in organizational contexts. We now turn to the second contribution of a PRW perspective: a more situationally embedded account of the nature and effects of organizational relationships.

PRW and Situational Embeddedness

Any work relationship is by definition embedded, meaning it is located in an evolving, interdependent, and nested set of contextual influences that are changing over time. Any full account of how PRW develop and change, and how they have impact, must in some way, take into account this contextual embedding or situatedness. Embeddedness focuses on the nested (or constitutive) aspects of contexts in shaping behavior or action (Dacin, Ventresca, & Beal, 1999). A focus on situated embeddedness of inter- and intraorganizational action is a topic of growing interest for organizational scholars (e.g., Dacin et al., 1999) who have been interested in the social embedding of individual and collective action. The chapters in this volume offer insight into three types of embeddedness related to PRW: cultural, historical, and structural.

Cultural Embeddedness. Relationship as an idea is culturally embedded in the sense that what relationship means and what aspects are valued are socially constructed (Gergen, 1994). The social embeddedness of both relationship and "positive" is a core theme in Duck's commentator chapter (chap. 9, this volume) and it is a theme that threads through many of the volume's chapters. For example, ideas of positive relationships that are created in a mentoring context are shaped by organizational and cultural contexts that create expectations about what mentoring is and what it can become (Ragins & Verbos, chap. 5). Similarly, Fletcher (chap. 19) discusses how ideas about and contributions from relational leadership are implicitly tied to the cultural construction of gender, and the identification of relational responsibility and competence with women rather than men. Heaphy's (chap. 3) chapter on bodily insights articulates how culture acts as a form of toolkit (Swidler, 1986) that constrains how individuals interpret bodily cues, consequently shaping how they interrelate with each other. From a different angle, Glynn and Wrobel (chap. 17) suggest that cultural constraints on an organization's identity shape how relationships can be used as a resource to cultivate trust and legitimacy. Although the kind of relationships that Glynn and Wrobel study differs from the other chapters (e.g., focusing on family relationships), their theory underlines the power of the broader culture in shaping the meaning of relationships and thus, the way that relationships are understood and acted on by people in them and people who observe them.

Historical Embeddedness. Relationships are created in a context with a past. Fragments and elements of the past shape the probability and form of PRW in the present. We see this historical embedding of PRW vividly in the accounts by McGinn (chap. 14) and Golden-Biddle, GermAnn, Keay, and Procyshen (chap. 16, this volume). McGinn (chap. 14) documents the role of shared history and the power of past accounts of collective action in fueling longshoremen's capacity to create a positive community in unsettled times. Golden-Biddle and colleagues (chap. 16) explain how the creation of cultural symbolic forms in the past shapes the possibility of creating positive relationships in the future for a community that was undergoing dissolution. In both cases, the shared meaning of the past around connection infused the possibly for relationship in future times because of how it shaped people's capacity to narrate themselves and their participation in collective action of some kind.

Other chapters emphasize that the history of a relationship is also an important consideration. Ragins and Verbos (chap. 5) propose that members' prior experiences and history of relationships shape relational knowledge that guides their current behaviors and expectations. Davidson and James (chap. 7) illustrate how prior experience in diverse work relationships creates personal learning that guides the development of future relationships. These chapters underline how history creates a type of path dependence that either fosters or diminishes the possibility of PRW in the future.

Structural Embeddedness. Social structures and practices also create the conditions for connecting in more or less positive ways. We see this theoretical claim in Baker and Dutton's chapter (chap. 18) which identified six features of organizational contexts (what they call enablers) that as institutionalized practices, make more probable the creation of positive social capital (as a form of PRW). Blatt and Camden (chap. 13) make a similar point by suggesting that organizational routines and practices make it more or less important for people with temporary membership status to build community in microinteractions. Some of the chapters (cf. Higgins, chap. 11; Kahn, chap. 10; Ragins & Verbos, chap. 5) point to the social embeddedness of any dyadic connection as situated in a system of other developmental connections, which they refer to as the constellation perspective. These authors point to the importance of considering the full range of developmental ties that underlie a PRW to understand the content and process of a particular relationship dynamic. In all of these chapters, structures of power, participation, and practice shape the conditions for interrelating, which make more or less likely the creation and sustenance of PRW. Scholars of PRW would be wise to consider the structural, historical, and cultural embedding of relational structures and dynamics. However, our chapters also hint at what we call mutual embedding in that relationships also constitute and affect social structure and culture, which is part of how they contribute to various generative (e.g., resource-producing) dynamics that we discuss next.

PRW and Generative Dynamics

One of the most exciting overall themes threaded in many chapters is captured by Rousseau and Ling's (chap. 20, this volume) summary point that "PORs substantially multiply the potentialities of people and organizations." Although this is referred to in different ways in the various chapters, the core idea is that PRW are resource-producing. Resources are assets (supplies or supports) that have economic, social, or emotional value. Resources are "entities that are centrally valued in their own right or act as a means to obtain centrally valued ends" (Hobfoll, 2002, p. 307). The claim about multiplying potentiality is at the core of the assertion that PRW are generative. Generative means a capacity to produce or procreate. Rousseau and Ling add that generative means "having the power to originate and propagate something that would not exist otherwise." Various chapters capture the generative possibilities of PRW in different ways.

PRW are generative through their capacity to enrich or energize. The connection between PRW and energy is one way of looking at PRW that allows researchers to consider how PRW are connected to life-giving dynamics. The most direct development of the tie between PRW and energy is presented by Quinn (chap. 4, this volume), who details how PRW create energy within the connection (by people interpreting interrelating in ways that foster autonomy, competence, or belongingness) and how this energy, through mechanisms of creating mutual resources, providing feedback, and fueling attachment, reaffirms and strengthens PRW. This assertion is also implied by authors who use the Stone Center relational theory (Jordan, Kaplan, Miller, Stiver, & Surrey, 1991; Miller & Stiver, 1997) where positive connections are defined, in part, by their zest or energy-producing qualities (e.g., see Baker & Dutton, chap. 18; Fletcher, chap. 19). In these authors' accounts, the generative capacities of PRW are created and sustained through the production of energy as resource in the connection, which in turn fosters other forms of resourcefulness (e.g., trust, inspiration, or positive emotions like contentment or joy). Heaphy (chap. 3) provides a means to more explicitly tie PRW to life-giving dynamics by developing the argument for how PRW are related to health-enhancing physiological changes for individuals in the connection. Ancona and Isaacs (chap. 12) also suggest that a PRW perspective facilitates thinking about teams as living systems that reflect on their own functioning and engage in creative actions that facilitate generative "alive" dynamics.

PRW are generative in the sense of creating meaning about the self, about others, or about a collective, which in turn cultivates additional resources (e.g., positive emotions, knowledge, or trust) that make more likely other generative patterns of interaction. For example, Roberts (chap. 2) suggests PRW foster positive self-meaning as individuals in PRW are more likely to share feedback about strengths, contributions, and other positive impacts that foster identity and behavioral changes. Awareness of the positive impact one has on others creates psychosocial resources that further allow people to take risks and move forward in ways that Roberts labels identity-enhancement processes. Blatt and Camden (chap. 13) suggest that if individuals behave in ways toward each other that cultivate a sense of value and worth, this positive meaning creates a valued sense of community (even among temporary workers) that further fosters contribution and task performance. McGinn (chap. 14) suggests that groups in or across organizations that share a history create a shared narrative for the community and for individual members that fosters effective responses when confronted with disruptive change. In this case, shared history among longshoremen cultivates positive self-narratives that foster community, which creates a capacity to adapt and respond. In all three examples the conditions of positive relationships contribute to a capacity to create a type of self or group meaning that further generates resources like a sense of community or a sense of positive identity, which in turn fosters adaptation, attachment, and successful task performance.

Some of the chapters imply PRW are generative through creating and sustaining various cultural and structural forms, which further sustain and fuel PRW. For example, Golden-Biddle and colleagues (chap. 16) use the Wetoka Health Unit to show how PRW both create and are sustained by various cultural symbolic forms. By symbolic forms they mean shared representations that direct experience and express meaning. They show by example and analysis that cultural forms (like a unit's mission) are enlivened and affirmed through PRW, and how these cultural forms, in turn, create and sustain PRW. The reciprocal dynamic between cultural form and PRW creates a type of resilience or capacity for a system (and its leaders) to endure conditions of extreme change. McGinn (chap. 14) argues that a community of works that is joined through PRW is generative through having a sense of identity that can empower and enable change, as well as by having a way of interrelating that cultivates trust, attraction, and communication that further sustains the community in times of change.

An important point for understanding the generativity of PRW is that within these kinds of relationships, the capacity to grow, change or evolve comes from within the connection (Feldman, 2005) because of the connection's capacity to produce other resources. A focus on the generativity of PRW centers on the endogenous resourcefulness of this form of human connection. For example, Glynn and Wrobel (chap. 17) show how family relationships (as positive organizational relationships) function as a kind of resource themselves, through the role they play in legitimating and conferring an identity for an organization. Baker and Dutton (chap. 18) argue that generalized reciprocity and high-quality connections are each generative forms of positive relationships that, through internal dynamics of the way that people behave with each other, produce further resources such as positive emotion, trust, knowledge, and creativity. Fletcher (chap. 19) explains how the enactment of fluid expertise in connection by a leader fosters a desire for more connection that generates mutual growth, which contributes to what Fletcher calls growth-in-connection spirals. Golden-Biddle and her colleagues (chap. 16) demonstrate the endogenous resourcefulness of PRW in the context of change. They argue that when PRW exist and organizational change is required, this kind of connection broadens people's capacity to undertake change by creating both hope and a sense of control, and thus, a heightened capacity for purposeful action. These four chapters and many of the others in this volume invite inquiry into different forms of endogenous resourcefulness in PRW that explain heightened capacities for action for individuals, and collectives who are connected to each other in mutually beneficial ways. As noted by Rousseau and Ling (chap. 20), these investigations should also consider limits on resourcefulness because of the scarce or fixed nature of some of the relationship-based resources (e.g., time, attention, or physical energy).

A PRW LENS EXTENDS

Inquiry into PRW also stretches and elaborates the possibilities for theoretical insights and empirical inquiry. We see four major ways that a PRW lens extends insights for organizational and management scholars: (a) by widening the scope of variables connected to relational processes and structures, (b) by enriching well-defined research domains, (c) by emphasizing the processual nature of relationships over time, and (d) by identifying new research topics.

Widening the Scope

Like a new camera lens for studying organizations, a focus on PRW broadens the view of what we see as important in organizations. A focus on PRW redirects attention to human growth and development at work, which as Rousseau and Ling (chap. 20) remind us, is an important but nearly forgotten focus in organizational studies. A PRW lens resurrects interest in growth and development both as an outcome of PRW and also as mechanism through which PRW affect a variety of other outcomes. Beyond growth and development a PRW lens invites consideration of how relationships at work connect to identity change (at the individual and organizational levels), authenticity, resilience, health and human physiology, psychological well-being, identification, engagement and attachment to an organization, task performance, effective team functioning and health, capacities and processes of individual and organizational change, leadership processes, and organizational legitimation.

A PRW lens also widens the lens for considering who is in relationship with each other. For example, a focus on positive community (cf. Blatt & Camden, chap. 13; McGinn, chap. 14) invites consideration of how temporary and ephemeral connections as well as long-term, institutionalized connections can be transformed in feeling and function by patterns of positive interactions and the structures that shape and sustain interaction. A focus on developmental networks (cf. Higgins, chap. 11; Kahn, chap. 10; Ragins & Verbos, chap. 5) extends consideration to how people inside and outside of an organization's boundaries are connected to one another in ways that create growth, development, authenticity, and successful performance on the job. A focus on family relationships as a particular form of PRW (e.g., Glynn & Wrobel, chap. 17) extends consideration of how the boundaries of different institutions (e.g., work organization and family) come together in creating legitimacy, trust, and other social assets that affect organizational as well as individual actions.

Enriching Current Domains

The focus on PRW does more than widen the scope of inquiry; it also deepens and enriches how organizational scholars consider current domains of research. Three of the many examples of domain enrichment involve mentoring, organizational change, and team dynamics. Ragins and Verbos (chap. 16) demonstrate that a focus on PRW enriches mentoring research by elaborating the characteristics and processes that underlie high-quality mentoring relationships. Further, a PRW frame draws attention to how relational cognition theory can explain the patterns in mentoring processes and the outcomes these forms of mentoring relationships facilitate. Golden-Biddle and colleagues (chap. 16) use a focus on how positive relationships shape culture, and culture shapes positive relationships, to explain how leaders are able to sustain organizational change in challenging times. Finally, Ancona and Isaacs (chap. 12) enrich how scholars think about teams by shifting the focus from " team dysfunction to team repair and improvement" through focusing on how the sequences of moves enacted by team members create a process dynamic that fosters effective and healthy team performance. All three chapters of these illustrate how a focus on PRW enriches current research domains by introducing new mechanisms of explanation, connecting variables that are not traditionally connected, and opening up the boundaries that surround a particular research topic. Other forms of domain enrichment are illustrated by Roberts's (chap. 2) enrichment of identity research, Greenberg's (chap. 8) enrichment of the justice literature; Pratt and Dirks' (chap. 16) enrichment of the trust literature; Higgins (chap. 11) and Kahn's (chap. 12) enrichment of the developmental relationships domain, Davidson and James's (chap. 7) enrichment of the diversity literature, Fletcher's (chap. 19) enrichment of the leadership domain, Glynn and Wrobel's (chap. 17) enrichment of theories of institutionalization, and Baker and Dutton's (chap. 18) enrichment of theories of social capital.

Emphasizing Process

Duck (chap. 9) reminds us that relationships are fluid, continuous, dynamic, and processual (and that relationships and the positivity of the relationships are continuously produced and reproduced over time). Several of the chapters in the volume have their eye on process—how PRW are created, sustained, repaired, renewed, and routinized or institutionalized over time. For example, Quinn (chap. 4) provides an explanation of the dynamics between PRW and energy, which helps to unpack the processual mechanisms that account for different relational trajectories (e.g., virtuous vs. vicious cycles) in people's patterns of interrelating at work over time. Pratt and Dirks (chap. 6) have an explicit process focus, and their chapter provides a commitment-based view of how the positive and negative in connection are important for sustaining commitment necessary to repair trust disruptions and violations. Davidson and James (chap. 7) open up a process lens by depicting the relationships built across differences as involving a continuous process of negotiating and learning from difference-related conflict and power dynamics. Golden-Biddle and colleagues (chap. 16) also explicitly focus on the process of organizational change, and how the dynamics of PRW are created and mutually reinforced through cultural symbols, over time in ways that enable large-scale changes to occur. Their account reminds us that understanding change processes within PRW also implies considering how PRW are nested within larger change processes. The chapters invite consideration of the embedded processual dynamics of PRW over time.

The interest in relationship processes is augmented by a focus on mutually reinforcing dynamics that alter the speed, form, and impacts of PRW. Many of the chapter authors use the term *positive spirals* to depict the presence of mutually reinforcing dynamics that accelerate or increase the impacts of PRW. Kahn (chap. 15, this volume) notes that PRW can become self-perpetuating as people engage in action toward each other in ways in which they both feel valuable, seen, cared for, appreciated, and engaged. These actions create momentum for more positive acts that create a pattern of what Kahn calls begetting. In his words "a positive movement from one group or community begets another until the acts take on a life of their own and become deeply woven into the life of the group or community." Roberts (chap. 2) describes a different kind of mutually reinforcing dynamic. She suggests that PRW activate an identity enhancement dynamic, where people move faster and more effectively in their own growth and development. She explains that in PRW, people experience more trust, which allows people to be more vulnerable with each other and self-disclosing, which aligns expectations and increases understanding, further strengthening PRW. Ragins and Verbos (chap. 5) identify a spiral associated with relational mentoring as a form of PRW. In their model, being in a relational mentoring connection with another could cultivate interdependent self-construals, relational identities, and a secure attachment style that affects one's relational mentoring schema, which further perpetuates the cycle of generative connection. A key question raised by these chapters is whether it is the positive spirals or mutually enhancing dynamics that help to explain the power of PRW. As Rousseau and Ling (chap. 20) put it, PRW are gifts that keep on giving. They are the kinds of connections between people that are expansive, producing opportunities for growth and the creation of new resources. Although different authors describe this amplifying and mutually reinforcing dynamic in different ways, a focus on PRW encourages consideration of the nonlinear effects of positive organizational relationships at work.

Identifying New Research Topics

The final point about how a PRW focus extends research is derivative from the first three; a PRW focus invites consideration of a range of new research topics. Each chapter explicitly addresses new research questions that arise from its particular take on PRW. Here we try to look across chapters to see some commonalities in the kinds of new research topics that a focus on PRW invites. The review of explanations and extensions that we have just completed suggests a variety of new research topics that include testing the newly identified mechanisms underlying PRW, testing the situationally embedded bases of PRW, and empirically exploring the generative mechanisms. However, we offer a few more invitations for new research that were not explicitly covered in our previous points but are brought up by the chapter authors.

Several of the chapters invite consideration of the antecedents of PRW. A core topic that several chapters suggest is a focus on relational competence, and a deepening of researchers' understanding of how people as individuals or as part of a connection develop knowledge and skills to interrelate positively more effectively over time. For example, Quinn (chap. 4) suggests that skilled conversational practice can enable PRW. Davidson and James (chap. 7) suggest processing emotion, reframing conflict, and giving and receiving feedback are core competencies critical to learning in relationships built across differences. Blatt and Camden (chap. 13) suggest that the ability to form connections quickly and to detach oneself effectively from organizations may be critical to building PRW for people involved in new forms of employment. All of these chapters introduce new research topics around relational competence: its origins, its form, and its effects.

Several chapters raise considerations about aspects of the context that foster and sustain PRW. For example, Heaphy (chap. 3) invites consideration of whether there are certain kinds of organizational conditions that strengthen the connection between PRW and the body because of culture's impact on how people are likely to see and experience their bodies. Golden-Biddle and colleagues (chap. 16) assert that different organizations have differing cultural capacities for building PRW. Kahn (chap. 10) reminds us of how formal structures of groups and communities can be impactful in terms of shaping the possibility of building PRW. The chapters by both Kahn (chap. 10) and Fletcher (chap. 19) suggest that leadership is important in both establishing conditions for PRW and interrupting negative spirals that could undermine PRW

Still another take on PRW is to consider what the base conditions are for this kind of generative connection between people. Kahn (chap. 10) suggests it is abundance, safety, boundaries, and positive spirals. McGinn (chap. 14) suggests it is shared history, a densely connected structure of interaction, and regular communication. Ancona and Isaacs (chap. 12) also cite the importance of safety but they wonder how attention, validation, empathy, and support also shape the possibilities of PRW in teams. Future research will need to sort out the relative importance of these different base conditions as a cornerstone for understanding PRW.

Several of the chapters encourage empirical inquiry into how positive and negative elements are combined in interrelating and their impact on the quality and outcomes of PRW. Kahn (chap. 10) reminds us that in PRW people are acknowledged for what he calls their shadow and their light, a view that usefully complicates the portrait of individuals when they are in PRW. Pratt and Kirks (chap. 6) explicitly suggest both positive and negative elements are essential to resilient relationships. Davidson and James (chap. 7) imply a connection between the positive and negative elements in connection by writing about the important role of conflict in building PRW across differences. Rousseau and Ling (chap. 20) invite consideration of negative feedback as important for explaining how PRW self-regulate and achieve equilibrium—implying that a focus on positive spirals, without attention to negative feedback as a corrective, would be an inaccurate and incomplete view of how PRW dynamics work operate.

Several authors make a call for a more contingent approach to PRW, asking under what conditions PRW and other variables are likely to be more or less related. For example, Roberts (chap. 2) inquires if there are certain conditions that foster stronger relationships between PRW and an individual's identity. Higgins (chap. 11) suggests consideration of people's career states and adult development stages is important for looking at how PRW are formed in developmental networks. Blatt and Camden (chap. 13) as well as Rousseau and Ling (chap. 20) encourage inquiry into how the nature of the psychological and employment contract of members within an organization affects the form and trajectory of PRW.

Finally, several researchers suggest that the meaning of *positive* in positive relationships is socially constituted. As Duck (chap. 9) suggests, "there is no such thing as inherently positive or inherently negative relationships." He suggests instead that societal standards for such judgments are important considerations for understanding how people come to see a relationship's goodness or benefit. Thus, scholars' interest in PRW needs to keep a theoretical and empirical eye on the shifting criteria for understanding a relationship's positivity.

CONCLUSIONS AND LOOKING FORWARD

Organizational and management studies have paid intermittent attention to work relationships under such diverse topical headings as networks, mentoring, leader–follower connections, alliances and partnerships, and social support. This volume attempts to fuse and energize this diversity through a focus on relational states and processes that are positive in the sense of being mutually beneficial in some way to two or more members who are interrelating or in connection in some way.

A focus on positive relationships at work explains and extends organizational scholarship in a direction that we find inviting and critically important for both the worlds of theory and practice in organizations. We close our concluding chapter with an explicit invitation to deepen inquiry into PRW as a research frontier that holds promise and possibility. The promise and possibility is partially revealed in four forms of improved understanding. First, by understanding how PRW originate, develop and change, organizational scholars can better understand how people's health, capability for action, resilience, career success, and task performance are shaped by the microrelational context of PRW. Second, by better understanding how PRW affect outcomes at the individual, dyadic, network, and organizational levels, organizational scholars can better understand the relational origins and relational supports for individual, group, and collective actions. Third, by taking a multilevel perspective that considers nested levels of communities and connections inside and outside the organization, we allow for a richer and more complete picture of the relational worlds of work. Fourth, and finally, by considering the dynamics of PRW over time, and the generativity in this form of relationship at work, organizational scholars get a better view and deeper understanding of the relational foundation of organizing, and in particular, the capacity for resourcefulness generated by PRW.

REFERENCES

Anderson, P., Blatt, R., Christianson, M., Grant, A., Marquis, C., Newman, E., et al. (2006). Social mechanisms in organizational research: Insights from a collective journey. *Journal of Management Inquiry*.

Bradbury, H., & Lichtenstein, B. M. (2000). Relationality in organizational research: Exploring the space between. *Organization Science, 11*, 551–564.

Dacin, T., Ventresca, M., & Beal, B. D. (1999). The embeddedness of organizations: Dialogue & directions *Journal of Management, 25*, 317–356.

Feldman, M. (2005, August). *Understanding endogeneity*. Paper presented at the National Academy of Management, Honolulu, HI.

Gergen, K. (1994). *Realities and relationships*. Cambridge, MA: Harvard University Press.

Hobfoll, S. E. (2002). Social and psychological resources and adaptation. *Review of General Psychology, 6*, 307–324.

Jordan, J., Kaplan, A., Miller, J. B., Stiver, I., & Surrey, J. (Eds.). (1991). *Women's growth in connection*. New York: Guilford.

Kahn, W. A. (1998). Relational systems at work. In B. M. Staw & L. L. Cummings (Eds.), *Research in organizational behavior* (pp. 39–76). Greenwich, CT.: JAI.

Leana, C., & Rousseau, D. (Eds.). (2000). *Relational wealth: The advantages of stability in a changing economy*. Oxford, England: Oxford University Press.

Miller, J. B., & Stiver, I. (1997). *The healing connection*. Boston: Beacon.

Swidler, A. (1986). Culture in action: Symbols and strategies. *American Sociological Review, 51*, 273–286.

Author Index

Subject Index